The culture of economism
An exploration of barriers to faith-as-praxis

STUDIEN ZUR INTERKULTURELLEN GESCHICHTE DES CHRISTENTUMS
ETUDES D'HISTOIRE INTERCULTURELLE DU CHRISTIANISME
STUDIES IN THE INTERCULTURAL HISTORY OF CHRISTIANITY

begründet von / fondé par / founded by
Hans Jochen Margull †, Hamburg

herausgegeben von / édité par / edited by

Richard Friedli
Université de Fribourg

Walter J. Hollenweger
University of Birmingham

Theo Sundermeier
Universität Heidelberg

Jan A. B. Jongeneel
Rijksuniversiteit Utrecht

Band 65

Peter Lang
Frankfurt am Main · Bern · New York · Paris

Jane Collier

THE CULTURE OF ECONOMISM
An exploration of barriers
to faith-as-praxis

Peter Lang
Frankfurt am Main · Bern · New York · Paris

CIP-Titelaufnahme der Deutschen Bibliothek

Collier, Jane:

The culture of economism : an exploration of barriers to faith-as-praxis / Jane Collier. - Frankfurt am Main ; Bern ; New York ; Paris : Lang, 1990
  (Studien zur interkulturellen Geschichte des Christentums ; Bd. 65)
  Zugl.: Birmingham, Diss., 1989
  ISBN 3-631-42563-5

NE: GT

ISSN 0170-9240
ISBN 3-631-42563-5

©Verlag Peter Lang GmbH, Frankfurt am Main 1990
All rights reserved.

Printed in Germany 1   3 4 5 6 7

ACKNOWLEDGEMENTS

I wish to record my gratitude:-

To Professor Hollenweger; without his encouragement, support
and affirmation this study would neither have been begun nor
completed.

To my friends and colleagues of the Adult Christian Education
Consultation at Upholland Northern Institute; many of the
issues discussed here have their roots in that process of
reflection.

To Lucy Cavendish College; membership of that college has
made it possible for me to use the University Library, which
must be the ideal place to do interdisciplinary research.
Lucy Cavendish provides a base and a support community for
academic women at all stages of their intellectual journey.
I and others are fortunate to have the advantage of belonging
there.

==

".....we invite the whole of society,
everyone, rich and poor, to begin a
practical process of personal and
collective conversion of the 'criteria of
judgement, determining values, points of
interest, lines of thought, sources of
inspiration and models of life accepted
in our society, which are in contrast
with the word of God and the plan of
salvation' (Paul VI, Evangelii Nuntiandi,
19)".

Extract from a Statement by the Bishops
of Chile, August 1980.

==

IX

PREFACE

Can economists be converted?

The entry entitled "conversion" in the Encyclopedia
Britannica is concerned with specialised financial
terminology. An additional note on "conversion, reaction"
refers to the main article on "hysteria". One gets the
impression that for modern man the conversion of pounds
sterling into American dollars is far more relevant than the
conversion of people, and much - though not all - of Western
literature supports this view. The Canadian theologian
Bernard Lonergan, on the other hand, understood conversion as
a process involving the whole person, including his/her
cognitive faculties. That is also the position which Dr.
Jane Collier takes in this dissertation.

Conversion is a 'turning from' and a 'turning to'.
This research originated in a dissatisfaction with the lack
of interest in technical issues demonstrated by some Church
statements on economic affairs. Economics is not just a
neutral science which informs on economic mechanisms. It
embodies presuppositions and a specific hierarchy of values
which are not only not openly discussed, but are
unconsciously held and defended by both economists and
economic agents in what Dr. Collier calls a 'culture of
economism'. In effect, they represent a secular
faith-option. Her disappointment with Church pronouncements
was based on the fact that they appealed to the moral
conscience of economists rather than to their scientific
honesty; in other words, they failed to call to conversion.

And that is exactly what Dr. Collier does in her
dissertation. She shows how decisions - whether economic,
scientific or theological - are always co-determined by faith
options, even - and especially - if these are unconscious.

She describes in particular the underlying premises of what she calls 'economism', and unmasks the culture of economism for what it is — a faith system rather than a simple description of what is the case. That the faith-option of economism is an option which the author hopes to transcend in her own life, and perhaps also in the lives of those who are open to her arguments, becomes clear in the chapter on conversion. She develops an understanding of conversion which is related not merely to the religious dimension of existence, but to our whole understanding of the world, including the structures which pre-determine thinking and acting.

This is, to my knowledge, the first time that a trained economist, whose daily bread it is to teach economics at a British university, tries her hand at arguing her case in an interdisciplinary dissertation and within the framework of missiological research. She shows convincingly that the tribes of Africa and the inner cities of Britain are not the only mission fields. In order to work within this field she had to know its culture, its language and its topography. She also had to offer something to help its inhabitants, economists and others, break out of the prison of 'economism'. Their freedom can have two results: the discipline of economics can become a true and honest science, and the economic dimension of social existence can become a sphere in which the Kingdom is more fully realised. Dr. Collier has convinced me that the process by which this can happen is one of conversion understood in the widest possible sense. To place conversion and mission in a context in which one would not expect it, is the fascination of this work. It enhances the understanding of both economics and theology.

Dr Walter J. Hollenweger
Professor Em. University of Birmingham
CH 3704 Krattigen (Switzerland).

===

CONTENTS

INTRODUCTION

Theology as faith seeking coherence.

This study originated as a dissertation submitted in the Faculty of Theology in the University of Birmingham. Since in a sense every dissertation is the story of the writer, it can be seen from one point of view simply as a reflection on the difficulties of living as a Christian and as a professional economist simultaneously. It represents an attempt to resolve a situation of 'cultural schizophrenia', contracted as a result of participating in a world deeply opposed to the value system embedded in the Gospel. It is, in other words, a search for coherence. Once I began this search, it became apparent to me that this dilemma is not one exclusive to economists, but a constitutive aspect of life for all Christians in a prosperous culture which functions under the dominant ideology of 'economism'.

From another point of view, however, the work addresses the more general theological problem of the relationship between faith and culture, and is submitted in the hope that its approach can help others who wish to reflect on the challenge of living as Christians in our particular cultural context. I have characterised this context as that of 'economism' because that it arguably the most powerful conditioning force in our environment. Economism, says the Oxford English Dictionary, 'imposes the primacy of economic causes or factors as the main source of cultural meanings and values'. This operates not only at the level of everyday living, but is also enshrined in the discipline of economics which both generates and articulates that ideology. E.F.Schumacher (1974 p.33) argues that −:

"Economics plays a central role in shaping the

activities of the modern world, inasmuch as it supplies the criteria of what is 'economic' and what is 'uneconomic', and there is no other set of criteria that exercises a greater influence over the actions of individuals and groups..."

In everyday terms, it is the 'economic' which defines the major preoccupations in a materialist market economy. It is not that these preoccupations, or the meanings and values on which they are based, are necessarily a bar to a faith commitment, it is that they create a gap which is difficult to bridge between a faith commitment on the one hand and its realisation in action on the other. This study suggests one interpretation of the way in which this happens.

I begin from the standpoint that the Gospel calls us not only to repentance, but to live out all the consequences of 'metanoia' as a praxis which is reflective, dialectical and transformative. What is required by the Gospel is not simply action in accordance with ethical norms. It is not enough to keep the commandments. What is asked is action which springs from our 'option for the Kingdom'. Such action, as a translation of grace, both liberates the person and, because it is salvific of 'self', is also salvific of 'world'.

The first chapter therefore poses the basic problem of faith-as-praxis in terms of Paul's confusion in Romans 7.14-25 - 'The good which I want to do, I fail to do; but what I do is the wrong which is against my will'. It suggests that the problem lies not only with the internal, but also with the external 'determinisms' which influence our action. In order to identify these 'determinisms', the second chapter develops a non-reductionistic view of action as grounded by consciousness, intentionality, and agency. Each of these is susceptible to cultural conditioning by presuppositions, values and institutional norms — these, in other words, represent for us the 'determinisms' of our environment.

The fact that the presuppositions, values and norms which support our daily existence are largely derived from the world of economics was borne in on me by the experience of teaching economics at university level over a number of years. Even before commencing their studies seriously, students' interpretative and judgemental processes are imbued with the logic of 'economism'. Economic issues prevail in the media, consumerism rules the pursuit of leisure, rewards for work are seen purely in monetary terms, virtue is perceived as material success. The Gospel is then heard and interpreted through a series of filters which distort its meanings and render its values at best unacceptable, at worst ridiculous. The three central chapters examine in detail ways in which this comes about, both on the level of theory and disciplinary thought, and on the level of everyday living.

Openness to the message of the Kingdom must therefore involve some kind of a deconditioning process, — "becoming like a child" — as a prerequisite for the experience of salvation as the power of God in human life. We cannot make that experience fully if our thought processes are such as to preclude the possibility of such an event, if the grids through which we interpret experience do not allow the experience to be formulated as a salvation experience. Nor can we experience God's liberation in our lives if the norms we use to judge the quality of that experience are those of our social and cultural environment which are alien to those of the Gospel. Such a deconditioning has to be seen as a continuous conversion at all levels of the personality. The final chapter explores the dimensions of this process, and implies that one of its main consequences is to challenge the dominant "economist" ideology itself to a total conversion which, if realised, must reshape the relationship between faith and economics both in theory and in practice.

The underlying theoretical perspective of the foregoing analysis can be stated as follows. The relationship between faith and culture is a dialectical theory-praxis relationship which structures the interaction between gospel and life. It can only be mediated by a systematic reflection which enables norms for action to be generated. Such action produces a coherence between faith and life — in this particular case between faith and the economic aspects of human life in our culture. The systematic search for coherence is nothing other than theological reflection, and the norms for action which it produces in turn change 'self' and 'world' in ways which challenge and correct that reflection. Insofar as the believer allows his actions to be grounded in authentic reflection, theory and praxis will be correlated so that each changes and transforms the other, and in the process there will also be a transformative effect in the world.

This dissertation is itself a witness to the existence of this dialectic. I did not begin my search with the intention of "theologising". The need for systematic reflection arose as the product of a need for a faith-life synthesis. This reflection has been assisted and illumined for me by the work of many writers in different disciplines. Three in particular have helped me to resolve some very basic intellectual and 'existential' puzzles. The work of Anthony Giddens has helped me to think in a concrete way about 'structural evil'. Documents of the Roman Catholic Church which concern themselves with issues of justice and peace in the world are full of references to 'structures'; as a social scientist I have always felt that these statements lack force because they fail to give this concept analytical and empirical content. Giddens provides a framework which might profitably be used by other theologians who wish to pursue this issue in greater depth.

The work of Arthur Rich has shown me that it is possible to find practical ways to build the Kingdom in the places where we are. I believe that his vision offers an antidote to the pessimism of the Christian who says 'but whatever I do can have no effect'. Finally, I owe the greatest debt to the work of Bernard Lonergan, who has taught me to think freely, critically and creatively. I belong to the very large group of people whose intellectual existence has been profoundly affected by his thought. It has been said by others, but it is perhaps worth saying again, that Lonergan was not concerned to found a school of thought, but to encourage others to think round the question of a 'metamethodology' which would bring the disciplines closer to one another and hence allow a dialogue to take place between theology and other disciplines. In a sense this study, however imperfect, is an attempt to put this idea into practice.

I write as a Roman Catholic and as a woman. The former perspective will be apparent on reading the dissertation — although I take a critical rather than a conformist view. The latter perspective is, I hope, in no way diminished by the fact that I choose to use the masculine 'he' throughout. If there were a word in the English language which had the connotations of our unity as God's children and co-creators I would use it — failing that, I simply choose the more convenient form. But it is as a Christian, rather than as a Catholic or a woman, that I believe that we cannot live in the freedom of God's Kingdom if 'metanoia' does not result in a praxis which is dictated by our 'option for the Kingdom' rather than by the requirements of the structures in which we live. What follows is in the last analysis a theoretical reflection on this personal viewpoint.

===

CHAPTER ONE - FAITH AS PRAXIS.

i. Introduction

This dissertation is about the problems faced in the living out of a faith commitment - in other words, about the gap between metanoia and praxis. This chapter attempts to establish a theological and scriptural basis for the detailed analysis of the difficulties involved in this. I begin by arguing that to see faith as primarily experiential is a perspective which unifies the subjective notion of faith with the objective notion of revelation. I then turn to the epistemological basis for a faith commitment, arguing that both historical and hermeneutical approaches are relevant when attempting to establish the content, meaning and relevance of the Good News. That 'evangelion' announces a kingdom which breaks into our world, changes our lives, and challenges us to respond in action. Our inability to translate the content of that message into faith as lived praxis is reflected on by Paul in Romans 7.14-25; the rest of the dissertation offers a suggested analysis of why this might be the case.

ii. Faith; some confusions.

As we begin the task of identifying the nature of the problem we have initially to admit that discussing Christian faith in terms of 'metanoia' and 'praxis' is not how the issue is usually approached. I propose to argue that this is because we do not always give due emphasis to faith as action because we see faith as a matter of reason or emotion rather than as a development of human personhood realised in the choices of concrete living and doing. (If faith is either purely rational or purely emotional the thesis expounded in the following pages becomes non-significant). One of the

factors which has contributed to this one-dimensional view of
faith is the linguistic confusion between notions of faith
and notions of belief. It is partly because these terms have
come to be used interchangeably (1) that we have witnessed
not only an obscuring of the understanding of faith as a
basic human quality, but also a devaluation of the status of
faith because the idea of belief has acquired connotations of
uncertainty. The result has been to emphasise the rational
in the faith response as opposed to the affective.

In universal terms faith as man's relationship to the
transcendent, as his response to the awareness of mystery, is
essentially a human and experiental quality - a 'gift to
humanity'(2). The awareness of mystery is prior to any
interpretative context; it is something we sense in our
lives, something to which we give a meaning which is
dependent on our own life experiences, on the concepts and
contexts which are available to us as interpretative tools.
In a religious sense that experience is shaped and elicited
by the particular traditions in which it exists, and the core
and content of the experience is articulated by the thought
forms and practices proper to that tradition. The 'inner
word' of faith is matched by the 'outer word' of tradition as
it speaks in personal, social and historical contexts (3).

The expression of faith in a Christian context has
always been primarily credal or propositional, rather than
primarily 'practical'. It has been articulated in dogma
since the fight against Gnosticism in the second century made
necessary a formal statement of belief. In other traditions,
however, faith is expressed in other ways. The fundamental
distinction between such forms of expression is between an
emphasis on 'saying' and an emphasis on 'doing', where the
focus is on faith as a way of life. In primitive tradition
the emphasis is given to the expression of faith primarily in
terms of ritual, in Judaism it finds its expression in
'orthopoesis' as opposed to 'orthodoxy'. For the early
Buddhists it was through the keeping of the moral law that

they were enabled to live lives of faith and thus to experience transcendence (4). For followers of Islam, on the other hand, faith is a way of appropriating the theocentric vision of the world presented in the Qu'ran. For them there is no belief system as such, only a set of presuppositions. In Hinduism faith is 'a placing of the heart'(5), an involvement, an engagement in doing what one knows to be worthwhile and thereby attaining truth. In all these traditions faith is equated with the human experience of transcendence which is then realised and lived out in concrete historical circumstances, expressed in ways of living rather than in verbal formulation as such. There is then an intimate link between doing and becoming, being and knowing.

Christianity, however, emphasises belief. It is peculiar to the Christian tradition that faith finds its traditional expression in terms of ideas, that words rather than actions are used as recognised expressions of faith. This is the basis of the implication that belief in a propositional sense is a necessary corollary of faith (6), and that rational assent is a prior requirement for the living out of a faith commitment. It is because of this centrality of the notion of belief within the Christian tradition that our whole view of faith becomes influenced by the way in which we conceptualise belief. It is possible to isolate two developments in particular which have been important here. One is the way in which the use of the word 'belief' has changed historically, the other is the way in which the relationship between faith and belief has changed over time.

The original meaning of the word 'belief' was engagement or commitment. When the early Christians said 'credo' as an act of faith they meant it in the sense of committing oneself to something, or setting one's heart on it (7). Faith was the act of the will which expressed itself as a commitment, an engagement with the object of faith proclaimed in the confession of belief. It was only later, with Thomism as the tradition which identified humanity with intelligence and will, that faith became an act of the intellect in which the will was explicitly involved. Faith and belief were identical, but the emphasis had shifted to cognition rather than commitment; faith became the cognitive component in Christian life, and belief its rational expression. The commitment of faith as a theological virtue given by grace was manifested by assent to 'truths' proclaimed by the Church.

It was also the case that the English word 'belief' had in its earlier forms such as 'belove' that same connotation of engagement as did the word 'credo'. It was only later that the 'beloved' or 'beliebt' object of that engagement became a proposition rather than a person. There was a consequent shift from belief in the sense of engagement with the object of faith as a person to acceptance of that person's word, and a further shift from that to belief in a proposition. Belief then becomes something objectified and descriptive rather than a subjective and experiential quality.

The 'objectification of belief was taken a stage further by the fact that the ordinary language use of 'belief' came to imply something separate and distinct from the notion of 'knowledge'. Knowledge is commonly taken to be something certain and correct; belief, however, came to be seen as involving opinions rather than certain knowledge and thus at best a minority aspect of cognition. Its usage in this way forms part and parcel of a particular historical ideology (8) which adheres to currently dominant concepts of knowledge and truth, and which excludes 'non-scientific' assertions from knowledge categories. Belief has thus become the category used by non-believers to discuss the faith of others in terms which make clear the supposedly tenuous relation between those ideas and 'reality'.

The outcome of this process of change was firstly that

faith came to imply the inclusion of the component of belief in a propositional sense, and secondly that the idea of 'belief' lost the connotations both of commitment and of certainty. There were other developments, too, which resulted in a polarisation of the relationship between faith and belief. On the one hand there were those, such as Luther and Kierkegaard, who emphasised the non-cognitive and relatively passive nature of faith; for them, the most important manifestation of faith was not orthodoxy of belief, but a trust which led to a freedom from anxiety. Faith is thus something both more fundamental and more elusive than simply an assent to propositions (9). On the other hand there was the ongoing attempt to establish the status of belief as a passport to faith. The result of this has been that the Roman Catholic tradition, for instance, has to some extent lost the understanding of faith as a basic human attribute, seeing it rather as contingent on belief in a propositional sense. It is true that we can look for the explanation for this in the fact that times have changed; during the first fifteen hundred years of the life of the Christian Church the 'truths' of faith were taken for granted and belief was not a major issue. It was only when changing presuppositions and ideals of knowledge made revelation appear more questionable that the primacy of belief began to be held and defended (10). But the consequence of this development has been to obscure the human and experiential nature of faith, and to create obstacles to faith in the real sense of living and doing. This is all the more damaging because of the dependence of faith on the religious tradition through which it is articulated.

In neither of the major traditions is the emphasis on faith as a way of life paramount. Neither faith in the sense of 'belief in'(Lutheran) nor faith in the sense of 'belief that' (Catholic) allow Christian faith-as-praxis as a way of life to flower. The confusion between faith and a belief in what appears to be empirically uncertain endows faith with a 'partial' quality and engenders actions which have the

quality of 'obligation' or rule-keeping rather than of
confident conduct. That confusion also leads to a fear
generated by the uncertainty of belief (11) if secular
criteria of certainty are adhered to. Fear is the antithesis
of faith, it generates the "mean faith of particularism"(12),
- a narrow faith which confines its manifestation to the
maintaining and reinforcing of the certainty of the 'truth'
of belief. It masquerades as faith or belief in order to
perpetuate an outlook identical to political or ideological
fanaticism, the kind of outlook condemned by St Paul
(Gal.2,15-16,1Cor.1,19-24) which sees faith only in terms of
rules or of intellectual understanding.

It is clear, then, that if we interpret faith as belief
in the modern sense we lose sight of the essential element of
engagement, and obscure the insight into faith as the human
relation to transcendent reality. If, on the other hand, we
emphasise faith as trust and confidence we may neglect the
power of faith to transform lives and empower action. In
either case we make it difficult for those who follow Jesus
Christ to find and articulate and live out their faith
experience within the context of traditions which fail to
mirror adequately the reality they signify. The real
problems within Christianity today are thus

> "not the result of real
> distinctions....expressed in traditional
> orthodoxy. The real problems result from a
> failure of Christians to pay the cost of
> discipleship (Bonhoeffer) or the price of
> orthodoxy (Metz)"(13).

In other words,the problem is to retrieve the essential
values hidden in orthodoxy, values which will cause faith to
be translated into action. The Gospel call to metanoia
requires us to look behind and beneath the institutional
rigidities of Christianity, to look further than confessional
proclamations and practices, to seek the real dimensions of
the repentance required of us in lived orthopraxis.

iii. The roots of faith; humanity and hope.

I have argued that faith entails a response which is more than simply credal, that our emphasis on credal formulation, although important in that it is essential for the articulation of faith, has nevertheless led to an obscuring of the expression of faith in ways of living, and that linguistic and ideological positions which cast doubt on the knowledge claims of credal formulations have further obscured our understanding of the reality of faith. That reality is clearly something more, and something deeper, than its credal expression within confessional contexts. Faith is in the first instance a human quality; 'the spark in our clod'(14); its existence has therefore to be explored in the context of an anthropology. We have to know something about who we are before we can talk about the quality of a 'faith experience', and if we can identify this quality as integral to human being—and—doing we can more naturally talk about faith as praxis.

Faith, says Panikkar (15) is like a hole in the human person, it exists as a question, a search, a need, a vacuum in the reality of personal existence. The components of this reality, our 'anthropological constants'(16), are shaped by our mutability and corporality, by our co—humanity within social and institutional structures, by our historicity and our own internal models of reality and hope. These are the dimensions, the parameters of our concrete human existence, within which we find our self—identity and self—understanding. They reassure us in the sense that they tell us who we are and where we belong.

But there is a sense in which we experience these parameters as threatening. They force us to experience ourselves as the product of something other than ourselves, to be explained and derived only in terms of the reflections of natural and social scientific findings (17). Nor do the

parameters of our existence remain static. The limits of our
own corporality are extended by the advances of medical
science. We can live longer, breed and even clone our
successors, cure sickness, modify behaviour. We have
extended the boundaries of time and space, we can talk to
people on the other side of the world, travel to other
planets, record history in the making. We are even aware that
social and institutional structures alter in ways which
appear to indicate a capacity for organic change independent
of human decision.

All of this gives us an illusion of autonomy, but at the
same time instils in us a feeling of powerlessness. We
realise how little we can do to alter the course of events;
we experience ourselves over against a world of impersonal
forces, both historical and natural, which determine our
destiny in ways over which we have no control. And yet this
is the very experience which can enable us to transcend
ourselves (18) and in so doing establish the reality of our
own personhood by experiencing ourselves as persons. The key
moment in that process is our affirmation of our own
experiential reality. Even when we decide that the
responsibility for our own self-determination does lie with
forces and circumstances outside our control it is we who
attribute that responsibility because it is ours to allocate.
By so doing we affirm that we are more than merely the sum
total of all the factors which determine our destiny. We are
persons, i.e. subjects who in the end bear the responsibility
for ourselves and thus transcend the finiteness of our own
existential reality. We have options, we can choose, even if
that choice is only to say 'yes' to the inevitable.

This kind of self-affirmation carries with it the
responsibility of analysing our own situation. As beings
conditioned by 'world' and by 'history' we need to ask
questions as to the meaning of our existence, questions
which in the end become questions about the meaning of all

life and all history. Our experience may be finite, but the horizon of our questioning stretches towards the infinite, because we ask about that which we do not experience. We question without restriction, we question the significance of our own questioning, and in the end we come inevitably to 'the question of God'(19). However, we are caught between "a transcendence in striving towards which man constantly exceeds himself, and a merciless confinement within the facticity of the existing order of things"(20). In terms of questions we may reach towards the infinite in self-transcendence, but in terms of answers we find nothing but the experience of finiteness and contingency.

Where then are we to seek answers? One thing is clear — everyone has to find their own answers. The 'turn to the subject' which was the product of the Enlightenment banished for ever the possibility that any external authority could provide us with acceptable answers. Modern man realises that it is he and he alone who fashions human events and states of affairs, that it is illegitimate to conceive of God as one who sits 'up there' pulling strings. The autonomous subject in a secular society can accept no answers which are not rooted in human experience, because experience is his only road to knowledge (21). Doctrine is at best only the interpreter, scripture only the mediator of experience. In the words of Bernard Lonergan, the critical exigence requires us to find meaning on a level which is based within the structures of our own differentiated consciousness, within the 'world of interiority'(22).

But what is it in our experience that can provide the answers to our questions? Answers do not come easily, and there is a great temptation to retreat from the area of human reflection where the questions arise. Retreat, as Rahner points out (23), is easy enough; we can simply be non-reflective, immersing ourselves in our daily concerns and refusing to bother about such things. Or we can postpone the questions (while at the same time admitting that they need to be looked at sometime). Or we can simply suppress them, regarding such issues as meaningless because they admit of no obvious answer —"whereof we cannot speak thereof we must be forever silent"(24).

If we do not evade the questions, if we do not dismiss them as worthless, if we open ourselves to their infinity, we experience the very real human phenomenon which Rahner calls 'transcendence' — the experience of being open to being, the infinity of reality as mystery (25). That experience arises out of our acceptance of the fact that there are no answers. That acceptance, and the risk we take in consciously admitting it, is the core of the faith experience, because it is "the act by which personal existence is accepted in trust and hope"(26). The ground of that hope is the mystery we call God (27). In the self-transcendence by which we allow ourselves to be seized by that hope we achieve authenticity as persons.

iv. The gift of faith; nature and grace.

We now shift the focus to the objective pole of the argument — the revelatory aspect of faith. To say that faith is the experience of transcendence is also to say that it is the experience of God's self-disclosure, his revelation of himself. In other words it is the experience of grace. If creation is God's first gift to humanity, then grace is his second gift (28). It is the gift which enables us to transcend the limitations of our own humanity as we respond to God's self-disclosure and are thus enabled to share in His life.

Scripture gives us models of this process (29). In the Old Testament, in Exodus, God pledges himeslf to redeem and deliver his people, thus binding man into a relationship with

himself. That relationship finds expression in worship
(Ex.19.5-6); its nature is likened to that of a father
(Deut.32.6), a mother (Is.66.13), a husband (Is.54.5-6). The
beginnings of a theology of grace in the New Testament are to
be found in the way in which grace forms one aspect of the
experience of early Christians of salvation in Jesus Christ.
St.Paul sees God's love for his people as demonstrated by his
choice (Eph.1.3-4) of those to whom he reveals himself
(Gal.3.23,25). This choice is particular or exclusivist in
the sense that it is those who have faith in Jesus Christ who
are 'elected', but it is also universalist in the sense that
it applies to all without discrimination
(Gal.3.28,1Cor.10.32). As such God's gift of faith is both
diverse (Rom.12.3-6) and unifying (Eph.4.13-16). It heals
divisions among men (Eph.2.14-16) and reconciles them to one
another (Col.3.11). For Paul, 'charis' or grace is the gift
by which God's saving power in Jesus Christ is made manifest,
the gift by which he reconciles men to himself
(2Cor.5.18-21,Phil.3.8f). Man is therefore 'justified' not
by any act which he may perform in accordance with the law,
but by faith in Christ (Gal.9.31, 10.3). Paul characterises
the gift of grace as the experience of salvation specifically
in terms of justification and of unmerited forgiveness
(Rom.5.6-8,3.23,8.28-30).

If faith is above all an experiential reality, it must be
the case that grace as God's revelation of Himself must also
be experiential. God's self-disclosure comes to us through
the written word of scripture, as well as through the lived
experience of the historical Christian community enshrined in
tradition. These are not two sources of revelation; they are
one. God's revelation becomes actualised in our lives in the
measure that we interpret these sources in the light of our
own lived experience (30), and use them to give meaning to
that experience. All revelation is interpreted; scripture
itself is an account of the way in which the early Christian
communities interpreted their own very real experience of

salvation in Jesus. It is thus a false dichotomy to attempt
to evaluate the authority of revelation as over against the
authority of our own experience. Revelation only comes to us
IN experience — there is no other means by which we can
apprehend it. We look to the sources of revelation to reveal
the significance of that experience. Revelation thus becomes
"the manifestation of a transcendent meaning in the dimension
of our historical horizon of experience and in the responsive
affirmation of that manifestation"(31). God reveals himself
to us in the measure that we have the means to interpret our
experience of the world as encounter with the transcendent by
using the religious language which carries the Christian
message.

This interpretation of grace and revelation as
experienced has its roots in the philosophical shift which
can be thought of as the 'turn to the subject', or the 'turn
to experience'(32). It is an interpretation which has only
relatively recently been represented in the mainstream of
Roman Catholic theology, and one which differs radically from
more traditional views. In medieval theology revelation was
a statement about the origin of salvation rather than about
the doctrine of salvation as such (33) — in other words, what
the believer believed in was the object of revelation. The
attempt of Vatican 1 (34) to establish the nature of faith as
belief in revelation was a rearguard action against fideism
and deism on the one hand and rationalism on the other.
Revelation was seen as codifiable in a set of truths and
statements. The counter-position to that was held by those
deists who maintained that there could be no such thing as a
supra-rational revelation. The truths of revelation must
therefore be seen as being already immanently present in
man's reason; the task of man-in-history was thus to discover
the content of that revelation. It was the deist thrust of
the Enlightenment which made the Roman Catholic church
suspicious of allowing a role to human experience, but in the
documents of Vatican II (35) the earlier scriptural view of
revelation as God's communication of himself to

man—in—history is restored.

This development highlights the ongoing tension which exists between doctrine as human formulation on the one hand and the redemptive reality which it claims to signify and witness to on the other. This tension has its foundations in the processes of historical and cultural change, which bring with them changing philosophical presuppositions which in turn necessitate a reinterpretation of previously valid doctrinal formulations of redemptive truths. The basic issue, which has run like a thread through all the historical changes, is the relation between nature and grace, long seen as two separate realities by Catholic theologians. The fundamental thrust of the work of theologians such as Karl Rahner has been to reformulate the dualistic relationship between nature and grace which was put forward by neo-scholastic theology, with its extrinsicist conception of God and its propositional understanding of revelation. Rahner's position (36) is that grace becomes an irrelevance for man if all that he has the capacity to know — other than verbal statements made about God by the 'magisterium' — is contained in the category of nature and immanently present in his reason. In that case he is and becomes so self-sufficient that he feels no need of grace. Grace, says Rahner, impinges on the area of human nature where man questions, wonders, searches for meaning — in other words, on his personhood. It is in the transcendence of the immediate in his nature that man's capacity for grace is seen. Rahner thus sees the cultural, moral and spiritual dimension of life as being animated by the movement of grace (37).

Once we locate grace within nature in this way we have definitively established the reality of their relationship (38), which is that grace as God's self-revelation presupposes the human person as the condition for its possibility. God can only reveal himself to us in the context of our own self-awareness, our understanding of ourselves as persons over against the world — in other words, in the

context of our experience. As Vatican II puts it, God
reveals himself precisely by revealing man to himself (39).
The particular context of that revelation, and the context
which gives it meaning, is our relationality, because it is
in relation with others that we experience encounter, the
paradigm experience of self disclosure of personhood. The
Christian revelation is revelation of a Person. In Christ as
revelation, and in the trinitarian dimensions of that
revelation God opens up to us the possibility of
understanding what being human really means (40), both on a
personal and on a social level. We are thus not only
justified but also sanctified, as our lives and our history
are transformed into a 'new creation'.

v. The content of revelation; history and hermeneutics.

This somewhat experiential view of faith would be
incomplete in anthropological terms if we neglected the
rational basis of faith. In order to be able to affirm the
foregoing we therefore need to reflect on the epistemological
grounds for that affirmation (41). The statement "we believe
that Jesus of Nazareth preached the coming of the Kingdom as
God's offer of salvation to mankind" requires validation not
only in terms of the possibility of faith, but also in terms
of its content as presented in scripture and tradition. In a
sense these issues can be tackled within the same context.
Faith, if it is anything within the range of human cognition,
is an experience which, like all other human experiences, is
self-authenticating. But the interpretation of the
experience, its meaning in the context of other life
experiences, its continuing significance as a creative force
which acts to encourage and sustain personal growth — all of
these must be based on the development of historical
knowledge. Historical study of Jesus is the key both to the
affirmation of our faith experience and to establishing what
it signifies; it is thus inappropriate to separate the Jesus
of history from the Christ of faith (42).

However, we must be aware of the tension between affirmation and significance. Historical study of Jesus may well give concrete content to faith, but it can never provide a verification of faith (43). On the other hand, the fact that the experience of God's offer of salvation is self-authenticating does not render it immune from the scrutiny of critical rationality. Here is where it is imperative to establish an adequate methodology which will cope with the different problems of validation. Our starting point has to be the realisation that the man Jesus has vanished beyond all recall; there is no contemporary written evidence, nor did he himself write anything (so far as we know). What we have is the 'historical Jesus' as presented to us in the writings of the early Christian communities. Access to that person thus requires a hermeneutical excercise – ie the development of a methodology for reaching an understanding of those texts (44).

This process will have a number of phases.

A. TEXTUAL CRITICISM serves both to retrieve meaning and to establish authenticity. In particular, it is important to establish the content of the symbols used, because it is this which will determine meaning. Proper exegetical criteria are needed – for instance, consistency of content will indicate authenticity, so will the existence of particular material in several sources. Editing criteria can serve to establish authenticity on grounds of 'queerness' or oddness of fit; 'formgeschischte' will do the same by deciding what can or can not be attributed to Judaism as opposed to primitive Christianity. Crossan (45) suggests how these ideas might be applied. We look first at the synoptics to establish the amount of 'creative reinterpretation' Matthew and Luke allowed themselves, and to decide which of the layers of interpretative restatement is earliest and best meets the criteria of historicity. We test for divergence between what is said there and the attitude of the early church – divergence suggests authenticity. This crtierion of dissimilarity can be applied not only to subject and content, but also to style and form.

B. HISTORICAL CRITICISM is required in order to analyse the circumstances in which the text might have been written and to evaluate the intent of its authors. An understanding of the text as historical artefact is a necessary part of establishing its authenticity; so is an understanding of its social and cultural context.

C. LITERARY CRITICISM is important because much of the scriptural material is presented in a form which requires literary analysis. For instance, as Perrin (46) points out, the Kingdom idea as used by Jesus is not a conception, but a powerful symbol which evoked a myth in the minds of his hearers (47). Furthermore, the parables which illumine that idea come to us in a form which is different to that in which they originated. As Jesus told them they were parable, oral and personal, but in the course of transmission through the oral and into the written literature they acquired a different status and meaning. They became allegorical rather than parabolic; the various elements in the story stand for something other than themselves. The story as a whole thus no longer functions in the same way — ie as an illuminating device to the participant hearer.

D.The final moment is the INTERPRETATIVE one. Literary crticism relies on historical, and historical relies on textual criticism as the dynamic interaction of text and interpreter finally comes into being (48). Not only does the interpreter interpret the text, but the text interprets the interpreter and his own experience.

We need such procedures in order build bridges back in time towards the circumstances of the life and death of Jesus of Nazareth. But there is a further problem raised by the tension — which has existed from earliest times — between the

process of historical reconstruction on the one hand and its
interpretation as governed by faith. The earliest accounts
we have are themselves governed by faith. History, as
Schillebeeckx reminds us (49) is always done by delineating
characters in ways which demonstrate what the historians want
to show. We can write the history of colonial Africa in
terms of the adventures of the intrepid explorers, or we can
write it as an account of imperialist oppression. Our
account will be theory- and value-laden, even if we believe
that we are doing history 'objectively'. Positivistic
approaches to history do not accept this point of view;
nineteenth century theologians thus saw no difference between
the historical and the earthly Jesus because they believed
that accounts by early Christian writers were faithful
reports by eyewitnesses of historical events.

All our historical accounts of Jesus come to us through
the grids and filters of early Christian perceptions as to
what the whole Jesus-event actually meant. The real
historical paradox here is that in spite of the fact that at
the time of Jesus there were a whole variety of widely
differing notions and perceptions in existence as to what
salvation might actually mean in practice, within five years
after his death there existed a group of people who
proclaimed as saviour a man who had actually failed in terms
of all the commonly acccepted perceptions about salvation.
But their proclamation was not committed to paper until years
afterwards, and by then those people had grown older and
others, who had never known Jesus, were committing the oral
tradition to paper so that their successors might have a
reliable source from which to teach. The stories they told
were stories which had been handed down to them, and they
told them in ways which were meaningful to them in the
context of their own life experiences and of their existence
as Christians in community. The gospels are thus testimonies
to faith rather than intentional historical accounts,
presented in narrative form and interpreted in the light of

faith. Because they are conditioned historical presentations rather than 'accurate' accounts they raise the whole question of disentangling what Jesus said and did from what the early Christian writers want to say when, for instance, they report the miracles or attribute certain attitudes to the disciples.

Our attempts to reach towards an understanding of Jesus and his message by using tools of historical and hermeneutical scholarship is thus an exercise which produces results which are themselves necessarily conditioned by the perceptions of the early writers. But this is only the first set of filters through which we see the 'historical Jesus', the first interpretative framework. The second framework is that which derives from Jesus' own understanding of himself. The categories which he himself possessed and used were themselves interpretative, drawn from his own Judaic background. The way in which he saw himself and conceived of his mission was determined by those categories — in other words, by the prophetic utterances, the messianic hopes and expectations which were common in the communities where he lived and taught. The story of Jesus is thus a story of how the key concepts and aspirations of his environment are translated into his activity and his message, of how the constraints which operated in his culture dictated the options open to him in terms of the way in which he could teach, heal and exorcise (50). He was surrounded by a whole complex of ideas about what salvation and the Kingdom of God might mean in practice — apocalyptic ideas, eschatological formulations, ethical prescriptions, politico-Zealotic and Pharisaic ways of thinking. How and why did he see himself as he did? To what extent can we penetrate behind his own grids and filters to reach the man himself?

Here is where the sharp edge of the interaction between faith and history takes place. Schillebeeckx summarises the problem

"....the sum of what historical inquiry may

> establish about a person is certainly not
> the same thing as understanding that person
> in his indivisible individuality"(51).

In other words, the Jesus we know is the Jesus of faith, not
the Jesus of history, and in the last analysis that
perspective is as important as all the scholarly evidence.
Schillebeeckx continues −

> "over against all the critical results (of
> historical scholarship) there will always be
> a residue, a surplus of meaning. A person
> can only be approached in personal trust or
> mistrusted in what is a similar attitude to
> commitment to a decision. Both the
> opposition of those who were scandalised by
> Jesus and the confident trust of those who
> found in him their salvation witness to a
> better understanding of Jesus of Nazareth
> than any neat and neutral account of him
> which the systematic methods of history
> might legitimately be able to give. In the
> end another human being can only be
> recognised in a disclosure
> experience..."(52).

In other words, there is perhaps a danger in trying too hard
to reach the historical Jesus. In the interaction between
faith and history it is finally faith which is primary,
although that faith receives essential validation from the
historical perspective (53).

The third interpretative framework within which we
operate is our own. The total hermeneutic process requires
us not only to examine the way in which Jesus interprets
himself in the light of his own cultural categories and the
way in which the early Christian writers interpret the
phenomenon of Jesus in the light of their aspirations and
expectations; it also requires us to look at the way in which
our understanding of the whole Jesus−event is conditioned by

our own particular personal, social and historic circumstances. How, in other words, does the dynamic interaction between text and interpreter work for us?

It is clear, first of all, that however methodically and objectively we approach the issue, we are working out of a background which, philosophically speaking, has undergone 'a number of radical changes over time. Philosophical presuppositions give historical study its particular focus and emphasis, as well as its interpretative content. Shifting perspectives have led to a variety of Christological perspectives which, as Schillebeeckx points out (54) are more or less heretical depending on whether they "give the last word (in Christological formulation) to faith (or) to philosophy". Over the centuries the focus has shifted alternately from the Jesus of history to the Christ of faith, we have 'seen the Lord' as Christ the victor, as Jesus our brother, as Christ the king, as Jesus the liberator, as Christ the incarnate word, as Jesus of the manger and of the cross .

Not only have philosophical stances shifted over the centuries, but so also has the nature of human experience. If the message of the Kingdom is really God's offer of salvation to us, we have to explore the whole question of what that actually means in our lives. We cannot simply assume that salvation is something for the future or for elsewhere or for some other time – this is the same kind of interpretation as allows us to think of the Kingdom as something not quite relevant to us here and now. What we believe about the Kingdom and what we believe about salvation are derived one from the other. If Jesus proclaimed a Kingdom which was to be inaugurated in human history then he was proclaiming the reality of a salvation which applied not in some abstract, other-worldly sense, but in the present historical, social and cultural perspective. Admittedly the eschatological dimension of Jesus' message allows the existence of a wide variety of interpretations. The Roman Catholic church, for instance, currently contains a diversity of belief on this topic as wide as that between the Latin American theologians and the more traditional forms of dogmatic belief. There is a diversity of opinion, too, concerning the question of whether or not God's offer of salvation in Jesus is made to all. The Catholic Church has widened its perspective on this issue since the Second Vatican Council (55), but other Christian positions might argue that the offer of salvation is made only to those who profess Jesus as Lord. There is also the possibility that God's offer of salvation is experienced concretely by some who do not adhere to any credal confession; who see Jesus as the embodiment of true humanity, as a guru, or simply as a reassuring myth (56). Nevertheless, taking the hermeneutical process seriously requires us to engage with the question of how our understanding of the texts is conditioned by our own 'grids and filters', of the extent to which we perceive the texts as interpretative of our own situation, and of how in turn we respond to that interpretation.

I have argued that the knowledge which provides the context of our faith comes to us through a set of grids and filters::-
(a) those of early church writers,
(b) those of the self-understanding of Jesus in the light of his own historical and environmental context,
(c) those of our own interpretative framework which is in turn conditioned by our own social and cultural context.
There are thus two quite separate problems in establishing this corpus of knowledge as rationally validated, one historical, one more strictly hermeneutical. Perrin argues strongly that these two aspects should be separately recognised (57), and that we should not simply assume that "there is an immediate ... correlation between a historical understanding of the messsage of Jesus and a hermeneutical appreciation of its possible significance for the present".

Taking the historical problem first, we analyse Jesus' preaching of the Kingdom in order to provide a basis for our analysis of faith as praxis. We shall do this by looking at understandings current in Jesus' environment which must have provided a background to his own understanding. We then look at the way in which modern interpreters have attempted to tackle some of the paradoxes of Jesus' message. Finally we attempt a literary analysis in order to retrieve some of the meanings of that message applicable to our own situation.

vi. The Kingdom of God; eschatology and apocalyptic.

The Kingdom is God's offer of salvation to man, finally and uniquely made in the person of Jesus of Nazareth. It is God's rule in the world as activity –
> "the power of God expressed in deeds: it is
> that which God does wherein it becomes
> evident that he is King. It is not a place
> or a community..not even the abstract idea
> of reign or Kingship of God. It is quite
> concretely the activity of God as King"(58).
Jesus proclaimed the inauguration of that Kingdom as the arrival of a state of affairs in which God would finally rule and redeem. This was not a proclamation of a better world, some utopia of freedom and love. It was the proclamation of the advent of a new world, which would shatter the existing world in a way that was hidden from human eyes, which would come in obscurity and failure, in scandal and folly.

Jesus chose to present his own particular experience of God to his hearers by using the symbol 'kingdom' – a symbol which powerfully evoked a myth in the minds of his hearers. It is clear that understandings of this symbol were not uniform – even among those who heard him there was a whole spectrum of interpretations of the idea, and he himself was clearly preaching an understanding which was not that uppermost in the minds of the majority of his hearers. But the use of the symbol enabled him to verbalise the message of God's eschatological kingdom as his "final and decisive activity in visiting and redeeming his people" (59). The terms on which this would occur were not necessarily those expected by his hearers, and much of Jesus' teaching was designed to make this clear.

How can we in our turn interpret these understandings? Modern biblical scholarship has concerned itself not so much with the question of what the realisation of the Kingdom would actually mean in practice, but rather with the conditions governing its realisation – ie when, how, where and by whom would it be realised. Each of these questions produces a tension within the interpretative framework; we shall deal with them in turn.

WHEN – present or future?
The key to understanding the controversy on the subject of whether Jesus thought the Kingdom was a present or a future reality is to realise that our own conception of time as linear is only one of several possibilities. In particular, our understanding differs fundamentally from that of Israel, whose concept of time was punctilinear. To quote von Rad –

> "The attitude of Western man to linear time
> is..naive; time is seen as an infinitely
> long straight line on which the individual
> can mark such past and future events as we
> can ascertain. The time span has a mid
> point, which is our present day. From it
> the past stretches back and the future
> forward"(60).

Cullmann (61) points to the fact that the structure of temporality is a culture-bound idea. For the Greeks time was circular; man was thus enslaved in a non-teleological historical process. Liberation could therefore only come from outside and be translated outside history (62).

The present/future tension in the literature is thus grounded in an understanding of time as absolute and linear − an understanding which precludes the possibility of the Kingdom being present and future at the same time (63). For instance, the 'consequent' eschatology of Schweitzer (64) sees the arrival of the Kingdom as embodied and expressed by the fixed eschatological expectations held by Jesus. His theory thus imposes a particular interpretation both on texts and on the behaviour of Jesus as conveyed by those texts. He believed that Jesus himself tried to translate his expectations into reality by acting in such a way as to bring about the 'messianic woes' and hence hasten the coming of the Kingdom. But, although immanent, it remained resolutely future, and Schweitzer sees the actions of Jesus in the latter part of his ministry as being determined by that futurity − in other words, by the requirements of Schweitzer's own hypothesis based on his notion of linear time.

The alternative position, adopted by Dodd (65) is that Jesus proclaims a Kingdom which has already been realised. This 'realised eschatology' view sees the prophetic/apocalyptic hope as a timeless reality which is thus already present although not necessarily fully realised. The Kingdom thus becomes present fact, and those sayings of Jesus which refer to the future coming of the Kingdom have therefore to be interpreted as referring to some reality beyond time and space. This view also clearly takes a particular implicit stance about the nature of time in that it implies that it is possible to talk about something in a 'timeless' context. There is thus the implication that it is possible to hold some kind of dualistic view about time − some things happen in time and some timelessly − ie outside the constraints of a time framework.

The compromise position to that taken by Schweitzer and Dodd — that of Jeremias (66), is based on a particular view of the tension between present and future in a linear-time framework. Jeremias argues that the Kingdom is in process of realisation (sich-realisierende Eschatologie), that it is a pronouncement to the present in view of the immanent eschatological future. In other words, this is a genuine acceptance of the present-future tension, and it is tempting to assume, as does Perrin (67) that we can go no further in resolving that tension. But such an unresolved tension leaves all sorts of questions unanswered. For instance, how can we assume that the two can exist independently, since a linear-time framework would lead us to suppose the the present in some way causes the future? Also, what kind of model of the Kingdom is presupposed — one which is only partially complete now and will be completed in the future, or one which is completely realised now and fulfilled in some indescribable way in the future?

Pannenberg's contribution (68) to the discussion enables us to resolve some of those problems. His basic point is that far from the present structuring the future, it is the future which structures the present. We find this perspective echoed in the way in which Jesus emphasises the present impact of an immanent future (Lk.12.40). The future, in other words, has an imperative claim on the present; it is the future which has ontological priority. All events are contingent until the possible becomes the actual. We can choose how to visualise this process; what happens can happen randomly, or deterministically, or by virtue of some power that gives contingent events a unity. That power exists, it is the power of God's future, the single future for all events, the future which lets go of itself to bring the present into being. So that God's presence in the world is seen not as primordial existence, as in mythic religion, but as the future of his coming Kingdom which manifests itself now. Jesus interpreted life in terms of eschatology, because he saw the revelation of God's love in the immanence of the Kingdom, in the ways in which the Kingdom manifests itself before it comes in power. And that, argues Pannenberg, is the way in which man gets a chance to participate in God's future, rather than being overshadowed by its sudden arrival. Man's response to the message of the Kingdom can be in terms of openness to that future. He can make the choices which create freedom and life, or those which build defences against God's future.

Taking the present-future tension seriously requires us to construct some explanation which accounts for the structure of relationship between them, but which is not based on simple causality. Pannenberg's contribution is particularly convincing because he does this in a way which not only explains the present-future relationship but stresses the key role of man's decision, choice and action in the realisation of God's kingdom.

HOW - apocalyptic/eschatological.

Did Jesus see the Kingdom as remaking the present world, or as a state of affairs which would reign once the present world had been brought to an end? The environment of his time would certainly lead him to favour the second interpretation, but Luke 17:20-4, Luke 11:20 and Mark 10:17-22 would seem to suggest that Jesus sees the Kingdom as God's power to break in and shatter the certainties of this world rather than to create a totally new order. Weiss, (and Schweitzer after him), held the view that the Kingdom was something which would erupt into history -

> "das Losbrechen eines ueberwaeltigenden Gottessturms, der vernichtend und erneuerend einherbraust .. den der Mensch weder herbeifuehren noch beeinfluessen kann"(69).

Much of the discussion for the first forty years of this century centred on the acceptance, rejection and modification of this view (70).

WHO — God's action/man's response.

The Old Testament understanding of the Kingdom is clearly one which emphasises God's action and power to rule and to subdue his enemies. Jesus on the other hand preached the Kingdom in action as well as word — by his own actions as well as by what he saw as appropriate action for others. Ritschl (71) saw the Kingdom as the moral organisation of humanity through action inspired by love. God redeems us, but we must act in such a way as to ensure that his Kingdom becomes established. He gives us dominion over the earth and sets us to work to accomplish that purpose. But Weiss and others of the apocalyptic school argue that this view places too much emphasis on the actions of man rather than God. It is God, they argue, who brings about the Kingdom by direct intervention in human history. Man only has to act in such a way as to show the repentance which the Kingdom's immanence demands (Interimsethik). Even Dodd does not see the Kingdom, permanently realised though it is, as being brought about by man's activity. The ethical teaching of Jesus is for him simply the new law of the Kingdom which has already been realised.

There is a clear tendency in this debate to regard eschatological interpretations as an alternative to ethical interpretations — to postulate another tension, in other words, between eschatology and ethics. But the issue is not so much whether God's action or man's action brings about the Kingdom, since it is always agreed that the Kingdom is primarily a manifestation of the action of God. The issue is much more whether, and the extent to which, the realisation of the Kingdom NEEDS man's collaboration. What, in other words, are we required to do? Bultman tackles this issue (72). The coming of the Kingdom places man in a 'crisis of decision', because this coming is an existential reality rather than a temporal one. The future as God's activity comes on man and demands the present existential decision. Accepting the challenge of the Kingdom therefore involves accepting the ethic of the Kingdom, and thus, Bultmann argues, the eschatological/ethical tension is resolved and transformed into a dynamic unity. Bultmann is thus interpreting the proclamation of Jesus as one which reflects a conception of human existence in the world as decision in the face of the challenge of God's demand — which is essentially also the position of Pannenberg.

WHERE — inside/outside.

Where exactly is the Kingdom realised? Some interpreters see the kingdom as God's reign over men's hearts. For Harnack (73) the Kingdom is to be interpreted individualistically and spiritually. It is a hidden life-force which guides the actions of men. For Schleiermacher (74) it is the corporate human God-consciousness which is the existence of God in human nature. This is brought into being as a result of Christ's God-consciousness — in other words, it is the result of the act of redemption. For Otto (75) the Kingdom is mystery, miracle, blessing, grace — something entirely numinous. The Kingdom, therefore, is simply a mythologisation of the holy, and as such is the expression of grace which motivates mens' individual lives.

Other interpreters, however, see the Kingdom as something to be built by man in the world. The 'social gospel' interpretation derives from Ritschl's idea that we are co-workers who collaborate with God's activity. Interpreters such as Ragaz (76) and Rauschenbusch (77) see the Kingdom as emerging specifically in history when God's will is done on earth, when the seed of the Kingdom sown in mens's hearts results in a gradual transformation of society and social institutions — ie when the liberation of humanity brought about by Jesus bears fruit in the realisation of a social ideal of Christianity. Dialectical theologians such as Barth (78), however, do not accept that the Kingdom is in the heart, or in society, or in some final cosmic state. The Kingdom is only in Jesus, and in the historical Jesus-event the Kingdom has come as close as it can come until time becomes eternity.

Theological discussion on this topic has not reached a consensus, nor has it resoved the inherent tensions which exist between the alternative poles of the different dimensions of Jesus' message. The majority of interpreters have adhered to one pole of the dimension in question rather than taking the tension seriously, and in so doing they have lost some of the richness and meaning which the scriptural texts convey. The very essence of the message of the Kingdom is contained in these tensions; the interpretative task is therefore not so much to ignore or resolve these tensions as to recast them creatively into a meaning structure.

For us as hearers of Jesus' message the idea of 'Kingdom of God' is also problematic. This is partly because of the element of tension and paradox, partly also because of the hermeneutical issue. But the major reason is because we have our own philosophical understanding of how things happen in the world (79). Jesus' preaching of the Kingdom conveyed the clear message that God's Kingdom was at hand now, that it was somehow to be realised within the circumstances of human history, and that it was therefore something relevant to our lives. But we have no way of seeing how this can be the case. For us, events and states of affairs in human history are the result of human actions, rather than the actions of God, they are a drama played out against a backdrop of natural happenings. Where in that picture is there room for an acting God?

Various solutions to this paradox have been adopted at various times in the thinking of the Christian community.
1. We can ignore any interpretation of God's rule as God's

activity in the world, and see it rather, as Schleiermacher
does, as simply requiring man's acknowledgement of God (80).
2. We can interpret the notion corporately, as Harnack does
(81), and see God's Kingdom in the world as the Christian
church; God's will is then manifested in the existence of
that church.
3. We can think of God as a supernatural being who 'makes
things happen' from outside the world. This is the
Hellenistic rather than the Judaic understanding of God's
power, which has served as reassurance to human powerlessness
throughout history, and which is deeply ingrained within our
own cultural thought forms.
4. We can simply adopt our own linguistic understanding of
'Kingdom' as a place. This parallels the Jewish apocalyptic
understanding of Kingdom as a new era. We tend to think of
that place as 'heaven' and we assume that we shall join God
there when we die, thus 'inheriting the Kingdom'.
5. We can adopt a more eschatological understanding and see
Jesus' proclamation as meaning that the Kingdom will be
realised sometime in the future, ignoring the fact that it is
also proclaimed for now (82). This finds echoes in our
cultural belief in human progress towards a better world – a
belief which is grounded in our understanding of evolution as
'onwards and upwards'(83). It also implies that we have no
need to worry about the coming of the Kingdom, because its
arrival is in some sense inevitable.
6. We can opt for an understanding of God's Kingdom as God's
reign over mens' hearts, something interior and
individualistic, a spiritual force with little, if any,
historical realisation.

All of these understandings have been propounded at one
time or another, all of them are current in our
understanding. And all of them, says Bonhoeffer, amount to
disbelief in the kingdom (84). Adherence to any one of them
allows us to sidestep the central issue, which is that the
challenge of Jesus's proclamation of the Kingdom demands a

response from us which has to be manifested in living and
doing, and that we have to rely on the fact that this is how
the Kingdom is realised. This is not to say that we create
the Kingdom by our actions –

> "..the Kingdom of God must always remain the
> Kingdom of God. It is not a construction
> undertaken by extending Christian virtue, it
> is not simply the Kingdom of better
> men"(85).

It is rather that the Kingdom becomes realised in history
only to the extent that faith becomes praxis, to the extent
that we translate our 'option for the Kingdom' into life and
action as we respond to the mystery of God and his future.
It is God's Kingdom, but our response.

We now turn to the texts in which Jesus preached the
Kingdom in order to disentangle a meaning structure which
might guide us in identifying the elements of such a
response.

vii. The Kingdom of God; the message interpreted.

The Jesus event is one single event; the man, his life
and message, his actions and words, form a single unity.
Because this message is proclaimed in word as well as deed
we need to pay some attention to the linguistic form of the
proclamation, and specifically to two issues–
(a) the status of the word 'Kingdom'
(b) the fact that the Kingdom is proclaimed in parables –
"in all his teaching to the crowds Jesus spoke in parables;
in fact he never spoke without a parable."(Matt.13:34)

(a) Perrin (86) argues that it is inappropriate to
think of the 'Kingdom of God' as an idea or conception, as
some authors do (87), because that implies that "for Jesus

'Kingdom of God' evoked a consistent well-defined understanding of the nature and form of God represented by that symbolic language"(88). If we adopt that understanding, Perrin argues, we prejudge the whole issue of what Jesus meant by 'kingdom'. Jesus uses the word not as concept but as symbol — something which represents something else, which evokes a myth, which points beyond itself to another reality. Symbols can evoke a very wide range of meanings. Paul Ricoeur (89) distinguishes between a sign which signifies something specific — ie has a one-to-one relationship with that which it represents, and a symbol which has a set of meanings which are not limited or exhausted by continual use (90). The 'Kingdom of God' is just such a symbol in ancient Judaism; its meanings, as we have seen, are created and reformulated within the overall mythic context of God's activity in the world. Although Jesus' use of the symbol is designed to evoke the myth as a whole, the range of meanings which he gives within that context are his own.

(b) These meanings were not entirely the expected ones. Jesus did not preach so as to recall the content of Judaic myth evoked by the symbol 'Kingdom'. Nor did he preach pedagogically, as did rabbinical teachers, where exposition is linked to specific biblical texts which are then interpreted, or to moral situations which are allegorised. (We have of course to be aware that much of the parabolic material was allegorised by later writers.) He taught in parables, a form of poetic metaphor (91) where the linguistic form is not a device designed to assist communication, but is itself the teaching. The image is the speech, the medium is the message (92). The use of metaphor (93) allows an extension of the normal use of language to reorganise or redescribe reality. It can be used to talk about known situations so as to create insight or to give an alternative to ordinary descriptions of reality. Alternatively it can be used to talk about new phenomena because the available conceptual structure is not adequate, thus enabling exploration of the unknown via the known.

Metaphor can appear as myth. Used thus, it creates a picture of the world which is characterised, as Levi-Strauss shows (94) in his discussion of the structure of myth, by reconciliation and the mediation of opposites. The character of myth is that 'it all works out in the end'. Stability is established, hope is fulfilled. But metaphor can also appear as parable, and here its function is very different. It appears as a metaphor of normalcy, because what is talked about are everyday situations; it thus invites the listener to participate in the world of the story, to situate himself within the action. But because its intention used as parable is to subvert all normal interpretations, the outcome of that participation is that stability is challenged, expectations are reversed, the fundamental mythic principle of reconciliation is overthrown.

Parabolic linguistic form conveys the whole message of the Kingdom; it conveys paradox, surprise, scandal, challenge. It demands the adoption of another paradigm, another framework of thought, one which will accomodate reversal of expectations about the future and reinterpretation of the past. It seeks to draw the hearers into an experience which is an experience of the wholly other, of the Kingdom, so that they can then draw from that experience their own way of living the message. Parable was the form Jesus chose to proclaim his own experience of God as Abba; the form of the proclamation reflected the experience just as his actions resulted from it. So that parable was, as Crossan shows (95) fundamentally constitutive of Jesus' own historicity, of his way of living his life in time.

This interpretation gives a much richer and more

central role to the form of Jesus' teaching than earlier
authorities were wont to do. Parables are much more than
Juelicher's timeless moral truths or Jeremias' stories which
contain the message (96). They express in their very form
Jesus' fundamental experience of God's Kingdom which comes
as unexpected future, which revises and reinterprets the
past, and which empowers life and action. It is from this
experience that Jesus' own life and actions spring; the
parables are the cause, not the consequence, of what he
does. As Crossan says, "he was not crucified for parables,
but for ways of acting which resulted from the experience of
God presented in parables (97). A parable", says Crossan,
"is the house of God "(98), and an investigation of the form
of the parables can thus be thought of as akin to an
archaeological undertaking.

What we find as we dig are characteristics or
attributes of the Kingdom which have in common the fact that
they are all linked to the idea of 'temporality'. In other
words, we find within the structure of the parables a
reconciliation of the present-future tension. We live in
time and act in history; there therefore has to be a
structure of temporality both to God's activity and to our
response. But neither of these happen as discrete events in
linear time. The future of God's Kingdom breaks into our
present as advent, forcing us to reverse our interpretations
of the past and destroying our plans for the future which
were based on those interpretations. The radicality of the
coming of God's Kingdom is the unexpectedness of the way in
which this process works out within the structure of our own
historicity. The challenge to our response is created by
the consequent necessity not only for seeing the world with
new and other eyes — not just the present, but also the past
and future, — but also for realising that God does not play
the game by our rules. Nothing is as we think it is, and it
is this realisation which will determine the quality of our
response in terms of action.

All this is seen by Crossan (99) as conveyed in the structure of the parables. Three of the parables are paradigmatic in that they embody all three key elements of advent, reversal and action. In the parable of the treasure (Matt 13.44) the man finds it, sells it, and remakes his life accordingly. The same pattern is seen in the parable of the pearl (Matt 13.45) and in the story of the great fish (Gos.Thom. 81.28-82,3). Other parables tend to embody one or other of these aspects. Parables of ADVENT are those which disclose to us something of the way in which the kingdom, God's rule as inbreaking into human reality, comes about. Most of the images come from nature: they portray the inevitability and the undeserved character, but also the normality of nature's bounty. The kingdom comes in HIDDENNESS and MYSTERY, we see the signs of its coming, but not the actual happening, (budding fig tree, Mk 13.28, Matt 24.32, Lk.21.29-30, leaven Matt 13.37, Lk.13.20-1, Gos.Thom.97.3-6) The kingdom comes as GIFT and as SURPRISE (sower Mk.4.3-8, Matt.13.3-8, Lk.8.5-8, Gos.Thom.82.3-13, mustard seed Mk.4.30-2, Mt.13.31-2, Lk.13.18-19, Gos.Thom.84.26-33) It also comes as DISCOVERY and as JOY (lost sheep Mt.18.12-13, Lk.15.4-6, Gos.Thom.98.22-27, lost coin Lk.15.8-9). The fact that in one parable the searcher is God and in the other it is man only serves to emphasise that the important thing is the quality of the finding experience. In fact, what all these parables convey is the quality of the human experience of the Kingdom, an experience which in spite of the radicality of what is happening is not shocking or startling, but at once reassuring and incomprehensible.

The advent of the Kingdom, although characterised as something which is essentially not traumatic, does have the effect of shattering our world, reversing our values, altering our choices, judgements and conclusions. There is an impossibility about it, a complete polarity of reversal,

which we can best see in what Crossan calls the parables of
REVERSAL, the Lukan stories which contain this insight.
The clearest example is the parable of the Good Samaritan
(Lk.10.30-7). It is easy to interpret this parable as
exemplifying one or other of several things - the way in
which the good are really bad, or the way in which those who
are unacccceptable are good, or the way in which love of
neighbour should be practised, or the fact that we should
love our enemies. On one level it is simply a moral story,
but an investigation of the structure suggests that something
more is being said. Crossan (100) suggests that what is
being conveyed is the impossible - the fact that a man who is
completely anathema can be good. The force of this is lost
on us unless we are prepared to translate it into our own
categories - can we for instance retell the story
substituting the word 'terrorist' for 'Samaritan'?

A similar reversal holds in the story of the rich man and
Lazarus (Lk.16.19-31). Here the situational reversal is
actually something immoral in the context of the thinking of
the time, because riches were seen as a sign of blessing and
sickness as a curse. The fact that Lazarus woke up in the
bosom of Abraham therefore reverses the values and judgements
which Jesus' hearers must have used when interpreting the
parable. Again, in Lk.18.10-14, the fact that God listens to
the sinful publican and not to the virtuous Pharisee can only
have caused the hearers to feel uncomfortable with their own
accepted norms, as must the fact that in Lk.15.11-22 the
wastrel son is inside the house eating and drinking what he
did not earn while the dutiful son is outside sulking. In
the parable of the great supper (Mt.22.1-10, Lk.14.16-24,
Gos.Thom.92.10-35) which has been used as an allegory by
Matthew and a moral story by Luke, the really disturbing
feature is that at the end of the day the invited guests are
absent and the uninvited are present. This feature of
reversal is something which is also seen in Jesus' use of
proverbial sayings within the context of Wisdom literature.

These sayings are used as paradox by Jesus in a way which challenges the basic presuppositions of Wisdom literature itself (101). This use of language as pushing language to its limits (it is easier for a camel to pass through the eye of a needle...) is analogous to the relationship of eschaton to world. The advent of the kingdom challenges world in the same way as paradox undermines language.

There is finally the class of parable which exemplifies the fact that the inbreaking of God's Kingdom which shatters our world demands a response from us in terms of living and doing. The parables of ACTION tell us that sometimes the decision is made, sometimes not, but that in any event we must be watchful and ready for the opportunity to respond. The friend at midnight (Lk.11.5-8), the unjust judge (Lk.18.2-5), the thief (Mt.24.43-4, Lk.12.39-40), the wheat and darnel (Mt.13.24-30, Lk.14.28-32) - all of these recount situations where successful decisions are made in response to the challenge of God's kingdom. In the rich fool (Lk.12.16-20) and the wedding garment (Mt.22.11-14) the wrong responses are made. In the parable of the bridesmaids (Mt.25.1-13) some respond adequately, some do not. But it is the nine servant parables which tell us something very important about the dangers of pronouncing a given response 'adequate'. In four of these parables - the doorkeeper (Mk.13.33-7 Lk.12.35-8), the overseer (Mt.24.45-51, Lk.12.42-6), the talents (Mt.25.14-30. Lk.19.12-27) and the throne claimant (Lk.19.12, 14-15, 27) the response of the servant is evaluated by the master (God) in the expected fashion. In other words we, the hearers, are on safe ground when we assume we know what an acceptable response to the challenge of the Kingdom would be.

But stranger things happen in the other five stories - the unmerciful servant (Mt.18.23-38), the servant's reward (Lk.17.7-10), the unjust steward (Lk.16.1-7), the wicked husbandman (Mk.12.1-12, Mt.21.33-46, Lk.20.9-19,

Gos.Thom.93.1–18), and the vineyard workers (Mt.20.1–13). In
the parable of the unmerciful servant the good man is going
to be rewarded and forgiven, but then there is a reversal. In
the parable of the servants reward even the good are not
rewarded, in those of the unjust steward and the wicked
husbandman bad servants do better out of being bad than they
would have done had they been good, and in the parable of the
vineyard workers, the story which grates so uncomfortably on
the ears of modern capitalist hearers, not only do the good
and hardworking not get what they deserve, but the layabouts
get what they have not earned.

What does all this tell us? It would appear that
although we must be ready and willing to respond in life and
action to the challenge of the Kingdom, "the eschatological
event of God will always be that for which wise and prudent
readiness is impossible"(102), because the event itself also
has the effect of negating our wisdom and our prudence. In
other words, it is not we who say what the correct response
to the challenge of the Kingdom is, it is God. It is not
only that the action demanded by the advent of the Kingdom is
never articulated within the parables, it is also that what
is conveyed is that we are not to use our own norms to judge
what action to undertake in response. It is not only that we
are given no guidelines which we can translate into rational
action – after all, to be told to turn the other cheek is, as
Crossan says "neither helpful moral admonition (nor) even
radical pacifist advice"(103). It is also that ethics as
such are deliberately overthrown. An ethic is a prop, a
system, a substitute for God's kingdom and God's
righteousness, and this was the basis of the challenge of
both Jesus and Paul to the moral guidance of the law as
expounded by the Pharisees. The only use for the law, as
Paul says, is to define wrongdoing. Obedience to a code does
not lead to God, God leads to obedience. It is not that a
good life makes the reward of God's presence inevitable, it
is that the gift of God's presence makes a good life

possible. The whole logic of ethics is thus undermined by the mystery of God, and that, if we can accept it, is "the most crucial moral experience of all"(104). The advent of the Kingdom as proclaimed in the parables shatters our world so that we experience God as distinct from world, so that God can act in the space which is left vacant. Our response in action to that advent must therefore be "to walk in utter serenity and utter insecurity, in total concern and total incertitude"(105).

The proclamation of the Kingdom is a proclamation in unity of word and action; Jesus lives as he preaches. He is a living parable, we watch what he does, listen to the stories and interpret them in the light of his actions. The whole complex reveals the message; by his actions as well as by his words Jesus makes the Kingdom present. Mark 1.27 sees his actions as a "new teaching with authority". His actions have the same structure of proclamation which is found in his parabolic teaching. His life is itself the ADVENT of God's rule; he is seen by scriptural writers as the eschatological prophet, the one who raises the dead (Is.26.19), makes the blind see (Is.29.9-10,18-29, 35.5-6,8), the deaf hear (Is.42.18,43.8), comforts those who mourn (Is.61.1-3) and proclaims the good news to the poor (Is.52.7). There is messianic significance in these acts, because "to be blind is a sign of separation from God, to see is to have access to salvation, and the 'eschatological prophet' is the 'light of the world"(106). The writers of scripture see Jesus' life and actions through the interpretative filters of their expectations about the coming of God's rule in the person of the messiah.

But there is a HIDDENNESS, a mystery about the inbreaking of God's kingdom in Jesus. Jesus is the ordinary man from Nazareth, a healer among many. To recognise his actions as signs of the Kingdom demands faith, not just in what he does, but in the power of God at work in him. Nazareth was the place where people saw him only as the carpenter, the son of Mary, the brother of James and Joseph and Jude and Simon. And there, although he performed cures, he could work no miracles because of their lack of faith — not in his ability to heal, but in the fact that in so doing he offered God's saving power to those who were sick. In the story of the lepers the same point is made — all are cured, but it is only one who acknowledges.(Lk.17.11-19), that Jesus has acted with the 'finger of God'.

The advent of the Kingdom in Jesus is thus mysteriously hidden within the happenings and actions of his life. It is easy even for those who are constantly with him to forget what it is all about, to lose faith. Jesus constantly asks that their faith be maintained (Mk.4.40, Mt.17.20, Mt.14.18-32). The stilling of the storm and the walking on water are not miracles designed to engender faith, but, as Schillebeeckx argues (107) acts designed to expose the inconsistency of faithlessness in an existing faith-sustained and faith-motivated relationship. And conversely, the power of a faith continually sustained, an ability to recognise the advent of the kingdom in Jesus, hidden and mysterious though it is, would be sufficient to move mountains. (Mt.17.20).

Jesus is in himself the advent of the Kingdom as GIFT and SURPRISE. "In Jesus something extraordinary makes its appearance in human history, something which his opponents traced back to demonic sources, but his followers to an inexpressible closeness to the deepest core of all reality..."(108). If Jesus is from God, he is God's gift and as such he can bring that gift to others. He can bring the saving activity of God in every human situation, the doing of good in manifestly evil situations, the gift to others of wholeness and of healing. The gospels see Jesus in specific conflict with the powers of evil (Mk.1.23-4, 5.7, 9.20-5) which manifest themselves as devils in those possessed — not a familiar idea to cultures unused to seeing sickness as a

curse from God. Jesus gives food, enough and more than
enough (Mk.6.34-44, Mt.14.14-21, Lk.9.11-17,) to those in
need, as witness to God's abundant care for people. It is
specifically in the context of acting as host at a meal, at
the lakeside (Jn.21.1-14), or at Emmaeus (Lk.24.13-35) that
Jesus is 'recognised' for what he is. And it is in the
foundation of the Eucharist that God's offer of sustenance
and nourishment for people in their lives is
institutionalised at the last supper (Mk.14.22-25, Lk.14.20)
in a way which can be historically perpetuated.

Jesus is the one who in the power of God enables people
to RECOVER what they have lost. In casting out devils by the
power of God (Lk.11.14-23, Mt.12.22-30) he restores lost
sanity. In raising the daughter of Jairus he restores a lost
life and a lost daughter (Mt.8.5-13, Lk.7.1-10). But above
all, his offer of God's forgiveness enables people to recover
lost fellowship with God. In the situations where Jesus
shares a meal with sinners he is the one who goes in search
of what is lost. He puts himself beyond the pale of Jewish
acceptability in order to demonstrate the unconditionality of
God's offer of forgiveness. God's forgiveness is extended to
all without regard for merit, and the one who is forgiven
most is the one who is greater in the Kingdom because
forgiveness is a two-sided affair - the greater the
forgiveness the greater the love and repentance (Lk.7.36-50).
The particular quality of Jesus' relationship with sinners
(Mk.2.15-17, Mt.9.10-13, Lk.5.29-32) as experienced by those
who followed him conveyed to them something of the power of
God's rule in human life - a power to redeem the most glaring
transgressions, to heal the bitterest feuds, to bring hope in
hopeless situations. That experience is what is expressed in
the question put in Mk.2.10 - "which is easier, to say to the
sick man 'you are forgiven', or to cure him? I cure him so
that you may know that there is nothing which God cannot do,
no limit to God's mercy".

But there is another aspect to Jesus' proclamation of the Kingdom which is shown in the character of some of the things he does as well as in what he says in parable. It is the aspect of <u>REVERSAL</u>. What Jesus does contravenes not only the law, but also what might reasonably be expected of a teacher. He did not behave as John the Baptist did, he feasted with his disciples, (Mk.2.18-22) when one might have expected him to fast, as a sign that his presence signified joy and savation (Mt.11.16-18). He reached out to people, particularly to women, in ways which must have caused raised eyebrows in the more conservative sections of the community. His actions offended, either implicitly or explicitly, against the sensibilities of that community. Explicitly and specifically, not only did he blaspheme by claiming to forgive sins (Mk.2.1-12) and break the law by eating with the tax-gatherers (Mk.2.13-17), but he engineered a direct confrontation with the norms of the society he lived in by walking through a cornfield on the sabbath and defending the actions of his disciples when they plucked ears of corn (Mk.2.23-8). Worse, he cured on the sabbath - a man with a withered hand (Mk.3.1-5) in a synagogue, a woman with a crooked back (Lk.13.10-17), and a victim of the dropsy (Lk.14.1-6). Why? Not in order to criticise the law as such, but to criticise the way in which it is expounded and applied by the Pharisees. We hear him condemning the legalism which makes of the law a burden rather than a vehicle for the expression of concern for one's neighbour and love of God (Lk.11.3-9, 42-4, 46-8, 52). The deepest purpose of the law is to create response to God's saving power, but that purpose cannot be laid down in any code. This is why it may be necessary - and Jesus shows it sometimes is - to do more than the law requires, or to go against the law, in the service of the kingdom. Jesus has thus both a practical reverence for the law and a critical view of legalism. In the words of Schillebeeckx -

> "All this would seem to support the
> conclusion that Jesus liberates the

individual from a narrow and oppressive view
of God by exposing (the) ideology as an
orthodoxy that stood in a ruptured
relationship to orthopraxis (praxis of the
kingdom), and furthermore, qua orthodoxy,
had established an ethic as an independent
screen between God and man, so that the
relevance of the legal obligations to man's
salvation had become totally obscured"(109).

The advent of the Kingdom shatters all worlds, reverses all
norms, exposes all ideologies to critique, even those
ideologies which are erected in the name of the kingdom The
actions of Jesus bear witness to this.

Finally, we can see the advent of the Kingdom in the
actions of Jesus as demanding our response in terms of
ACTION. Specifically, the whole process of sending out the
disciples (Lk.10.2-12, Mt.9.37-8, 10.7-16) is only the end
result of the call which they experienced - a call which is
also experienced in the Old Testament as God's activity by
Elisha (1Kings 19.19-21). The point about this call is its
quality of ultimacy. It takes prior claim over other
obligations - not only work and unfinished business, but even
burying the dead (Mt.8.19,21-2, Lk.9.57-60) which in Jewish
law is an obligation preceding all others (110). As ultimate
call it demands ultimate response, unconditional and complete
surrender of all relationships and possessions. In the story
of the rich young man who asks Jesus what he must do to
attain eternal life (Mk.10.17-31) the surrendering of
possessions in order to follow Jesus would have been the sign
that following the law assiduously was not sufficient for
salvation. The essence of that response would have been lived
out not in poverty as such, but in a praxis which involved
sharing the life of Jesus by doing what he did.

To conclude, then, Jesus is the salvific event. He

proclaims the Kingdom in word, parable and action. His proclamation delineates for us the shape of God's offer and our response. Salvation is offered as the Kingdom's advent, which comes in hiddenness and mystery, in gift and surprise, in discovery and joy. Its advent reverses and shatters the shape of our world, in that advent and reversal we are freed for action and response. Jesus tells us these things in parable and proverbial saying, but he also lives them in his daily life and actions. Word and action are unified message, whose source is the ultimate human experience of God.

viii. Faith as praxis; some difficulties.

Jesus could have chosen to preach the good news of God's offer of salvation in many different ways. The linguistic form which he used — that of the parable — serves to convey the whole message of the Kingdom: the manner of its coming in hiddenness and mystery, its inbreaking into the world as surprise and gift, our joy at its discovery. It also conveys the element of paradox and scandal as expectations and judgements are reversed, and it ultimately presents us with God's demand that we respond to his offer in life and action. The quality of that response is not dictated or indeed predicted by the standards of our world — in fact, it may often involve a rejection and reversal of what is normally defined as appropriate action. It will be characterised rather as the living out of a new life in love and freedom, as 'doing the truth' — orthopraxis — in a way which is transformative of self and world. It is not simply that we translate our faith into our lives, it is rather that our lives become translated into a faith response.

But the practical implementation of this may be more difficult than it appears; what do we actually have to do? An adequate response to the challenge of the Gospel is not simply a matter of making the right choices, although the issue has always been presented in terms of a choice between good and evil. That interpretation is Pelagian. Pelagianism (111) takes the view that the point of God's gift or 'grace' is that it helps us to keep God's law more easily. Grace is seen as something superimposed on our nature which reinforces our own efforts in that it helps our 'weakness of will' and makes it easier for us to choose the good. However, the problem is much more subtle than this.

The first problem about the Pelagian view is that it relies on the assumption of a prior good, formulated within an already defined and existing set of laws to which we have to conform. As we have seen, this was not the thrust of Jesus' preaching. Nor is it the stance taken by Paul. With the legalistic morality implied by that view comes a correspondingly defined set of sins. The law, as Paul points out, (Rom.3.20), not only brings consciousness of sin, but sin actually gains its power from the law (Rom.23.2) in that it becomes defined and judged by the law (Rom.2.13ff, 5.18-21, Gal.3.19). We are then 'under the law'; we live with the understanding that the law is there to be kept, and this leads us to think that our 'righteousness' depends on our success in keeping the law — i.e. on our own merit. The law establishes the possibility of legalism (112) in a way which gives rise to the temptation to use our adherence to the law as a claim on God — we think that we 'deserve' reward for having kept the law; that we have 'earned' our salvation. But if that were the case, argues Paul, Christ would have died in vain (Rom.3.21-6), because we could have saved ourselves by our fidelity to the letter of the law, and would have had no need of God's salvation. As Sanders says — "Paul's view that attempting to do the law is itself sin is not the cause of his view that keeping the law and being Christian are incompatible, it is the consequence of it"(113).

It would appear, then, that 'doing good' is not the crux of the matter. The fact is that without the help of the

Spirit God's law in the real sense of that word cannot reign over our hearts because it is rendered impotent by our adherence to the sin which has been unleashed by our human interpretations of that law. Paul argues that the Spirit shifts our relationship with the law onto a different plane (Rom.8.5.) -"if you are led by the Spirit you are not under the law" (Gal.5.18). We are now under God's law, and the kind of law which has to do with recording transgressions has been ended and annulled by Christ (Rom.10.4, Eph.2.15), in whose Spirit we can satisfy every claim of God's law simply by loving our neighbour(Rom.13.10). Jesus witnessed to this by his action. However, the Pauline understanding of the nature of a faith response was not the one which prevailed historically. It was not until Luther, who saw the sin which lurks in the depths of every good act, that Christianity recovered the understanding of the relationship between grace and free will embodied in the Pauline texts. (Rom.3.20-8, Gal.3.11-12, Phil.3.9, Eph.2.9-10, Gal.3.22). Faith-as-action is thus not seen as a matter of choosing a prior defined good, but of responding in love to the given situation.

There is a further problem about the Pelagian view of grace and salvation. It is assumed that because we are transformed by grace, we can achieve the good, whatever it is, simply by our own efforts. Again, it is Paul who defines the complexity and exposes the weakness of this view. As well as being 'under the law' we are also 'under the flesh'. The liberty which grace gives to us is not total, because we cannot do in an exterior sense what we desire interiorly to do (Rom.7.14-25)(114). We are divided beings; in the duality of our human existence there is something which precedes and limits our liberty. Paul's anthropology is precisely characterised by Rahner -

> "What is certain is that all nature, which
> precedes liberty, offers resistance to the
> person's free and total disposability over

himself. Thus the dividing line between
person and nature is vertical over against
the horizontal line that separates the
spiritual from the sensible in man"(115).

Whatever our right intention as motivated by God's love in
our hearts, only the wrong is within our reach (Rom.7.21),
because in order for our response to God's grace to be
translated into action we have to work through the
instruments of nature – our 'bodily members', and our nature
lets us down (116). We need the external instruments of our
natural lives to carry out our human projects and under God's
grace to make ourselves into the persons we are in God's
eyes. But because our nature exists prior to our liberty in
the Spirit (Rom.8.5, Gal.5.18) it places a constraint on the
development of our own personhood.

This whole idea of a 'nature' which constrains the
realisation of our personhood and the exercise of our liberty
is seen by Paul as 'flesh' – our creatureliness, our
sensibility and affectivity which constrain our liberty. Our
being may be penetrated with love as the spiritual law, but
our actions are imbued with egotism because we choose the
easy solutions and avoid the creative ones. Egotism
alienates us from ourselves because we fail to realise the
intention conceived as a loving response to grace. We can see
this kind of thinking as representative of the 'already/not
yet' tension in Paul's soteriology. The spirit is already at
work as the first fruits, but the process will not be
completed until the eschaton (117).

But being 'under the flesh' cannot be the only factor
inhibiting our response? To believe that would be to see us
as creatures of impulse, without reason or intent. Whereas
in Romans 6.14 the struggle against the flesh results in
victory "sin shall not have dominion over you...", in
Romans 7 there is no sense of victory. The 'bondage'
(Gal.2.4, 4.4–8,24,25, 5:1) imposed by our nature must surely
therefore be more than the 'passions and lusts' of Romans

6.14; the problem cannot only lie in 'weakness of will'.
Paul acknowledges the existence of a further constraint when
he discusses the phenomenon of bondage to the ambiguities of
nature and environment. His 'ta stoichea tou kosmou'
(Gal.4.2-4, 8,10,19, Col.2.8,16-33) are those cosmic elements
central to his own thought system - 'powers of the world' -
which enslave created man even though he delights in God's
law and tries to fulfil it (118). Paul perceives these
powers as forces, elements, principalities, authorities,
spirits; the concept conveys a complexity of meanings
understandable only in the light of contemporary mythologies.

However, we need to attempt some interpretation of this.
There are close parallels between Paul's concept of 'slavery
to the law' and his perception of 'bondage to the elements'.
We are dead to the law (Gal.2.19), dead to the elemental
spirits (Col.2.30), we are confined under the law (Gal.3.23),
slaves to the elemental spirits (Gal.4.3,8ff). The law is
our custodian (Gal.3.24), the elemental spirits are our
guardians and trustees (Gal.4.2). The law is weak (Rom.8.3),
the elemental spirits are weak and beggarly (Gal.4.19). It
follows, then, that when we die with Christ we die to the
elemental spirits of the universe (Col.2.20). Adherence to
Christ can thus liberate us from the tyranny of something
which is basic, inherent and powerful in our world, because
Christ in dying stripped himself of those powers as well as
of the flesh (Col.2.15).

These elements are clearly not desirable influences. But
whereas 'the law' is unambiguous in meaning, then as now, the
concept of 'ta stoichea' needs interpretation in a modern
context. Suggestions as to its meaning have depended on both
the world-view and the theological stance of the interpreter
(119). 'Elements' can be seen as principial - rudiments of
teaching or instruction, as cosmological - forces or heavenly
bodies (Eph.6.12-13), or as personal powers - angels or
demons. It is clear from Paul's use of the phrase that,

although they have clearly some relationship to the cosmos, the elements have also something to do with the world of man, - which is the sphere of the 'rulers of this age' (1Cor 2.6,8) - whether they be foundations, principles or material elements (120). Nor is Paul using the phrase in a neutral sense; there is a clear theological implication that "the world and its elements are considered to stand in a state of opposition to God and his saving grace" (121). Paul's view of 'world' was multidimensional (122); he saw it not only as that which was earthy and fleshy, but also in terms of political, economic and social patterns, as well as those structural intellectual and institutional systems which hold men in bondage - the 'world rulers' who were responsible for the crucifixion (1Cor 2.7-8).

Liberation must therefore be more than just a personal matter. For Paul, man and the cosmos are inseparable: salvation involves not only personal liberation from the powers of darkness but also the final cosmic victory over those powers (123), because Christ in dying stripped himself of those powers as well as of the flesh (Col.2,15). Adherence to Christ thus liberates us from the tyranny of something basic, inherent and powerful in our world; when we die with Christ we die to the elemental spirits of the universe (Col.2,20).

The question as to whether the concept of 'ta stoichea' implies the existence of angels and demons is irrelevant. Paul was using his own particular mythological framework, (based to some extent on Gnostic astral religious beliefs), to express a truth which he saw as central to salvation. We therefore have to make a distinction between what Paul believed and what we believe Paul to have been talking about. What is clear is that he was convinced of the existence of 'objective' forces which held sway over mens' minds and hearts, conditioned their thinking and actions and caused them to misinterpret the essential truths about their own existence. For the Jews such 'forces' were contained in the law, for the Gentiles they were embodied in the impersonality of their philosophical systems. For us, they exist in the structures of our world as surely as they did for Paul —

>"...we only have to look into our own hearts to be confronted by the principalities and powers.... It is little comfort to us that the inexorable fate which was once expressed in terms of the influence of the stars, conceived of as personal demons, is now expressed in terms of psychological, physical or economic determinism. We still ask how a man is to triumph over an evil heredity, or how he can be free and victorious in a world of rigid law and scientific necessity. We still suffer from 'astronomical intimidation' — terror at the insignificance of man and the vastness of the material universe encompassing him"(124).

Paul's view of man as being 'under the flesh' and 'in bondage to the elements' thus amounts to seeing our whole nature as a complex of 'determinisms'(125) — powerful interior and exterior systems functioning independently of free will and inhibiting our liberty to respond to the message of the Kingdom. These 'determinisms' have their parallels today. In order to see how and why this might be the case we need to construct a typology of these 'determinisms' so that we can examine the ways in which they inhibit our actions.

A modern classification of these determinisms might run as follows —:
1. Physical determinisms: our biological and instinctual drives which, if allowed, encourage rooted egotism. This is Freud's 'id', our own animal nature. For Paul, these

determinisms place us 'under the flesh'.

2. Psychological determinisms: our preconscious/ subconscious/ unconscious motivations, fears and drives stemming as much from our personal histories as from our physical make-up. Paul sees an inner man stripped of control by forces more powerful than his conscious self, and thus subjected to a process which results in his own alienation.

3. Cultural determinisms: the ways of thinking, the presuppositions embodied in images and concepts which structure our responses in action in ways of which we are not even aware. Nygrens (126) argues that for us these forces are the twentieth century myths which limit our vision in such a way as to make the Christian message incomprehensible to us. The overriding myth of the twentieth century is the set of self-evident presuppositions by which this epoch lives. It is these that make the Gospel appear mythological and thus irrelevant. We can include under this heading religious 'determinisms' as the systems of thought embodied in ecclesial structures and sacramental and ritual worship which above all lead to the belief that salvation can be attained by devotion, by faithful practice, and by righteousness as comunally determined.

4. Moral determinisms: the tendency to follow the 'law of minimum effort' (127) by slavishly adhering to moral codes and social values, and thereby shutting out the radicality of the Gospel call to love.

5. Structural determinisms: required ways of acting as embodied in economic and political structures, as well as in the institutional and organisational framework of society. Norms of attitude and behaviour are expressive of the way in which society conceives of social relationships, but they also provide a justification of those relationships and hence are ideological — i.e. prejudiced in favour of vested interests. The Gospel may require us to act in ways which contravene accepted norms, to challenge existing social relationships and ways of behaving by making an option for those marginalised and rejected by society

Paul's anthropology suggests that these determinisms provide one way of picturing man's 'existentially hopeless situation'. His explanation accords with our experience of our own personal limitations. We live with the fact that our actions are not, either in their execution or their consequences, what we might have intended. We realise that our own physical and psychological natures are flawed. We battle with our subconscious motivations, the egotism which governs every conscious choice, the bias which limits our creativity. We fail to make the responses which could lead to possible good (128). These things we know already. What is perhaps less apparent to us is the way in which our actions are conditioned by the determinisms of the world external to ourselves. Action is the outcome of a complex of rational and affective processes. Each of these is 'conditioned' by our cultural environment. Our presuppositions structure our experience and understanding, our values influence and distort our judgement, and the structures of our world limit our actions. It is the task of the following chapters to examine in detail how, within one historical and cultural context — our own — this conditioning occurs. Before we do this, however, we must develop a formal model of action in order to identify the precise effects these distortions can have on our actions — and hence on our response to the Good News of the Kingdom.

===

NOTES—CHAPTER ONE

1. Whereas in English and Spanish there are two words for these differing concepts, in German there is only one. For a discussion of the concept of praxis see Appendix 1.

2. Panikkar (1971) p.223. The basic approach to faith expounded here is outlined in Smith (1979).

3. Lonergan (1971) p.113. Lonergan, who acknowledges the primacy of faith in that 'love precedes knowledge', acknowledges also that the tradition which identifies faith and belief is older and more authoritative.

4. Smith (1979) p.32ff.

5. Ibid p.67ff.

6. Ibid p.15.

7. Ibid p.76. Smith points out the word in this sense is 'first cousin' to the Hindu 'sradda'.

8. Ibid p.144.

9. See argument in Metz (1965). Metz's discussion lays bare the fragility of our existence in faith at any time, even as believers: he reminds us of the words of the father of the demoniac in Mark 9.23 — "Lord, I believe, help thou my unbelief".

10. A transformation which can be characterised as a shift in the content of a faith declaration from — "Given the reality of God as a fact of the universe I hereby proclaim that I align my life accordingly", to — "Given the uncertainty of God, as a fact of modern life, I declare that the idea of God is part of the furniture of my mind". Smith (1979) p.118.

11. For contemporary problems of belief see Koenig (1972).

12. Smith (1979) p.13.

13. Lamb (1981a) p.75.

14. Lonergan (1971) p.103.

15. Panikkar (1971) p.245.

16. Schillebeeckx (1980) p.734.

17. Rahner (1978) p.30.

18. 'Transcend' in this sense refers not to any reflection on the conditions of possibility of a more than empirical reality. It refers simply to the fact than man experiences himself and his life as something other and more than the everyday realities of his existence.

19. Lonergan (1971) p.103.

20. Kasper (1980), p.15.

21. It is the job of theology to articulate this 'crisis of faith'. See Dorr (1972) for an account of the theological basis of faith as experience. Also see Lane (1981)

22. Lonergan (1971) p.83.

23. Rahner (1978) p.32-33.

24. Wittgenstein (1961) p.74.

25. Rahner (1978) Ch.1.

26. Rahner (1979) p.14.

27. Rahner (ibid p.17) puts it as follows: -"The cross means the stark demand for a man to surrender himself unconditionally before the mystery of his being which he can never bring under his control since he is finite and burdened with guilt. The resurrection means the unconditional hope that in this surrender the ultimate acceptance of man takes place through this mystery." For an account of the anthropology on which this is based see Johns (1976) Ch.2, also Rahner (1968).

28. See Yarnold (1974) for an account of the theology of grace.

29. Ibid.Ch.1.

30. This position differs from earlier understandings. Aquinas' distinction between infused and created faith was taken further by Vatican 1's Dogmatic Constitution on Catholic faith, which maintained a distinction between supernatural and natural faith. The latter can be known by reason, the former comes directly from God rather than from scripture and tradition as sources of revelation. Faith is thus located somewhere beyond our

experience.

31. Schillebeeckx (1980) p.48.
32. See Lane (1984) Ch,1. On the newer Catholic theologies which emphasise experience see Lane (1981)
33. Schillebeeckx (1980) p.43-44.
34. What the Council proposed was a quantitative extension of the content of revelation beyond what was accessible to reason.
35. Notably in Dei Verbum: Dogmatic Constitution on Revelation.
36. This issue is well discussed in Avis (1982) p.530.
37. See Rahner (1965) p.297-317. Also (1966) p.165-188,
38. See Schillebeeckx (1968).
39. Gaudium et Spes para.41.
40. Schillebeeckx op cit. 52p.
41. This section is based partly on the ideas discussed in Schillebeeckx (1983) Pt.1
42. This separation formed the basis of the discussion between Bultmann and Kasemann; Bultmann's position is that our faith is in kerygma rather then in person. See Bultman (1951/5)
43. Schillebeeckx (1983) p.73.
44. Perrin (1976) p.2ff.
45. Crossan (1973) p.5.
46. Perrin (1976) p.2.
47. Weiss (1892) and others have seen Jesus' use of the term 'kingdom' as a conception — thus necessitating a discussion as to what the concept might have meant.
48. This, in Bultmann's terms, is the excercise which is necessary to bridge the 'hermeneutical gulf' between the mythical teaching of the New Testament and modern man.
49. Schillebeeckx op.cit.p.77ff.
50. For a discussion of this issue see Harvey (1982).
51. Schillebeeckx op.cit.p.87/8.
52. Ibid.p.87/8.
53. See Hollenweger (1982) Ch.9.
54. Ibid. p.61.

61

55. See Lumen Gentium, Ch.2.
56. See eg.Machovec (1976).
57. Perrin (1976) p.32.
58. Perrin (1967) p.55.
59. Ibid. p.57. For an account of contemporary understandings which provided the context of Jesus' teaching on the kingdom see Appendix II.
60. Von Rad (1965) p.99ff.
61. Cullman (1951).
62. This type of hellenistic thought forms part of the background to our modern understanding of salvation as happening somewhere else, and must surely also have contributed to the background of Jewish apocalyptic thought.
63. The arguments of the protagonists in this discussion were also influenced by the way in which Jesus himself was clearly wrong in his own expectations about the timing of the coming of the kingdom. See Harvey (1982) p.88ff. for a discussion of this point.
64. See Schweitzer (1911).
65. Dodd (1935).
66. Jeremias (1954).
67. Perrin (1976) p.38.
68. Pannenberg (1975).
69. The quote is from Perrin (1963) p.18, who takes a footnote from Weiss (1892) 2nd.ed.p.5.
70. The arguments are given in Perrin (1963) p.18ff.
71. Ritschl (1900).
72. See Bultmann (1951/5).
73. Harnack (1901).
74. Schleiermacher (1928).
75. Otto (1923).
76. Ragaz (1971).
77. Rauschenbusch (1919).
78. Barth (1936).
79. Marshall (1977) points to the difficulties this raises for those who try to preach the Kingdom nowadays. For

one thing, kingdoms are a vanishing reality in the world
of today. Also it is difficult to recreate in people's
minds nowadays the sense of crisis which would lead them
to see God's intervention in human history as something
new and decisive.

80. Schleiermacher (1928).
81. Harnack (1901).
82. A point of view which would reflect early Christian
    eschatological expectations.
83. See Crossan (1975) for a refutation of this.
84. Bonhoeffer (1965).
85. Pannenberg (1975), p.33.
86. Perrin (1976) p.33ff.
87. In Weiss (1892).
88. Perrin op.cit.p.34.
89. Ricoeur (1969).
90. Lonergan notes (1971) p.66 that symbols evoke not only a
    multiplicity of meanings but also conflictual meanings –
    their meaning-structure does not obey the laws of logic,
    nor is it static.
91. Crossan (1973) Ch.1.
92. Here we are talking about 'medium' in the sense of
    linguistic form rather than in the sense of a medium of
    communication.
93. See Rikhof (1981) p.83ff.
94. For a discussion of his work in this topic see Leach
    (1970).
95. Crossan (1973) p.33.
96. Julicher (1888), Jeremias (1954).
97. Crossan op.cit.p.32.
98. Ibid.p.33.
99. Ibid.p.31.
100. Crossan (1975) p.106.
101. Ibid. p.76. Crossan cites Beardslee (1970) in support.
102. Crossan (1973) p.120.
103. Ibid.p.82.
104. Ibid p.82.

63

105. Ibid.p.83.
106. Schillebeeckx (1983) p.187.
107. Ibid.p.199.
108. Ibid.182.
109. Ibid.p.256.
110. Ibid.p.221.
111. Segundo (1973) p. 16ff.
112. Cranfield (1964) p.47
113. Sanders (1977) p.443. Sanders points out that Paul's understanding proceeds from solution to plight. He deduces man's existentially hopeless situation from the fact that Christ died for all, as opposed to basing his soteriology on the existence of man's plight.
114. Whether the 'I' of Romans 7:14-25 means the 'universal person', Paul prior to his conversion or Paul after his conversion is not important in this context. What matters is the continual existence of the 'human condition' even in the person of faith.
115. Rahner (1965) p.369. Paul clearly does not accept the postulates of 'conscious intentionality': he does not see the subject as being able to will or intend in freedom. Man wills and acts either under the lordship of the flesh or under the lordship of the spirit.(Rom.8:5,12, Gal.5:16) In his existence 'under the flesh' or 'under the Law' he is constrained by forces which designate his possibilities of action, See Bultmann (1967)p.37.
116. Segundo op.cit.p.22 sees this as a more authoritative interpretation of the idea of 'concupisence' than that which sees it as representing the attraction of evil.
117. Dunn (1975) p.265.
118. Kasemann (1980) p.198ff.
119. Interpretations are dealt with in Bandstra (1964).
120. Reicke (1951) p.264.
121. Ibid. p.265.
122. Wilder (1956) distinguishes the senses of 'world' used by Paul.

123. McGregor (1954) p.25/6 gives examples of the way in which that thought was developed in early christianity.
124. Ibid. p.27.
125. Segundo op.cit p.30.
126. Nygrens (1951) p.372.
127. Segundo op.cit.p.33.
128. See Lonergan (1957) Ch.7 for a discussion of group bias.

==

CHAPTER TWO - THE ACTING PERSON.

i. Introduction

The analysis presented at the end of the last chapter lacked any account of the way in which these 'determinisms' actually function as impediments to faith-as-praxis. For this we need to develop a model of human action which is adequate in terms of the Christian idea of personhood in that it gives importance both to the rational/intelligent and to the affective/emotional aspects of the person. We can find such a model in the thought of Bernard Lonergan (1), whose account of action as the outcome of the processes of experience, understanding, judgement and decision makes it possible to identify the ways in which the limitations placed on us by our nature and our world inhibit our response to the message of the Kingdom.

However, it is necessary to justify this choice of approach by contrasting it with various philosophical accounts of action. I argue that these attempts to deal with the problem of action fail as heuristic devices because of their reductionistic views of the acting person — ie. they see action as 'determined' rather than 'conditioned'. An adequate account of action from a faith perspective has to be based on notions of consciousness, intentionality and action-as-agency. Consciousness forms the basis of the cognitive component of action, intentionality grounds the affective element, and agency is the basis of free and responsible choice. It is the whole person who responds to the call to live out the commitment of faith in action, however flawed that response may be.

ii.   The analysis of action.

Any discussion of human action which is undertaken with
the purpose of illuminating the idea of faith—as—praxis has
to be undertaken within the framework of three requirements.
(a) An emphasis on the person 'man acts' as opposed to an
emphasis on action or behaviour as such.   The ontology
required is thus an ontology of persons rather than of states
or events.
(b) An emphasis on the cognitive component of action.
(c) An emphasis on values as the ground of action.   These
three perspectives enable us to develop an approach based on
notions of agency, consciousness and intentionality.

However, action is not to be seen only in a personal
sense, because the acting person is inextricably linked to
his social, cultural and historical environment.   There are
two obvious ways in which this is the case. One is that any
person's referent concept of self—identity by which he knows
himself to be a person is derived to a greater or lesser
extent from the view of 'person' current in his environment.
The other thing is that his completed actions are seen as
'acts' within a social context, and are given meaning and
interpretation by that context.

There are other ways, too, in which action   is
conditioned by environment. Both the cognitive and the moral
processes which ground human action are themselves subject to
such conditioning. This is discussed in the following three
chapters, which look at the way in which experience,
judgement and decision—taking are conditioned by the social
and cultural environment, and how such conditioning
structures action. This chapter concentrates on laying the
foundations for this analysis by developing a theologically
adequate approach to action.

In a methodological sense this is not an easy task. The
main reason for this is that the focus of this kind of
enquiry into action differs from the understanding of action

current in philosophy and the social sciences. Action is
usually analysed in ways which consign the person to the
background, or reduce him to a manageable number of
dimensions or attributes (2). These approaches often focus
on action as constituting an event (without any account of
the meaning of that event) rather than on the process of
acting as such. This is largely because the acceptance of
science as the cognitive ideal dictates that action is seen
as appearance, as something external, rather than as
something having to do with the person (3). Scientific
understanding tends to deal with the states of affairs which
are constituted by linked complexes of events; action then
becomes just one event in a world of events (4). Science is
nomic; it therefore needs to be able to construct reality as
interrelations between physical entities and events which
have a causal character so as to make explanation and
prediction possible.

Fitting any notion of human agency – ie of personhood –
into this picture presents difficulties. We can take the
option of regarding the agent as a kind of pseudo-entity, an
appearance whose reality is the action performed by him which
constitutes an event. This gives us a manageable ontology
delineated in terms of events, but eliminates the agent. Or
we can invoke agency to explain action, but that involves us
in the task of redescribing agency in some way with which
science is familiar – for instance, in terms of physiological
events. That again reduces the agent in that it ignores or
denies the existence of inner mental states (5). The
prevalence of both of these approaches can be seen as the
consequence of

>"a tendency during positivistic periods in
>the human sciences to retreat to a
>conception of man as automata and to
>experimental methods of investigating their
>behaviour commensurate with that conception.
>It is not difficult to pass from despairing
>of penetrating to the core of human

physiological functioning to an effective
denial that it exists"(6).

Yet it is clear that some reconciliation between the
explanatory power of science and the obvious explanatory
value of agency is necessary. The philosophy of action has
attempted to do this by seeing mental states (beliefs,
desires, etc.) as themselves events which either occur in the
mind or are definitive of it (7), and by then analysing
action in terms of the connections between these events as
causally related (8). This allows 'event causality' to be
maintained in its most rigorous sense, but it consigns
intentionality to a different sphere of analysis. The only
way in which agency can be dealt with without categorising
mental states as events is to introduce 'agent causation' in
one of two ways. Either (a) the agent is a causal power, an
entity who causes a state of affairs (rather than an event)
(9), or (b) the agent causes something which is part of his
action (10). In the former case action is seen as the upshot
or physical result of a mental state because of some 'law of
nature which dictates that that action follows from the
mental state; in the latter case action is identical with the
mental state that has the physical result (11).

Objections to these approaches all revolve round the
problem of the restrictiveness imposed by the philosophical
parameters. The first objection is that the notion of
causality used presupposes that Humean causality is the only
possible way of interpreting the power of an agent to act
(12) in a world where every event is seen as having a cause
(13). But even a Humean relation is not nomic if no
mediating processes can be identified and nothing can be said
about efficacy. Another problem arises from the fact that to
take action as something caused by agency within a world
categorised by an ontology of events contains an implicit
metaphysical assumption which when explicated takes the form
of materialism or physicalism. Taken to its extremes, such a
position empties the notion of 'agent' of responsible
content, and therefore regards the category of 'action' as

spurious (14). Yet another objection centres round the inability of 'agent causation' to incorporate adequate accounts of the mental aspect of action (15) because it presupposes a fundamentally Cartesian view of human nature. Action is presumed to occur as a consequence of the existence of wants or beliefs without any intervention of will or choice.

However, it is not only the philosophical positions imposed by the commitment to science as the cognitive ideal which restrict inquiry into human action to a non-personalist focus. Philosophy itself makes any appeal to the prima facie quality of rational action impossible because the focus of English-speaking philosophy has been confined to 'second-order' considerations such as the logical structure of language, conceptual frameworks and 'language-games'(16). As a result, analytic philosophy's investigations of 'agent causation' have been formulated in terms of relating the concept of action to the empirically perceived data of action in the light of their causation by mental states(i.e. wants and beliefs) as mental events (17). The other focus contained within this philosophical paradigm centres on the framework of explanation of how action is produced, in terms of a discussion of the logical relations between wants, beliefs, intentions and so on (18). The emphasis is on the structural features of the mechanics of decision-taking in logical and linguistic terms (19), but again the acting person is pushed into the background.

Other disciplines, too, offer little in the way of enlightenment (20). Psychology, which is the obvious discipline to study the workings of inner mental states, lacks any approach to agency in action. Behaviourism, which studies action as an external stimulus-response pattern, accepts an implicitly non-cognitive concept of action based on reaction and interaction. Behavioural psychologists have seen their scientific aspirations fulfilled by their ability to reduce human action to observable phenomena and hence manageable statistical variables which can be used for explanationa and prediction. Attempts by psychology to move 'inside' the acting person are found only in the field of psychoanalysis, which sees human action in terms of unconscious motivation, thus implicitly denying any role to conscious intentionality or to cognition.

The approach of sociology to human action, on the other hand, has always focused on the importance of action as a social phenomenon. The difficulty here has been to develop an adequate approach to the study in a social context of what is in the first instance an individual attribute without at the same time negating the importance of agency (21). The main interest of sociology has thus been centred in the explanation of action in terms of its meaning as conditioned by the circumstances in which it is constituted. Action is then studied as completed 'acts' within a social framework.

Where does this leave us? It would appear that neither philosophy nor the social sciences can offer an account of action which is based in the common-sense observation that action is done by people who are agents, who have beliefs and feeling which in some sense structure or determine that action. In other words, none of these approaches to action start with what is the logical first reqirement —i.e. an adequate model of man (22). In their efforts to conform to the canons of scientific respectability or the requirements of a particular philosophical programme, they present reductionistic views of man which locate action as the causal outcome of brain states (mechanism) or of animal drives (behaviourism) or of subconscious urges (psychologism) or of social conditioning. Action then becomes deterministic — intention, choice and freedom play no part, inner mental states as such are ignored. Action theory in the philosophical sense devalues the importance of such inner mental states by focusing on their outcome in terms of event causation, thus ignoring the cognitive and effective element in action. Analytic philosophy is not interested in inquiry as self-corrective, or philosophy as practical, and action is of necessity a practical issue.

A theological perspective on human action as the articulation of a faith commitment imposes the requirement of finding an adequate account of acting personhood as a 'model of man'(23). The dimensions of that requirement are that our model of man should be anti-reductionistic, that it should give a clear account of the significance of the moral in action and that it should unify the affective, or 'feeling' component with the cognitive component in action as a basis for responsible choice. On the other hand, it should not disregard the importance of the social, the cultural and the historical. We do not exist as persons of faith in a vacuum, we cannot stand outside the context of our own action. What we are and what we do are products of that context. We therefore have to recognise the importance of the dialectical relationship which exists on a 'micro' level between 'person' and 'action', and on a 'macro' level between human action and social praxis. That reflection continually reminds us that

>"man is not just his own potential, but---he
>is also the direction he chooses to give
>that potential---he can make himself what he
>is through each choice he makes---we become
>ourselves through each particular action, we
>choose ourselves in each act of
>becoming"(24).

Where are we to find the basis for such a perspective? It is tempting to begin the search within the confines of philosophy, but this is to implicitly accept the traditional conception of philosophy as 'the mirror of nature'(25), as a general theory of representation which enables the variety of cultural claims to knowledge to be adequately adjudicated. The assumption, and the potential criticism (26) of this approach is that it takes a view of inquiry as being conducted within a framework of a priori propositions about the person. If we want to adopt this view we have to conform to the conditions of the possibility of such an approach. Rorty puts the problem as follows — his point is worth quoting in full —

> "It is the notion that human activity (and inquiry, the search for knowledge in particular) takes place within a framework which can be isolated prior to the conclusion of inquiry — a set of presuppositions discovered a priori — which links contemporary philosophy to the Descartes—Locke—Kant tradition. For the notion that there is such a framework only makes sense if we think of this framework as imposed by the nature of the knowing subject, by the nature of his faculties or by the nature of the medium within which he works."(27).

According to Rorty, then, these would provide the only justification for an approach which makes such prior assumptions. Rorty does not accept that it is possible to argue for the existence of such presuppositions. I want to maintain that such presuppositions are given not only by the nature of the knowing subject but also by the nature of his social and cultural context — i.e. the medium within which he functions, and that we can discuss the acting person within this framework. I want to argue that the pre—understanding which must lie behind any notion of 'person', including 'person of faith' is culturally given, that a 'person' is "not a natural object but a cultural artefact — a being who has learned a theory in terms of which his or her experience is ordered"(28). In other words, our cultural parameters determine our self—identity. But having said that, the basic structures which ground that person as actor are to be found in the dynamism of his own conscious intentionality, where cognitive and affective processes combine to produce action. The structures of human consciousness and intentionality are thus the a priori presuppositions to which Rorty refers (29), and they provide the basis for the account of action which will be developed. However, before doing this I look at three representative accounts of action in order to highlight their reductionistic nature.

iii. **Man as machine.**

A 'scientific' approach to human action requires that its explanation should be causal in the strong sense. One way to achieve this is to look at action in mechanistic terms by seeing it as a response to a stimulus. If the stimulus is seen to emanate from the functioning of psychoneural processes in the brain, action can then be seen as triggered by brain function. But we normally think of action as somehow originating in the mind. Mechanism therefore presupposes a certain view of what philosophers call the 'mind-body' problem. We can set this problem out in the form of the inconsistency of a number of propositions (30). We accept that the human body is material and that the human mind is spiritual, we know from experience that mind and body interact, and we believe it to be impossible for spirit and matter to interact. Clearly not all of these four statements can be true at any one time – any three of them can hold, but the fourth is inconsistent. Attempts to reconcile this inconsistency can take one of two forms. We can deny that mind and body are interconnected and see them as totally separate entities – this is the dualistic solution. Or we can deny that the mind is a spiritual entity and see it as part of matter. This is the materialist solution.

Materialists see mind as a bodily process, in other words as an activity of the brain. Behaviourists (see next section) take this a stage further in that they see mental states only in terms of their behavioural manifestations. But it is not necessary for the materialist position to reduce the notion of mind to behaviour. We can maintain, as does the 'causal' theory of mind (31), that mental states are simply states which dispose men to certain sorts of behaviour in either a strongly causal sense or in some sense which simply correlates mental states and behaviour patterns.

To talk about mental states or characteristics in this context is thus to talk about mechanical matters, about what 'makes men tick'. Central-state materialism (32) takes a more precise view of how the mechanism works. It identifies mind with the central nervous system, seeing the workings of that system as expressions of mental states. The mind then becomes simply that part of the body which controls behaviour; its functioning is identical with the brain's neurological impulses, and since the brain itself possesses no non-physical properties, mind turns out to be wholly matter. Action is therefore controlled by something material — i.e. matter.

The materialist position is reductionist — i.e. it embodies the idea that there is no essential difference between all the things which exist in the universe. Everything is matter. Armstrong (33) reminds us that all developments in the natural sciences are in some sense reductionistic in that they have led us to understand biological processes in terms of their chemistry, and chemical processes in terms of their physical characteristics. Why then should it be the case that the only kind of happening in the universe not reducible to physical processes should be mental processes? Why should the outcome of mental processes be any less predictable than any other occurrence? Armstrong bases his argument not on logical necessity, but on what he calls 'the supremacy of physics'; and he claims for the conclusions of science a force possessed by no other type of argument on the grounds that they have their basis in public discourse and the possibility of objective validation. If science believes that matter is the universal category then is it not at least likely that mind is also matter?

Whether or not we accept this argument, (given that
scientific reductionism is a fact of our intellectual
environment), it clearly bypasses the central problem, which
has to do not with the conclusions of reductionism, but with
how it is used as a method. In Greek philosophy reduction to
essentials was used for explaining, but also for eliminating.
Now there is obviously a great deal of difference between
saying that we can explain behaviour in terms of brain
functioning on the one hand (i.e. in terms of simple physical
processes), and saying that that is all there is to the
explanation of mind-generated behaviour (34). In the first
case we try to reduce the cause of human behaviour to
something which we can physically identify and measure, but
in the second case we eliminate from discussion any cause
which is non measurable. The explanatory reductionist says
'matter thinks', but the eliminatory reductionist says man
does not think at all — that he only responds to trigger
mechanisms in his skull. Although these approaches seem
different, it is easy, as Agassi warns (35) to slide from one
to the other. Reductionism is metaphysically positivist
(36), the methodology of reductionism becomes the explanation
and hence determines reality, rather than the reality
determining the methodology (37).

Central-state materialism takes the full reductionistic
position in that it argues (a) that mind causes behaviour —
matter stimulates behaviour response, (b) that mind is
nothing other than the central nervous system — mind is
matter, matter therefore thinks. It is, however, to be
distinguished from behaviourism in that the mind is
identified not with behaviour itself but only with the cause
or principle of that behaviour. The attraction of this
argument is that it provides a solution to the mind/body
dilemma, but it comes under fire from two separate sources.
One is that of the empiricist/analytical philosophers (38)

who talk about perception, sensation and mental images in a non-physical sense. The other is that of the more traditional philosophers (such as Thomists in the theological field) who attack central-state materialism for its failure to talk about thought and the relationship between 'inner states' and physical states. But it is also possible to criticise central-state materialism on the basis of what it does as well as what it does not do. Most of the specific objections have to do not so much with the fact that the brain is said to cause behaviour, but much more with the fact that the brain is identified with the mind and that there is thus no possibility of independent mental function.

The first problem relates to freedom. Central-state materialism appears to leave no room for the possibility of human freedom. As Skinner says of the materialist position in general —"A scientific analysis of behaviour dispossesses autonomous man and turns the control he has been said to exercise over to the environment"(39). The world acts on the person rather than the person acting on the world, because brain function is externally stimulated. Behaviour need not, however, be entirely determined. It is possible to introduce limited notions of freedom into the materialistic framework by, for instance, allowing choice within rule-governed situations such as games (40). Chess is played by rules, the player assesses his options and chooses a particular course of action (41). Central-state materialism is compatible with freedom of choice in this sense, where choices are the deterministic outcomes of probabilistic calculations.

A more profound objection centres round the question of whether the statement 'the mind is the brain' is a logically or a contingently necessary truth. It is clearly not the former. If it were to be a contingently necessary truth it would be possible, as Armstrong argues (42), to give accounts of both mind and brain which are mutually independent. We can clearly explain 'brain' in a physical sense, but how can

we explain 'mind' other than in terms of the brain and still
adhere to central-state materialism? Armstrong, whose
concern is to defend that position, argues that the way to
deal with the explanation of mind is to regard it as a
mediator between stimulus and response. There would be
several advantages to this approach. It would allow for the
possibility of having a mental state without having the
resultant behaviour. In other words, it allows for the
possibility of 'phenomena' — characteristics of mental states
which are apparent to the person but not to those who observe
the behaviour of that person (43). It also allows one to
postulate more or less causal mental state/behaviour
relations in the ordinary sense of efficient causality. We
may question the validity of this argument on the grounds
that it separates mind from brain, but there is a deeper
sense in which the argument appears inconsistent. If the
whole point of the materialist explanation of action is to
establish a connection between measurable brain activity and
measurable response, the categorisation of mind as mediator
in that process is surely either to describe it in terms of
some brain functioning or to revert to the kind of
non-materialist interpretation of mind which central state
materialism tries to resist. Armstrong is aware of this
difficulty, and attempts to find its solution in a linguistic
reformulation. "The concept of a mental state", he says, "is
primarily the concept of a state of the person apt for
bringing about a certain sort of behaviour" (44). This way
of putting it allows both for the logical possibility of
disembodied mind — i.e.mind independent of brain, and the
fact that mental states qua mental states are incapable of
existence independent of the brain. In other words, it
allows one to maintain that something is and is not the case
simultaneously.

A related objection concerns the potential impact on the
materialist position of proven parapsychological findings.
If evidence for the existence of telepathy, psychokinesis, or

survival after death were to come to light and be accepted by the scientific community as a whole the materialist position (that mind is simply bodily process) would be no longer tenable. This objection, however, does not stand up to close examination, because there is a close connection between what we take to be philosophically adequate stances and the present state of scientific knowledge. If telepathy and other such phenomena were found to exist beyond any scientific doubt this would imply that we would have found a scientific explanation for them, and their existence would thus be compatible with our present materialist concept of mind. Alternatively, if our conception of science changed to permit the acceptance of paranormal phenomena our philosophical positions would alter accordingly. After all, television is a paranormal phenomenon with respect to Newtonian Physics (45)!

Consciousness is perhaps the most central of the problems faced by materialists. Does an acceptance of central state materialism imply a denial of the existence of consciousness, or does it simply ignore its existence, as does behaviourism? Again, Armstrong (46) argues that we can resolve this difficulty by simply assuming that consciousness is itself another mental state, possibly existing in some kind of hierarchical relationship to other mental states in the sense that consciousness is prior. But what kind of mental state can consciousness be? It can only be the state of introspection, and if we argue that we immediately run into a logical difficulty. If consciousness qua introspection is a brain mechanism, it should be possible for it to fail, to make mistakes in the same way as for instance neurological processes do. But introspective knowledge is 'selfauthenticating' — we know what we know about ourselves until circumstances cause us to revise our opinions. It is therefore impossible for our consciousness qua introspection to make mistakes, and if that is the case we cannot accept central state materialism's view of consciousness as a mechanism which is fallible like any other mechanism. In spite of the attempts of materialists to argue this point we must conclude that central state materialism fails to deal with the problem of consciousness so central to any adequate account of the acting person.

iv. Man as behavioural

Behaviourism abstracts from all the problems of action theory and simply regards action in terms of a description of behaviour. Action becomes that which is observable and measurable, and is studied in this way in the hope that it will ultimately be possible to derive completely general laws of behaviour. In metaphysical terms this approach is positivist; it attempts to redescribe mental states and behaviour in terms which are publicly accessible and 'objective' because they are operational. All concepts and all verbal reports of subjects are synonomous with operations insofar as they lend themselves to measurement.

The basis of this approach is psychology's understanding of itself as scientific. The experimental work done by I.P.Pavlov in Russia (47) established connections between behaviour and patterns of neural responses. He demonstrated that the nervous system adapts so as to be able to anticipate events on receipt of a signal — the 'conditioned' reflex. Pavlov worked with dogs, but B.F.Skinner (48) extended his conceptual analysis to the study of human behaviour. He argued that behaviour is a function of the consequences of previous behaviour. and that a manipulation of these consequences — i.e. of the environment — can therefore determine behaviour. In particular, it is possible to reinforce preferred behaviour patterns by rewarding appropriate behaviour — a technique known as 'operant conditioning'. Behaviour can thus be predicted and controlled if reinforcements can be understood and delivered as necessary. The study of behaviour thus becomes something which "in its exclusiveness tends towards robotism" (49).

The approach of behaviourism as a method of studying human action is based in the cultural faith in science. However, there have been two other influences which have helped to establish its supremacy in scientific terms. One is philosophical materialism, and the other is the perception of man-as-animal.

The philosophical basis of behaviourism is the belief that the mind-body problem is irrelevant because 'mind' is not a thing. But unlike the mechanists who identify mind with brain and therefore believe that mind causes behaviour, the behaviourists believe that mental activity and behaviour are identical. Mental activity is behaviour, a description of mental states is a description of behaviour and dispositions to behave in a certain way, and differences in mental states are visible as differences in behaviour patterns. "Having a pain" is thus behaving in a way which indicates a state of pain (50).

It is true that it is not possible to explain mental states in the abstract without some reference to behaviour — it is difficult (51), for instance, to talk about anger without talking about angry behaviour. But the behaviourists are committed to a position which does not allow them to say that anger caused the angry behaviour — behaviour for them is the same as mental activity. They are thus in opposition to the common tendency to talk about mental states as 'mental objects' and to regard them all as causing behaviour in the strongly causal sense. For instance, we tend to say that anger caused someone to kill, or jealousy caused him to be unkind (52), but whereas the strong notion of causality applies to the first statement, the second statement is not causal in that sense because the unkindness is part of the jealousy. Behaviourists will admit of neither statement as causal; they see mental events as gaining or losing dispositions to behave. But this places them in a somewhat odd position. They need causality as part of the scientific image, and if mental events are simply dispositions to behave they must themselves therefore be effects of whatever causes behaviour. Whatever these causes are, they cannot be non-physical, so behaviourists are driven to seek the causes of behaviour in patterns of behavioural effects. Behaviour is then 'caused' by conditioning and reinforcement of behaviour patterns; it is a response to the stimulus occasioned by past behaviour.

There are problems about this account of human action. It is clear that linking mental states to behaviour in a one-to-one correspondence leaves out of account those mental descriptions which refer to events which are not behavioural. 'Having a pain' does not just refer to pain-behaviour, it also involves a sensation which is very real to the person experiencing it, although it may not be observable. Furthermore, mental sensations can occur which are not translated into behaviour - although the behaviourists would argue that they would probably be visible in terms of some physiological manifestation (e.g. raised blood pressure). However, two other considerations weaken that argument. One is that a given mental state (e.g. of anger as measured by rises in blood pressure) can in fact result in very different kinds of behaviour, so that it is difficult to see in what sense the mental event can be said to be identical with the disposition to behave. The other is that for the behaviourists having a pain and imitating someone with a pain is the same thing, and this is clearly not a commonsense conclusion.

We should not infer from this that behaviourists (e.g.B.F.Skinner) deny the existence of thought processes. It is rather that they think it legitimate in the conduct of research to ignore the acting person as agent. They thus eliminate the whole question of consciousness and cognition as factors in the origin of action (53). 'Inner life' is thus effectively discounted -

"The best way to deal with consciousness or

introspective subjective experience, they tell us, is to ignore it. Inner feelings and thoughts cannot be measured ... or otherwise recorded or dealt with objectively by any scientific methodology ... Consciousness, in the objective approach, is clearly made a second-class citizen in the causal picture. It is relegated to the inferior status of (a) an inconsequential by-product, (b) an epiphenomenon (a sort of outsider on the inside), (c) just an inner aspect of the one natural brain process.. Once we have materialism squared off against mentalism in this way, I think we must all agree that neither is going to win the match on the basis of direct factual evidence (54)".

Skinner justifies this on scientific grounds (55). He argues that to be scientific any study of man must disregard all 'prescientific' anthromorphic ways of talking about human behaviour. But the fact that discourse is 'prescientific' does not necessarily brand it as 'unscientific'. His mistake, as Flew shows (56), is to argue from analogy with the physical sciences where prescientific notions are not appropriate. But in any study of man they are crucial to understanding, and to exclude mental states not expressed in behavioural terms from consideration is to limit the potential for understanding human action.

However, the primary agenda of behaviouristic research is not understanding but control. Skinner argues (57) that the findings of such research can be used to condition people in ways which will promote the good of society. Aggression and conflict can be eliminated, cooperation can be fostered by the inculcation of appropriate responses. Behaviourism thus not only ignores problems of understanding action, but seeks to find ways of determining it and thereby to substitute for human processes of intention and decision.

v. Man as psychological

The view of man which has entered, perhaps most deeply, into the twentieth-century consciousness originates with the work of Sigmund Freud and his school. This perspective sees man, not as a whole person, but as divided within himself not just in a dualistic, body/mind sense, but in a fragmented and 'layered' fashion. These aspects of man, the layers of his being and personality, are not his in any unique and subjective sense, but are rather objects whose interrelations lend themselves to scientific study and to the establishment of general laws governing their behaviour.

Such analysis identifies first man-as-ego, subject to pressure from all sides. The ego is pressurised by the id, the subconscious store of past experiences, hereditary influences, even the 'race memories' identified by Jung as the collective unconscious. The id is the origin of instinct, of fear and of impulse; it is inaccessible to processes of conscious thought, its influence is 'sub-conscious'. On the other side stands the superego, which controls by setting 'ideal' standards. The superego is shaped by father-identification and mother-love repression on the one hand, and by externally-given but internalised religious and social norms on the other. The ego tries to be moral, but its strivings are menaced both by the amorality and libido of the id and by the censure and severity of the superego. The superego is the origin of guilt; conscience is now "no longer the still small voice, it is (rather) the brute force exercised by the powerful over the powerless (58)". The ego, caught between two subconscious poles, and threatened by the demands of the external world, becomes a prey to subconscious fears and nameless anxieties which can find an outlet only in dreams since conscious expression is barred to them. These fears and anxieties are as much the ground of action as are rational conscious thought processes — indeed, for Freud, they were the only ground of action.

Freud was not the first to use the idea of the unconscious as a force governing man's actions (59). However, what is unique about Freud is the way in which he marries the force of the subconscious with its analysis in terms of symbolic significance. As Friedman points out (60), this kind of approach has the effect of synthesising mechanism and rationalism, which are the basis of behaviourism and operationalism in modern psychological thought and practice, with the romanticism and mysticism more properly associated with the name of Jung. For Freud, the attraction of the subconscious was that it was accessible to scientific study, and the only way to study action scientifically was to ground it in the subconscious. He saw all transcendent notions of man deriving from philosophical anthropology as 'prescientific' from the point of view of the study of action. Man thus becomes something other than his own view of himself. "Man to Nietsche is the valuing animal....but to Freud he is the animal who thinks he values, but whose valuations are really (only) the product of psychological forces "(61).

The agenda of the practice of psychoanalysis which originated with Freud is the explanation of action in terms of subconscious reason or motive by the use of the above 'model' of man. From the philosophical point of view — i.e. in terms of the philosophy of action, this line of approach presents two fundamental difficulties (62). One is that it uses the concepts normally used in the explanation of action — reason, intention, motive, purpose, wish — in a context which implies that the subject does not know or is not aware of the fact that he or she possesses those attributes or feelings. It is easy enough to imagine that one might not be aware of the fact that one had a secret desire to do this or that, but it is surely less possible to envisage a situation where one was unaware of an intention to act. Freud's approach thus requires the meaning of the familiar concepts to be 'stretched' in unfamiliar ways which diminish if not negate their content. Furthermore, it is clearly a linguistic fallacy to say that unconscious motives are the basis of action if we accept that thought can only be conceptual, because in that case motives have to be articulated in order to exist, and articulation brings them into the forefront of consciousness. There are clearly difficulties here.

A second difficulty is that to regard actions as being governed by the subconscious requires a basic shift of the conventional perspective on the nature of mind. Freud's conception of mind is much nearer to the notion of psyche or soul than to the Cartesian concept of the mental. Mind for Freud is in the first instance not accessible to conscious knowing, although he does distinguish between the preconscious content of that mind, which can become conscious, and the unconscious, which stays for ever repressed below the level of consciousness. Because the subconscious mind lends itself to scientific study action becomes intelligible in terms of objectively observable 'reasons' for action in a way which can never be the case if reasons for action are consciously and subjectively formulated and articulated. It is clear that in this sense the 'hidden agenda' of the Freudian approach is scientistic. Conscious motivation for action is seen as scientifically inadequate in that explanation cannot be given in terms of reasons which can be objectively analysed, and incomplete in the sense that it does not allow for the analysis of unconscious forces. Behind this reasoning clearly lie the assumptions about causality, objectivity and reality which ground all scientistic thought.

For the purpose of the argument here the most fundamental issue concerns the question of human freedom and the responsibility for action. It would appear at first sight that the existence of unconscious compulsion implies the impossibility of conscious freedom of action, because it suggests that actions are determined without any kind of choice being possible – in the extreme case action then simply becomes a reflex response to a subconscious stimulus (63). But the issue is more complex than that. Complete freedom of choice has never been held to be a live option. Classical philosophy has always interpreted freedom of choice to exist within the framework of whatever external constraints were operative in the particular situation; Catholic theology has always seen the necessity for God's grace to guide that choice. In that context we can see the contribution of Freud as

> "the insight that, although we are indeed
> free, we are not so totally free as to be
> liberated without effort from the
> biological, social and psychological
> conditions of human existence, which are
> internal conditions of our human
> freedom.... there is (thus) the possibility
> of accepting as one's own the restrictions
> on our individual freedom – whether they are
> imposed from within or are inescapably part
> of our own human constitution – by means of
> a fundamental and free option which sets our
> course consciously in the direction of human
> growth and achievement (64)".

Human reality, in other words, is a mixture of freedom and compulsion. The strength and the usefulness of psychoanalysis is that the ego can be helped to integrate the demands of the id and superego and search for the full identity found in replacing the id by the ego. Psychoanalysis, in other words, is for making rational agents, who can decide to do this rather than that, and have recognised reasons for doing so.

None of the three models of man which have been examined here provide us with an adequate basis for a discussion of the determination of human action. Materialism negates the existence of consciousness, behaviourism adds to this the aim of replacing processes of intention and decision by the influence of conditioning. Psychologism, as we have just seen, renders notions of freedom, responsibility and choice ambiguous. We must now attempt to develop an alternative view which will remedy these deficiencies.

vi. **Man as person.**

No account of human action can be acceptable in theological terms unless it starts with an account of the person who is aware of himself and of the world, who uses his cognitive faculties to assess, and his convictions to judge, what he ought to do. This common-sense type approach to action needs to be unpacked into its various components — into an analysis of personhood, consciousness, intentionality, and agency.

Consciousness, awareness, presupposes that we are aware of something. In the first instance that something is ourselves. Cartesian dualisms always cast this problem in terms of the subjective and objective focus of experience, the 'inner' and the 'outer' of awareness. This kind of dualism fails to cope with a prior problem, which has to do with the way in which we experience ourselves, i.e. with the interpretative context of our own experience. The experience of self-identity is not merely preconceptual. We need words to describe what we experience about ourselves, and categories by which to analyse ourselves. In other words, in order to be able to have a concept of self identity we need some concept of person, and this we can only get from our environment, from what is socially defined as such (65), and social definition includes definition within a religious tradition. The way in which we see ourselves is thus culturally conditioned. We learn how to think about and how to manage ourselves by using the model of personhood given to us by our social/cultural experience (66). The realisation of our own personhood is thus not some kind of empirical discovery, it is merely the adoption of a way of thinking which is given to us by the context of our existence. The operative principle here is "nothing in the mind that was not first in the conversation"(67). Just as we get minds by acquiring beliefs as well as linguistic and practical skills, so we become persons by getting a theory about ourselves which we learn from the public concept of person, and that theory enables us to order our experience of ourselves. Our concept of 'self' as a subject of experience thus becomes operative by a kind of displacement from our model of 'person'(68) by a kind of analogical understanding.

However, our sense of personal identity is not merely passive. The social concept of person includes action, so that our concept of self will be one where there is a unity of consciousness and of agency (for which personhood is a precondition). This unified notion of personal identity will not, however, be a merely transcendental one whose structures are given in an a priori sense, but will have properties and attributes culled from the social environment and will be fully realised only in action. Action, in other words, is a particular moment of apprehending the person (69). We only give our particular theory of personhood empirical content when we act; our action reveals our own personhood to ourselves because it is inherent in the quality of action that it has to be done by a person. Action thus reveals rather than presupposes the person; the real concept of person lies in the person-action unity, still more so for the person of faith. Our self-conception thus works by "conceiving of ourselves as personal beings by appropriation of the concept of social being from our public/collective activities for the purposes of organising our experience as the mental life of a self-conscious agent (70)". In particular, identity can be linked to institutional roles.

The socially-defined sense of 'person' thus gives us the

model for self-identity on which our own experience of ourselves as conscious subjects is based. We use public and collective notions of person to gain a conception of our own personal identity. Our idea of 'self' is thus developed in the interaction between our experience and the interpretative frameworks at our disposal which enable us to give form to that idea. Berger argues (71) that modern self-identity can be seen as having particular characteristics; on the one hand it is open and differentiated by virtue of the plurality of culture, but it is also reflective and individuated.

But our actual awareness of that identity belongs in a different realm of understanding, that of self-consciousness. We can think of ourselves as existing in a mental sense within different spheres (72). These spheres have two axes, the public/private axis and the individual/collective one. Our concept of person is gained from the public/collective sphere of existence and structures our self-identity in the private sphere, but this understanding still belongs within the 'collective' realm of existence, since that is where action takes place, and action/agency is central to the concept of person. Self-consciousness, however, is the interior translation of this self-identity, our own conscious awareness of what we are as defined by the prior theoretical model. Whereas consciousness is simply an awareness, an attending to states and conditions of that which is other than oneself, self-consciousness is the awareness of our own states and conditions. In other words, we make the distinction between self as object and self as subject.

vii. Man as conscious.

We now explore the way in which this self-consciousness is arrived at, using the analysis presented by Bernard Lonergan. Consciousness, as awareness of the self, is a basic attribute of the acting person (73). We can make a fundamental distinction between two senses of consciousness

(74) in ordinary language usage — 'consciouness of'(thing) and 'consciouness that'(state). In other words, consciouness can be perceptual or cognitive (75). We can be conscious in the sense that we are 'aware of' something or 'aware that' something is the case (76). In relation to actions the distinction is between the fact that we are conscious of acting and that we act consciously. Our awareness' of ourselves is gained by the fact that we use the theory of self which we have acquired from our social and cultural context to structure and organise our experience round this'self' in some sort of cognitive fashion. This theory and the empirical experience are both linguistically mediated (77), and serve to develop an awareness of ourselves and our acts. Consciouness, in other words, is a primary component in knowing.

This view forms the basis of Lonergan's position on consciousness (78). He sees consciousness as the condition of possibility for all intellective and cognitive activity and in highlighting this he implicitly affirms its central importance in the analysis of action (79). However, it is neither the product of nor identical with the content of any cognitive activity. It is a kind of empowering force in the process of knowing rather than the actual process itself. Nor is it the case that consciouness enables the subject to experience all his cognitive activities to the same extent — these activities are done consciously, but it may be easier for the subject to experience himself being rational or intelligent or sensitive than to experience himself having an insight. However, it is the factor which ensures that the whole notion of the subject is a dynamic and developing one. Once the subject is awake he is an experiential subject, open to perception, experience, imagination. He is intelligent, and as intelligent subject he sublates the experiential — i.e. he goes beyond experience while retaining and preserving its essentials as he grows in the understanding of that experience. As rational subject he judges, and as rationally self-conscious and responsible he acts on the basis of those judgements.

However, Lonergan distinguishes a further development of
consciousness whereby consciousness is, so to speak, opened
to the ego by self-knowledge in the moment in which
self-consciousness is constituted (80). Consciousness lets
us experience our knowing and doing - in that sense we are
'self-conscious', but there is a further consciousness of
self which allows us to distinguish between ourselves (the
ego) as subject, and ourselves as acting persons (agent), and
to evaluate our actions as good or bad. The difference is
between being conscious THAT we know and do, and being
conscious of HOW we know. What is happening, in Lonergan's
terms, is that instead of the knowing/acting subject being
self-consciously present to himself as subject, he is present
to himself as object; he is the object of his own cognitional
processes and can affirm that fact. He comes, in other
words, to know how his mental life is organised.

Such 'second-order' consciousness can be
'differentiated' into its component parts. Knowing and doing
involve the subject in different operations, the quality of
consciousness changes as these operations, cognitive and
others, are performed (81). These qualitative differences in
consciousness can be highlighted by objectifying them into
their empirical, intelligent, rational and responsible
components (82).

Consciousness is clearly basic to any theological
understanding of action, because such an understanding has to
include a cognitive component. Lonergan's work outlines in
structured fashion the essential role that consciousness
plays in cognitional theory. It not only grounds the
performance of cognitional operations, it also supplies the
basis for the reflective awareness of the self as conscious
centre of the cognitive act. Consciousness is thus essential
to notions of belief, reason, intention, deliberation,
willing. Self-consciousness is the precondition for notions

of desire, want, motive and choice. Consciousness thus grounds both the cognitive and the affective element in action. But consciousness is not sufficient to account for that affective element. For that we need an account of intentionality.

viii.   **Man as intentional.**

Lonergan's acting subject is thus before everything a conscious subject, promoted to different levels of consciousness by the unfolding of his cognitional processes. The factor which unites and provides the dynamism for this movement is intentionality (83). Cognitional processes are viewed as transitive in two senses; they are transitive in the grammatical sense in that they have objects, but they are also transitive in the psychological sense in that by them one becomes aware of their object, one 'intends' their object (84). Intentionality is thus a mental state, a property of the knowing subject, by which "one has an awareness or conception of some object or kind of object, or of some state of affairs involving some object or kind of object" (85). We can even go so far as to say that it is a 'mark of the mental' (86).

Intentionality has to be distinguished from merely intending to do something, as well as from intending to bring about certain ends while doing something (87). In other words, we can intend the action, or intend the consequence of action. Neither of these are the same as intending the object of cognitional processes. In the case of intending to do something the object of intending is simply the action; there is an 'external' teleology in the intending. In the case of the intention in action the object of action is the state or event it is to bring about — the teleology is 'internal' to the action. Intentionality in the sense that Lonergan uses it is teleological in a much more diffuse sense — i.e. the account of action needs to be much more

93

intensively developed before that teleology can be exposed (88).

The telos of Lonergan's concept of intentionality is the transcendental notion. Intentionality makes the objects of the cognitional process present to the subject. Just as the subject is conscious in a different way of the different states of his own cognitional activity, as successive levels of consciousness sublate the previous ones (89), so do the objects of that activity unfold as transcendental notions of being and value. The first three levels of consciousness 'intend' being as the intelligible, the real and the true - i.e., as the objects of experience, understanding and judgement. On the fourth level of consciousness it is the good as value which is intended. Human consciousness is not only intelligent and rational, it is also responsible. Any cognitional process which establishes 'what is so' (90) generates a further set of questions of the form -;' because of what I know and because I know it, what ought to be done, is it worthwhile to do it'?(91) Value is 'intended' in these questions for deliberation. Judgements of value enable us to say whether something is good or worthwhile. These judgements promote us to moral self-transcendence in the same way as judgements of fact promote us to self-conscious ness - i.e. cognitive self-transcendence. In both cases we make a transition to an objective world.

This is the basis of Lonergan's approach to the affective side of human action. Instead of developing a psychology of motivation for human action (92) he uses what might be termed a 'psychology of orientation' (93). In Method in Theology (94) Lonergan outlines the way in which values are the object of the process of deliberation, and feelings are the intentional response to those values(95). The apprehension of value given in feelings - in other words, the objects to which feelings point us are a series of notions of 'good' (96) which exist in a variety of ever-widening contexts (97). Finally there is the good of

value itself, which as a transcendent notion enables us to
discriminate between and identify the worthwhileness of
particular goods and various versions of the good of order.
The good of value is transcendental in the sense that we can
intend, but we cannot know value; it is thus the principle
which drives us towards the realisation of the good.

Here we can identify a point which is fundamental to
Lonergan's whole position on the acting subject as moral and
therefore authentic. The good for which we strive in action
is not something external and objective in any empirical
pre-defined sense, it is what we come to know and eventually
to do by a process of intending the good. Lonergan cites
Aristotle as holding the same view, as being unwilling to
speak of ethics apart from the ethical reality of good men
(98). The good is realised in the structures of the
subject's existential consciousness as the truth is
established by rational consciousness -

> "... the notion of intention of the good
> functions within one's human acting, and it
> is by reflecting on that functioning that
> one comes to know what the notion of the
> good is...just as the existential subject
> freely and responsibly makes himself what he
> is. so too he makes himself good or evil and
> his actions right or wrong... the subject is
> good by his good choices and good
> actions"(99).

Action, in other words, is self-transforming, and Lonergan's
analysis of the good gives us an interpretative framework
with which to handle that idea.

However, Lonergan takes the idea further. Conscious
intentionality is ultimately self-transcending. Our response
as authentic knowing and doing subjects becomes more
authentic as we progress - we endeavour not only to 'know the
truth' but also to 'do the truth'. Lonergan's notion of the
acting person is thus of a subject who realises himself both

in cognitive self-consciousness and moral self-transcendence,
in knowing and doing. His approach combines the use of the
traditional 'faculty psychology' concepts by which action was
always analysed in Catholic theology with the moral
component, to describe a subject whose choices determine his
own authenticity as he becomes ever more conscious of the
significance of personal values and the meaning of personal
responsibility in his dealings with others. The richness of
this approach in relation to approaches such as mechanism or
behaviourism lies in the emphasis on the importance of the
cognitive in action – not only in relation to the action as
such but in relation to the mental processes on which it is
grounded – as well as on the role of what is intended. These
together form the basis of authentic personal choice; we now
look at how such choices are made.

ix. <u>Man as agent.</u>

We are knowing beings and moral beings. Action
therefore springs from both cognitive and moral decisions.
But a psychology of action does not reduce to a psychology of
decision-taking, because decision-taking explanations say
nothing about how decisions are actually executed (100). We
need a conception of person-as-agent, rather than simply
'passenger on a mental vehicle' (101) to explain how decision
is translated into action. Cognitive and moral beliefs
provide reasons for action because they enable the actor to
say what he wants to achieve in teleological terms, that he
wants that outcome, and that he knows how to get it. He
thus has both a disposition and a tendency to act in a
certain way. But reasons for action do not necessarily
explain action – in particular, they do not explain failure
to act. We need some notion of 'agency', of power to act, as
an explanatory device. We need a "conception of ourselves as
agents (which) should .. be understood as the employment of a
theory with the active and willing self as its prime

theoretical concept"(102).

First, however, we need to examine the way in which our cognitional processes give rise to the beliefs which form the basis of action. Lonergan, as we have seen, regards these processes as a set of interlinked activities. Seeing, inquiring, imagining, understanding, conceiving, reflecting, and judging form a self-assembling and self-constituting set of functionally interrelated activities (103). They can be used to monitor, to steer or to evaluate action; they can precede, accompany or follow action. They are of three basic kinds, experiential intellectual and rational. Intellectual acts presuppose experiential ones — we have to experience what we understand — and rational acts presuppose intellectual ones - we have to understand before we can affirm. The process of 'coming to know' requires all three moments.

The motivating force for such acts is that of the question. Knowledge cannot be imposed or imparted (104); it begins with the attempt of the conscious intelligent and rational subject to make sense of his experience, with his 'unrestricted desire to know' (105). This 'making sense' process is what Lonergan calls insight. Insight happens by means of 'the pivot between the concrete and the abstract (106)' — in other words by the way in which the flow of sensations interacts with imagination, memories and associations (107). Understanding is what we make of the insight as formulated conceptually; it stands to the object of understanding as sight stands to colour. Further questions will arise, however, because understanding as conceptual formulation must be verified. We form a hypothesis, we reflect on the conditions necessary for that hypothesis to be verified, we then investigate as to whether those conditions are fulfilled. We thus make a judgement which takes the form of affirming that the conditions necessary for that judgement to be made have been formulated and verified. This is judgement as a 'grasp of the virtually unconditioned'. What we conceptualise is what we reflect on, what we reflect on is what we grasp the virtually unconditioned in, what we grasp the virtually unconditioned in is what we affirm (108).

Judgement is an answer to the Aristotelian question 'an sit'. It is the act that changes a proposition from an object of thought to an object of affirmation. It is the part of cognitional activity which establishes truth; truth is thus the implicit content of every judgement as opposed to its explicit content (109). It is therefore also an act which places the responsibility for a commitment to truth on the knowing subject. Judgement rests, says Lonergan, on "the absence of further questions" — as such, it is the act which establishes rational beliefs (110).

Theories of rational action (111) have as their first requirement that the beliefs held by the acting agent should be rational. They normally require that the agent should have a defined goal which it is rational to pursue (112), and that he should hold beliefs about how that goal is to be achieved. Rational action is then simply the implementation of that strategy (113). But this is necessarily an incomplete account of action insofar as it fails to take account of the moral component. It is possible to introduce this dimension by widening the concept of rationality in judgement to include the establishment of beliefs by all processes of judgement — not only judgements of fact but also judgements of value. For Lonergan, judgement establishes not only what is so but also what is good. Beliefs are the outcome of that process (114). Just as judgements of fact are grounded in the norms of the cognitional process, so judgements of value are grounded in the norms inherent in the social, religious and cultural heritage (115). We believe what others have established because a judgement of value grounds our acceptance of their conclusions. Belief is therefore a compound of what we establish by judgements of fact and judgements of value.

Rational action is normally taken to imply a connection between rational beliefs and action; beliefs provide us with a 'reason' for action (116). But if we say that having a reason for action necessarily results in that action we ignore situations where action cannot be explained by the logic of the means-ends relationship. We also ignore situations where the means-ends argument does not result in the expected action. We must therefore look for some intervening factor, some kind of 'activity principle' (117) which can explain the connection between belief and action — in other words, for some principle of agency. If we regard beliefs as providing the disposition and the tendency to act, action will require the empowerment of those tendencies.

In order to analyse what the notion of agency might mean we can use analogies of process borrowed from the natural sciences. The cause-effect principle presupposed by rational action theories can be seen as having the form —
BELIEF.....ACTION
This is an example of what Harre (118) calls the 'patient' idea of the acting person. The schema for action of a patient is —
BEING + STIMULUS.....ACTION
The patient will be quiescent until some stimulus, perhaps the acquisition of beliefs, reasons for action, leads him to action. But the stimulus here, the action, is essentially applied to the patient. The stimulus realises in the patient the passive dispositions he possesses which then become tendencies to acquire a particular state or attribute. This formulation gives no account of agency because it attributes to reasons the status of causes of action. Acting persons are clearly more than mere 'patients'.

An agent, as opposed to a patient, already possesses the disposition and the tendency to act which only need in some sense to be released (119). An 'agent' schema for action might therefore be of the form —
BEING MINUS RESTRAINT = ACTION

The stimulus in the patient case relies on the acquisition of beliefs, whereas in the case of agents the beliefs are already there. Action happens because of a chosen release of blocked powers. It is, of course, perfectly possible that in any one person the two identities are sequential - a person is first a patient, then as they acquire tendencies and powers whose realisation requires the removal of some restraint, they become agents. A person is a 'perfect' agent if he controls both the tendency to act and the release of that tendency. Sometimes one or both are outside the agent's control - one may have a tendency (such as a neurotic compulsion) which one cannot control. Alternatively, one may wish to do something but be restrained by outside circumstances (e.g. we may wish to work but fail to find employment).

The release of the tendency to act, the crucial moment of activation between decision and action, can be discussed in terms of the will (120). The will is the basis of freedom in action. We can avoid the problems associated with the hypothetical existence of a mental organ called 'the will' if we think of willing as self-exhortation - telling oneself to do something (121). It is always possible for the agent to choose to do something other than the obvious action, to will himself to do something which is unpleasant or patently irrational. Harre argues that there is no mystery about the mechanism of willing - it is no more difficult to understand how we come to obey ourselves than to understand how we obey others, given that the command is given in the context of the same kind of moral order as exists between persons. Akrasia, weakness of will, powerlessness to act when action is indicated, is then simply to be understood in terms either of a cognitive failure (the agent knows what he ought to do but is impetuous or wicked) or of a general moral failure centred round concepts of lack of effort (122).

Willing is the act which reveals the self-transcendence of the person in action. As we respond to values we can choose to say no rather than yes — I may but I need not (123). It is the moment of self—determination in action, the moment when as well as opting to execute the action the agent constitutes himself as agent and as self—transcendent. The will is a power rather than a property, the power which is released in the choice of action. It is guided by cognition — of self, of reality, of values, but the characteristic trait of the will is the ability to respond to presented values in the object (124).

But there is also a prior objectivity of the will. In the act of willing the acting person constitutes himself and reveals his own self possession. In Wotyla's terms, acts of willing form the ego, the object of the act of will (125). The ego, in other words, is the object of the will — it is what is willed, chosen before any object. In willing to do something I determine myself and reveal my own self—transcendence in action — not in any horizontal sense as indicated by intentionality, but in a vertical sense of going beyond my own subjective preferences in striving for the good. The process of choosing the good in action reveals the way in which action is dependent on the ego — i.e. on the acting person, in a sense which is absent in any purely causal account of action. It is that dependence which is the ground of personal freedom to 'do the truth'. As the person becomes conscious of this power to choose he experiences

> "the fact that he is the one who is
> determined by himself and that his decision
> makes him become somebody who may be good or
> bad — which includes at its basis the
> awareness of the very fact of his being
> somebody (126)".

It is the concept of will as interpretative of the notion of agency which forms the basis of the idea of action as self—transforming praxis.

This chapter has attempted to develop a philosophy of action which is on the one hand rational and cognitive and on the other hand takes into account feelings, beliefs and values as the basis of the ultimate moment of decision whereby all this is translated into action. But even this framework cannot cope with Paul's dilemma in Romans 7.14-25. In terms of the material explored in this chapter his problem would have to be analysed in terms of cognitive irrationality or confusion, or indecisiveness or weakness of will. If Paul had seen his plight as being solely due to being 'under the flesh' the account of action given in this chapter would have sufficed. But Paul is also 'under the law', and so are we, in the sense that no amount of cognitive or moral freedom can guarantee 'orthopraxis'. This is because the cognitive processes which ground our action are structured by the presuppositions and models of reality which are built into our cultural ways of thinking, as well as by the theories by which we analyse our world. Our values too are given to us by the notions of the 'good' which prevail in our culture. And our decisions and actions will be both enabled and constrained by the social and institutional norms which constitute our society. The next three chapters explore these 'determinisms' as limitations on our freedom of action; they focus particularly on the way in which the 'culture of economism' generates specific influences on thought and action.

==

1. This model is developed in (1957), extended in (1971), and completed in (1985).
2. See Bernstein (1972) Pt.1.
3. This is a focus with which both phenomenonalists and realists are happy. See e.g. Pols (1982) Chs. 5 and 6.
4. Emmet (1984) Ch.4.
5. Kockelmans (1983) argues that these perspectives have not only provided the foundations for research in science but have also influenced the way in which we have come to conceive of and to understand ourselves.
6. Von Cranach and Harré (ed) (1982) p.9.
7. Davidson (1980). especially the paper on agency. The problem about this is that we put agency into an event—causation world.
8. The causality here is the strict Humean notion of causality where one event or state is the cause of another if its occurrence is both necessary and sufficient for the occurrence of the other. Pols (1982) p.10.
9. See e.g. Davidson (1980), Sellars (1966).
10. See Prichard (1949), Chisholm (1976).
11. Davidson (1980) p.53 says there is no point in using causation to explain relations between the agent and his act because nothing is thereby explained.
12. See Pols (1982) p.10. Also Hornsby (1980).
13. Harre (1984) p.183. cites Taylor's criticism of the principle that every event must have another event as cause. See Taylor (1966).
14. Pols (1982) p.13.
15. Aune (1977) sees this as the central question in the philosophy of action, but focuses his attention on only one specific problem within that field — i.e. on the logic of deliberation and reasoning.
16. Pols (1982) p.16.

17. See Davidson (1980), Goldman (1970). What Davidson is basically concerned with is analysing the logical structure of action described conceptually. But this contributes little to an understanding of real-life situations where happenings are complex outcomes of actions and natural processes. Lonergan (1974) in "The Subject" argues that it is useless to try and understand the acting subject by analysing concepts of action. Concepts are 'immobile', they remain what they are defined to mean; they change as understanding and the mind that forms them change. Conceptualism ignores both the concrete and the questioning in the ontological reality of action.

18. See Aune (1977) for an account of this issue.

19. E.g. von Wright (1971). Explanation here is fundamentally functional as opposed to causal, as Elster (1983) points out. Von Wright argues that it is not the action of interfering with the world which is the 'cause', it is rather the state of affairs produced by the action — i.e. the 'event'. to speak of actions as causing results is thus a 'bad mistake'. (p.68).

20. See von Cranach and Harre (1982), Preface and Introduction.

21. Ibid. p.xi. Ethnomethodology, for instance, postulates a hierarchy of control in motivational terms from society to self to act.

22. See Hollis (1977), Dageneis (1972) for accounts of what this might entail.

23. For a grounding of this statement see Gaudium et Spes Part 1, Ch.1. Man is made in the image of God (Genesis), and redeemed by Christ (Paul); he is thus not less than 'person'.

24. Friedman (1967) p.25.

25. See Rorty (1980).

26. Made so cogently by Rorty throughout his book.

27. Ibid. p.8/9. Rahner (1965) pp.33-4. would argue that there exists such a framework: the nature of the knowing

subject determines the limits of the possibility of knowledge.

28. Harre (1984) p.20.

29. Lonergan's work on the subject as knower was concerned with the search for criteria which could be used to ground transcendental method. He sought these criteria in the a priori conditions of human knowing, and found them in the recurrent and related operations of human cognitional activity.

30. Campbell (1971) p.15 calls this the inconsistent tetrad.

31. See eg. Davidson (1980).

32. See Armstrong (1968) for an account of this.

33. Ibid Ch.4.

34. See Agassi (1977), who makes this point throughout his book.

35. Ibid. p.49.

36 Ibid. p.42/3.

37. See Centore (1979) who discusses this point in his conclusion.

38. Such as Davidson (1963), Danto (1973), von Wright (1971).

39. Skinner (1971), p.205.

40. See e.g. Ryle (1949).

41. This is the strong notion of rational action — the inevitable outcome of rule-governed choice.

42. Armstrong (1968), p.77.

43. However, awareness by phenomenal properties ('having a pain') is actually incompatible with a purely materialist conception of mind. See Campbell (1971) Ch.6.

44. Armstrong (1968) p. 82.

45. Campbell (1971) p.97.

46. Armstrong (1968) p.92ff.

47. For an account of this see Simon (ed) (1957).

48. Skinner (1948), (1971).

49. Dageneis (1972) p.16.

50. Again, for the behaviourists pain is pain-behaviour, for

the mechanists pain is a brain impulse which causes behaviour.

51. See argument in Campbell (1971) p.75.

52. Ibid. p.65ff.

53. See Agassi (1977) p.159 fn.80.

54. Spery (1965) p.75/6.

55. For an account of this see Flew (1978) Ch.7.

56. Ibid. p.141/2

57. Skinner (1948).

58. Friedman (1967) p.196.

59. See Dageneis (1972) p.56.

60. Friedman (1967) pp.191-209.

61. Ibid. pp.194/5.

62. For a discussion of this and related issues see Flew (1978) pp.151-171.

63. Psychic determinism would thus become a special case of physical causality.

64. Dageneis (1972) p.74.

65. Harre (1984), Ch.1. Harre suggests (p.167) that the origin of this notion of person may be found, as Mead shows in Mind, Self and Society, in intersubjectivity. But Harre's self is much more of an abstraction than Mead's 'self', who can find out only in the concretely intersubjective situation who he is.

66. Ibid p. 22.

67. Ibid. p.116.

68. Ibid p.79. Harre points out that the concept of self can be stronger or weaker in a culture depending on the kind of concepts used — linguistic forms, in other words, determine psychological structures. Examples can be given of societies where 'self' is merged with the general group entity, as well as of societies where group life is primarily individualistic (Ibid p.87ff.). 'Self' is the inner, person is the outer aspect of self-identity.

69. Wotyla (1979).

70. Harre (1984) p.108.

71. Berger (1974) p.73/4.
71. Adapted from Harre (1984) p.44.
73. Although in the literature not a popular one. "Let me just mention that the characteristics 'intended' or 'conscious' are often theoretically derived or silently neglected, because they are erroneously thought to constitute a menace to the scientific causalistic concept of man, since they presuppose assumptions of conscious steering and free will ". von Cranach and Harre (1982) p.36.
74. Harre (1984) p.147ff.
75. This more or less approximates to the Thomist categories 'conscientia perceptio' and 'conscientia experientia'. it is only the second of these with which Lonergan concerns himself.
76. Usage in German makes this clear. the word 'bewusst' is clearly related to the word 'wissen'. The root 'sci' in conscious has the same connotation, but it is lost in current usage, which in English tends to emphasise the perceptual rather than the cognitive end of the concept. See Harre (1984) p.151/2.
77. Ibid p.146.
78. See Appendix III
79. See Lonergan (1957) Ch.11, (1971) Ch.1.
80. Ibid. (1957 Ch.18, (1971) Ch.1.
81. Ibid. (1971) p.8.
82. See Appendix III.
83. Doran (1981) Ch. 2 points out that this idea marks a movement, a horizon-shift in Lonegan's thinking which happened in the period between the publication of Insight and the publication of Method in theology.
84. Lonergan (1971) p.7.
85. Aquila (1977) p.ix. The notion of intentionality must, however, be seen as prescinding entirely from any discussion as to the sense in which such an object can be said to exist. We can discuss intentionality without engaging in that issue.

86. Harre (1984) p.115 uses Brentano's notion of the mental as the intentional specifically to argue that if a person displays an intention as the conceived, proposed or declared outcome of an action (practical) he must also be displaying some representation or sign of that intention and that sign is the intentional activity (extra-practical).

87. See von Cranach and Harre (1982) p.40.

88. Lonergan's account of intentionality is borrowed from Scholastic philosophy, as well as from Husserl. For an account of the development of the idea see Spielberg in McAlister (1976). Scholastic philosophy conceives of intentionality along the whole spectrum from act to object, relation and concept. It is essentially cognitive. Brentano saw intentionality in terms of 'mental inexistence' or 'immanent objectivity'. However, he disliked the word 'intentional' as descriptive of the process by which the object is present in consciousness. It was Husserl who finally separated the concept of intentionality from the notion of immanent inexistence, and refined it as relatedness towards an object.

89. In the sense of a lower level being retained, preserved, yet transcended and completed. Lonergan (1974) p.80.

90. As to how that is finally established, see Lonergan (1957) p.332 on self-correcting process of learning.

91. Lonergan (1971) p.

92. See Doran (1981) p.68 for an account of possible psychologies of motivation. Abstracting from the idea of motivation also allows Lonergan to avoid the problem of unconscious motivation. "In talking about the intentional self we raise causality to the human level and protect the consideration of motive from reductionistic interpretations." [Winter (1966) p.149]

93. Doran (1980) p.68. See also Crowe (1968).

94. Lonergan (1971) pp.30-4.

95. We should distinguish here between feelings and emotions. Harre (1984) p.123 makes that distinction, arguing that emotions are in fact culturally conditioned — 'accidie' and 'melancholy' are no longer fashionable conditions. Feelings are what one experiences, emotions are the response to that feeling. Feelings in Lonergan's sense are one's experiencing of value.

96. For structure of the human good see Lonergan (1971) pp.47–52.

97. Lonergan (1974) 'The Subject' p.81.

98 . Ibid p.82. Aristotle in Nichomachean Ethics II (iii) 41.1105 b 5–8, II vi 15.1106 b 36ff. We find the same point in Rahner (1967). However, there is also a sense in which values can be said to exist objectively.

99. Lonergan (1974) 'The Subject' pp.82/3.

100. Harre (1984) p.181.

101. Ibid. p.185.

102. Ibid. p.193.

103. Lonergan uses the analogy of a scissors, where the lower blade represents the data and the upper blade the questions of cognitional activity.

104. I.e. it is something internal to the subject.

105. Lonergan presupposes a particular view of experience as cognitive. Dewey (1916) p.11 (see discussion in Bernstein p.204) argues another view — viz. that most of our experience is non-reflective and non-cognitive, and that inquiry is something we undertake only when 'something is the matter'.

106. Lonergan (1957).

107. This is the way Lonergan handles the fact that we can only make sense of our own experience in the context of prior interpretative frameworks. These frameworks would include linguistic ones for the majority of thinkers. Lonergan, however, explicitly takes the view that no conceptualisation happens prior to insight.

108. The conditions for a judgement to be correct are established by experience, the 'conditioned' by a

question for reflection. How do we establish the fact
that it is raining?

109. Here is where Lonergan establishes his own position on
truth. His position exposes the fallacy of the old
syllogism – what God has revealed is true, God has
revealed the mysteries of faith, therefore the mysteries
of faith are true. Truth exists formally only in
judgements, judgements exist only in the mind. God's
truth is thus truth in God's mind and in my mind, but
not in the minds of non-believers, whose judgement
dictates an alternative conclusion. See (1974) p.71.

110. If we are to say beliefs are dispositions to act we need
to explain how they are grounded. See Crowe (1968).

111. See Benn and Mortimore (1976), Elster (1979) for
accounts of these.

112. This is substantive formal rationality. For instance,
if hedonism is assumed, utility maximisation is a
rational goal.

113. But see Simon (1957) for reasons why rational action may
be 'bounded' by practical considerations, also see
Elster (1979) pp.65-77 for the restrictive requirements
as to agents preferences.

114. We can then extend the concept of rationality to define
it as 'following one's conscience'. See Wotyla (1979).

115. Lonergan (1971) pp. 41-7.

116. See Aune (1971) for an account of the debate as to
whether reasons are the cause or merely the explanation
of action. Also see Bernstein (1971) p.252 for the
distinction between acting for a reason and acting with
a reason.

117. Harre's terminology (1984) p.188ff.

118. Ibid. p.189.

119. For this notion of power to act as release see also
Harre in von Cranach and Harre (ed) (1982). The notion
is based on Fritz Heider's idea of personal power,
conceived of as effort plus ability. See summary by B.
Harris and J. Harvey (1981).

110

120. Harre (1984) p.194. See also Aune (1971) pp.65-74.
121. For this idea see e.g. Kenny (1979).
122. Harre (1984) p.195.
123. Wotyla (1979) Ch.3, especially pp.124ff.
124. Ibid p.135.
125. Ibid p.108.
126. Ibid. p.113.

===

CHAPTER THREE - THE CONDITIONING OF EXPERIENCE AND
UNDERSTANDING.

i. Introduction

Our response to the message of the Kingdom is a response
in action. Knowing is basic to action (1), and the basis of
decision-taking, as we have seen, is therefore to be found in
the combination of experience, understanding, and judgement
as affirmation of that understanding. These together
establish 'what is the case'. This chapter will argue that
the process of coming to know is dependent on the way in
which we 'see' the world, and that in turn is structured for
us by the 'determinisms' of our cultural context. Our
experience is interpreted in the light of our
presuppositions, our understanding of the world is formed by
our theories and culturally given models of reality, and our
processes of judgement are influenced by cultural ideas of
truth and culturally established methods of verification.

This chapter analyses the properties of a world view
given by the wider context of a scientific culture, and more
particularly by the 'culture of economism'. The framework of
thought embedded in the discipline of economics itself
provides the thought forms central to a materialistic
culture, where economic concerns tend to dominate all areas
of life. The presuppositions, models of reality and ways of
establishing rational conclusions which most influence our
thinking are to that extent exemplified by those generated
within the discipline of economics.

I begin by using Lonergan's notion of 'horizon' to
analyse the parameters of our thought. I then look at the
particular presuppositions which ground our experience,
arguing that whereas their prevalence and continuation is
ensured by their ideological status, their nature presents
basic problems for a faith stance. I use the idea of a

paradigm to outline the framework of thought used in economics; here too presuppositions give us ways of interpreting the world inimical to the way of faith. I then discuss the thought forms – theories as models of reality – which help us to understand our world, adopting the post-empiricist view that theory is in one sense or another socially dependent, and the main sense in which this is true is that meaning is socially created. I look at ways in which economics contributes to this creation of meaning in our culture; I take the position that it impoverishes rather than assists our understanding because it precludes ways of seeing and modes of interpretation basic to the message of the Gospel.

ii. Thought and experience.

The process of coming to know, of establishing 'what is the case', is a process which begins with experience. But no experience is unproblematic (2) in the sense that it comes to us as 'brute fact'. We never experience the world 'barely and purely', but rather in a way which depends on how we interpret that experience. This is the view taken by post-empiricist philosophers of science (3); they maintain that experience comes to us through conceptual frameworks which structure for us the form our experience takes (4), that the meaning of the terms we use to describe our experience is dependent on the theories we already hold, and that we can experience or observe nothing unless we have a prior interpretative framework within which to make sense of it. Language, theory, text and sign make all knowledge claims unavoidably reflexive, because we cannot talk about the way in which language structures experience without using that language. On the other hand, there is clearly a dialectical relationship between such frameworks and our experience; whereas our new experience is always in some sense related to the knowledge we have already gained, it in turn adds to the fund of that knowledge. Thought, as

Schillebeeckx says (5), "makes new experience possible, while on the other hand it is experience which makes new thinking necessary".

What kind of interpretative frameworks are in question here? One way of approaching this is to visualise ourselves as thinking on several different levels, or, more properly perhaps, at different depths. Much of our thought is ephemeral, fleeting and thus non-reflective and non-interpretative. We ask ourselves what there will be for dinner or whether it will be fine on the week-end. This is, so to speak, the 'grid' of immediate thought. At a deeper level thought is done within the bounds of 'models' of reality, of interpretative frameworks. This is the kind of thinking by which we attempt to make sense of or give meaning to our experience. In a pre-critical or pre-reflective sense these models may remain hidden or unnoticed, but they are there nevertheless, and serve to give structure and coherence to the flood of experience. At a still more profound level there is a structural level of thought which dictates the parameters within which all thought is done. This is the level of basic presuppositions (6), and it is the level with which I shall be concerned in the first part of this chapter.

These levels of thought, and therefore the particular shape they give to our experience, are clearly conditioned in the first instance by our historical and cultural environment. The circumstantial background to our lives provides the material for the disconnected series of superficial thoughts which continually run through our minds. Our conjecturallyconditioned models of reality, our 'theories', also come from our environment. Here the word 'theory' is used not in the narrowly axiomatic sense but in the much broader sense used by philosophers of science such as Feyerabend, who says that theories are simply sets of general assumptions (7), Hanson (8), who sees theory as a conceptual organiser, and Bromberger (9), who regards theory as a puzzle-solver. We can thus talk about everyday actors' theories, commonsense theories and implicit theories without implying that they are in any sense structured or formalised (10). They are simply the 'shape' into which we pour our experience.

The deepest, 'structural' level of our thinking is formed by the 'world-view' of our history and our time. But world views are much less the product of history than of culture. It is culture which is the fundamental formative influence on our presuppositions and our prejudices (11). It is, for instance, far easier for us to understand the presuppositions which grounded Greek philosophy or biblical thought than to engage in dialogue with present-day cultures other than our own, simply because our own culture is derivative of these former influences (12).

We can look more closely at this idea of 'levels' of thought and their determination by using Lonergan's concept of 'horizon'(13). Lonergan defines horizon as "a maximum field of vision from a determinate standpoint"(14) — i.e. our own. We can use this idea to distinguish between the grids and filters of our own thought processes and the cultural influences which condition them by separating the 'subjective' pole of horizon' from its 'objective' pole. In objective terms we can identify the way in which our own cultural world-view or cosmology has undergone a number of fundamental changes from Aristotelian to modern times (15) — shifts which have radically altered the bases of peoples' frameworks of thought so that, as Wittgenstein says, "what were ducks before the revolution were rabbits afterwards"(16). The objective pole of 'horizon' is then structured by the resultant models of reality — theories — which provide the basis of our reflection. Scientific thought sets the parameters of these frameworks of thought within what Thomas Kuhn calls a 'paradigm'(17) — an overarching 'way of seeing' which governs the way in which a discipline or cluster of disciplines is done. We are thus already provided with a 'context' of thought.

The objective pole of 'horizon provides the conditions of possibility for the personal or 'subjective' pole — in other words, for the thought frameworks of the person. "Horizon", says Tracy, "is the limit or boundary between the questions I ask and can't answer and the questions I can't ask because they're meaningless for me"(18). Each of us has such a horizon, the outer possibilities of which are set by cultural factors, but the limitations of which are our own. The ground of that subjective pole is the consciousness of the intentional subject; it is that consciousness which, according to the degree in which it is 'differentiated', sets the limit to the possibility of enquiry by establishing the finite world of meaning relevant for that subject. Our own subjective horizons of thought are thus not only dependent on social and educational factors, not only the result of past experience and achievement, but they also provide both the conditions for and the limitations to further development of thought. They form our 'relative' horizon, within which we think on an ordinary commonsense level, on a theoretic-interpretative level, and on a cosmological level — the level of basic presuppositions.

We now look at these frameworks in turn. We focus first on the cultural presuppositions which play such a large part in influencing our thinking. The wisdom of doing this lies in the fact that, as Torrance says (19), cultural assumptions are most dangerous precisely when we are unaware of them. Our faith response is likely to be more critical, more reflective, in the measure that we understand the influence of these presuppositions on our actions.

iii.   World views in a scientific culture

    All our thinking takes place within an overarching
framework of metaphysical presuppositions which we can
designate as a world-view, a world-picture, or, more
properly, a cosmology, since it comprises fundamental ideas
about the structure and function of 'world'(20). World views
play a central role in a culture where the demise of belief
has left us with a psychological void, where rationality
precludes reliance on myth, and where "the challenge of the
increasing fragmentation, specialisation and babylonisation
of knowledge systems and languages" (21) creates an ever
greater necessity to make sense of the world. The
interaction between cosmology and culture is two-way; on the
one hand 'world-pictures' express a set of presuppositions
about the way the world hangs together in a causal sense –
this in turn enables more specific theories about such
interconnections to be formulated (22). On the other hand,
however, the resulting product of knowledge systems helps to
form the metaphysical framework within which such knowledge
is culturally acquired (23).

    Our presuppositions are those of a scientific culture,
or, more properly, those of science as a cultural system
(24). They have their roots firstly in the long development
of scientific thinking (25),and secondly in the philosophical
framework which grounds the doing of science (26). Science
bases its endeavours on the premise that there is an external
world, that it can be accessed by capturing the facts of the
world in true propositions, and that those facts can be
described in scientific language. At its most extreme,
science is taken to be a linguistic system in which true
propositions are in one to one relation to facts. Facts in
turns can be described and predicted by means of theories,
and these theories can be observed in operation. Science
thus aims to uncover the hidden mechanism of the world. The
presuppositions which lie at the root of this endeavour serve

to support the cultural belief in the validity of this mode
of knowing, in the rightness of scientific endeavour, in the
power of science to change the world for the better, and in
the ontological order as expressed by the structures of
scientific thought (27). They are also self-reinforcing in
that they serve to structure and limit the direction of new
thinking by precluding developments in thought which do not
accord with, or which conflict with, the expectations which
they embody (28). We now look at 'scientific'
presuppositions in turn.

A. Because intelligibility is an important attribute of a
material 'world' we need to hold views on its structure and
substance. The Greeks were not concerned with substance,
only with structure. Aristotle believed that there was a
correlation between the structures of reality and the form of
an axiomatic system – the principles of thought corresponded
to the principles of being, and being was thus intrinsically
intelligible (29). Knowledge of the world was certain and
unchanging, truth was necessary and universal, there was
therefore no metaphysical issue. But the rise of scientific
thought meant that the isomorphism between the structures of
reality and cognitive structures could no longer be
maintained (30); empirical discovery and controlled
experiment made it necessary both to redefine the link
between thought and reality and to hold a view about the
substance of reality. Our beliefs about substance are
fundamentally antimetaphysical; we believe only what we see.
What we cannot actually see – i.e. 'world' as a whole –, we
tend to visualise as a homogeneous, one-layer system (31)
composed of a substance or unit built into structures. This
is 'metaphysical monism', which is the only presupposition
which accords with the materialist conception of the universe
we inherit from the rise of empirical science (32). The
conception of the universe as a closed system capable of
mathematical formalisation leads to the view that in terms of
substance it can be broken down into particles whose
interrelationships can be explained by the causal laws of

physics and chemistry. Torrance (33) points to the way in which thinkers such as Michael Polanyi have seen the deficiency of this position because it fails to take into account the personal rational nature of the human spirit. It has also been undermined by developments in modern physics, which replaces the materialist conception of the universe by a view of universe as field, and by the substitution of ideas of field structures for causal mechanistic laws.

B. It is a basic presupposition of our thinking that we have no problem in expressing our knowledge of reality either in theoretical structures or in language. In other words, we assume the relation between the structures of thought and the structures of reality to be unproblematical. This assumption bypasses two kinds of problem, one connected with the relation between theoretical structures and the reality they conceptualise, the other connected with the language used in theoretical reflection and the way in which it maps or reflects the logical structure of the reality it describes.

(i) There have been a variety of approaches to the problem of expressing the relationship between a reality which can only be partially known empirically and the thought forms, or theoretical constructs by which that reality is conceptualised and analysed. Duhem (34) saw the role of theory as setting up a series of mathematical propositions designed to yield hypothetico-deductive experimental formulations. Mach (35) saw reality as defined in terms of the operations and experiments by which it was apprehended. An alternative view (36) saw theories simply as agreed conventions by which the facts of reality could be handled. Realist views bypass the theory-reality problem by simply assuming that it is possible to describe an already 'out there' reality, and that theory in no sense creates the reality it describes. Anti-realists, on the other hand, see theories simply as tools or instruments for handling data and deriving predictions.

(ii) Scientific knowledge is entirely conceptual: empirical reality has to be handled by natural or artificial language in a hierarchical conceptual structure. The problem of the relationship between reality and the language in which it is described is approached in a particular way by the programme of logical empiricism, which attempts to propagate a world-view which sees reality purely in terms of a logical structure which can be linguistically handled by mathematics (37). There is thus an isomorphism between linguistic structures and the structures of reality. Logical empiricists such as Russell attempted to find metaphysical structures in language systems. Wittgenstein held that logic mirrored the world, that the world is a collection of facts, that facts are the existence of a state of affairs, that states of affairs are combinations of objects, so that theories therefore simply specify the pattern of propositions which give the simplest description of reality. For logical empiricism, the structures of the world are thus to be found in the logical syntax of the language of science; science is unified in its method and axiomatic in its foundations. Current philosophical thinking rejects the agenda of logical empiricism, but fails to offer an alternative metaphysical paradigm. There is still a linguistically-orientated emphasis on analysing the logical structure of scientific systems. Scientific method is either theory-centred, with theory- and language-dependent observation, or observation-centred, where theories have abstract calculus, observational frameworks, and correspondence rules linking the two.

C. We believe in a strong version of <u>causality</u> (38) as a foundation for the order of the universe. We see the universe as a causally-related system which is governed by immutable laws which are fixed and unchanging (39). There is a natural order to the universe which is best conceptualised in mechanistic terms (although we tend to use more organic formulations when we think about society). This implies that it is seen as possible to control reality by identifying and manipulating the mechanical process. Our choice of a naturalistic model of order (rather than a historical or an idealistic one) thus justifies and legitimates our choice of science as method (40). The image of the machine is a powerful one in the common understanding of science and of empirical reality. Its influence even extends to the way we create our own self-image, in the sense that we automatically tend to envisege our minds as computers and our bodies as machines (41)

D. Our presuppositions with regard to time and change are much more relativistic. We see the physical laws of nature as fixed and unchanging over time (the 'container' notion of time and space), but we see biological processes as evolutionary and social processes as subject to constant change. The fact that unchanging time and space were identified with the unchanging reality of God led Newton to maintain that it was impossible to have a notion of God becoming incarnate in historical time. Kant took this conception of unchanging time and space and transferred it from the mind of God to the mind of man. The fact that knowledge then becomes knowledge of things only in their appearances means that knowledge is possible neither of God nor of Jesus Christ (42).

E. We assume that the way to get knowledge about the world is to come to understand the laws which govern its operation. Science, which sets out to derive and test causal relations between variables, is thus the valid method of gaining knowledge and attaining truth. Science uses as its source of knowledge experience, the evidence of the senses, and rational analysis; these are combined with the method of science to yield knowledge which is more reliable than that stemming from revelation, authority or tradition. The consequence of this is that we find it difficult to believe in the possibility of acquiring one type of knowledge — i.e. scientific knowledge — by sense experience, while acquiring another type of knowledge — i.e. religious knowledge — by revelation, because our presuppositions as to the validity of the knowledge claims of science preclude a recognition of other types of knowledge claim. This dichotomy (based as it

is on the dualism inherent in the distinction between
theoretical and empirical aspects of reality) exists even for
the person of faith; — "for those who can tolerate such a
distinction (between knowledge claims) it is quite easy to
trust the senses in the lab, to believe in God's miracles in
Church... if, however, a direct conflict occurs endangering
life or some of the other basic values, then the chips will
be down" (43).

F. The perceived power of science to solve problems and
fulfil human needs has created a nexus of cultural beliefs
which revolve round the image of science—as—knowledge. Those
beliefs are in the first instance held by those who support
science and at a further remove by the public at large to
whom the politicians are accountable. (They are 'beliefs'
rather than certain knowledge, because the evidence that
science is "a good thing" is by no means conclusive). This
cultural faith in science in turn seems to sustain the faith
of scientists in what they are doing. The most central of
these 'beliefs' is a belief in progress. Science has given
western thought a concrete foundation on which to base its
belief in notions of utopia. Technology translates the
potential of science and articulates its nature so as to
explicate it in terms of progress. In other words, technology
ensures that science produces the results expected of it in
the control and use of nature. Science and technology thus
act as instruments which link our conception of 'world' to
our conception of desirable ends — they thus create both our
ontology and our eschatology (44). What this amounts to is
that we tend to think of progress as equated with an ever
greater ability to manipulate the world, rather than in terms
of increasing human welfare.

    The second of these is a related belief in the power
of science. We believe that science will eventually be able
to solve all our problems, and that therefore nothing must be
allowed to impede the march of scientific knowledge. This

uncritical acceptance of the 'goodness' of knowledge tends to conflate scientific knowledge as the theoretical side of technology with the technological diffusion and application of that knowledge - i.e., it does not distinguish between power and the use of that power. After all, the splitting of the atom does not imply that nuclear weapons have to be built, advances in genetic knowledge do not mean that they inevitably have to be applied to problems of genetic engineering. There is a cultural belief in the premise that because scientific knowledge is good, its applications are inevitable and therefore legitimate - a belief which ignores the fact that the applications of science are society's choice. Science as a pragmatic enterprise is thus much more ambiguous than it is culturally perceived to be. We may have better medical care, but is modern medicine treating the disease or the person? (45). We may live longer, but do we live happier lives? We may live better, but are we not at the same time more anxious about material welfare? We may travel faster, but does it not often take us longer to get there? (46). Our belief in the power of science extends to a conviction that science will somehow compensate for our depletion of the earth's natural resources and fossil fuels, that it will inevitably find ways to avert the threatening catastrophes of famine, atmospheric pollution and nuclear waste.

Our belief in the desirability of scientific knowledge, in the face of all the evidence to the contrary, has much to do with the increasing subjection of science to political decision. In the last fifty years it has become more and more the case that science must be pursued at all costs, because scientific knowledge gives an advantage over one's rivals, whether political or industrial. The 'independent' nature of scientific knowledge has become subordinate to the requirements of national security, to the decisions of industrial companies and the whim of politicians who cannot afford not to support science. The common image of the scientist in his laboratory acquiring 'objective' knowledge does not take into account the realities of how his research is funded. There is thus an ideological component in our view of science as desirable. However, we also consider it desirable because we are in fact detached from its acquisition. Science and the results of science are for us not an 'object of contemplation'. We cannot experience the 'facts' of science unless we are scientists, whereas we have a variety of ways of experiencing other aspects of life, whether directly or indirectly — for instance, through literature. We have thus no directly experiential way of evaluating science.

It is partly because of this that we hold a naive conviction that science can attain <u>truth</u>. The belief in science which forms part of our world-picture has at its core the idea that it is possible to verify scientific statements empirically, and that such verification will render both the statement and the hypotheses which generates it 'true'. It is this notion of truth which has passed over into all disciplines, including theology, where the 'truths of religion' are established rationally rather than by empirical processes. Except in mathematics — where a statement can be proved 'true' in a mathematical sense — such notions of truth entirely ignore both the ontological status of what is proved and the intelligibility of the facts which are established. Scientific confirmation is in practice always conditional; facts are theory-determined, and thus the problem of truth resolves itself into the problem of determining conditions under which a statement can be validly asserted. Scientific statements are 'true' if they fulfil the demands placed on them — the more precise they are the easier they are to falsify (47). Ordinary language statements are often 'true' because minimal demands are placed on them. This leads to the kind of imprecision contained in ordinary notions of truth as, for instance, when we declare a statement to be true if it corresponds with the world, or when we think of truth as semantic — p is true, therefore there is a state of affairs p. Ontologically these senses of 'true' are inadequate; the first assumes a world which can finally be known and truth which is eternally true, the second assures a world represented by statements and mirrored by language. Scientific truth is never universal or eternal, it is limited and conditional, and hinges on the degree to which statements can be specified in such a way that they are testable. All that testing then establishes is the validity or otherwise of that statement within those conditions and constraints.

Empiricist and rationalist notions of truth and its attainability have formed the basis of our belief in the objectivity of science. The belief that objectivity has something to do with truth is accompanied by the belief that objectivity has something to do with agreement between scientists. Scientific agreement on choice of research, method of analysis and interpretation of results ensure that what is established by science carries no component of 'subjective' evaluation or decision. It is clear that this argument cannot withstand the obvious criticism that it is possible for all scientists to be equally misguided – or equally corrupted (48). It is also possible that agreement represents consensus rather than objective judgement. Furthermore, science in any society works to establish conclusions which are useful from an instrumental point of view, and to avoid problems which can create divergent points of view. No science is 'value-free', nor would value freedom establish objective truth.

We have, finally, an overriding belief in the hegemony of science. The 'two cultures' referred to by C.P.Snow are not held in equal respect in the popular mind. The educational system fosters a hierarchical evaluation of scientific and non-scientific achievement which has roots not only in the cultural preference for 'rational' rather than 'irrational', but in the pragmatic option for 'useful' rather than 'non-useful' knowledge (49). Because the scientific approach has yielded successful results in the field of empirical science, it is assumed that it can do the same in

social science, psychology, and even aesthetic fields of
knowledge; the scientific attitude thus promises a whole new
vision of life and the world (50). And yet science fails to
live up to its promise. As the tool of society it fails to
contribute to a clear improvement in human welfare, creating
luxury goods for some rather than attempting to satisfy the
basic needs of others, discovering the cure for fatal illness
yet supplying the means for wholesale destruction of natural
and human life. The US spends two thousand times as much in
any one year on alcohol and tobacco as the sum estimated by
the WHO to be necessary for the eradication of major third
World diseases. Lack of scientific knowledge is not the
problem, the ambiguity lies in how society chooses to apply
it (51).

All these presuppositions together form the framework
within which we think about the world and interpret our
experience. The status of these beliefs is 'ideological'
because they are generated by society and culture. The
concept of ideology (52) can be loosely interpreted as
'Weltanschauung', the sum total of ideas about social life of
all kinds, which is generated actively or passively by those
whose interests are expressed by the ideology (53). More
negatively, ideological beliefs mask or distort reality; they
create 'false consciousness', where people believe that they
have an accurate or true perception of reality because they
fail to see the social origin of their beliefs. They can be
individually or socially held, they can refer to a specific
element in society or to the totality of the social structure
(54).

Ideology is functionally related to the social order;
society constructs and propagates the kind of beliefs which
are necessary to enable it to function in a given fashion
(55). Usury, for example, was always held to be immoral
until the needs of industrial society for venture capital
gradually made the lending of money for interest by those who
had it to those who needed it acceptable. In our day

technological progress is accompanied by an emphasis in education on the priority of mathematics and a belief in the intellectual superiority of those with mathematical ability. How such beliefs actually get established depends on the actions of those whose interests are served by the process. Ideological formulation can be something passive and diffuse, where ideological reflection is simply the reformulation of the 'horizon of meanings' in a society, or it can be more positive and more manipulative — "the conceptual dominance of the material situation by an elite that equates social reality with the characteristics of its own system through particular abstractions"(56). Marx himself made that distinction; he saw the urge of political economists like the Physiocrats, Adam Smith, and Ricardo to grasp the inner connections of economic phenomena as a very different thing from the actions of the 'vulgar economists', who simply tried to translate the common consciousness of capitalists into a doctrinaire language, concealing social contradictions in the interests of the dominant class (57).

I have argued that our presuppositions are those of a 'scientific' culture, that they serve to underpin the accepted view of science as knowledge, and that they are socially generated — i.e. 'ideological' because it is in the perceived interests of society that they should exist in the form that they do. But if our presuppositions are ideological what is their status — to what extent are they 'true', 'rational', or to be trusted? Are we looking at the world in the 'right' way, through the 'right' set of spectacles? What, in other words, is the distinction between ideological content and the cognitive value of thought? The empiricist answer to this is that the gap is unbridgeable. Empiricists equate myth, ideology and everything metaphysical; they see science as the antithesis of a mythical world and reject any possibility of an ideological component in science. World' for them stands outside the knowing subject; there is thus a clear distinction between ideology, which is subjective, and fact, which is objective.

Mannheim made the same kind of argument (58). He saw ideological influences as sub-conscious and therefore a deviance from the norms of rational thought. Ideological belief can thus to be contrasted with scientific or 'true' belief - the implication is that it is possible to have a non-ideological , non-distorted view of reality which is 'true'.

The 'strong thesis' of the sociology of science (59) is that this belief is itself ideological. Sociologists of knowledge point to the fact that there are no extra-natural or extra-social grounds for rationality or truth. There is no way in which we can reach 'truth' in some transcendent sense. All our knowledge is gained and all our science done in a social context which is permeated by a mixture of true and irrational belief. Rationalists will argue against this on the grounds that logic and empirical knowledge are universal and free from ideological bias. They argue that logic is an a priori necessity for language - but they neglect the fact that the kind of logic embodied in the language will depend on the way in which the language is structured. The Nuer, for instance, say that twins are birds (60). They do not mean that they are like birds, but that they are birds. Yet they acknowledge that there is a clear distinction between twins and birds. Their language allows them to maintain the existence of logical contradictions as ours does not. Logical truth is thus a contingent rather than a necessary requirement for language.

Rationalists would also argue that empirical knowledge is possible on a non-ideological level. However, that argument overlooks the way in which the validity of knowledge is language- and culture-bound. Knowledge is simply that which is accepted as such in any given culture, and the rules for its establishment are given within that cultural context. For us, knowledge is science, rational rules - or rules which we hold to be rational - are evolved and generated within our society. They will not necessarily be the same for other

128

cultures. Models of knowledge emerge from a social milieu which determines both what counts as knowledge and what knowledge is possible. Rationality is thus itself culturally generated, so that science and ideology in fact share the same roots

The genesis of science itself can thus also be thought of as more or less manipulative, more or less 'idelogical'. Habermas (61) argues that the way in which sciences 'rationalise' society through technocratic abstraction, and the way in which science as a mode of thought becomes institutionalised within society both result in the establishment of science as the ideology of society. The process operates through mechanisms of cultural domination, by the way in which people are depoliticised and by the extent to which the consequences of scientific endeavour are legitimated by technological rationality. These processes happen in a manipulative fashion; it is not that science provides the basis for ideology, it is that bourgeois ideology invests itself with the appearance of science and thereby becomes respectable. In other words, it is not that "science has replaced class-contradictions as the source of ideology, but the dominant class has instrumentalised the name of science to pretend it has" (62).

Science thus casts its mantle of respectability on 'bourgeois' ideology. That respectability is in part seen to stem from its rationality, its objectivity, its 'value-freedom'. But value-freedom is neither desirable nor necessarily present. The value-freedom of science can be seen as itself ideological (63), in that it legitimates a social outlook which is pragmatic and thus antipathetic to the essentials of human dignity and freedom. Because science is objective it is thought to be authoritative, its conclusions beyond question. Society accepts this because science makes society richer, but in doing so it legitimates the use of instrumental reason which in itself is incapable of deciding between social goods. The ideological element in science exists whenever values creep into scientific endeavour (64). This happens at every level. What counts as a research problem is socially determined whether the choice is made by individuals or by a group of scientists. Theory choice and construction are grounded by the metaphysical presuppositions and cognitive interests of scientists. Theory can thus be seen as "a conscious attempt to explain the relationships between the appearances that form the basis of ideologies" (65). Hypotheses and conjectures are influenced by what the scientist wants to prove, data choice, classification and the presentation of results are all structured to fit into that already existing framework.

We can look, too, for concealed social influences on the culture of science – for instance, the way in which social factors making for hostility to cannabis users as a dominant group bias the popular presentation of research findings, or, at the other end of the scale, the way in which research into the connection between smoking and cancer is presented so as to leave open the possibility of scientific doubt. Science, in other words

> "as it is accepted within the scientific
> community and hence by the wider public, is
> the result of a complex of decisions and
> persuasive arguments of individual
> scientists which reflect their ideological
> and evaluative commitments as well as their
> instrumental motivations" (66).

It is not that science is powerful because it is true, it is rather that it is true because it is powerful.

At this stage it is possible to draw a number of tentative conclusions concerning the way in which our overall world-picture can influence our faith response.

1. Our position on the nature of reality is defined by science. It is very easy, as Gilkey points out (67), for science 'as an attitude, a method and a body of conclusions'

to expand itself into a view of the whole of reality. This process happens in stages.

(a) We begin with the conviction that science has no cognitive limits, that it can do everything and solve every problem and that eventually it will progress to that point.

(b) We proceeed to the plausible assumption that science represents the only cognitive access to reality – after all, if science has no limits must it not know everything, so that there is nothing which it does not know (positivism, instrumentalism and naturalism are all positions which take this view).

(c) The ultimately real is therefore matter, the processes of nature, and nothing else. The consequence is that only what is seen can be believed, only what is proved can be held as valid. Faith in 'what is not seen' thus becomes much harder to maintain.

2. We reject the validity of attempts to mirror reality in myth or symbol. Scientific beliefs and presuppositions about reality fulfil the functions which earlier mythic accounts, including biblical myths, fulfilled in more traditional societies. "A scientific culture produces its own myths just as a fishing culture does, and it is quite natural that as the myths of a fishing culture have a base in fishing, so in a scientific culture the myths have a scientific basis" (68). A major myth in our culture is that myth itself is to be discounted as non-rational (69). The consequences are that earlier myths such as biblical accounts of creation are held to be non-rational and therefore non-cognitive and thus without status.

3. We have a narrow empiricist view of the nature of truth. The success of 'objective' empirically-based science in control and production has given us a conception of truth which is so narrow that it cannot encompass any statement of faith and so restrictive that it requires empirical evidence to establish it. Mary Hesse points out that this is the biggest problem in creating an interaction between science

and faith as cognitive systems -

> "we need quite a different theory of truth
> which will be characterised by consensus and
> coherence rather than correspondence, by
> holism of meanings rather than atomism, by
> metaphor and symbol rather than literalism
> ..by.. judgement of value as well as fact"
> (70).

4. Science fills the gap left by the demise of the sacred. Our scientific models serve the same function as the more sacred images of reality used in earlier times. They enable us to represent the world to ourselves, thus acting as "a way of perceiving and making intelligible our experience of the society in which we live" - the role which Durkheim ascribed to religion (71). Science is also sacred in that we appeal to it for strength. Scientists receive some of the adulation previously reserved for priests, primarily because they appear to have a more certain method for arriving at the truth than do churchmen. Furthermore, that truth is reliable in that it is verifiable.

5. Theology has to make a response to this. When we look at the presuppositions of our scientific culture we realise that they have their roots to some extent in the very development of Christian theology itself. For instance the idea of inertia or of an inertial system which lies behind the conception of a closed mechanistic universe can be traced back to the notions of immutability and unmoved mover applied to the doctrine of God. It is all the more important that Christian theology undertakes the task of reformulating our understanding of faith which is in accordance with changing scientific presuppositions (72). As cultural perceptions move away from scientism and mechanism (which automatically exclude any possibility of interaction between God and his universe) and human spirit is liberated from the cause-effect continuum, the verbal formulation of Christian faith can also be liberated from excessively restrictive formalism, and can

engage in the prophetic task.

6. Our own theological understandings have become flawed by these presuppositions. The dualism inherent in our scientific culture has the effect of encouraging the substitution of a mythological understanding of incarnation and creation for a realistic theology. The tendency is to detach Christ from God, relegating him to a being who mediates ideas about God and about humanity, and thus to detach Christianity from Christ, placing it either within the bounds of the Church or secularising it within society. We thus lose the essence of the Christian message.

7. Our self-understanding has become equally flawed. The combination of dualism and deism (God as outside the natural laws of the universe) drove a wedge between belief in God as Creator and the rational order of nature, and therefore between faith and reason (73). Locke took this further by drawing the distinction between rational knowledge and belief, because belief is only an opinion and not based on evidence. Faith thus becomes subjective and non-cognitive (74). Empiricism leaves no room for God, but also no room for a full conception of the human person, because the only allowable characteristics of 'person' are those which can be observed by science.

iv.   The economic world view.

In the previous section I discussed the way in which the most global of our horizons of thought is formed by the presuppositions of a scientific culture. Individual sciences or disciplines are done within their own particular presuppositional frameworks which derive from the overall nexus of beliefs. These frameworks serve to direct and legitimate the scope and direction of 'normal' science within any discipline; they are thus closely related to the theory and practice of that particular field of knowledge. The

corollary of this is that the acceptability and prevalence of
any one approach within a discipline hinges not so much on
its success as on whether its philosophical and ideological
premises are consonant with society's viewpoint (75). There
is thus a close interaction between cultural presuppositions,
disciplinary presuppositions and the way in which knowledge
is acquired in that discipline. This interaction is
reinforced by the fact that the kind of presuppositions which
ground the doing of any discipline serve to structure the way
in which society thinks about that particular area of human
experience; i.e. they provide pre-scientific 'images' which
shape the way in which such experience is conceptualised
(76). For us, given the structures of our world, the
economic area of our experience is paramount. Progress,
virtue, well-being, happiness – all are defined in economic
terms: getting, having, using, spending are the ideas which
form the basis of our thought and the focus of our actions.
We thus tend to use 'economic' thought forms even when we are
thinking about non-economic areas of experience.

In analysing cultural presuppositions I used Lonergan's
model of 'horizon'. We can analyse the idea of disciplinary
presuppositions in a similar fashion by looking at the way in
which they are handled in the work of Thomas Kuhn and Imre
Lakatos. Kuhn offers the notion of a 'paradigm'(77) as a
tool for analysing what 'goes on' in science. Normal
science, he says, is a puzzle-solving activity done within
the context of an overarching 'paradigm'. The definition of
paradigm, however, proves elusive – Kuhn uses the idea in no
less than twenty-one senses in "The Logic of Scientific
Discovery". This variety of interpretations can be reduced
to three major categories (78). A paradigm is either
something operational in theoretical terms, or it is
something sociological (where it refers to the approach
shared by a community of scientists) or it is something
metaphysical. In this latter sense, the sense of
'presupposition', Kuhn equates a paradigm "with a set of
beliefs (p.4), with a myth (p.2), with a successful

metaphysical speculation (p.17), with a standard (p.122), with a new way of seeing (pp.117-21), with an organising principle governing perception itself (p.120), with a map (p.108), and with something which determines a large area of reality (p.128)" (79). Paradigm as presupposition must arguably be considered the primary sense of the word, because "the paradigm (as presupposition) has got to exist prior to the theory" (80). Theory as structured insight into the problem will then be generated by the interaction between the metaphysical presupposition and the concrete problem addressed by the scientist.

The same idea of a disciplinary world-view is to be found in Imre Lakatos's (81) analysis of how science is done. Any science, he says, has a hard core of non-falsifiable theory, a 'protective belt' of theory which can generate falsifiable hypotheses, and a 'positive heuristic' which links the two. The role of the positive heuristic is to set out the way in which the research programme should unfold.

There has been considerable disagreement as to how to interpret Lakatos's model in the context of economics. In particular, there have been a variety of views as to what can be said to constitute the 'hard core' of the discipline (82). These disputes have made it particularly difficult to distinguish between the metaphysical beliefs on which economic theory is based and the assumptions which it incorporates (83). However, Fulton (84) suggests an interpretation which clarifies the problem. He argues that Lakatos' positive heuristic should be thought of as including the presuppositions on which disciplinary endeavour is based. Presuppositions belong more properly to the heuristic of a discipline than to its hard core; they are prior to any statements contained in the hard core (just as paradigm is prior to theory) because they help to provide a justification for and an understanding of the research programme on the one hand, and they clarify and illuminate the positive heuristic

on the other hand. This distinction enables us to see
presuppositions as being part of the heuristic of a
discipline, while locating assumptions firmly in the hard
core and the protective belt.

Economics is a discipline where it is particularly
important to distinguish presuppositions - what Leijonhufvud
calls "cosmological expressions and beliefs" (85), because
"political economy has always been a discipline with strong
normative implications in spite of persistent effort on the
part of its practitioners to develop its scientific and
objective aspects" (86). These beliefs reflect images of the
economic world, the way it is structured and the way it
functions, and they both determine and are derivative of the
way theory is formulated. From a faith perspective, too, it
is essential to examine these presuppositions, because
economics, as the discipline which concerns itself with
material welfare, deals with issues basic to the thrust of
the Gospel message.

The ruling paradigm in economics is that of the
neo-classical school; it remains relatively unchallenged by
other alternative paradigms such as Marxian, radical or
institutional economics. The reason for this is clearly the
fact that the neo-classical paradigm satisfies the need
within the discipline for intellectual consistency, i.e. for
an adequate 'hard core'. But it also serves to fulfil the
function of an ideology in social terms, of a belief system
in political terms, and of a puzzle-system in intellectual
terms. Most important of all, it enables economists - and
others - to see economics as 'scientific' (and therefore
epistemologically and culturally respectable) because
neo-classical economics resembles physics, the ideal science,
in structural and conceptual terms (87).

The presuppositions of neo-classical economic theory
provide us with the images and frameworks we use when we
think about the economic dimension of human experience. They

form the 'Gestalt', the world-pictures we make of the economy. This Gestalt is self-fulfilling in the sense that it forms the basis for individual and political action. Political decisions adapt a constantly changing economic reality to make it accord more perfectly with a metaphysical or ideological image; individual actors thus find their presuppositions confirmed by their own experience (88). But there is a sense in which these presuppositions are deeply misleading. Our commonsense tells us that economic life is concerned with human and institutional activity undertaken for the production and distribution of goods. But neo-classical economics analyses the world in a way which actually precludes discussion of human action as the basis of economic activity (89), because action is reduced to a deterministic outcome. We are thus forced to think in structural and functional, rather than in human terms.

In _structural_ terms the world-image of neo-classical economics is that of a giant machine. Newtonian physics provided Adam Smith with his model of an economy where the decisions of a myriad of self-seeking individuals combined to create order and harmony – i.e. equilibrium between the forces of demand and supply in interconnected markets – and thus stable prices. In his vision of the economy as "a great, an immense machine, whose regular and harmonious movements produce a thousand agreeable effects" (90). Smith offered an alternative view to that of the mercantilists of his day, who believed that unfettered private enterprise would result in social chaos. Smith attributed the fact that order and harmony would prevail to the fact that the system was in some sense architected by a 'divine being', an 'invisible hand', whose intervention fulfilled the same function as the laws of physics (91).

Smith's notion of a mechanistic economic universe is the basis of the subsequent belief that any market system will tend to converge towards stability, matching what is offered with what is required at the right prices (92). In fact, his 'hidden agenda' was to legitimise the working of the free and uncontrolled markets of his day by proving that the mechanics of the market are rooted in human motivations which are universal and hence beneficial (93). No arguments exist to support either of these contentions. Polanyi (94) points to the fact that all the evidence we have from other cultures prove that the motivations which form the basis of economic activity are culturally determined rather than in any sense 'natural'. The behaviour of economic agents is thus in general determined by the way in which the economic system is embedded in social relations rather than by personal motivation as such.

Nor is it possible to accept that the unfettered workings of the market mechanism are necessarily beneficial. They may be efficient in an allocative sense, but they are not equitable. The whole idea of 'laissez-faire' neglected the fact that with a market context some people are more able to act in such a way as to ensure their own interests than others. Low standards of living result in a lack of ability to work and thus a lack of income to fulfil basic human needs. When needs are not satisfied people are less able to compete because of poor health, poor education, poor information and an inability to understand the complexities of the system. The ideology of free enterprise assumes that the stronger will break out of this vicious circle and claw their way upwards – a kind of social Darwinism. But this assumption neglects the fact that free markets are never free. They are controlled by power blocs – large companies, trades unions, media influences, pressure groups (95). The result is that any order which does exist in markets exists in such a way as to allow the strong to benefit at the expense of the weak (96). Smith's assumption that a 'natural' order implied a 'just' order was therefore simply incorrect.

The philosophical vagueness which characterised Smith's account of the workings of an exchange economy was sharpened

by the work of later economists (97) who used the device of
the differential calculus to give a precise mathematical
formulation of the individual behaviour patterns which
supposedly underlay the functioning of the market 'machine'.
This was an attempt to provide a scientific statement of the
'laws' governing the economic universe. Since such laws
could not be observed, they had to be constructed in
axiomatic form. Economic theory thus enshrines one
particular interpretation of social process, because these
laws are based on a particular conception of motivation and
behaviour. The substitution of abstract scientific
formulations for societal process is at best ambiguous (98).
At worst it is manipulative, since it encourages the creation
of social process to accord with that interpretation.

The image of the market economy as a self regulating
mechanism is a powerful one (99); it continues to function
both as belief and as theory — "Newtonian physics, just
because it has lasted so long, is in the unique position of
being able to be regarded either as quasi—metaphysics or as
the very prototype of deductive theory" (100). But it exerts
a limiting and stultifying influence on economics as a
discipline, and has a damaging effect on popular thinking.
There is a tendency to see the market as a 'natural'
mechanism whose workings must not be impeded, simply because
if it is the 'natural' form of economy it must be the 'right'
form. 'Market' remains a static conception of 'world' (101),
embodying as it does tendencies towards 'equilibrium', and
this in spite of the fact that the mechanistic image
stimulated both Darwin's thinking on biological evolution
(102) and Marshall's interest in the possibility of
biological change within the static mechanical economic
universe once time is introduced (103). The specification of
this mechanistic cosmology in terms of an economic model
requires assumptions of no time, no space (so that all market
participants have perfect information), no social
interaction, and some kind of gigantic auctioneering process
to ensure that markets 'clear'. And yet it is the belief

which form the basis for current political thinking and
policy in both the US and the UK - policy which

> "rests on the fundamental belief that a
> market economy has self-regulating
> properties of astonishing refinement -
> properties which if formally laid out make
> the performance of an automatic pilot in an
> aeroplane or the guided mechanisms of an
> intercontinental missile look like child's
> play" (104).

More important, perhaps, is the fact that our retention
of the image of the machine carries with it the assumptions
on which it is based - assumptions which reduce the notion of
human action to a predetermined stimulus/response behaviour
pattern, where the stimulus is the price signal and the
response is in terms of demand or supply of goods or work.
It ignores all institutional and class relationships, and
neglects the issues of power and conflict in society (115),
categorising relationships only in terms of those between man
and thing.

In _functional_ terms the presupposition of a
mechanistic economic universe rests on individualism as a
vision of society. It is utilitarianism which gives us the
assumption that the individual is the unit of human society,
and the notion that individuals acting in their own
self-interest can achieve the maximum benefit to everybody
was a powerful defence of laissez-faire (106). Individualism
is thus part of the dominant ideology of capitalism (107).
In disciplinary practice it translates into 'methodological
individualism'(108) - a principle which, while accepting the
truism that the world is made up of individuals, maintains
that the facts of the world can only be explained in terms of
facts about individuals. This is a positivist understanding
of the world, which sees individuals as real, but social
phenomena as constructs of the mind and therefore meaningless
in empirical terms. (Mrs.Thatcher is on record as saying

that there is no such thing as society). The consequence of
this for economics is a form of reductionism whereby
aggregative propositions are derived simplistically from
individual propositions and empirical laws are derived from
the aggregation. Economists are thus enabled to retain the
idea of free will and at the same time to have a
rationalistic explanation of economic equilibrium.

Individualism in turn rests on asumptions of
self-interest and rationality. The assumption of
rationality has two aspects. We assume that the rational
thing for agents to do is to maximise their utility given
their preferences ('epistemic rationality'). We also assume
that the rational thing for them to do is to buy or sell in
the way that they do ('practical rationality')(109). The
concept of utility is thus endowed with what Joan Robinson
calls 'impregnable circularity' — "utility is the quality in
commodities that makes individuals want to buy them, and the
fact that individuals want to buy them shows they have
utility"(110). The situation is deterministic (111) in that
both the ends from which the economic agent has to choose and
the selection criteria are given, and the means relative to
each are known. Rational economic man (112) is thus no more
than a robot — he cannot be said to be an actor in any human
sense because the actor/action relationship is invariant. As
a thinking person, an 'intentional self', he is purely
passive. Winter comments (113) on how strange it is that in
an age where the natural sciences gave such powers of
autonomy and control to man, the 'social science' of
economics should see him as enslaved by personal wants and
market forces. By denying any choice-governed behavioural
underpinnings to economic theory and neo-classical theory in
particular, economics ensures its own inability to be
'scientific' in terms of prediction and control (114).

The presupposition of rationality has another and deeper
implication. It implies that we assume that the solution to
all problems can be found by rational thought and analysis,

that if we only really understood what 'made the machine
tick' we could manipulate it. Those who dislike state
intervention and are suspicious of socialism are those, as
Munby points out (115) who are keenest to discover this
mechanism. But it is also possible (116) that "The good
society is to be regarded as an artefact...the state of
nature as a poor business. Not only the good society, but
the market itself is an artefact"(117). It is fundamental
rationalism which leads us to believe and to seek for an
automatic self-regulating mechanism which on the one hand
absolves us from the responsibility of creating/managing our
own world and on the other hand is arrogant enough to assume
that we can understand such a mechanism.

Individualism and mechanism as basic metaphysical
presuppositions of the economic world both rely on one other
assumption - that of certainty and perfect foresight (118).
The assumption that the future is known has "probably been
the most important and pervasive single simplification,
bearing more logical weight than any other, in the whole
range of economic theorising, analysis or model-building"
(119). The proper functioning of the market - in the sense
that it establishes the market-clearing price - requires that
people have perfect knowledge of all available alternatives
in the market situation - i.e. that information flows are
perfect with regard to the present situation. The market is
then assumed either to exist in a context of timelessness -
i.e. the future is now - or it is assumed that the
probabilities of future events can be calculated, so that
choice becomes probabilistic. In challenging this belief,
J.M. Keynes provided what has probably been the most
fundamental refutation ever to have been offered to the
ruling paradigm. He pointed out that since it is a
commonsense fact of life that we cannot know the future,
economic agents must be assumed to act under conditions of
uncertainty. This means that they cannot make the choices
which are required for markets to reach equilibrium (120).
Choice is thus no longer rational in a neo-classical sense -

it is much more a matter of guesswork, or custom, or even following a hunch. Furthermore, the economy exists in a situation of 'machine malfunction' on a permanent basis, because allowing for the existence of time enables us to recognise that prices and quantities adjust at different rates. Markets thus trade at 'false' or non-market clearing prices; this results in shortages and surpluses, i.e. in phenomena such as unemployment. Capitalism, Keynes argued, was thus inherently unstable.

Keynes' perspective was coloured by the fact that he saw economics primarily as a moral science (121) which was obliged to address itself to a situation where the existence of unemployment signified that people's needs were not being fulfilled by the system. He sought to change the prevailing set of beliefs, but he did so without providing any means of falsifying them. Scientific revolution is a process, not an event; it requires an underlying system of analysis to elaborate its tenets and justify its rationale. The fact that Keynes continued to think in terms of the existence of markets allowed his work to be re-interpreted (122) in terms of an extension to the market system. The neo-classical cosmology has thus survived unscathed; perfectly functioning markets continue to hold the centre of the theoretical stage, and the economic world-view rests on premises of mechanism, self-interested individualism and rational choice under conditions of certainty as the norm.

The prevalence of this cosmology has an ideological explanation: economics is no less ideology-ladden than other disciplines. In fact, the scope for ideological influence is wider than in other disciplines, simply because on the one hand it treats of 'social' states of affairs but on the other hand it purports to do so 'scientifically'. The fundamental ideological component of economic thought, and hence of the presuppositions which ground it, is the agenda of providing a justification for the workings of a capitalist economy and defending what is thus the dominant political faith. An important part of the myth of the market is its claim to efficiency. The corollary is that the myth persuades people that state allocation of goods is unnecessary, because governmental decision will of necessity achieve an allocation which is inefficient. The problem of economics is perceived — and stated by all the textbooks — as that of producing as much as possible from a limited number of scarce resources. Allocative efficiency is thus perceived as important, in spite of the fact that in human terms it has nothing to do with equity or social justice. Efficiency is the market's definition of welfare. Child labour, for instance, was considered legitimate in early industrial society (even by Christians) on the grounds of efficiency, and because economic analysis dictated that efficiency was to be pursued at all costs. We see the equivalent in a society which applies the logic of the market to every area of social functioning. In universities and polytechnics in the UK education now becomes a 'product' packaged in discrete units called 'modules' for 'delivery' to consumers who are to be provided with the cash in the form of loans or vouchers to buy what they choose. Institutions will put in competitive tenders to government funding councils for monies with which to provide the service. This, it is hoped, will generate an educational provision which is market-driven. Cost-effiency may be achieved, but at the expense of a welfare loss to society — ;

> "the risk that we shall lose one of the most
> valuable features of our universities and
> polytechnics — their power to pursue
> knowledge and ideas for their own sake and
> to look independently and critically at the
> world around them. At their best, they
> explore the uncertain, track down the
> unknown, unmask the dangerous and illuminate
> the beautiful. Markets tend to abhor the
> uncertain, avoid the unknown, conceal the
> dangerous and ignore the beautiful"(123).

Market functioning serves primarily the interests of those with power. The 'myth of the market' provided a justification for the status quo of income distribution in early capitalist society. The labour theory of value justified differences in prices and incomes by relating reward to merit; Ricardo thus argued that producers were entitled to profits (124). (Marx, on the other hand, pointed out that the 'surplus' which profits represented had in the first instance been created by labour — profits were thus immoral). Nowadays we justify inequalities on functional grounds by saying they are necessary as 'incentives', thereby making the implicit assumption — also ideological — that people have a natural property right in the fruit of their labour. Western countries maintain the necessity of freeing world trading structures of restrictions, knowing that they will benefit at the expense of the Third World primary producers because of the way the mechanics of free market systems work.

These are the presuppositions which provide the parameters to our understanding of the economic dimension of our existence. They are likely to create an inherent conflict at the deepest level of thought between what appears to be self-evident and necessary in a social context and what appears to be required of us as persons of faith and hearers of the message of the kingdom of God. They are also likely to structure our understanding of the Gospel itself. Poverty is the antithesis of all that is understood by us to be good, and yet Jesus came to preach to the poor. Our cultural understandings give us no guidance as to how to interpret the meaning of that.

v. Models of reality — theories

The way in which we see the world is not simply contingent on the presuppositions we hold and the kind of filters they create. It is also determined by the way in which we make sense of and come to understand our experience. The models of reality we have, our 'theories' (125) shape our experience into something comprehensible. They enable us to interpret the interconnections between events and states of affairs, to give significance to what we observe, and to assess the likely outcome of any given situation. 'Theory' in this sense has a conjectural or speculative dimension to it; it is 'theory' in the Greek sense of the term. For Plato and Aristotle theory was for understanding the world; the criteria of theory are thus coherence and the ability to illuminate reality, as well as the power to direct the knower towards a knowledge of the good. Theory thus enables us to understand.

But there is a narrower interpretation of theory which derives from science. Theory in science serves to link together the laws and generalisations which can be made about events on the basis of observation, and to deduce consequences which are verifiable or testable, thus yielding reliable knowledge. The standard empiricist account of science is that there is an external world which is 'already out there real' (126), which can be described in scientific and therefore value-free language, that the scientist can capture this world in true propositions which mirror facts, that those facts can be strung together in theoretical explanations which can yield verifiable hypotheses. The basic assumptions are thus that experience is 'objective' and independent of theoretical explanation, that law-like relations between empirical facts are external both to the object and to the investigator, that language is literal and there is thus no problem of meaning, and that meaning itself is independent of fact. Theory therefore, is for establishing truth, and for gaining objective knowledge, as well as for enabling science to predict and control.

There are thus two views of 'theory'; an empiricist culture tends to accept the second one, and to incorporate

its assumptions into everyday speech. We talk about what we
know in terms of 'fact', about establishing knowledge in
terms of 'proof', - the only acceptable answer to the
question 'how do you know? runs in terms of empirical
verification. We thus restrict the domain of certain
knowledge to what can be deduced rationally and verified
empirically.

This account of knowledge, as an account of the way in
which we perceive and assimilate the world, is not only
inadequate to explain the way in which the range of our
ordinary knowledge comes to us, but it is also an
impoverished and outdated account of scientific knowledge
itself. It relies on assumptions of ideal language, unified
method, and 'naive verificationism', since all the primitive
terms of the language used are related to observable
categories. It involves an ontological commitment to a
logical world whose form makes it acessible to the
operationalism of scientific method. Man the scientist thus
stands over against that world, and creates his own power of
access to it, as well as the possibility of manipulating its
processes.

The post—empiricist account of knowledge acquisition
refutes this perspective. It argues that theory is
culturally given in a number of ways relevant not only to our
experience of the social scientific world but to the
empiricist account of natural science itself (127).
1. Quine argues (128) that the theories by which we interpret
the world are empirically underdetermined in the sense that
any one observation can be accounted for by more than one
'theory' or model. Alternatively, it is not possible to
falsify any one single hypotheses by observation because
hypotheses are interdependent, they 'hang together', and it
may be another hypothesis which is responsible for the
observational anomaly. "Total science", says Quine, "is like
a field of force whose boundary conditions one experience. A
conflict with experience at the periphery entails adjustments

in the interior of the field...reevaluation of some statements entails reevaluation of others because of their logical interconnections" (129). There is thus no one-to-one correspondence between 'theory' and the empirical reality it seeks to explain; theories are logically constrained by the 'facts' of the world but underdetermined by them. The consequence is that although it is possible to adopt a 'realist' stance to the relationship between knowledge and experience it is no longer philosophically valid to maintain a purely empiricist view of explanation.

2. Experience comes to us through the filters of language; it is presented to us in the form of the concepts by means of which we are enabled to think about reality. We cannot think without concepts; there is thus no possibility of preconceptual experience (130). Concepts settle for us the form our experience takes (131). But since concepts in everyday language depend for their meaning on the kind of social interaction they represent, the way in which we think is inextricably bound up with the form of social life and behaviour in which we participate. A new way of talking sufficiently important to rank as a new idea will thus have its counterpart in a new form of social interaction; concepts thus mirror social life and enter into it (132). There are thus two separate facets to the establishment of experience – one is the conceptual enquiry which determines what it makes sense to say, and the other is the empirical enquiry which is answered by experience itself.

3. These two issues are in fact interconnected. Just as there is no possibility of preconceptual experience, so also is there no possibility of empirical enquiry conducted in an independent observation language. Even descriptive terms derive their meaning not only from their empirical associations but also from the interpretative frameworks which support the investigation (133). It is clear that some observational terms (e.g. 'red') are less theory-dependent than others (e.g. 'ultra-violet'), and that some are more

clearly indentifiable than others in an empirical sense. But all the terms in which we describe experience derive their meaning from the theories by which we interpret them. Meaning is thus a matter of theoretical coherence rather than empirical correspondence. Observation therefore involves a kind of pre-interpretation on the basis of background theories as well as on the basis of other interpretations (134). This view, as Mary Hesse points out (135),commits one, in scientific terms, to a 'network' rather than a 'layered' version of theory, and to a view of theoretical explanation as redescription rather than an attempt to establish isolated 'facts'(136). There is thus no theory-independent access to reality, as empiricists claim.

4. If our concepts are grounded in social interaction and the empirical terms we use to describe our experience are theory-dependent, it then becomes clear that the models we use to think about the world are themselves to a greater or lesser degree socially conditioned. There are various ways in which this can be the case. Our theories can have their roots in forms of social structure and experience (137), in belief systems, or in the technological conditions which prevail in that particular society (138). We can also look for their roots in the social interests which guide their acquisition and development (139). If the primary interest of society is technical — i.e. an interest which seeks to manipulate and control the world, then ways of interpreting the world will be 'scientific'. If, on the other hand, the primary interest of society is in the handing down of tradition, then the focus of interpretative endeavour will be hermeneutic, aiming at the mediation of understanding of what has gone before.

But the social origin of theory — i.e. of interpretative frameworks — is not universally accepted. The most usual argument against it is that insofar as theories are 'rational' they do not require explanation in terms of their social origin. Protagonists of this view argue that ways of interpreting the world can be classified into those which are rationally well-founded and those which are socially generated. But there are at least two reasons why social explanation of theory is still needed even when standards of rationality are adhered to. One is that scientific observers are not detached from the reality they are observing (140). It may be the case that the form of theoretical construct differs as between the natural and the social sciences, in the sense that whereas the natural sciences can make statements which prescribe the nature of the world in terms of the logical interconnections between events, the social sciences cannot do this because external observation of the social world would preclude its understanding. But natural science itself is also done within the context of shared understandings, shared presuppositions, and shared norms, all of which are socially generated (141).

The other reason to maintain the necessity of the social explanation of theory is in order to refute the argument that any 'social' component of interpretation distorts the 'truth' of scientifically acquired empirical knowledge. This argument draws a distinction between modes of thought in Western 'rational' societies and those in primitive non-Western cultures on the grounds that our methods of acquiring knowledge are scientific whereas theirs are not (142). This is an argument which confuses the accepted manner of justifying beliefs with their actual basis. It is true that in our culture we set about the process of acquiring knowledge in a more or less systematic fashion, but this does not in itself guarantee that the frameworks within which we process that knowledge are any more rational or logical than those of cultures which do not think in 'scientific' terms. They are simply different because their social context is different, and it may well be that this introduces the possibility of 'misinterpretation' - i.e. giving the wrong meaning to what is observed. If a tribal chief injects a chicken in order to ask a question of the oracle, and if the chicken then dies, he sees the oracle as

having given a negative answer to his question, whereas we
simply say the chicken has been poisoned (143). But that is
simply because the context of interpretation is different.
The tribal chief is not interested in whether or not the
injection caused the chicken to die – he is simply interested
in the answer to his question to the oracle. That is the
piece of knowledge he wanted to acquire. The kind of
criticism which argues that his interpretation is 'false' is
the same kind of criticism which sees 'truth' in terms of
empirical verification, 'knowledge' in terms of rationality,
and the language and science of Western society as the high
point of the historical evolution of ideas (144). Theory
derives its validity from the usefulness of the purpose it
serves in the particular social context in which it operates,
and that is as true of Western scientifc theory as it is of
any tribal society. Theories and models of reality have thus
an essential social component; they have not only a social
origin but also a social purpose.

The upshot of all this is that the process of making
sense of our experience happens through a nexus of
interpretative grids composed of theory–dependent observation
choice, language– (i.e. concept–) dependent formulation of
experience, theory–dependent observation language, and
socially–conditioned models of reality. The factor common to
all these is the category of meaning. Reality. or world, is
mediated to us by meaning, and the constitution of meaning is
prior to any knowledge (145). It is meaning which makes the
world accessible to us insofar as we participate in its
meaning. In the case of scientific knowledge this involves
our participation in the community of knowledge which shares
these meanings. In the case of our everyday or commonsense
knowledge this simply involves our existence in the context
of shared everyday meanings. The meanings hidden in the
lived world are taken for granted by its participants, but
require interpretation by social science (146), because those
meanings are not unambiguous. The scientist as a person
lives both in the world of commonsense meaning and in the

world of scientific meaning — he sees material objects both as sense objects and as collections of particles, he experiences social situations both as participant and as interpreter. This dual role requires what Lonergan calls a 'differentiation of consciousness' — i.e. a conscious awareness of moving from one realm of meaning to another. For any human person meaning is constituted within different 'realms' in a widening series of contexts — social, scientific, cultural, historical. Each of these contexts possesses a nexus of meanings which will inform our own particular consciousness.

vi. Models and concepts in economics.

Economics does not subscribe to the post-empiricist position — it believes that it is possible to gain knowledge about, and to control, a world 'out there' of which the economy is part. Economic theory is of two kinds. Axiomatic 'high-level' models are formalised in terms of functional relationships between variables which are 'mental constructs'(147) rather than concepts which are operational in terms of data or descriptive in an experiental sense. Low-level theoretical generalisations, on the other hand, are specified in terms of concepts which have an empirical equivalent in terms of data. As Loasby puts it (148), we have a disciplinary community where "the High Churchmen of axiomatic economics emphasise the necessity for public and formal ritual, and the select status of the priest in his mathematical vestments, while the positivist 'Low Church' is a priesthood of all believers, sceptical of vain ceremonies and relying for divine guidance on the personal revelation of the correlation coefficient".

Axiomatic economics sees 'truth' as being contained in and generated by the logical and behavioural axioms which were developed by the classical and neo-classical economists.

Truth thus exists independently of experience; it requires no inductive approach for its establishment. Ludwig von Mises (149), for instance, argued that "social and economic theory is not derived from experience — it is prior to experience...no kind of experience can ever force us to discard or modify a priori theorems". The axioms may not be 'realistic' in the sense that they accord with experience, but the explanation for that is that the world is sub-optimal and therefore does not measure up to the perfect world of economic theory. Realism is gained only by simplifying and generalising to the point where the kind of statement made is of the nature of self-evident truth (150).

The more empirical focus in economic theorising is grounded in the programme of logical positivism, and it is here that we find the roots of the idea that economics can be 'value-free'. Because of a particular semantical confusion, logical positivism as a philosophical position has become enshrined in the discipline as the distinction between 'positive' and 'normative' economics, rather than as a set of norms for demarcating the scientific from the non-scientific. The distinction between 'positive' and 'normative' was originally drawn by J.N. Keynes (John Maynard's mathematician father) to distinguish "economic uniformities, economic ideals and economic precepts" (151) — in other words, to distinguish the 'science' of political economy from the ethics and the art of political economy respectively. 'Positive economics' thus originally referred to the descriptive empirical side of the subject which would be used as a basis for the more evaluative exercise of saying something about the problems of political economy. It was the aspiration of economics to 'scientific' status which led to the acceptance of the canons of philosophical positivism and to a consequent confusion between 'positive' in the sense of non-normative (J.N. Keynes' view) and 'positive' in the sense of observable and testable (the view of philosophical positivism) (152). Schumpeter sees this confusion as misleading —

"The word 'positive' as used in this
connection (discussing J.N. Keynes) has
nothing whatever to do with philosphical
positivism. This is the first of many
warnings about the dangers of confusion that
arise from the use, for entirely different
things, of the same word used by writers who
themselves confuse the things" (153).

In terms of positivist thinking economics should not concern
itself with the normative — ie human welfare — if it is to be
validly scientific — a position which neither J.N. Keynes nor
any of the classical political economists would have
accepted. The whole meaning of 'positive' economics has thus
shifted —

"from being the opposite of normative it has
moved — because the normative is
non-observable and non-testable — to being
the opposite of non-observable. The logical
positivist or radical empiricist will not
recognise that there is a range of meaning
involved; normative equals metaphysical
equals non-observable equals non-testable
equals meaningless" (154).

The consequence of this is to equate the normative with the
meaningless and thus to establish value-freedom as an
essential characteristic of scientific respectability in
economics, in spite of the fact that in philosophical terms
the fact-value distinction in general is no longer accepted
as legitimate. In this way the discipline perpetuates the
belief that economics has not and must not have anything to
say on the question of values.

This peculiar mixture of idealism and empiricism
dictates the agenda of the discipline which Shackle
characterises as "the science of the quantification of the
unquantifiable and the aggregation of the incompatible"
(155). Economics sees itself as scientific; theory is
therefore important. There is thus an ongoing attempt to

extend the domain of the application of theories, to suggest restrictions of their parameters, to provide criteria of coherence, define logically coherent assumption sets and reconcile theoretical conflicts. There has been a serious attempt to define theoretical acceptability – and profesional competence – by the extent to which arguments are expressed mathematically. The use of mathematics restricts fields of interest to those which can be expressed in mathematical terms. It also restricts the form of the economic 'world' to that of the mathematical model, thereby imposing notions of equilibrium and excluding the possibility both of historical and organic change and of the consideration of concepts which are non-quantifiable, such as the concept of power in markets.

But there is more to scientific respectability than maintaining a scientifically impeccable "hard core". There is a social requirement of instrumentality for a discipline which bears so closely on the fulfilment of social aspirations (156). Economics has got to be seen to be 'useful' for purposes of prediction and control; its own positivistic self-understanding also requires some bridge to be built between theory and reality. It is therefore vital that reality is accessible. Economic reality is handled conceptually – this in fact is the essence of 'economic analysis' (157). Theoretical formulation is relevant to reality only to the extent that the concepts used give some kind of grip on the real world. It is our concepts which shape our vision, enable us to formulate policy recommendations and evaluate their results, and nowhere more so than in economics because

> "there is no immediate grasp of the
> economic; there is no raw economic (reality)
> any more than there is any immediately given
> effectivity in any one of the levels. In
> all these cases, the identification of the
> economic is achieved by the construction of

> its concept, which presupposes a definition
> of the specific existence and .... of the
> different levels of the structure of the
> whole as they are necessarily implied by the
> structure of the role of production
> considered" (158).

Concepts in economics are ordinary language concepts: their use in ordinary language situations thus exerts an influence on perceptions within the discipline. In other words, they come loaded with ideological 'baggage' in a way which is frustrating to those who would prefer a pure observation language. Concept choice is dictated by the focus of disciplinary interest as well as by real-world problems. Two kinds of concepts exist — those which have an 'operational' dimension (i.e. they can be linked with experience or observation by means of data) (159) and those which are pure mental constructs. Unlike the other social sciences, economics already had a whole range of technical concepts with which to work before the discipline ever acquired a scientific focus. Land, capital, rent, profits, markets — these were all concepts used in everyday discourse. It subsequently acquired a range of conceptual categories created by generalisation from sets of categories or events. Some of these concepts translate into data by means of statistical measurement. Some are used in primarily non-observational sense unless they refer to a particular situation — e.g. 'price'. Some, such as 'liquidity' or 'company objectives' have no empirical content whatever, unless such a content is specifically defined as such.

What kind of grip do our concepts give us on 'world'? How well do they convey meaning, act as perceptual filters? The empiricist answer to this runs in terms of the extent to which concepts have empirical content. 'Experience' for economics comes through statistical data which are centrally collected according to a prior classification system whose basis requires a great deal of simplification and

homogenisation. It is thus not necessarily suitable for
analytic use; the pouring of data into conceptual categories
is often an ad hoc procedure (160). Data collection is in any
case subject to problems of error, of misrepresentation, of
non-reporting (161), and insofar as it is produced by survey
techniques rather than by observation it is subject to the
fact that people have very little awareness of what affects
their own behaviour. Above all, data can be politically
manipulated. The basis of calculation for UK unemployment
figures has been changed a number of times in recent years.
The rate of inflation is dependent on what is included in the
Retail Price Index. Poverty no longer exists as an economic
'reality' in the UK because since 1988 poverty statistics are
no longer collected, so there is no empirical basis for
discussion of policy initiatives (162).

There is yet another problem with economic concepts. We
have a difficulty in demarcating and establishing definite
individuality, separating one entity from another, the whole
from the sum of its parts. When does a car become a car?
Furthermore, classes and aggregates are inexact. If we count
the unemployed as those who are without work for fourteen
days, is the person who has been without work for thirteen
days employed? 'Loose concepts' is the term coined to mirror
this problem of the indefiniteness of individuals and the
inexactness of classes. A real example of 'loose concepts'
is the money supply. Definitions of the money supply
proliferate, their content changes constantly with the
exigencies of policy expediency. Any measurement of the
relation of money to GDP, or to any other aggregate, is
therefore no more than notional.

Statistical data are thus a very imperfect mirror of
economic reality, not only because of the practical problems
connected with their collection, but also because of the very
weak link between concept and data. The general practice is
to fit data to the conceptual framework dictated by the model
specification and then construct hypotheses which yield

behavioural results in accordance with the predictions of the hypothesis (163). Concepts are connected to data only in the sense that they 'correspond' to them. Data as such have no 'meaning'; it is not possible to establish any economic 'fact' unless one has a prior set of concepts by which to interpret it and contextualise it. A money transaction conveys no information to the observer unless he/she has notions of purchasing power, price, sale, barter and acceptability within which to interpret it (164). A figure for the capital/output ratio in any given industry says nothing unless we also know the extent of spare capacity in that industry.

What all this implies is that the empiricist view that the meaning of economic concepts is to be found in their empirical counterparts is untenable. The economic 'facts' which data collection provides us with are not the 'brute facts' of logical positivist philosophy. Facts are established only conceptually, and concepts derive their meaning from their theoretical context either in an operational sense or a logical sense. The 'objective facts' required by the canons of scientific respectability do not exist as such (165); they are established only by the way in which the theory links the concepts together. What counts as 'fact' may have very little to do with what is happening 'out there'. It is possible to argue that this is an indication of

> "the immature state of social inquiry, which
> may be measured by the extent to which the
> operations of fact-finding and of setting up
> theoretical ends are carried out
> independently of one another, with the
> consequence that factual propositions on the
> one hand and conceptual or theoretical
> structures on the other are regarded each as
> final and complete in itself" (166)

But this is a view which fails to take account of the complexity of the "quantum-leap" required to bridge the theory-reality gap. It is not just a question of the way in which data are handled to fit the concept by statistical technique. There is also the fact that it is often difficult to choose data which will adequately mirror the conceptual content (167).

A more fundamental issue is the way in which concepts which are technically operational can give rise to deeper and more metaphysical problems of translation. Capital, for instance, has no ontological existence as such. There are things such as buildings and machines, but there is no way in which they can be validly aggregated into a homogeneous item of data which takes account of the variety of their characteristics. This means that the concept of the aggregate production function (a 'mental construct') has not only no empirical validity but also no analytic meaning in anything than a purely logical sense. As Chase points out (168), it does not even have the status of something which can be accepted on faith, because faith assumes that what is seen does exist.

A related issue concerns the question of time. Data mirrors the 'state of play' at any one time period only. Using data for explanatory purposes therefore always means that explanation is 'after the event'. Hicks points out that "economics is in time in a way that the natural sciences are not. All economic data are dated, so that inductive evidence can never do more than establish a relation which appears to hold within the period to which the data refer, - economics is thus on the edge of time and on the edge of history" (169).

We are thus forced to the conclusion that we are witnessing in economics what might be termed a "crisis of abstraction" (170). The concepts we use lack real world content; they also lack empirical content due to generalisation and oversimplification. Concepts such as 'efficiency' or 'competition' are difficult to pin back into everyday experience. But abstraction also has a theoretical face. It refers to the unreal nature of the axiomatic frameworks of analysis made possible, in particular, by the mathematisation of the subject (171). The kind of models used in general-equilibrium economics are logical and elegant. They seduce us into losing sight of "the full extent of the limitations for real-world relevance and policy which the nature and degree of the abstractions inevitably impose" (172). But they explain nothing because they specify no causal process, they abstract from time, ignore uncertainty and informational constraints. However, the anti-realist bias in economics (173) is due much more to the impurity of operational concepts — i.e. to their 'unreal' nature — than to the excessive purity of abstract models.

The concepts we use may give us little grip on the lived realities of economic life, but they serve to shape they way in which we think about that reality. The concepts we use are chosen to fit the overall image which mechanistic theoretical approaches present. Equilibrium, stability, elasticity, expansion, inflation and contraction are all words in the everyday vocabulary of economists and journalists. They are all borrowed from mechanics and thus, although they have particular technical meanings in economics, they carry with them connotations of economic process as mechanistic and deterministic rather than as the outcome of human action. And the importance of this lies in the way our thought processes are influenced and our experience shaped. Economic concepts support overall images, they also help to bend our perception of our own everyday participation in economic life. Work, for instance, is something which in general terms is often — perhaps usually — experienced by people as life-enhancing (174). But neo-classical economics considers work to be a disutility. People require to be compensated by higher pay for working harder or longer hours. A job, on the other hand, is something which has no neo-classical connotations. A job — i.e. permission to work — is something which we consider desirable, but work itself is considered undesirable. The value of work done is assessed on the basis of its market value — i.e. value as equated with price. The work of a construction engineer is considered 'better' or more worthwhile than that of a dustman or a canteen worker or even a nurse — not just subjectively, but even in terms of social valuation. It is, however, usually true that our society tends to value jobs which result in concrete products more highly than those which involve repetitive service to other people (175). Our whole experience of the world of work is thus moulded by a 'received' viewpoint.

The concepts which we use also limit the ways in which we can think about what are becoming ever more urgent issues. Changing social, cultural and technological conditions present economists with the necessity to analyse problems of ecology, of long-term unemployment, of pollution (176). We have, for instance, no way of distinguishing conceptually between a resource which is renewable and one which is not. The only way we can discuss pollution is in terms of social costs, or "externalities" — i.e. via a technique which seeks to quantify the costs arising from the particular situation, but which is totally inadequate to cope with the longer-term aspects of these problems.

There are other ways in which the concepts we use encourage a reductionistic view of economic existence. Because all our evaluations are market-based we are unable to use our concepts to include wider dimensions of any given issue (177). We think about efficiency — a concept which is always defined in an allocative or technical sense — in a way which makes us unable to evaluate meaningfully the relative efficiency of nuclear power and solar energy; if we think that nuclear power is more efficient simply because it can produce more energy, do we make allowances in the evaluation procedure for potential long-term hazards and for costs of subsidisation? We measure potential industrial success in terms of productivity, but to what extent can we validly use an overall index of industrial productivity as an indicator of the state of the economy when there are people unemployed and therefore not productive? How can we use profitability as a concept with positive connotations when profits are bought to the expense of incalculable social costs? (178).

It is also possible to fall into disciplinary forms of ordinary language speech which show the way the world is seen (179). The tendency to reduce everything to quantification leads to depersonalisation; the economy is viewed as being made up not of people and what they do, individually and institutionally, but of aggregates such as unemployment, labour, consumer demand saving, expenditure and so on. The other face of this is the tendency which has crept into ordinary-language use of personalising the institution. We talk of unemployment rather than of people who are unemployed, but we discuss the way in which the economy can become 'leaner, slimmer, fitter' as a result of government policy. Companies are healthy, or competitive, marketing policy is aggressive, sales or profits 'forge ahead'. Ordinary language speech tends to ascribe personal — and usually masculine — attributes and attitudes to institutions, while at the same time discussing people as a non-personal aggregate.

This kind of language use is ideological in that it mirrors the evaluative basis of thought. The kind of symbolism mirrored in language derives its nature from the social context, in particular, from the system of production (180). But the language of economics can be used in a more overtly ideological fashion — witness the way in which current usage works to convey an idea of the sacred, to sacralise the secular. Politicians talk about "pontificating on economics" (181), about the Church being "cheapened" by its involvement in social and economic affairs. Much of the monetarist rhetoric, as Seabrook says, has been drawn from "incursions into the territory of the spirit", a plunder of religious terminology and imagery. We talk about the

Japanese "economic miracle", we "prevail" against striking miners, "rejoice" at the victory in the Falklands. Wealth is "created", the economy is subject to "laws" which have the force of moral sanction — woe betide those who hinder the workings of the market. Capitalism is no longer seen as a bringer of insufficiency and hunger, but as a provider of all good things — salvation comes through abundance, and is made possible by money. The symbolism of economics has become quasi—religious, a conflation of values with value, which "plunders the symbolism of Christianity to dignify its ideology"(182).

vii.   Postcript: the relation between thought and world.

The argument of the preceeding sections has maintained that, contrary to empiricist views, we cannot accept that 'world' exists independently of thought. It is constituted by the meanings given to experience by the ideologically determined grids and filters of cultural perceptions. These 'filters' structure the way in which we 'see' the world. But they do more than this. There is a dialectical relationship between thought and world which is completed by the way in which thinking can be said to actually constitute the object of experience. Thought, in other words, both structures the form of experience and constitutes its object (183). The way in which we think creates and shapes the reality we think about.

We can regard the question of 'object constitution' in three ways. Thought constitutes the object of experience in an epistemic sense, where the activity of mind constitutes or creates the known object by means of interpretation or structure. This is the sense which has been touched on at several points throughout this chapter. This is 'theoretical' object—constitution, which imposes order on the chaos of human experience by allowing it to be meaningfully interpreted. It incorporates a fundamentally anti—empiricist stance insofar as it assumes that the object of experience is not knowable unless it is so constituted by thought.

However, we can also think of the way in which thought constitutes the object of experience in an <u>ontological</u> sense. This is the sense associated primarily with the thinking of Marx, the sense which sees men as making their own history and constructing their own destiny. Both of these ways in which thought constitutes reality are interlinked. It is the meanings and interpretations given by people to their experience which enable them to constitute and sustain the ontological reality of their lives. This is the more idealistic view of the connection between the two senses.

On a more practical level, the ontological constitution of reality requires thought to generate the required <u>practical</u> action. This is precisely the point on which the entire argument of this chapter focuses. I have tried to isolate the different biases in our cultural mode of thought on a presuppositional, a theoretical and a conceptual level; I have also tried to indicate the way in which this 'matters' insofar as it is thinking rather than any external empirical reality which dictates the form our experience takes. We can now see the way in which that process of thought can actually be said to constitute the object of experience. In an interpretative, a historical and a practical sense how we think creates the reality of our lives, a reality which is both 'self' and 'world'.

It is clearly possible to interpret this idea in a strong or in a much weaker sense. In a strong sense we can see people as free to constitute their own 'world'. Their 'world' is their invention, they actively constitute it rather than merely seeking to gain knowledge of it. This is the view taken by phenomenological sociology, which argues that the reality of the social world hinges on the fact that it is constituted by meaning; cognitive processes thus produce 'real' things. This is clearly a non-positivist, although no necessarily a non-naturalist, view of thw world.

In a weaker sense people only exercise their creativity in a way which is guided by the nature of the object or the conditions of human perception. This was Kant's view; he saw categories of thought as regulating rather than constituting the object of experience. 'Object constitution' in this sense is thus no more than description. At its weakest it fades into empiricism, and this in turn raises the question of the nature of the object. Do we believe that the object of experience is real, or merely apparent, phenomenon or appearance.

The importance of all this is central. Whether we think of 'world' as being constituted by meaning or by practical action, thought is the operational factor. The kind of thinking we do will determine the kind of world we and others participate in, because we tend to fashion our world after the manner in which we conceive of it.

==

NOTES—CHAPTER THREE

1. Fisher and Murray (1969) p.39.
2. See introduction by A.Montefiore and C.Taylor to Kortian (1980).
3. See e.g. Achinstein (1968), Hesse (1980), Thomas (1979).
4. Lonergan's notion of preconceptual insight is contradicted by the basic point made in Winch (1958). See Lonergan (1968).
5. Schillebeeckx (1980) pp.31ff.
6. It is possible, as Schillebeeckx does (1983 p.577), to extend this analysis to the historical development of thought.
7. Feyerabend (1962), see Achinstein (1968) p.132.
8. Hanson (1958), see Achinstein op.cit p.133.
9. Bromberger (1963), see Achinstein p.134.
10. Thomas (1979), p.5.
11. Kroeber and Kluckhohn (1952) distinguish over 100 uses of the word 'culture'. Quoted in Geuss (1981) p.4 fn.
12. Schillebeeckx (1983) p.578.
13. This is a concept which, as Schillebeeckx points out, (1983 p.732 fn.2) is used frequently by both J-B. Metz and K.Rahner. The idea is central to the thought of Bernard Lonergan, who uses it in two ways – as a heuristic for analysing the growth of scientific knowledge and as a notion which explains the growth of a person's capacity to know. See Tracy (1970) Introduction.
14. Lonergan (1967), 'Metaphysics and Horizon'.
15. See Tracy (1970) Ch.4.
16. Quoted by Schillebeeckx (1983) p.581.
17. Kuhn (1961). For the ambiguity of this idea see the creative essay entitled "The nature of a paradigm" by M. Masterman in Lakatos and Musgrave (1970).
18. Tracy (1970) Introduction.
19. Torrance (1980) p.13.

20. We must make a clear distinction between the idea of a presupposition as the ground of belief, analysis or enquiry, and what is assumed, implied or contextually implied – i.e. what we normally call assumptions. See Edel (1979) p.37/8.

21. Radnitsky (1970) p.90.

22. "In any analysable sense of 'see' we see the world organised and classified in systematic ways, defined by attitudes and principles that may genuinely be called 'metaphysical'". Ross (1971) p.4/5.

23. Or, as Elkana (1979) p.276 says, "An attempt to explain change and growth of knowledge cannot separate ideas about the world and men from the ideas about knowledge in which the first is embedded".

24. See essay by Y.Elkana – "Science as a cultural system", in Mathieu and Rossi (ed) (1979). If a cultural system is one which is historically constructed and subject to historically defined standards of judgement, then, it can be argued, science itself is such a system. On that criterion, medieval culture was a theological culture.

25. "The use of idealised scientific images as a source of authority.....has become known as 'scientism'". Richards (1983) p.137. Antagonism to the growth of science as a world-view came not only from religious sources but also from secular quarters – witness the 19th century antagonism associated with literary romanticism, political conservatism, and philosophical idealism. See Shils (1974) p.1.

26. Philosophy produces these world-pictures by applying philosophical argumentation to existing knowledge systems. The images of reality they produce in turn influence the growth of knowledge because they are used by scientists and researchers. Radnitsky (1970) p.4.

27. "Beliefs held about the task of science (understanding, prediction, etc.), about the nature of truth (certain, probable, attainable, etc.), about the sources of knowledge (by revelation, by ratiocination, by

experiments through the senses), are all part of the time-dependent, culture-dependent images of science." Elkana (1979) p.276.

28. E.g. paranormal scientific investigations.

29. "For Aristotle, the unbridgeable gap between things as experienced and the same things as known vanished in the realisation that this separation derives from the nature of the complex human way of knowing the real rather than from any simple diversity or absolute discontinuity in the sections of the real". Fisher and Murray (1969) p.40. Lonergan too (1957) enviseages an isomorphism between cognitional structures and the structures of the real.

30. This was Kant's problem in the 'Critique of Pure Reason'. He could not see how experience is possible when nature is governed by empirical laws (whether diverse or universal) and understanding has its own a priori constitutive principles of knowledge. Subjectivity — i.e, the excercise of the faculty of judgement — therefore becomes a requirement for knowing. See Outhwaite (1983) p.78.

31. Radnitsky (1970) Vol.1.p.73.

32. This contrasts, for instance, with the notion of 'world' as a living entity which is found in traditional cosmologies.

33. Torrance (1980) p.16.

34. Duhem (1906).

35. Mach (1906).

36. Machlup (1978) represents this position in economics.

37. Radnitsky (1970) Vol.1.p.56.

38. See Emmet (1984), Hesse (1980).

39. Not the view held in modern physics; but there is a lag between 'growth in science' and its popularisation. Heisenberg has not yet penetrated into common consciousness. See Capra (1979).

40. Kinloch (1981) p.27ff.

41. Barzun (1964) p.20ff.

42. Torrance (1980) p.19.
43. Elkana (1979) p.282. Those who are not Jehovah's Witnesses regard with amazement and distaste decisions of parents to deny blood transfusions to their children.
44. See Skolimowski (1982). But this author argues that these beliefs of ours are in fact shaken by the continuing failure of science in cognitive terms because absolute knowledge remains an elusive goal.
45. Barzun's comment (1964) p.170. on this is – "the stumbling block of (any) science of man lies at the point where one must distinguish between what exists and what is said to be measured. In physical science the nature or reality of the object is of little importance. But when man is the object, shrugging off his nature or reality is a form of conduct that ranges from cavalier to dangerous".
46. For a discussion of this and related issues see Mishen (1969).
47. Ross (1971) p.325.
48. E.g. racist research in Nazi Germany. For a general discussion on scientific objectivity see Lawson (1986).
49. See essay by J.Rigaud "Science and culture" in Mathieu and Rossi (ed) (1979).
50. See Barzun pp.33/4 for an example of an unqualifed acceptance of the hegemony of science.
51. Richards (1983) p.145.
52. A warning is given in Manning (ed) (1980) on the anarchy of linguistic differences which bedevil the concept of 'ideology'.
53. Barnes (1974) p.129 gives the example of the way in which the belief that all men are equal can give rise to appropriate theories about social structure.
54. For a careful classification see Larain (1979).
55. See Pratt (1978) p.103ff. Marx believed that idea systems were the product of economic structure. Weber, on the other hand, saw social structures as the product of ideas.

56. Kinloch (1981) p.6.

57. See Larain (1979) p.188.

58. Mannheim (1936).

59. See Hesse (1980) p.30ff.

60. Pratt (1978) p.61

61. Habermas (1970).

62. Larain (1979) p.210.

63. Barnes (1974) p.216 fn.2.

64. Ibid. p.176.

65. Fine (1980) p.8.

66. Hesse (1983) p.52

67. Gilkey (1983) p.66. See also Lonergan in Insight.

68. Ibid. p.66.

69. See Hollenweger (1982).

70. Hesse (1983) p.54.

71. Durkheim (1915) p.257.

72. Torrance (1980) p.14.

73. Ibid.p.44.

74. Ibid. p 43.

75. Deane (1978) p.xii.

76. "Given the primacy of the 'economic' view in the modern world, the hypothesis is that this view must be deeply rooted in the mental constitution of modern man, that it must have for him particular and not insignificant implications that are apt to escape him". Dumont (1977) p.26.

77. Kuhn (1962).

78. As categorised by Margaret Masterman in Lakatos and Musgrave (ed) (1970).

79. Ibid. p. 65. The page numbers refer to Kuhn (1962).

80. Ibid.p.69.

81. In Lakatos (1978).

82. See refs in Fulton (1984) for the dispute in economics.

83. Particularly because much intellectual effort has been expended on interpreting the argument made by Milton Friedman (1953) in an article entitled 'The Methodology of Positive Economics'. Friedman claims that it does

not matter whether the assumptions made by a theory are realistic or not, so long as the theory yields true predictions. Most of the confusion arises from the fact that Friedman talks about both theories and assumptions in several different senses – in particular, he loses sight of the distinction between the presuppositions which provide the parameters for theory construction and the assumptions which are particular to the theory. For summaries of this discussion see Boland (1979), Nagel (1963), Musgrave (1981).

84. Fulton (1984) draws the distinction between the world-picture of neo-classical economics and the research programmes within it which form the disciplinary 'hard-core'.

85. In Latsis (1976) p.72.

86. Deane (1978) p.xii.

87. See Nield (1982) p.9.

88. "These assumptions are used by economists in their work almost unconsciously. In fact, in many economists' minds they have ceased to be assumptions and have become a picture of how the world really is." Capra (1982) p.209.

89. Even Eichner (1983) p.11/12, who is a critic of the received view, argues that since the only necessity in economics is to predict the behaviour of groups, the only requirement is to be able to predict the response of people in a social context rather than actually to develop any "psychologistic explanation of individual behaviour".

90. Quoted in Deane (1978) p.7/8.

91. The world-vision thus sees action as determinate, never the result of free choice. The observer can never influence the reality he observes, he can only predict the future course of events. For the distinction between the Newtonian and the Heisenbergian view of order see Weisskopf (1979).

92. See Leijonhufvud in Latsis (1976) p.71.

93. See Weisskopf (1973) p.8.

94. Polanyi (1945). But, as Winter says (1966) p. 202, we have to see that every model of society reflects its own ultimate horizon of meanings and contains its own idea of social fulfillment.

95. See eg. Galbraith (1952).

96. In a way which is demonstrated by historical examples, both past and present. E.g. Winter (1966) p.8/9, referring to the export of grain from Ireland during the Irish Famine — "No other historical example illustrated so well the obliteration of the human subject matter through preoccupation with a 'science' of man and with establishing an understanding that economic laws were laws of nature".

97. E.g. Jevons (1871).

98. Winter (1966) p.12.

99. As argued by Lowe (1951).

100. Masterman in Lakatos and Musgrave (1971) p.71/2.

101. Capra (1982) p.196 argues that economics changes much faster than natural sciences, because the ecological and social systems in which it is embedded change as well as the institutional and informational systems. Witness for instance the recent development of sophisticated and world-wide financial markets. We therefore need a conceptual system which is capable of accomodating that fact.

102. See e.g.preface to Eichner (1983). It was while Darwin was reading an article by Malthus that the idea of natural selection came to him.

103. Foa (1982) discusses Marshall's fascination with biological Darwinism.

104. Nield (1982) p.5. it has to be said, however, that there is a sense in which this belief serves as a legitimating device for social and economic engineering designed to introduce the logic of the market into areas where it does not exist in an institutional sense. National Health hospitals in the UK are an obvious

example.

105. Hollis and Nell (1975) base their arguments on this issue.

106. See Lowe (1983) pp.88-90.

107. See e.g. Foley (1975).

108. See Ryan (1970) Ch.8 for an account of the debate on methodological individualism.

109. Recent developments in the concept of rationality have led to the introduction of a concept of procedural rationality, where rationality is discussed in terms of decision-taking proceedures under uncertainty. See essay by Simon in Latsis (ed) (1976).

110. Robinson (1964) p.48.

111. Latsis (1976) p.16ff discusses the trade-off between situational determinism and the extent to which agents' actions can be rationally explained.

112. For a very full discussion of this idea see Bensusan-Butt (1978).

113. Winter (1966) Ch.1.

114. As Rosenberg (1979) puts it - "Economists seem to be faced with the following difficulty. Their employment of any law-like claim to the effect that actions reflect the maximisation of preferences, subject to belief about alternatives, requires a specification of the beliefs and desires in question. And yet none of the specification of desires that trade on our commonsense understanding of this notion seem to confirm the maximisation hypothesis... Accordingly the maximisation hypothesis can be preserved only on the condition that it is not actually applicable to the practical prediction and control of any human action.

115. Munby (1956) p.67.

116. Munby quotes this as the view expressed by Robbins (1932) Essay 2.

117. Robbins op.cit. pp.55,57.

118. "Those who foretell the future lie, even when they foretell the truth". Arab proverb, quoted in Wiseman

(1983) p.36.

119. Hutchinson (1977) p.79.

120. For a recent account of this see O'Donnell (1982).

121. See Deane (1978) p.181/2.

122. Misinterpreted is perhaps a better word. the so-called 'neo-classical synthesis', effects a marriage between two systems of thought with fundamentally different cosmologies. See Leijonhufvud in Latsis (ed) (1976) pp.98ff. Keynes was a Marshallian, but the neo-classical systhesis is Walrasian in character. The synthesis ignores the non-rational decision element in Keynesian theory, loses the dynamic of his 'process' analysis, and serves only to replicate the whole dichotomy which Keynes rejected.

123. Kellner (1989).

124. See Eichner in Eichner(1983).

125. See Bunge (1979) Ch.5 for 'scientific' distinctions between theory and model. Even in the strictly scientific sense different authors tend to make different distinctions. See also Hausman (1981) p.44ff., Suppe (1977). For looser interpretations see Achenstein (1968), Winter (1966) p.236 for the variety of social models.

126. Lonergan (1957) uses this expression throughout Insight.

127. See Knoor-Cetina (1981), Hesse (1980) p.167ff.

128. Quine (1980).

129. Ibid. p.41.

130. Lonergan, as we have seen, has another argument.

131. Winch (1958) p.15.

132. Ibid. p.123.

133. Einstein - "It is the theory which decides what can be observed". Quoted in Trigg (1980) p.63. See also Hesse (1980) p. 63ff. Hesse also points out that the idea of theory-dependent observation language invalidates Aristotle's idea of discovering essences by intuition - the idea which forms the basis of Lonergan's idea of pre-conceptual insight (1957 p.3ff.,1968).

134. A central point in Feyerabend (1962).

135. Hesse (1980) p.63ff.

136. Ibid.p.63ff. She makes the distinction, as Duhem does not, between a fact and the linguistic expression of a fact.

137. For different ways of thinking about society see Bunge (1979). We also find our models which we use to think about knowledge in the social context. See Bloor (1976) for the way in which the thought of Kuhn and Popper is derived from social forms.

138. Bloor (1976) Ch.1.

139. Habermas (1971).

140. See Lugg (1983) for a discussion of this point.

141. See Filmer (ed) (1972) pp.33ff.

142. See Horton and Finnegan (1973). We also, as these authors point out, draw other distinctions between ourselves and these societies – for instance, that of true/false belief systems based on the secular/religious-magical distinction.

143. Bloor (1976) p.21.

144. Hesse (1980) p.48ff.

145. "We have known ever since Husserl's 'Ideas' that meaning-endowment is an act wherein pure sense-experiences are animated. What in a cursory glance we see as meaningful has already been constituted as such by a previous intentional operation of our consciousness...I am only aware of this process of the constitution of meaning insofar as I attend to it, otherwise I look at the world and take it for granted that it is meaningful". Giddens (1976) p.44-6.

146. For an account of this see Taylor (1971).

147. The term is Machlup's – see his essay "Operational concepts and mental constructs" in (1978).

148. Loasby (1976) p.28.

149. Von Mises (1933) p.190.

150. Loasby (1976) p.22-3.

151. Machlup (1978) p.490.
152. The confusion is perpetuated by Lipsey, who reinterprets the programme of scientific positivism as value-freedom rather than testability. "Positive statements are about what is or will be ... normative statements are about what ought to be. They depend on our judgement about what is good or bad, and they are inextricably bound up with our philosophical, cultural and religious positions."(5th ed. p.7).

Lipsey admits, however, that economics can never be 'positive' in the strict philosophical sense - " all that the positive economist asks is that something which is positive and testable should emerge from his theories somewhere"(Ibid). He does not pursue the issue as to whether one might wish to verify or falsify the theories by empirical testing - wisely, perhaps, since economics never considers that a falsified hypothesis should lead to theory modification. See also Wiseman (1983).

153. Schumpeter (1954) fn.p.8.
154. Machlup (1978) p.438. For the same argument see Coddington (1972) p.2.
155. Shackle (1972) p.360.
156. This explains the fact that theories become more or less fashionable depending on real-world problems and on political interests - witness the revival of interest in the theoretical underpinnings of classical monetary economics.
157. See Edel (1979) Ch.1.
158. Althusser (1979) Quoted in Outhwaite (1983) p.7.
159. Strictly speaking 'operationalism' states that the meaning of concepts is defined by their operations - see for instance Machlup's essay in (1978) called 'Operationalism and pure theory in economics'. Operationalism is the option taken by a discipline which cannot attribute meaning by means of verification. Operational concepts are linked by means of statistical correlation, whereas mental concepts , having no

operational dimension, can only be linked by means of logical necessity.

160. As Eichner points out in his introduction to (1983) economists originally turned to deductive reasoning because government statistics did not really give them an understanding of the structure and function of the economic system as it functioned in an everyday context. This led them to proceedures of aggregation, of fitting the aggregates into economic models by the device of 'least squares' which reduces the equations so that the original variety of data is lost.

161. Hollis and Nell (1975) p. 81 for problems of identification and specification.

162. Morgenstern (1963), also Waterhouse (1989). Research by the Independent newspaper has uncovered allegations by statisticians of "political manipulation of statistics, selective and misleading use of figures, failure to collect information which reflects badly on the government's record, and constraints on research". (Waterhouse op.cit).

163. This technique can generate some very odd research approaches. See for instance Becker's work on marriage and other topics in (1976). Rosenberg (1979) p.522 says of Becker's work — "after all, it is only a matter of ingenuity, and no real scientific achievment, to erect an axiomatic system that is merely compatible with any finitely large body of available data. Axiomatic systems are not falsifiable — only the hypotheses they generate. Becker can thus propound a theory which is not open to challenge, even though his analysis is neither economic, nor a theory of human behaviour, nor a theory proper..."

164. Hollis and Nell (1975) p.104.

165. Shackle (1972) p.118. Although Friedman makes the same point in (1953), he tends to obscure the argument by talking about facts, evidence, experience and observation interchangeably.

166. Dewey (1938) p.507.

167. As in the case of 'life-cycle' consumer behaviour.

168. Chase in Eichner (ed) (1983) p.144.

169. Hicks (1979) p.38.

170. Hutchinson (1977) uses this phrase to discuss problems of realism in economics.

171. See for instance Blatt's essay in Eichner (ed) (1983) on how economists misuse mathematics, also Georgescu-Roegen (1979), Munby (1956) p.73 for problems arising from the imperialism of mathematics in the subject. The trend began with the work of Pareto, but it has been reinforced by the subject's bid for scientific respectability.

172. Hutchinson (1977) p.92.

173. Machlup (1978) p.183.

174. See the arguments presented by Pope John Paul II in Laborem Exercens, also see Schumacher (1980).

175. See Capra (1983) p.246.

176. Ibid. p.200ff.

177. Ibid. p.243.

178. By, for instance, the 'new international division of labour', whereby multinational corporations relocate production processes to low-wage countries in order to increase profits, thereby creating unemployment throughout the advanced countries.

179. Althusser (1979) says — "knowledge is not just a relation between a knowing subject and a known object, but rather an effect produced by certain concepts which make it possible to think certain facts or states of affairs and not others." Quoted in Outhwaite (1983) p.35.

180. Kinloch. (1981) p.11.

181. Seabrook. (1984). Some of his examples are stretched, but the overall picture conveyed is convincing.

182. Ibid.

183. This section leans heavily on Outhwaite (1983).

CHAPTER FOUR - JUDGEMENT AND VALUES.

i. Introduction.

Action is dependent on belief and desire. The last
chapter examined the bases of 'belief'; this chapter looks at
the basis of 'desire'. I focus in this chapter on the way in
which we make 'judgements of value', decide what is
'worthwhile'. I argue that the values which ground such
judgement are culturally given, that an important segment of
that cultural influence for us is constituted by the economic
dimension of our social existence, and that the values
embedded in the ways in which we think about the economy thus
tend to pervade our evaluational processes in general. I
argue in particular that the intrinsic social values of
welfare, justice and freedom are given a particular
interpretation in the economic context, and insofar as this
interpretation prevails we are led to adopt a particular set
of instrumental values which are alien to those central to
the message of the Gospel.

ii. Valuing.

Judgements of value are an answer to the question 'is it
worthwhile'? The process of judgement here involves both
using the values we hold to determine how the good as we see
it is manifested in any particular situation (established by
judgement of fact), and deriving an imperative, moral or
otherwise. There are many kinds of 'good, so the basis of
such an imperative is not necessarily moral, although in
practice it may be difficult to separate the axiological from
the ethical. Judgements of value will be moral judgements if
the good is defined in a moral sense, but they can also, for
instance, be aesthetic or pragmatic judgements.

Judgements of value in any particular instance are made on the basis of values already held. In this chapter I want to discuss the origin of those values – in particular, the extent to which they are culturally conditioned in general and conditioned by sub-cultures in particular. Evaluations thus take place within a given 'moral practice'(1), and the norms within this practice establish the criteria for judgement in any given situation. A given 'moral practice', whether it be that of a group or class, provides the spectacles through which we view the facts of any given situation in order to evaluate them, and the criteria by which we judge them to be 'good'. Each of us belongs to a variety of such groups; our total vision will thus be composed of an amalgam of values culled from our environment. For each of us, however, there will be a dominant perspective, a way of valuing based on ideas about man and about the 'good' in the widest sense, which will provide the foundation for our particular valuing stance and hence for the basis of action.

The perspective I would want to maintain in the face of the current ethical pluralism can be characterised as cognitivist but not universalist, pluralist but not relativist, and emotivist insofar as it gives credence – although not predominance – to the role of feelings in value judgement (2). Judgements of value, including moral judgements, are cognitivist in the sense that they are made on the basis of what is judged to be the case – i.e. they are based on facts – including facts about human welfare – as well as values (3). One can thus speak of such judgements as being consistent, or ill-founded, or even 'logical'. To do this is to reject the claim that facts and values are logically independent (4). It is also to reject the idea that value judgements are only emotive, or intuitionist, or have simply the status of commands (5). On the other hand, such judgements are clearly not universalisable in the sense that exactly the same judgement will always be made given exactly similar circumstances, because both what counts as a

relevant fact and what count as important values can vary
from culture to culture, as well as from group to group
within a culture. I would thus want to maintain the
possibility of pluralism in such judgements, but with two
caveats. One is that this position is seen as reconcilable
with maintaining a position of ethical naturalism in the
widest sense. It should be possible to make statements of
the form 'everyone needs justice, love and peace' while at
the same time being clear that these concepts will be
differently interpreted in different social and cultural
contexts and within the different factual perspectives (6)
which these contexts will deem as relevant. Diverse patterns
of life and fulfillment in different vocations, careers and
sub-cultures will give rise to different value preferences,
because although basic human urges are common to everyone,
the emphasis on each varies, as does the set of wants in
terms of which each person interprets his need.

The other caveat is that pluralism should not be equated
with relativism. Relativism in the strict sense involves
believing that moral judgement is dictated by convention, or
by 'what the group says'(7). But this is not the role which
pluralism assigns to convention. Pluralism sees convention
not as dictating what is right or good, but as establishing
the criteria for making judgements of value. It establishes
ways of deciding which criteria are relevant for evaluative
purposes. Pluralism thus involves a distinction on the
meta-ethical level rather than implying ethical relativism as
such.

I also want to argue that judgements of value are based
on deliberation which is affective as well as evaluative in
the rational sense, which involves heart as well as mind,
feelings as well as convictions. To say that judgements of
value involve emotional responses is not, however, to argue
that the source of such judgements is to be found exclusively
in the emotions. We can adopt Dorothy Emmet's analogy, and
see the overall value stance of the valuing person as

splitting, like the colours of a prism (8), into values which
he feels more deeply about and values which are primarily
rational rather than affective (9). There will always be a
response to values which is to a greater or lesser extent
affective, because we are 'engaged' with the values we hold.

The bulk of this chapter will be concerned with the
central argument — viz. that within the practices and codes
which ground our evaluative processes there is clearly
identifiable an influence which stems from the valuations
embodied in economic thought and practice. In a cultural
sense these values have been retained and perpetuated because
they are enshrined in ways in which we think about the
economy. My aim is to identify those valuations. They
appear to exist on both the axiological and the ethical
level; in economics we find embodied both judgements of value
in the sense of evaluating the permanent dispositions behind
actions, and judgements of 'oughtness' which pronounce on the
value of isolated acts. Economics thus provides one source
of the values on the basis of which we make judgements of
value; it forms, as it were, one 'culture' within the wider
culture. However, it is an influence which is perhaps more
pervasive than perhaps any other, simply because it reflects
the core concerns of a materialist culture, and therefore
engages both minds and hearts.

iii. <u>Values and their origin.</u>

Whatever we hold to be the 'ultimate good' in terms of
life as it is to be lived will dictate the kinds of values to
which we subscribe (10). Historically this 'ultimate good'
has received a variety of definitions, all of them to a
greater or lesser extent relating to human well-being.
Aristotle and utilitarianism provide two clear examples of a
definition of the good in terms of 'happiness', but whereas
for Aristotle happiness meant human perfectability, for the

utilitarians it meant simply material well-being. For Aristotle, virtues are values because they signify the achievement of perfection, for the utilitarians, however, virtues are at best instrumental (11). At the other extreme, G.E.Moore sees the notion of 'the good' as a non-natural quality, without independent existence, attaching to persons, things or states of affairs, to be apprehended intuitively and achieved practically (12).

These positions are not as far apart as they seem to be. The set of values to which we subscribe can usefully be thought of as a hierarchy. Given 'goodness' as the primary value, intrinsic values can be thought of as qualities in persons, things or states of affairs which foster, embody or achieve — and thus define — goodness. There will then be a whole range of intermediate values, or instrumental values, which contribute to their achievement. All sorts of classifications are conceptually possible. For example, Smelser cites representative typology by which the intrinsic value of freedom is realised by the instrumental institutional value of free enterprise (13). This latter is legitimated by the value of profit making, and by individual commitment to the value of personal success. Other instrumental values which support this hierarchy are those of efficiency and personal responsibility. Other versions of value classification abound. American values have been classified on the basis of a survey by Rescher (14) as

 — individual rights values — privacy, equality, personal integrity, welfare, freedom,
 — life-setting values — public order, pleasantness of environment,
 — personal characteristic values — efficiency, rationality, social adjustment, education, intelligence, talent.
Rescher notes that what is remarkable about this value set is the absence of the traditional virtues — i.e. qualities, such as kindness, which can be cultivated. The personal values in this list are either ones over which people have no control — i.e. natural ability — or they are socially

engendered. Value classification itself is thus a function of social and historical circumstance.

As well as discussing the classification of values, it is possible to discuss the force exercised by different types of value judgement. Hare (15) distinguishes between value terms which have purely prescriptive meanings and those which are evaluative in the sense that they contain both descriptive and prescriptive meanings. Sen (16) uses this distinction to establish separate classes of value judgement. To say that capital punishment should be abolished is a purely prescriptive judgement, to say that it is barbarous is an evaluative judgement. It is not always easy to distinguish clearly between the two categories – some sentences can stand for either type of judgement. To say that hard work is good is both descriptive and prescriptive. The distinction can be defined more closely by classifying such statements by whether or not they imply an imperative. 'Compulsive' judgements have an affinity with Kant's categorical imperative in the sense that they imply an overriding imperative, whereas non-compulsive judgements have the status of a hypothetical imperative – it may well be qualified by other value judgements. Compulsive judgements extend the prescriptive to the imperative, whereas non-compulsive judgements can have both prescriptive and evaluative elements.

Compulsive judgements clearly rank as judgements which will have a very clear outcome in terms of action. But Sen makes a further qualification in the sense that he distinguishes between judgements which are 'basic' – i.e. they hold whatever the factual circumstances – and judgements which are non-basic in the sense that the facts of the case can alter the judgement. It is possible to move from a non-basic to a more basic judgement by moving to a more general statement. Value conflict can be coped with in this way; since it is not possible to hold two value positions which are both compulsive and basic judgements – one of the

judgements involved must be non—basic. For instance, it is
not possible to maintain both that human life is sacred and
inviolate and that women have an absolute right to determine
what happens to their own bodies. One of those judgements
must be non—basic in the sense that it can be qualified.
Judgements about ends are not all basic judgements — it is
therefore possible, for instance, to argue about the ends of
social policy by determining whether it is a basic or
non—basic statement which is being made (17). Analyses such
as this enable us to be more precise about the way in which
values held might actually influence action, because they
enable us to reflect on the relative importance of the values
we hold.

Two questions now arise. Firstly, what is the source of
such values, and secondly, what determines the particular
value stance of any one person? If we regard values as
related to whatever we define as 'good', we are led by a
system of regress through the hierarchy of values to seek the
source of 'good', as has been done historically, in God, in
human nature and purpose, in society, or merely in the
individual conscience. Aristotle's notion of human
perfectability, the Platonic idea of perfectability divorced
from cultural influences, the Christian notion of the will of
God, all involve identifying the good as being that which
most centrally serves those purposes, thus defining the value
set. But it would be naive to suppose that such notions
provide externally given sources of value. If we ask
ourselves where our ideas as to what is good come from, we
have to answer that these ideas are themselves culturally
given (18). Notions, concepts and meanings of 'good' all
arise in the interaction between cultural thought forms and
their articulation on the one hand, and lived experience
within that culture on the other. These are the notions
which form the basis of the social norms which come into
being in the form of obligations to behave in a certain way —
which may not be the way individuals wish to behave, but

which is the way seen as indispensable for the proper functioning of that society (19). We tend to overlook this, to believe that our own sources of value in our culture are absolute and exogenously given while at the same time perceiving the taboos and norms of other cultures as culturally determined. To the extent that we are unaware of the cultural origin of our own values we can regard discourse on values as a subset of ideological discourse in general. Such discourse serves to legitimise the cultural values which condition and mould our ways of evaluating. Social control is then contingent on the extent to which we internalise these values.

There are two possible approaches to the explanation of why values emerge in a particular society/culture. One is the historico/sociological type of account which looks at conditions which led to the emergence of that value. The other kind of explanation focuses on the more formal structures common to the situations in which values emerge — i.e. the 'conditions of possibility' for their emergence. Ullman-Margalit (20) distinguishes three types of social interaction which will generate patterns of behaviour which will give rise to social values. What these situations have in common is that they are 'problem' situations whose solution requires that particular type of behaviour and the resultant values which will dictate it. This is a type of functional/structural explanation of the emergence of values, which can be contrasted with more specifically mechanistic accounts of the way in which values are generated.

Nor is this process in any sense static (21). Processes of valuing change as political ideologies change — Thatcherism turns the optional values of initiative, competition, hard work and enterprise into specifically instrumental ones. Such changes happen as values are eroded due to boredom, disillusion or reaction, as the operating environment of society changes. or as information within society improves. Different segments and institutions within society also play their part in value formation. Kaysen (22), for instance, discusses the ways in which business corporations act as shapers of values. Their products assist in shaping the material environment, providing the images on which we base our valuations, our assessment of what is beautiful or ugly. They shape our symbolic environment by providing verbal, visual and auditory forms of articulation for those values. Their production processes define what is thought of as work in our society, how work is evaluated, and what work is deemed to be worthwhile. And finally, corporatism provides society with the value of novelty, the evaluation that product and process innovation is good in itself, even though, for instance, it may create unemployment or develop and market inappropriate or injurious products, as in the case of Nestle's babymilk products in developing countries. The extent to which overall social change will induce value change will depend on the costs of adopting and maintaining that value over against the benefit to be derived in terms of realising the basic social requirements of survival, welfare and advancement.

The 'good' is therefore what is culturally defined as such, and valuations in society will be based on what is required to achieve it. Both the choice and the interpretation of intrinsic values will be socially determined. But what determines the particular value stance of any individual person? The key factor in value constitution on the individual level is 'interest'. Aristotle's answer (23) to the question 'how do we know the good?' is that the good appears to each man in a form answering to his character. In fact, there is a real similarity between the ascription of values to a person and the ascription of traits of character. What we are will determine the way in which our sensitivity to values comes into being and grows, because it will colour our interests. The cohesiveness of groups in society depends to a large extent on a shared nexus of values, and we are therefore likely to share the broad value bias, or ethos, of our primary social grouping. On the other hand, our cultural environment is not only complex, it is also pluralistic, and to that extent it is possible for people who are linked closely together by family or professional ties to hold widely differing value stances. It is also possible for our involvement as valuing agents to vary — we can act as advisers or purely as spectators as well as actual agents; or we can make an interior distinction between the values and norms implicit in the ethos of our subculture and the obligation to adhere to them in a practical sense. The process of commitment is necesssary before the values can become operative in us — this issue is dealt with with in the next section.

The valuing agent functions in a dynamic sense within two contexts. One is the context of his own development. Insofar as his sensibility to values develops, insofar as he adopts values, insofar as he bases his judgements of value, and consequently his actions, on those values, he will become what he does (24). The other context is that of the hierarchy of values with which he himself is confronted. These are his own personal values, the values of the group or subculture, and the values of his culture or nation. Value conflict is inevitable, because value orders refer to different levels of the moral personality. Any single decision will be viewed in the light of a fragmentation of value, as in the analogy of the prism. Conflicts can arise because of conflicting obligations to others, because of conflict between one's own projects and wider obligations, because of constraints on action deriving from the rights of others, or because of the claims of perfectionist ends.

There is a further complication to the extent that valuations can be mutually shared on a cultural level, but differently internalised in each person. Myrdal (25) cites the Negro problem in the United States as an example of the way in which valuations are preserved on a general plane but not acted out on an individual basis. This is clearly a situation where there is a contrast between

> "what America thinks, talks and acts under
> the influence of high national and Christian
> precepts, and on the other hand the
> valuations on specific planes of individual
> and group living where personal and local
> interests, economic, social and sexual
> jealousies, consideration of comunity
> prestige and conformity, group prejudice
> against particular persons or types of
> people, and all sorts of miscellaneous
> wants, impulses, and habits dominate his
> outlook (26)".

General cultural values are given the sanction of
legislation, but individual values often conflict with these.
The upshot can be either a process of interior moral
struggle, which can only be resolved by a process of
Aristotelian judgement, or — more likely, perhaps — a
side-stepping of the problem. One way of doing this is to
choose a focus for evaluation, and consign conflicting planes
of evaluation to the background. In our culture, the
conflict is often resolved by accepting the one-dimensional
scale of values provided by utilitarian forms of thought.
Utilitarianism is one-dimensional in that it conceives of
only one definition of value — there is hence no value
conflict. It is also restrictivist in the sense that it
assumes that everyone has the same status as valuing agents.
It also negates the context of the development of moral
sensibility. It fails to take account of the fact that there
is both a quantitative difference between people in terms of
the degree to which they are sensitive to values, and a
qualitative difference in terms of the fact that they have
different value perspectives or 'spectacles'.

I shall argue in later sections that the influence of
utilitarianism on our valuations stems largely from its
importance in economic thought. But I now want to take up
the issue of commitment. There is a basic inadequacy in the

above account of how value stances come to be held.
'Interest' structures the thrust of moral development within
the context of the subculture: the rate at which that
development takes place is some function of personal and
moral development in general. What is not clear from the
account is the process by which values are actually adopted.
We need some account of absorption, of apprehension, of
motivation which will explain commitment to value. It is to
this that we now turn.

iv. Intentionality.

The concept of intentionality gives us a mental
construct by which to analyse this process. There is a sense
in which values 'exist' prior to their recognition or
apprehension by any one person. They are 'out there' in a
societal or cultural context before we adopt them. To
maintain the existence of 'objective' value involves
challenging those who maintain that desire alone gives worth
or value to an activity, non-cognitivists who hold that there
is no value prior to commitment, existentialists who say
essentially the some thing, classical utilitarians who
maintain that happiness is the sole good, and 'neutral'
utilitarians who see the good as the maximisation of desire
satisfaction. For all these, value has existence only
'inside' the agent, and is brought into existence only as it
is realised. But to maintain that valuation is
phenomenological as well as attitudinal implies that values
have an existence independently of our affirmation of them,
as qualities or characteristics attached to persons, objects
or states of affairs. The sense in which we can affirm
values — or disvalues — does depend on 'subjective' inward
processes; it is contingent on how such values conform to
what we regard as 'the good', and it is a process which is
constantly changing as our own value set is reinforced or
modified in the interaction between experience and the lived

situation. But our affirmation is of values already 'there', and that affirmation has two moments. One is the moment of affirmation itself, the moment of judgement, where we rationally, as it were, decide that whatever is in question corresponds to what we believe to be 'the good'. The other simultaneous moment is the affective response. Valuation in an attitudinal sense is primarily a matter of feeling and secondarily a matter of desire. We respond to, apprehend value in feeling, and the isomorphic element in that response stems from the fact that we have ourselves already affirmed that value, so we in some sense already embody it. This idea of the recognition and apprehension of value in feelings is analysed in the notion of 'intentionality' (27).

Intentionality is mental directedness, a 'reaching out towards'. It is a modification of a scholastic notion of "a form in the mind which enables the mind to refer to what is not part of itself, and to what may or may not exist in the real world beyond itself" (28). Values, once we recognise them as such in the given situation, are not simply qualities or properties we rationally analyse. They are responded to as felt, with emotion, and this response itself is experienced as self-transcending as we reach out towards that which is extra-mental.

Brentano (29) envisages three stages in this response. There is a moment where what is intended is simply 'vorgestellt', simply recognised as being there. There is the moment where it is acccepted or rejected by a process of belief and judgment, and a further moment where it is responded to with feelings of acceptance or rejection, love or hate. In other words, there is both a rational and an affective response to objective value. Meinong (30) takes this idea further by postulating a 'two-sided' or interactive process of intentionality, whereby our response to value in these different senses is not just a passive process, but undergoes whatever modification is necessary in order to make the presentation of the objective data of value possible.

The subject—object distinction thus becomes blurred; value has an objective foundation in the character of objects, but the objective basis of value will determine the appropriate value experience, so that the essence of value lies in its derivative characteristic arising out of the relationship of objects to people. This approach has the advantage of stressing the non—uniform characteristic of value as apprehended. Not only can value be embodied in things, patterns of things or states of affairs, but we can also distinguish, as Meinong does, between objects of value apprehended in feelings, which he terms dignitatives — i.e. what is agreeable, true or good, and those apprehended through desire, which he terms desiderative.

The concept of intentionality provides an explanation of the way in which the values which form the basis of value judgements are recognised and apprehended. It also, as we have seen, plays a key role in the later development of Lonergan's thought. The rational basis of action remains, but feelings are the medium through which we apprehend the values which ground our action. Such feelings can be transient, but they can also be ones which "are in full consciousness so deep and strong...that they channel attention, shape one's horizon, direct one's life. Here the supreme illustration is loving... "(31). Lonergan sees a dynamism here akin to that dynamism which pushes people to the point of developed rationality, but in this case the point reached is that of responsibility (32). Just as there is a dynamism in the human spirit which manifests itself as 'the unrestricted desire to know' — i.e. an openness to being, so also there is a dynamism which manifests itself as an openness to the good, and this has the effect of creating a continuous response, a continuous reaching out, not towards the good in any particular situation, but towards the good as such.

Intentionality, in emphasising the role of feelings as response to values, has something of importance to contribute to our understanding of the Christian faith response. It becomes possible to love our enemies, not out of duty or out of fear, but because the value 'good of others', and in particular 'good of enemy' elicits in us an attitudinal or emotional response. It is here that we see the extent of the process of conversion necessary if we are to become 'conformed to Christ'. Conversion entails adopting gospel values in such as way that they become normative for action, not just in the purely deliberative or rational sense but because they become simply the ground of inclination. We love our enemies because we feel love for them; we do whatever that love prompts us to do. The ground of morality thus becomes not the right action, but the moral man whose inclinations have been transformed by his internalisation of Gospel values.

v.   The values in economics.

We now turn to more specific issues. If we accept that values are objective, that they are culturally given and interpreted, that they arise in the interaction between society's needs and the ideological formulations which result, we are led to focus on the way in which the major one of these needs — ie. the economic — creates a nexus of values within society. Habermas (33) sees the technological interest as being the basic, and in our society the most overriding, of the survival needs. The economic/technological aspect of human existence thus holds a monopoly over all other aspects in terms of social discourse. Knowledge systems, in particular the discipline of economics, provide the thought forms, the concepts and the values which form the context of that discourse. Communication systems — media, education — disseminate these ideas, and in the course of this process values are transmitted and reinforced. People adopt the values of the system even though they may criticise it on ethical grounds; they tend to attribute the failings of the system to selfishness or other human failing, rather than assuming that it is the system itself which lacks ethical principles. Insofar as this discourse takes precedence over other interest areas in society the value set on which it is based becomes the most central in terms of determining thought and action.

We have, however, to distinguish the levels on which this operates. There is firstly the question of the values embodied in the 'doing' of economics. The economists who generate knowledge systems are themselves part of the culture; they inherit the value premises inherent in the discipline, but they also bring to their endeavours their own particular set of values. This will introduce the kind of dynamic element into the discipline which is necessary to ensure that it responds to changes in cultural institutions and values. The interaction between the object of knowledge, disciplinary thought forms and the value set of the economist - i.e. the axiological layer of his mind - will create new ideas and forms of expression which will in turn become part of the disciplinary system of operation (34).

Judgements made by economists are both methodological and normative (35), for disciplinary endeavour itself involves value-based choice. The economist demonstrates his own particular bias in his choice of problem for research, in his selection of hypothesis by which to test his ideas, in his choice of data to fit the hypothesis, in the interpretation of results, and in the language by which all this is described (36). Description itself involves selection. Sen (37) reminds us of the ways in which description can be good in the sense of appropriate without being a good (in the sense of truthful) description of what is being described. Usefulness and realism are not the same thing; we can describe a selective educational system as efficient without saying anything about its divisiveness, or unemployment as rising without indicating how it is distributed within households or by region. In economic research, as in social research in general, there is an inextricable link between theory and practice, fact and value. Practical problems invite theoretical reflection which can only be done by analysing the facts, and ultimate practical conclusions are based on value premises as well as on factual analysis. Value-laden description is an inherent part of this process.

At a deeper level, the economist demonstrates his own bias by the degree to which he can comfortably subscribe to the research paradigm within which he operates. Research paradigms in economics contain their own value premises, not the least of which is the fact that they are defended and defensible in terms of disciplinary cohesiveness and scientific respectability rather than in terms of their usefulness, their empirical validity or the appropriateness of the values they embody (38). A pluralism of competing and conflicting paradigms persists in the discipline — unlike other disciplines where dominant paradigms tend to render others obsolete — precisely because of the heavy axiological content. They continue to exist side by side because they represent different interpretations of what the problem situation is and different views of what ought to be the goal of the economic evlution of society. They have, in other words, a differently defined vision of 'good' and 'bad'(39).

These paradigms form the framework of thought within which the individual economist operates, and to which he must subordinate his own value bias if he is to operate effectively — i.e. acceptably in disciplinary terms. Their value-loading is implicit and diffuse, and impossible to separate out from the scientific process in general. Myrdal (40), who is prepared to allow for the existence of values but considers that their 'anti-scientific' effect can be negated if value premises are explicitly identified as such, freely admits that the difficulty with these recommendations is that values are not only difficult to isolate from other issues, but they also exist in suppressed and unacknowledged forms in both person and paradigm, whether they are about ends or means to achieve those ends.

When we look at the values within the discipline itself, the first thing to be said about the value bias there is that there is a bias towards the achievement of value-freedom. The most fundamental expression of this bias within economics is formalism: i.e. the requirement that economic behaviour be studied as an isolated and independent form of human behaviour in general. In our experience of everyday living we do not consciously distinguish economic acts from non-economic acts - indeed, it might be difficult to do so. Economic behaviour on any common-sense interpretation forms a continuum with social behaviour in general. Such a perspective can be termed 'substantivist'(41). But conventional economics isolates economic behaviour from social behaviour in general and attributes to it law-like regularities. The categorisation of economic behaviour in stimulus-response terms enables economic analysis to be conducted in terms of impersonal mechanisms, thus allowing the establishment of a science of economics which could exist separately and independently from its subject-matter - i.e. human behaviour. This view, as Andreski points out (42), can be plausible only when the sociological assumptions of economic theory accord with the dominant characteristics of the societies where the theory originates. Where this is not the case - i.e. as in the case of third world countries - the arbitrary nature of the approach is revealed.

One of the purposes of formalism is the desire to eradicate valuations and to demonstrate that what is discussed is purely factual - price determination, income distribution, even economic welfare. The philosophical warrant for this derives from Hume's statement that norms or 'ought' statements cannot be logically derived from descriptive statements with truth-value. These latter are held to be 'value-free'(43). The warrant has been used to establish the hegemony of a 'positive' economics which is independent of normative questions and value judgements and which therefore conforms to the logical positivist idea of science. It is true that the central programme of the fact-value distinction in economics has been to establish logical independence rather than ethical neutrality (44). However, its philosophical underpinnings have been discredited (45), and this allows us to admit that values are embedded in even the most formal economic reasoning.

Value judgements are located at both ends of the chain of reasoning. Normative assumptions about welfare, for instance, underlie the most aprioristic of economic models. As Gordon puts it –

> "Paretian welfare economics is a conspicuous offender in this regard. It begins with some quite clear value assumptions, then goes on to construct an elaborate logical system ...emerging ...with specific prescriptions for policy which are treated as if they were undeniable. The history of scholastic philosophy teaches that one should never embrace an assumption until one sees what a clever logician can do with it"(46).

Policy prescriptions emerge from economic analysis simply because as evaluative statements they are analytic – they follow logically from the reasoning within a context of institutional facts and constitutive rules (47), as well as "by virtue of forms of reasoning embedded in ordinary language, in established concepts and the standard meanings of certain words"(48). But this does not negate the value-loading of the conclusion. There is a confusion between laws in the sense of norms and laws in the sense of regularities, and this accounts for the way in which formal economics claims to have access to scientifically observable facts, which then become political precepts – such as, for instance, the 'necessity' to provide incentives for highly-paid managerial workers so that they will work more effectively.

    The programme of formalism has thus two aspects. Not
only is there an effort to distinguish 'positive' from
'normative' economics in the sense that facts are held to be
value-free, but there is also an attempt to establish the
factual as normative (49). Evidence of the prevalence of
women in low-pay trades (50), for instance, can provide a
warrant for the employment of women in those trades - it is
seen as 'normal'. This is an example of the way in which what
'is the case' becomes what 'ought to be the case' simply
because 'this is the way it has always been'. This has the
effect of discouraging challenges to the status quo.
Furthermore, it is frequently the case that factual and
empirical conclusions are constructed in support of a
particular political programme. For instance, Minford (51)
uses the argument that people do not seek low-paid jobs as
grounds for the political recommendation that social security
benefits ought to be cut so that people are forced to take
such jobs. Economic analysis abounds with such examples; they
provide evidence for Sen's comment that "the implicit
assumption seems to be that if everyone agrees on a value
judgement then it is not a value judgement at all, but is
perfectly 'objective' (52).

    To say that the eradication of values is itself a value
in the discipline may sound like a contradiction in terms.
Economics is - and has to be - deeply normative, not just in
the sense that facts and values are inextricable, but in the
sense that 'value' itself is what economics is concerned
with. Just as concepts of right and duty are central
political concepts, so also is the concept of value the
central economic concept, because, as Myrdal points out, it
is the concept for describing the social 'ought'(53). But
which concept of value is relevant? What is value? Is value
simply the price at which the good exchanges on the market,
or is it something deeper, something to do with worth? If
value is simply to be equated with price, then its normative

content is light. But economics has never been content to see value as purely exchange value. It looks for the source of inherent or intrinsic value in commodities, value which is enduring or necessary as opposed to accidental or ephemeral price value. This then becomes the 'right', 'natural' or 'just' value — heavily normative concepts. The source of this value could be located in use or need—fulfillment. But classical economists — Ricardo in particular — took the option of seeing the source of value as the input of labour required to produce the good — thus establishing what Myrdal calls an 'empirical fiction (54)' which still grounds much of economic theory. The assumption that value stems from labour derived from the natural law assumption that property has its justification in the labour bestowed on the object, but it remains the rationale for the institution of private property and, by implication, inherited wealth. The concept of value—in—exchange is also normative (55), and also derives from the idea of property rights. Traders who exchange goods in the market have a 'right' to be compensated for the value of what they exchange by the price they get, even though the goods are of no 'personal' value to them. Economics thus adopts a particular value stance in the way in which it conceives of value.

We now come to the question of the source of the valuations implicit in economic reasoning. Again, such valuations are culturally generated in the interaction between the real—world problems which economics seeks to solve and the basic world—view or philosophical perspective of the time. Every age sees its own economic problem through the lenses of its own value—set — its tacit assumptions about human nature, about the goals, aspirations, impulses and drives reflect the subculture of the historical period in which they develop. Economics is simply unusual in that an outdated complex of disciplinary paradigms survives virtually intact and unchallenged, a relic from a historical period where both the problem and the perspective were very different from today.

The philosophical framework which grounds economic valuations is that of utilitarianism. For utilitarians, the end or purpose of all activity, including economic activity, is pleasure. In terms of classical political economy pleasure comes from material goods; it is defined as being achieved by means of acquisition of goods made possible by people's property rights over their own efforts. Psychic satisfaction is gained by an ethos of Puritan impulse control (56) – which engenders thrift – combined with the Calvinist virtues of hard work and discipline. Add to this the free market/laissez-faire view of the economy which was utilitarianism's import from natural law philosopy and the result is a prediction that the welfare of all is ensured by the exercise of self-interest. What is natural becomes what is right, moral conduct can be deduced from the requirements of social utility, private vice becomes public virtue (57). The individual economic agent, as Smith argued, is not himself subject to moral decision. "In this case, as in many other cases, he is led by an invisible hand to promote an end which was no part of his intention ...I have never known so much good done by those who affected to trade for the public good"(58).

Economic theory adopted the method rather than the philosophical postulates of utilitarianism. The attraction of utilitarianism from the economist's point of view is that it uses rational ways of testing the good, as, for instance, intuitionism does not; ethical behaviour is then seen as a subset of the general theory of rational behaviour (59). As a theory of personal morality utilitarianism values actions in the basis of their consequences – an 'outcome morality'. As a theory of public choice utilitarianism is used to assign values to states of affairs on the basis of satisfaction. Sen and Williams (60) term the resulting combination 'welfarist consequentialism'. The procedure involves a set of value judgements which allow the assumption that it is possible to aggregate and homogenise individual satisfactions in order to get a sum of social satisfactions. It also allows the belief that the correct distribution of income is that which maximises the total, irrespective of its distribution - i.e. an unequal distribution is better than a more equal one if it results in a greater total satisfation level. All of this makes theory easier to manipulate and hypothesis formation more manageable

Trenchant criticism of utilitarianism as an ethical system has been provided by Sen and Williams (61), who argue that the main problem lies in the fact that utilitarianism imposes 'informational constraints', the most important of which is the narrowness of its conception of personhood. People are seen only as the location of their utilities; information about people is thus reduced to a homogenous vector which can be ranked with other people's utility vctors. The result produces a norm by which actions and states of affairs can be evaluated - i.e. the evaluation is in terms of the consequences for utility. All information with regard to a person's autonomy as an agent, his integrity and his attachments is considered unimportant. In particular, utilitarianism is not interested in the how and why of the qualities of personhood. This leads to a disregard of the sources of desire and satisfaction, of the extent and intensity of preference, and of the interdependence of people's satisfactions. We lose the people, we see only the choices.

Utilitarianism treats desires and preferences by means of three devices. The first is that of reductionism. Wants are homogenised; there is no way in which utilitarianism can distinguish between trivial preferences and deeply-held ''basic' judgements of value. Secondly, the move towards idealisation restricts the kind of preference that is allowed to count in various ways; in general terms utilitarianism accepts only preferences which are formulated after reflection and with full information. And thirdly, utilitarianism relies on the fiction that preferences can be

viewed as existing independently of the social context which
conditions them and which they help to shape. This makes
utilitarianism anti-liberal, because utility functions may be
interdependent. How can I allow someone to do what he
chooses if it reduces my pleasure? In its disregard of the
source of satisfaction and its concern for the consequences
utilitarianism can, for instance, be used to legitimise
slavery or torture - all that is important is the sum total
of utility. Such, as Sen points out (62), is the philosophy
which grounds the free market system and 'consumer
sovereignty, the economic cornerstones of modern democracy.
Not only does it lack a psychology and a politics, but it
ignores the relationship between politics and moral
reflection.

We have looked at the sources of the valuations implicit
in economics as a discipline. We now look at the way in
which the prevalence of the 'culture of economism' leads to
particular cultural interpretations of welfare, justice and
freedom, the most basic of the social values, and the way in
which these interpretations designate as instrumental values
efficiency, rationality, merit and competition.

vi. Welfare - the value of self-interest.

The word 'welfare' has connotations which are wider than
the purely economic. However, in social and political terms
welfare as an intrinsic value is defined as economic welfare
and culturally interpreted as pleasure/happiness defined
specifically as 'more is better'. The instrumental values of
self-interest and acquisitiveness provide the motive and
engender the action which will achieve welfare maximisation.
I want to argue in general that our view of welfare is an
impoverished one, not only because of the limitations
inherent in the way in which we interpret it, but because of
the reductionistic view it takes of 'economic man'. Our view

of welfare as 'more is better' causes us to institutionalise
the value of economic growth to the point where it becomes
ideology, cultural belief and commitment. It also causes us
to minimise the distributional aspect of welfare. And
finally, our view of economic man as rational serves to empty
action of moral content.

Immediate practical problems arise in the context of
giving empirical content to the notion of economic welfare.
If we accept that 'more is better' we have to ask 'more
what'? Welfare on a national scale is generally defined as
GNP. But this measure (63) is flawed. It counts only value
added in a market context — it does not, for instance, count
household activities as creating value. It counts inputs as
a surrogate for value added in e.g.educational activities —
no attempt is made to easure output or benefits. It includes
what is not actually desired — i.e. the cost of clearing up
pollution and defence costs. It gives no account of the
wastage of natural resources, and there is no attempt made to
value family/neighbourhood or environmental/political assets.
The conception of welfare is always defined in terms of
empirical preferences. But there is no consideration of how
preferences are generated, of whether it is possible to say
that preferences and welfare are mirror images, or of whether
it is possible to extrapolate from individual to social
welfare. As Scitovsky says (64) — "The national income is
at the very best an index of economic welfare and economic
welfare is a very small part, and often a very poor
indicator, of human welfare."

Even given that we have a satisfactory definition of
welfare, we still have to ask what more of anything brings
us. The answer of economics is that it brings us 'utility'.
Utility is the index of welfare. Quite apart from the fact
that in terms of policy evaluation this is a totally
one-dimensional view of welfare (65), there is also the
question of the relationship between the objective notion of

human welfare and the subjective notion of human happiness. Admittedly we are the best judges of what makes us happy, but how then is one to cope with the case of the poor man contented with his simple diet, as over against the rich man who is miserable because his champagne is not of the right vintage? Whose welfare is greater? Because of the difficulaty of making such an evaluation, some objective standards (eg measures of poverty) are necessary in order to talk meaningfully about welfare. This is particularly the case if we believe that subjective perceptions of welfare may not be reliable for one reason or another. Rescher (66) argues that not only may people not necessarily be the best judges of their own welfare, but that the welfare/happiness relationship may be very loose. Nevertheless, it should not be assumed that because a person is not necessarily the best judge of his own welfare others can judge that for him. The assumption that welfare and happiness stand in a one-to-one relationship is at best simplistic, at worst dangerous.

How is welfare maximisation done? 'Pareto optimality' provides the economic definition of optimum welfare - a situation where no-one can be made better off without someone being made worse off. There is both an allocative and a distributional aspect to this. Productive resources are optimally allocated in the sense that as much as possible is produced, and from a given set of resources distribution is such that welfare is maximised. Pareto optimality rests on assumptions that agents always act in their own self-interest, that they know what that interest is and will be in the future, and that they have no interest whatever in the welfare of others, neither benevolent nor malevolent.

The problem here is that it is possible to have a variety of distributions which satisfy that condition and Pareto rules cannot rank them in order of desirability. Optimality thus refers only to efficiency and not to equity. Welfare is defined in terms of a sum total, thereby making no

allowance for the way in which individual welfare might vary
as between people. Gross inequality of income is as
desirable as an equal distribution. As Sen says, a society
or economy can be Pareto-optimal and still be 'perfectly
disgusting'(67). Furthermore, Pareto-optimality implies
that social choice is made on the basis of majority decision,
without any regard to overall criteria of equity or justice.

>"A fatal defect of naive utilitarianism is
>its incapacity to provide adequate
>accomodation for the pivotal facet of
>justice. No acceptable ethical theory can
>articulate its principle of choice among
>alternative distributions of goods and evils
>in abstraction from a consideration of the
>legitimate claims of the individuals at
>issue...(but) for the naive utilitarian,
>justice and obligation are always
>provisional matters..."(68).

Welfare maximisation as an objective thus ignores the
question 'whose welfare'. A related, and perhaps more
intractable problem, has to do with the question as to what
is actually being maximised. Here there is a real ambiguity.
Even assuming that we have found an adequate answer to the
welfare/happiness problem, do we know what it is that the
economic agent values? Is it pleasure, however defined, or
is it opulence in a material sense? Traditional welfare
economics, which is centred round the analytical apparatus of
'Pareto optimality' opts for the first possibility. The
economic agent aims to maximise the sum total of his pleasure
or satisfaction as measured by utilities. What he values is
then different kinds of pleasure; different lifestyles can be
evaluated in terms of how much utility they provide. Utility
is therefore used both as a measure of satisfaction and as a
kind of device to homogenise satisfactions. But problems
arise when we try to compare the utility gained from, say,
eating an orange, with that gained from, say, listening to a

concert. The problem here is a conceptual rather than a practical one. On the practical level economics manages the comparison by looking at the price the agent is prepared to pay for the different kinds of pleasure, but on a conceptual level doubt remains as to the sense in which it is valid to talk about such satisfactions as in any sense comparable. Economics responds to this problem by seeing utility in two ways (a) as a mental state triggered by the consumption of commodities, the state being the same irrespective of what gives satisfaction, and (b) as an evaluational (homogenising) device used to evaluate objects of value – i.e. commodities. It then becomes unclear whether we value utilities as such, or value commodity bundles in terms of utilities. Do we want happiness or what brings us happiness? The distinction is a real one, but it is glossed over in welfare economics and in the everyday understanding of consumer behaviour in general. We are left with no clear understanding of our own bases of evaluation in a material sense.

There is a further problem when we come to unpack the notion of what it is of which utility is regarded as an index. Are we talking about pleasure, happiness or satisfaction on the one hand, or are we talking about desire fulfillment? Pigou (69) saw the strength of desire as providing an index of utility. But desiring itself is a valuational exercise; it is a consequence rather than a source of valuation. We desire what we have already established to be 'good'. Nor is desire itself foolproof evidence of valuation. It represents only one aspect or part of valuation; it is, for instance, possible to value something without desiring it. It is also possible to desire what is not necessarily 'good' in the sense of good-for-us. How much utility is gained from a shot of heroin by an addict?.

The problems raised by seeing utility as an index of happiness (whether as mental state or evaluational device) or as an index of desire fulfillment can be avoided — and much of the literature takes this escape route - by a simplistic use of choice as an index of utility. The attraction of measurability and observability leads to a conflating of choice and benefit. The major problem here lies in the variety of motives which can trigger choices, not all of them leading to beneficial outcomes in a personal sense. What about the case, for instance, of the person who choses to give up his life for his friend? The use of choice as an index of utility ignores the complexities of rationality and freedom.

The metaphysical problems associated with the notion of utility can, of course be bypassed if we regard the aim of welfare maximisation as opulence. This, however, encounters the problem of mindless materialism. Can we equate well-being with being well-off? Goods and services are valuable, but not in themselves, only to the extent that they can contribute to people's ability to live well (70). What is the point of having a bicycle if I am crippled and cannot ride it? We run the risk of 'commodity fetishism' if we regard commodities as anything other than means to ends. Opulence is thus a measure which conveys very little information about welfare in a subjective sense.

I have discussed the way in which economics sees the 'object of value', and the difficulties inherent in giving content to the concept of utility as an index of welfare. I now come to the question of the 'subject' — ie.how economics evaluates human behaviour?. More particularly, what are the values embedded in assumptions about how welfare is achieved? Neo-classical economics is subjectivist, and focuses on behaviour using a particular image of man to derive behaviourist conclusions (71). The basic assumption derives from the insights of utilitarianism. Economic man is assumed to act in such a way as to maximise welfare as the sum total of his satisfactions. Furthermore it is a theorem of this

particular type of analysis that, provided certain conditions
are satisfied, such preference-based behaviour will lead to
the most efficient allocation of resources (goods and factors
of production) in the economy (72). 'Efficiency' here is
defined as meaning that the economy arrives at a situation
where it is not possible to make anyone better off without
making someone else worse off - i.e. there is no wastage and
no slack. At this point the sum total of social 'happiness'
will be maximised, whether in terms of getting the most
output for a given quantity of inputs, or alternatively
getting a given output at the lowest possible resource cost
(73).

Welfare maximising behaviour is seen as 'rational'(74).
Rationality as a normative characteristic is part of the
programme of formalism in economics. Just as economics
isolates economic behaviour and action from human behaviour
in general, so the notion of rationality isolates a
particular type of motivational basis for that action -
welfare maximisation, a particular type of mental process
associated with it, and a particular form of consequentialist
act evaluation. The criticism to be made of the assumption
of rationality is not so much that people do not behave like
this, the criticism is rather that it is unrealistic and
reductionistic to believe that people always behave like
this in the relevant circumstances. Intentionality does not
presuppose rational actors; to assume that rational action is
normative, as economics does, is as much to discount the
importance of feelings in values as to discount the
significance of values in action.

Problems about the particularly narrow interpretation of
rationality with which economics is saddled fall into a
number of classes. In philosophical terms rational action
must be seen in a wider context than purely instrumental
rationality - 'rational man' is a bigger person than
'economic man'. Many of our actions are done without the

calculative procedures assumed by instrumental rationality —
gearchanging while driving a car, for instance. In practical
terms it is doubtful whether rational action of the type
assumed by neo-classical economics is achievable. Perfect
knowledge is itself an unattainable binding constraint.
Information, if available, has to be gathered and processed
in ways which cost time and money. Decisions are thus taken
on the basis of imperfect information — agents 'satisfice' as
opposed to maximise, and rationality is no longer unbounded,
but bounded and procedural (75). Some information is
unobtainable whatever the financial outlay — e.g. information
about the future. The best that can be done there is to
calculate probabilities, but subjective probabilities do not
appear to provide effective bases for rational action. As
Elster points out (76), decision theorists do not appear to
perform as well as "ordinary people selected for that crucial
and elusive quality — judgement".

Furthermore, action in any context need not be entirely
rational in the sense of being consistent. People take
decisions on impulse, behaviour can be random in a
statistical sense. Part of the reason for this may be that
people do not actually always know their own preferences
which are assumed to ground choice behaviour. Preferences
may not emerge till after the event — 'I never knew I liked
asparagus till I tried it'(77). Choices may form or change
preferences — one may 'acquire a taste for something. Tastes
and hence preferences may change with circumstances and over
time, not least because of persuasive influences such as
advertising or social pressures — 'keeping up with the
Joneses'. Rational choice may thus clearly have an element
of inconsistency.

The converse is also the case; choice may be consistent
but not rational. People may act 'irrationally' in the sense
that they act out of regard for the welfare of others rather
than in their own interest. Choices can be consistent

without being egotistical. Two situations can be
distinguished here. There is a sense in which actors can be
altruistic in the sense that they act out of sympathy for
others, but their self-interest is served by the increase in
the welfare of others. But there is also the situation where
altruism is seen as commitment, where action on behalf of
others actually diminishes the welfare of the agent, or at
least does not increase it. It is not possible to categorise
such action as self-interested; the commitment to the welfare
of others drives a wedge between personal choice and personal
welfare. Choice can thus be consistently guided by values
other than egoism (78).

Economic analysis cannot allow for the possibility of
altruism. Efficiency in the sense of the optimum allocation
of resources - the overall economic goal of neo-classical
economics - relies fundamentally on the instrumental value of
self -interest as the motivating force of economic behaviour,
and on the agent's rationality in implementing it. The
reason for this is that it is self-interest which triggers
the requisite positive or negative responses to price
changes, and which thus provides a 'signal' to the market.
Self-interest will dictate that if prices fall, more is
bought, and if prices rise, less is bought. But if, for
instance, self-interest is replaced by altruism then the
individuals' response to price changes will be indeterminate.
It will be impossible to know the direction of response
without knowing how the price changes are related to the
satisfaction of others. Matthews (79) sees other reasons,
too, why altruism would provide an inadequate basis for the
analysis of economic behaviour. Are we actually competent,
for instance, to judge what will best contribute to the
welfare of others - do we not know our own requirements best?
(He cites Hayek as originator of this argument, which is
often used as an argument against state intervention). Even
if we were competent to judge the interests of others, would
organising the economy on the basis of altruism actually

contribute to effiency?

The discussion so far has dealt with the way in which rational action as defined by economics is normative because it maximises the welfare of the group. This already establishes it as moral action. Two questions then present themselves. Firstly, is it always the case that rational action on the part of the individual leads to the best outcome for the group? Secondly, do rational action and moral action always coincide? An intuitive response to the second question might well be in the negative; if morality is defined as concern for others and rationality is defined as self-interest then clearly they can conflict. But the intuitive response is inadequate; it may be the case that rational self-interested action takes the form of sympathy. A clearer perspective is gained by tackling the second question in the context of the first, and postulating a situation where paradox is introduced because of the interdependence of choice.

In the well-known 'Prisoners' Dilemma' situation two prisoners are held in separate cells and informed that there is conclusive evidence against them of having committed a minor crime and that both are suspected of murder. If neither confesses to the murder, they will each receive six months imprisonment for the minor crime. If one confesses and the other does not, the one who confesses will go free, and the other will get a sentence of twenty years. If both confess, each will be sentenced to ten years imprisonment. What are they to do? In the absence of a contract between them the best solution for each man is to confess, even though he gets a ten-year sentence. If he does not confess, he risks having to serve a twenty-year sentence if the other man confesses. Although technically non-confession should allow him to get off lightly, he cannot risk the possibility of the other man not thinking strategically or being malevolent. The rational thing to do is thus to confess even though confession results in an inferior welfare situation for all. Rationality in this instance fails to bring about optimum social welfare - who wants to go to prison?

The prisoner acted rationally . But do rationality and morality coincide in this instance? Sen (80) lists the possible criteria which might be used to judge whether the chosen action in this case was moral or not. In terms of the Kantian imperative the moral thing would be not to confess. Sidgewick's principle of equity, which advises us to do what you judge to be right for others to do, would also advocate silence. So would Hume's principle of universalisability, Rawls' principle of maximising the welfare of the worst-off and the Pareto principle of maximising one's own utility. Rational and moral action are thus not necessarily coincidental, not does rational action necessarily yield either the individual or the socially optimum outcome. It is clear that there may exist a kind of schizophrenia in our moral perspectve between the kind of action we are required to perform as moral agents and the kind of action which 'economic' behaviour requires. Utilitarians have no problem with this; Harsanyi (81), for instance, argues for the existence of a two-tiered system of valuation - including moral valuation, which would encompass subjective preferences about personal and social utilities and satisfactions on one level, and (possibly different) ethical preferences on a more idealistic level. But this simply introduces another kind of schizophrenia. A more likely reconciliation is the one which Matthews postulates (82), where ordinary morality becomes corrupted insofar as the morality of the market-place becomes normative for private moral dealings.

Rational economic man is thus not necessarily moral man, and even if morality is defined in the terms in which utilitarian rationality defines it, economic man is still not behaving morally. This conclusion becomes intuitive if we remember that the pursuit of Pareto optimality is defined as rational, but may clearly not be moral. It can thus be argued that morality is not rational. In a society where rationality is the dominant instrumental value, such a conclusion would be profoundly disturbing.

vii. Justice - the value of merit

As in the case of welfare, justice has both wider and more narrowly economic connotations. The interpretation of 'justice' in an economic sense is dictated for us by the distributional system within capitalism. Beliefs as to who should get what are embedded in that system, articulated by economics, and implicitly adopted by the culture. The factual becomes normative as people adopt the values generated by the instrumental requirements of the system. The historically relative nature of those judgements becomes absolutised as they are universalised and given an 'objective' moral standing (83). The value-ladenness of the issue becomes suppressed; distribution is viewed simply as an efficiency problem. But the distribution of income and wealth is not only a moral issue, it has also a central role to play in the message of the Gospel.

A critique of this approach normally takes the form not so much of fundamental criticism of the system itself, as of the effects, in terms of injustice, which it brings about. Society's response to these effects is to try to remedy them by welfare provision, while at the same time remaining firmly wedded to the values which brought about their existence (84). But the real point at issue is not this; it is rather the understanding of justice and the values which underpin it conveyed by the system. Any society has a number of alternatives as to how to distribute what is produced. It can either use principles based on merit /work /sacrifice, or it can distribute according to need, or aim for equality of distribution, or distribute according to rank or the social usefulness of the recipient (85). The fundamental difference between these ideas is whether or not the aim is to achieve distributive justice in the sense of just distribution, or commutative justice in the sense of just procedures for distribution. Capitalism opts for the latter alternative.

In our system the right to what is produced stems from legal entitlement based in property. Property is a socially defined bundle of rights rather than an absolute and immutable entitlement as such. What each one gets depends on possibilities for acquisition and transformation of property as well as on rules as to how the product should be distributed. Doing justice, therefore, becomes a procedural matter — it is commutative rather than distributive, non-consequentialist rather than consequentialist. Here, oddly enough, capitalism departs from the consequentialist framework of thought which characterises the interpretation of welfare as a social value.

For the majority of people the only property rights which they possess are those over their own labour. They will thus be entitled to rewards in proportion to that labour. But labour only becomes a 'factor of production' when it is used — i.e. where work is performed. It is thus work which brings entitlement and determines claims to distributive shares. It is not too much of a leap from the fact of work as the basis for claims to distribution to the value of effort as meritorious, and therefore praiseworthy in an ethical sense. Since reward is assessed on the basis of effort, differences in reward are then indicative of, and seen as, differences in merit. Effort, as measured by productivity, and merit thus become synonymous (86). Since wages depend on productivity, those who are more productive are entitled to a greater share of the product. What is earned and what is deserved become two aspects of the same reality; capitalism thus clearly embodies the logic of Pelagianism.

But the connection between reward on the one hand and

effort—as—merit on the other can be challenged on at least two grounds. One is that the amount of product for a given amount of effort may well depend on factors other than hard work — i.e on ability, education and training, and often on sheer luck — for instance, being born into a family where children are genetically and socially advantaged. Also, the value in money terms of labour depends, other things being equal, on the scarcity of that particular kind of labour rather than on any effort made by the worker or on that worker's productivity. Surgeons and steeplejacks are highly paid because, for different reasons, their services are in short supply. In what sense can we therefore maintain that we 'deserve' what the labour market entitles us to? Furthermore, our productivity may involve social and private costs — if, for instance, we work in a cigarette factory, if we make armaments, or aerosol sprays, or fur coats. In what way is this meritorious?

The other problem is that, even allowing for these complications, productivity is primarily determined not by the amount of effort but by the amount of the other factor of production (capital) with which labour is employed. The neo—classical principle of productivity as a function of factor ratios in use is simply expressive of the common sense principle that for a given amount of effort more can be produced with better tools or a greater quantity of tools. This is the point at which the fallacy of the 'effort as merit' reasoning underlying the system becomes exposed. Capitalism is above all a system where a particular type of technology (machines) requires that the tools with which people work are owned by others prepared to make the initial outlay and take the risk involved in setting up productive enterprises. People are thus no longer in control of their own lives as far as work is concerned. Whether or not they can be at all productive is determined by whether or not they are invited to work — i.e. employed. How much they can produce is determined by the amount of capital (in the sense of machines) with which they are employed. People are thus, as Pope John Paul says, subordinated to the interests of things – they are no longer masters of their own productive output (87). The choice of technology therefore plays a crucial role in the determination of relative productivities. Neo-classical economics argues that that choice is itself influenced by factor prices. But it may also be influenced by the maximisation of profit, power and size in the corporation. Technological choice is often determined by the desire to replace workers by machines or make the worker easily replaceable and dependent on machines and capital by minimising the need for skills and qualifications (deskilling).

Productivity thus bears little relation to effort. Even if it did, the worker would not be entitled to the value of everything he produces (88). Smith's theory of 'natural price' was an attempt to cope with the fact that under capitalism part of the product is diverted to those who owned the tools – i.e.the machines – on the grounds that they must make a rate of return on the resources which they devote to capital formation and accumulation. The economy thus, as Habermas pointed out, has to develop a principle on which the surplus can be legtimately distributed (89). That principle is the profit motive. Economics sees profits as being the return to capital justified by the 'productivity' of capital. Profit theoretically provides the incentive for capitalists to remain in business or invest further. It uses the word 'productivity' which has connotations of work, effort, merit to describe how capital 'earns' a rate of return. The word itself is suggestive, it conjures up the magic of abstinence – Locke's image of sweat poured out. But what we are really doing, argues Ayres (90), is translating the mythology of agency, which we use to ground our version of inalienable rights, into inanimate machines. We impute causal efficacy to capital as a factor of production simply in order to have a formula for distribution. As Ayres points out, productivity and creativity are not attributable directly to agency, even in a human sense; they are attributable primarily to the technological, knowledge and communicative environment in which we function. Our attempt to justify the existence of profits by the productivity of capital is simply an attempt to legitimate a pragmatic and ad hoc feature of capitalism, just as our attempt to justify labour rewards on the basis of labour productivity is a pragmatic and very largely arbitrary approach to just distribution.

But again, there is a fallacy in this type of thinking which has been exposed by post-Keynesian economists such as Joan Robinson. To say that profits are the returns to capital as a productive factor assumes that we are talking about something which exists - specifically, something which exists in a quantifiable sense. In this sense capital turns out to be a kind of 'will o' the wisp'(91) - how does one measure a unit of capital? It has to be in money terms in order to 'homogenise' it, but how do we value a unit of capital in a way which is independent of the returns to capital which that valuation will help us to establish? Land and labour are measurable in terms of their own technical units - acres, hours, - so that we can define their productivities independently of the returns to them. This is not the case with capital; the theoretical justification for profits thus rests on a set of unresolved metaphysical problems. Nevertheless, profits remain the driving force of the system.

The primacy of the interests of capital is demonstrated by the way in which structures of value and power operate in industrial enterprises. A common-sense perspective on productive enterprises might distinguish between people on the one hand and things on the other. But productive enterprise sees labour simply as a cost, the work which the company has to buy; labour is then only a means to an end. Goods and labour services are both commodities; the enterprise sells one and buys another in different markets. The aim of business activity is to maximise the monetary difference between the two operations — i.e. to maximise profits. This is done by producing cheaply and selling expensively on the one hand, and by maximising productivity and minimising wages on the other. The central problem of production is thus seen as profit - all other problems are secondary.

Capitalism thus embodies a view of justice which emphasises the commutative aspect. Justice is defined in terms of fulfilling people's rights to a return rather than in terms of the consequences — rights which stem from labour rights and property rights. In moral terms rights-based moralities are non-consequentialist and hence potentially detrimental in terms of human welfare. An inventor of an essential drug, for instance, would be perfectly within his rights to sell it for the highest price he could obtain, even though that would exploit the need of other people. A society might give certain classes of people rights to oppress others (as in South Africa). It is thus clearly important — and recognised to be so — that society is at least consequence- sensitive in distributional terms even if it is not actually consequentialist — i.e. even if its distributional system embodies commutative rather than distributive notions of justice. A consequence-sensitive society will try to embody practices of distributional justice at least in its taxation and welfare systems, and this is to a greater or lesser extent the solution adopted by Western market economies.

The alternative would be to adopt a system based on distributive justice, but this is not so easy. Any attempt, for instance, to move to a system of greater equality meets the question — equality of what (92)? Suppose, for instance, one redistributes income in some utilitarian fashion so that marginal utilities are equalised. The problem about that is that we do not know enough about the different kinds of utilities, about the source of such utilities, and about the different capacities people have to gain such utilities. A further problem with equality, as well as the 'equality of what' problem, is 'equality for whom'. Sen points out (93) that traditional economics ignores the family. What, then are we to assume about how welfare is allocated within the family? Are we to think of a 'glued together' family where the is no allocation issue, a 'supertrader' family where allocation is done on the basis of bargaining (94), or the despotic family, where one altruistic person (the woman?) is sufficient to create a despotic situation?

Another possibility is to consider distribution on the basis of need, but here too there are difficulties. What is 'need' and who defines it as such? Real needs are in fact those which are dictated by survival in a human sense, but that means whatever is necessary to "provide all human beings with the opportunity for a fuller life"(95). These needs are clearly culture- specific, and it will be that which will determine which commodities are relevant. A needs-based distributional approach is essentially concerned with commodities, but which commodities fulfil needs, and is it possible to rank needs? Commodities function in an interlinked fashion — nutrition requires both food and medical care, so that ranking may not be possible. It may not even be possible in a community to satisfy all basic needs (how much resources do we devote to taking care of the old?). Also, needs have a psychological element and are thus socially interdependent — I need to be able to function in the community for psychological health. It is also the case that a needs-based approach is a 'passive' concept which encourages people to think in terms of what can be done for them rather than of what they can do for themselves, and above all for others. In an objective sense it encourages minimalism — so much and no more.

An attempt to envisage a system of distributional justice which avoids the problems created by difficulty of achieving equality, but which defines needs in a particular way, is suggested by Rawls (96). Rawls argues that if we set up a system which contains inequalities they must be such as to be in the interests of a representative member of the public. We distribute in such a way that any of us would be content to be the person made worst-off by the distribution. Rawls stipulates welfare in terms of 'primary goods'; any claim to more must then arise as a result of a shortage of primary goods. Given even that we could find an adequate definition of primary goods, his notion of welfare is clearly biased in the direction of fetishism — he is concerned with goods rather than with what they do to people. Furthermore, his suggestion involves the establishment of a method for achieving distributive justice rather than an outline of what that distribution would look like. His principle is insensitive to the diversity between people, particularly to the problems of those who need more because they are disadvantaged in terms of how or where they live — those who are ill or handicapped, for instance, or those who live in inner city areas.

Another argument against the possibility of achieving a wider or more equal distribution of goods is that certain types of goods depend for their value on being scarce. Education, for instance, loses its job market value if everyone is a graduate. If everyone has a car no-one will be able to get to the West country at holiday time or to work in cities. Hirsh's argument (97) deals with the general issue of limits to consumption, either because goods are scarce (old masters) or because satisfaction derives from scarcity (snob goods). The distributional significance of his argument arises from the fact that the more widely certain goods are distributed the less is their value, so in distributional terms nothing is gained by redistribution. In fact, the increasing prevalence of social security in Western society only serves to aggravate distributional competition at the expense of collective struggle for growth.

Distributive justice is not guaranteed by capitalism,

not advocated by economics, not valued by our society in general. However, there is a general socially-determined but historically variable commitment to correcting the worst excesses of capitalism. But not everyone subscribes to that; some argue that a move towards distributive justice would be positively harmful. Hayek (98) points out that you could only get social justice in a command economy, and claims for such justice must therefore be rejected because they conflict with individual liberty. The value of individual liberty he sees not as a right but as the way to progress. Free markets increase wealth better than planned economies, he argues, and the benefits gradually spread downwards. Individual liberty is thus an instrumental value because it ensures property rights. The case for individual liberty is seen by Hayek as entirely resting on the fact that it results in a successful manner of living. The justice of market allocation is thus unquestionable because it is determined by a system which secures the necessary procedures for the generation of growth through successful entrepreneurial activity. He can therefore attack the legitimacy of distributive justice as a moral claim. His morality is thus a 'morality of intent' rather than of consequences. Hayek's views provide a justification of Habermas' comment (99) that the growth of free economic activity has led to the development of moral individualism — a situation brought about by a lack of restraint to self-interest by any moral or religious influence.

Capitalism as a system, and economics as its mouthpiece, thus sees justice as a value in commutative terms only — ie.it is seen in non-consequentialist terms. The fundamental problem with any attempt, including that of the welfare state, to introduce egalitarian or needs-based notions of distributive justice is that they conflict with notions of fairness based on effort and merit, notions of rights as embodied in property, and notions of market efficiency which rely on the provision of incentives. Insofar as this is the case, there is an inconsistency between our ideas of economic

justice which involve giving people their rights as opposed
to what they need, and our notions of welfare and freedom
which are defined in consequentialist terms. There is a
further conflict between our valuation of the importance of
merit and our understanding of a Gospel based on the gratuity
of God's gifts.

viii. <u>Freedom - the value of competition.</u>

The functioning of the market mechanism is the way in
which resources are allocated and wants are satisfied in the
context of freedom of choice. Entitlement to goods is
determined by income; income is determined by productivity.
Allocation of goods is then achieved by the interaction
between preferences on the one hand and market prices on the
other. People compete with one another freely for what is
available, producers compete to sell cheaply; this process of
competition establishes price. There are two problems here;
one is the fact that the market mechanism creates has
problems of its own, the other is the way in which its
desired or actual existence structures our evaluations. The
argument in this section maintains that the interpretation of
the social value of freedom - as freedom <u>from</u> restraint in
the market and freedom <u>to</u> compete - is flawed and
impoverished.

There is no other part of the capitalist economic system
which is so deeply imbued with ideology as the notion of the
market. It embodies not only Newtonian conceptions of order
and harmony, but also Darwinistic notions of human progress
and development. Competitive striving is essential to market
functioning, but it also becomes something more, something
seen as essential to the process of human growth and as a
spur to personal and social development. The idea of the
market is then absolutised, market thinking is reified and
applied to other disciplines (100) and areas of social life.

What is fundamentally a social institution becomes a kind of universal human situation with almost biological connotations. Our thinking is thereby encouraged to make the factual/normative shift, from a position where the market exists to one where it is legitimised, from a position where it is legitimised as a social institution to one where the human attitudes necessary to function in it and to make it function are held to be good because they make the market work. This in turn gives a particular connotation to the socio/political value of freedom, and causes it to be interpreted in a particular way.

Para-ethical criticism can be made of the market both on the basis of the behaviour it deems to be good and because of the results it brings about. This criticism serves as a basis for a critique of the values associated with the market. Market functioning relies on the prevalence of certain attitudes which are then themselves held as instrumental values (101). Selfishness and avarice are exalted to the rank of virtues, competition – which is really strife – becomes praiseworthy. There is a cultural assumption that it is 'natural' to be competitive, and that what is natural is right.

The market values competitiveness because it is competition which weeds out the inefficient and drives prices lower. But do people compete on equal terms? The argument that competition brings efficiency always assumes that power is equal in the market, that people are not being squeezed out simply because they are weak. People may be given equal rights in a market system, but they differ in their ability to use those rights. In parts of the market – i.e. in the labour market – there is clearly an inequality of power when it comes to wage bargaining. Ability to compete for goods depends on income; some are strong enough to compete for jobs and wages, some are not. In the case of non-price competition it is companies with the most money to spend on advertising who can compete most efficiently. Monopoly and the consequent exercise of power are the inevitable outcome.

It is not only inequalities of power which can lead to competition on equal terms. The allocative consequences of market functioning must also be called into question, because the dynamics of the market mechanism itself can result in an widening of inequalities. This is particularly the case in an international context. Market responses in trading terms vary in their sensitivity to price changes. Third world countries selling primary products on world markets face a no-win situation. If they increase their production in order to make more money world prices will fall because world responsiveness (or elasticity of demand) to commodity price changes is low, and incomes of primary producers will therefore fall. The rate of growth of world demand for primary products is slow enough to ensure that there is a continual downward pressure on the relative incomes of primary producers. The prices of manufactured goods, on the other hand, are not determined by the free play of markets, but by costs of production, and these are continually rising because of world inflation. The gap between rich and poor, North and South, therefore widens because markets work to the advantage of the North.

The ideological status of the market and the normative power of the values which underpin its functioning can be challenged on the grounds that in reality markets do not actually work. Given the fact that the market mechanism is believed to be the central device for the allocation of society's resources this is a serious charge. It is not so much that markets fail to function, but that they do not function in the way supposed by neo-classical economics or political ideologies. There are several reasons for this. One is the fact that the assumption underlying market allocation and behaviour is that there is perfect knowledge of what would happen if, for instance, quantities offered for sale were to be different. This assumption does not hold, not only because we do not know the future, but also because information is neither perfect nor costless. The consequence is that prices and quantities tend to adjust at different rates. The other reason is that in normal circumstances the market lacks a co-ordinating device which will ensure that the right price is established for what is sold (102). Trading thus takes place at non-market-clearing prices, which means that the equilibrium necessary for optimum allocation to take place is unattainable even in a conceptual sense. A particularly interesting case arises in the situation — such as in the case of financial markets — where the above problems have in fact been overcome. Computer systems provide perfect and costless information and instantaneous adjustment, and yet the market does not stabilise. In fact, prices become highly volatile. This happens because when markets do work perfectly expectations are the major factor governing behaviour, and in conditions of uncertainty expectations work to destabilise the market.

We can also query the status of the market as an allocative device because the fact is that markets are not capable of allocating all resources. In the case of 'public goods', for instance, the market, if left to itself, would fail to purchase the adequate amount of street lighting or defence equipment, simply because people would take advantage of the fact that they were being provided anyway by the cooperation of others and would refuse to pay their share. This is the 'free-rider' problem, which has to be overcome by governmental provision of these goods. The market cannot allocate in this instance.

The role of governments in the market is essential, not just to provide these 'public goods', but also to enforce standards, prevent restrictive practices and monitor the adverse effects of competition. For instance, the prices established in a market context can fail to reflect the true costs to the community of producing the goods. The cost of a nuclear power plant, for instance, is not only compounded of the market costs of inputs, but also of the social costs which its operation may incur. Social and private benefit may also diverge; the building of a new underground line or bypass, for instance, can benefit those who do not use the facility directly as well as those who pay for its use. Government intervention is required in order to ensure that private benefits are not purchased at the expense of social costs

Governments may also choose to remove from market allocation goods considered by society to be a basic human right - eg. education, health - and to allocate them on a non-market basis rather than on the basis of ability to pay. Proponents of 'market ideology' argue against this on the grounds that non-market allocation removes 'incentives' within that sector, encourages inefficiency and waste, and diminishes peoples' personal responsibility for their own need-provision (103). But why is it assumed that need is better fulfilled, or more responsibly fulfilled, if people pay? Perhaps it is because people have established a rank order of priorities in their expenditure and paying is a signal of the degree of need. People will then consume exactly what they need of the service, and no more. But can we take it for granted that needs are comparable, that people are not ignorant or inarticulate, and that there ability to pay for basic human needs is not in question? It is possible to argue strongly for non-market allocation of education and health on the basis of the arguments made earlier about the inability of some market participants to compete successfully.

There will also be problems about market allocation if the goods are such that their allocation via the price mechanism is unsuitable. In the case of blood, for instance, if it is sold and bought donors will have an incentive to sell it even if it will bring harm to those who use it (eg AIDS). Should it be the case that people can sell their

kidneys for transplant purposes?   If the market is permitted
to allocate resources in those areas it encroaches on spheres
of human interaction in which market relations have no place
(104), and it also exploits those who need to sell.
Allocation via the market mechanism is not always ethically
desirable, and once that it admitted it may be difficult to
draw the moral line between differing market situations.

     We now come to the question of the degree of freedom
assumed and guaranteed by the market. The whole conception
of market freedom hinges in the first instance on the
assumption that people <u>can</u> participate in the market.   In
other words, it may be that people are free from constraints
on choice, at least notionally, but they may not be free to
exercise those choices. Freedom of choice exists in the
market only on the neo-classical assumption of given tastes
which are stable, measurable and objectifiable.   Economists
and politicians envisage producers and consumers as acting in
the full knowledge of what they want, and as knowing how to
get it.   But the link between choice and tastes or
preferences is not always predictable, and in any case how
'free' is our freedom of choice? In the first place, we may
choose what we do not actually prefer because of impulse or
ignorance of the complexity of goods. How capable are most
of us of judging the relative merits of hi-fi systems or
cameras?   Also, how extensive is the choice set, do you have
a genuine option?   In what sense are you 'freer' if you
choose the obviously more desirable - i.e. longer life?

     Nor do tastes remain stable - they are affected by
advertising, by the tastes of others (105) as well as by
technocracy and the way in which we perceive the performance
of the system as a whole. We tend to prefer those goods
which are likely to give us status in the eyes of others,
even when in an objective sense they do not appeal.   We
become more sensitive to our relative position in the
'possessions' stakes the more able we are to compete.   Does

economic progress actually exacerbate the resentment of inequalities? Free markets give participants freedom of choice in the negative sense — i.e. freedom from constraints. But that freedom is illusory if choices are structured, manipulated and thus inadequate reflections of real wants.

The importance of all this is that the system determines not only tastes, but actual wants. The market dictum that producers produce what the market wants is in practice untrue. It is much truer to say that producers decide what to produce on the basis of corporate objectives, technological objectives and power choices and they persuade consumers that this is what they really want. Galbraith (106), for instance, questions the assumptions that consumers are not influenced by producers. Producers seek security, they have a protective purpose and will seek to control quantity and price. Large producers will dominate the system, with small firms operating at the periphery. Large firms also have a persuasive influence on the public authorities. The total selling enterprise serves the real goals of the system. Advertising and market research are used to sell; innovation is used to create wants even when consumers resist, as in the case of electronic banking.

The link assumed by the market between tastes and welfare is also open to challenge. What we freely choose may not be what we want in the end. Hirsch argues (107) that whereas basic needs are satisfied by the intrinsic characteristics of commodities, other needs are satisfied by their extrinsic characteristics — eg the social context of their use. This satisfaction is limited firstly by the fact that the oversupply of commodities causes a diminution in their value because of congestion, and secondly because an increase in their supply causes them to be held in less esteem socially. Hirsch's theory is about what one might term externalities in consumption brought about by the extent to which others also consume them — one satisfaction characteristic is therefore assumed to be exclusivity. It is therefore not the case that the market's allocation of goods is necessarily beneficial. The cultural commitment to growth begins to look like an individualist fallacy — a case of the individually rational pursuing the collectively unattainable. Even if we have more our welfare may be less.

Freedom to choose also implies that we can operate in the market within the constraints dictated by income. But even when we have acquired what we want we are still constrained. Consumption is an activity which is done under constraints imposed not only by income but also by time. Becker (108) distinguishes between 'high-time' and 'low-time' goods. The rich have to spend a great deal on goods which are quickly consumed, because otherwise they would not have the time to consume their income. Schumacher (109) makes the distinction between optimum consumption and maximum consumption. Orthodoxy maximises consumption by the optimal pattern of production rather than maximising satisfaction by the optimal pattern of consumption, which could involve actually limiting consumption of goods. such as fatty foods, which bring costs as well as benefits. Maximising satisfaction in this sense might well involve consuming less rather than more.

In a foundational sense market economies fail to guarantee real freedom. If our interpretation of the value of freedom is grounded only by our experience as market agents it can only be an impoverished one. Any adequate interpretation of freedom, even in a market context, would have to include the concept of positive freedom as well as negative freedom. Sen (110) has developed an approach which focuses on a person's 'capability' as an index of his welfare — capability to do or to be. This idea extends the notion of freedom beyond the simplistic idea of freedom of choice. Freedom is capability; capability in a market context is determined by a persons entitlements, which are made up of income from labour or produce from land (his 'endowment'), combined with his exchange entitlement — what he can lay claim to in exchange for that. These depend on the characteristics of the society and a person's position in it. Many options will not be available to the poor, but the freedom of the rich and famous may also be limited — for instance, because it will be impossible for a king to go to a public bar. Entitlements also depend on production and earning opportunities, as well as trading opportunities, social security provisions, and taxation. In advanced societies the state provides minimum entitlement guarantees, but in third world countries famine as a phenomenon can still exist side by side with adequate food supplies (111) simply because people's entitlements are inadequate to purchase food. This is an example of the fact that the market paradigm fails to explain much of what actually happens. The economic problem is not always shortage in relation to wants, but failure of ability to play the market game.

But 'entitlements' in the sense of fredom to participate in markets only partially of guarantees real market freedom. The conversion of commodities into capabilities depends on a complex series of interlinked factors. For instance, the ability to benefit from food (nutrition) depends on one's health situation (body weight, metabolic rate, activity level), as much as on food intake. Real freedom is defined as much by the capability to benefit from commodities as to purchase them. Capability is about functioning; capabilities can be thought of as allowing the attainment of 'functioning bundles'. It is much more sensible to think of capabilities as objects of value than to think of commodities as happiness. Capabilities are valued because they reflect freedom to live well, to achieve happiness, to control one's own life. Different commodity bundles can produce the same capability — i.e. to be healthy (112); and any given commodity bundle can produce different capabilities. The possession of a car, for instance. can open up new employment and new leisure possibilities. Capabilities are thus the negative reciprocal of powerlessness — not being in control of one's own life.

The interpretation of freedom as 'freedom to choose' in a market context is an inadequate notion of freedom because it is achieved only at the expense of others — i.e. by competition. But to see competition as a value or a virtue ignores the reality of inequalities of power and the constraints on freedom which come from both inside and outside the person. Furthermore, freedom to choose and to compete in the market has a hollow ring to it when we remember that it is based on entitlement, and this for us stems from property rights. But these are themselves a restriction on the freedom of someone else to use what we claim — in other words, our freedom is founded on a limitation of freedom for others. The fact that we accept both the desirability of this 'ideal-type' allocative system in the face of theoretical and practical evidence of its implications for human welfare says much for the extent to which we are wedded to the values it embodies. It is only when we widen our notion of freedom in the market to include ideas of 'capability' that we gain some insight into the poverty of our cultural understanding of freedom.

===

NOTES—CHAPTER FOUR.

1.   This view is argued in Phillips and Mounce (1970).

2.   See MacIntyre (1981) p.18 for a discussion of what
      should be accepted or rejected in emotivism.

3.   We can see not just the relevance but also the authority
      of moral judgement as being grounded in the facts.   See
      Hughes (1979)

4.   See essays in Hudson (ed).(1969).

5.   As argued by Hare (1952), (1963).

6.   Phillips and Mounce (1970) p.54.

7.   Cooper (1980) p.97.

8.   For the analogy see Emmet (1979).

9.   The rational component in value judgement allows Sen 's
      distinction between basis and non-basic judgements.   See
      Sen (1970) Ch.5.

10.   Taylor (1980) p.35 discusses the criteria for what is to
      count as an evaluational   principle.   His   criteria   of
      generality, universalisability and priority status for
      such principles do not, however, cope with the problem
      of conflict and hierarchy of values as well as does
      Sen's notion of basic and non-basic judgements.

11.   For a discussion of the role of virtue see MacIntyre
      (1981).

12.   See Olthuis (1968) for treatment of this.

13.   Smelser (1962).

14.   Rescher (1969) Ch.3.

15.   Hare (1952), (1963).

16.   Sen (1970) Ch.5.

17.   This contradicts views such as those of Robbins (1932)
      p.62, who says that such arguments are simply a matter
      of 'thy blood or mine'.

18.   See e.g. Fourez (1979) for the idea of 'cultural
      stories'.

19.   Ullman-Margalit (1977) p.13.

20.   Ibid. p.9ff.

21.   Rescher (1969) Ch.3 argues that value change is endemic

in social process.

22. Kaysen (1967) p.35.

23. Nichomachean Ethics Bk.3. Ch.5. 1114 a 30f.

24. See Kohlberg (1976) for the basis of this in terms of a theory of moral development.

25. Myrdal (1958) Ch.5.

26. Ibid. p.58.

27. For an account of the development of the idea of intentionality see Findlay (1970). As we saw earlier, Lonergan uses this idea.

28. Ibid.p.17.

29. In Brentano (1874). Discussed by Findlay (1970) p.16-24.

30. In Meinong (1969). See Findlay (1970) pp.24-36.

31. Lonergan (1971) p.32.

32. Ibid. p.240.

33. Habermas (1961).

34. Werner (1958). Quoted Tarascio (1980) p.169 fn.3.

35. Tarascio (1980).

36. See eg. Heilbronner (1973), Machlup (1978), Klappholz (1964).

37. Sen (1982), in essay entitled ' Description as choice'.

38. See Loasby (1976) p.194-8.

39. Problems have been variously seen as efficient transformation, allocation of scarce resources, distribution, market failure, and incompetent market performance. Goals have been visualised in terms of opulence, growth, efficiency, equality, justice, need provision.

40. Myrdal (1953) Ch.7, Section 3.

41 . This is the view taken by Karl Polanyi, in (1945) who saw economic behaviour in terms of reciprocity and redistribution within a social context. For a discussion of this point see Schneider, (1974) Ch.1.

42. Andreski (1972) p.140/1.

43. See Klappholz (1964) p. 98/9. Hume's dictum was meant in a purely logical sense - i.e. in the sense of seeing

233

'ought' statements as isolated from rule, practice, value system or culture.

44. See Lipsey's distinction between the logical and the ethical 'ought' (1979 fn.p.7.)
45. See essays in Hudson (ed) (1969).
46. Gordon (1977) p.540.
47. Hudson (1969) (ed) p.146.
48. Mackie (1977) p.73.
49. Korff (1968) cites the Kinsey report as an example of this point.
50. Evidence on women in employment is presented in Rubery (1988).
51. Minford (1983) on unemployment.
52. Sen (1970) p.57.
53. Myrdal (1953) p.56.
54. Ibid p.66.
55. See Deane (1978) – chapter on Ricardo.
56. See Weisskopf (1977) who argues that people have been 'bent' in psychological terms in the interests of economic progress.
57. See Brittain (1973) for survey of opinions on relationship between public welfare and private avarice.
58. Smith (1776) Book V Ch.2.
59. By eg. Harsanyi in Sen and Williams (1982).
60. See introduction to Sen and Williams (1982).
61. Ibid.
62. Ibid p.21.
63. Nessel (1984) in Boulding (ed.)
64. Scitovsky (1977) p.145.
65. Sen (1984) p.513.
66. Rescher (1972) pp.15ff.
67. Sen (1982) esp.pp.339ff.
68. Rescher (1966b) p.58/9.
69. Pigou (1952) p.24.
70. See Sen (1984), essay entitled 'Rights and Capabilities'.
71. See Hollis and Nell (1975) p.19 for a discussion of

these differences.

72. This approach sees preference as revealed by choice. In
     this context values are simply what dictates choice, the
     value system is simply the system which generates rules
     for choice. The programme of general equilibrium relies
     on the existence of a connection between choice and
     preference, and between preference and welfare.   But
     these connections are not necessarily operative; choice
     behaviour may not represent preference (altruism), and
     preferences may not reflect welfare (alcoholism).   See
     Sen (1982) — Behaviour and the concept of preference.

73. Lowe (1967) queries why maximum output is seen as
     optimum. In a situation where resources are limited and
     survival depends on getting as much as possible out of
     what is available, products become imtermediate goods
     essential for realising the good life.   But where
     resources are plentiful why should welfare be defined
     solely in terms of getting most from least?

74. All of the meanings of the word 'rational'   are
     value—laden. 'Rational' can be taken to be the converse
     of irrational, non—rationl, emotional,   immoderate,
     unreasonable, or empirical. For a discussion of the
     main issues concerning economic rationality see
     C.A.Tisdell — Rational behaviour as a basis for economic
     theories, in Benn and Mortimore (1976).

75. See Simon (1976) in Latsis (ed).

76. Elster (1979) p.113.

77. Sen (1982) — essay entitled ' Rational fools'.

78. The actual example Sen gives of commitment is that of
     workers in China who were asked to make a commitment to
     the values of the group but failed to respond with
     increased effort.
     There are other ways, too, in which welfare can be
     interdependent. Our welfare may increase, for instance,
     only if B's welfare diminishes (malevolence), or if B's
     welfare increases (sympathy). Our we may value B's
     welfare, but not our own, or we may even get utility

from a diminution in our own welfare (masochism). See Boulding in Hook (ed) (1967).

79. Matthews (1981).

80. Sen (1982) essay entitled 'Choice orderings and morality'.

81. Harsanyi (1982) in Sen and Williams (1982).

82. Matthews (1981), p.300.

83. Blum (1970) p.160 sees Christianity as challenging what is seen as a universal moral position rather than a historically relative one.

84. For the tensions and conflicts inherent in this approach see Peter Taylor-Gooby (1983) in Ellis and Kumar (ed).

85. See Acton (1971) p.58ff.

86. Schumacher (1980) p.28.

87. Laborem Exercens pps.15-17. Technology can be the enemy as well as the ally of man.

88. Habermas (1974) Ch.6 points to the way in which capitalism splits up the metabolic circle described by Marx whereby man as subject separates himself from the object of his creativity by production and reunites with it by consumption — (the Hegelian subject/object split translated into the language of production and consumption.) Because of the idea of 'surplus value' what went away is not what comes back.

89. Habermas (1970) p.66.

90. Ayres (1980).

91. See Sen (1984) essay entitled 'On some debates in capital theory'.

92. Sen (1982) essay entitled 'Equality of what'.

93. Sen (1984) essay entitled 'Economics and the family'.

94. Becker's work on the family exemplifies this assumption. See eg (1976).

95. Streeten (1981) p.21.

96. Rawls (1972). For a critique of Rawls see Rich (1984).

97. Hirsch (1977).

98. Hayek (1960), (1976).

99. Habermas, eg.(1976) pp.82/3.

100. See Barber (1977) in Dworkin (ed.)
101. Acton (1971) p.8.
102. Traditional alternative explanations of this mechanism are Marshall's 'auctioneer', and Walras' 'tatonnment' process.
103. Acton (1971) p.33ff.
104. Titmuss (1973) Ch.1.
105. Duesenberry (1962).
106. In eg Galbraith (1952).
107. Hirsch (1977).
108. Becker (1976).
109. Schumacher (1974) Ch.4.
110. Sen (1984), Essay entitled 'Goods and people'.
111. See Sen (1981), Woodham—Smith (1962). This latter is the authoritative study on the Irish famine of 1945—50 caused proximately by the failure of the potato crop, but intensified by the insistence of the British Treasury that wheat should be exported from Ireland because it could command higher prices in the UK.
112. Sen (1984) p.512.

==

CHAPTER FIVE - ACTION IN A SOCIAL CONTEXT.

i. Introduction.

This chapter focuses on the moment of action, the moment
where we enquire what has to be done, how we ought to respond
in action to the exigencies of the situation. Just as the
two previous chapters explored the consequences for action of
our cultural context, so this chapter explores the
consequences for action of our existence as social beings. It
would be illegitimate to discuss action without setting it in
its social context, because we are never individuals acting
in isolation. Our actions are always 'situated' in the sense
that our decisions are influenced by, and form part of, the
rules and social practices of the social structures within
which we live.

Action in a social context is interaction with others,
and there is no satisfactory way of describing or
interpreting that action except in terms of the meaning given
to it by the social actors themselves. We can distinguish
between two types of interaction - even though the
distinction may in practice not always be watertight. Some
social interaction happens in an institutionalised context -
within organisations such as companies or educational
establishments, for instance. There interaction is quite
closely patterned, conforming to the norms laid down by that
particular organisation for the performance of those roles.
This is in part a functional type of interaction, designed to
achieve the goals of the organisation. There, social actors
play roles which are more or less closely defined.

Not all social action is functional in that narrow sense.
Much of our daily lives are spent interacting with people in
situations where roles are not so clearly specified,

interaction not so closely patterned. We can think, for instance, of the supermarket, the pub, or the church as locations for this type of interaction. Interaction in those cases is simply a kind of interdependence which can be direct, as in face-to-face 'positioned' encounters, or it can be indirect, where people do not actually interact on a personal level — in a football crowd, for instance.

The fact that action happens in the context of interaction has two consequences which are important for the argument of this study. The first of these is the issue of the unintended consequences of social action. Interaction constructs a chain of consequences which are neither predicted nor intended by actors. Not only do the consequences of action structure outcomes, but they provide the context for choice of future action in a social context and thus act as carriers of social change. Both role-type and non role-type interaction will give rise to unintended consequences, but in varying degrees, because institutions as functional social systems are deliberately constructed so as to be able to monitor and eliminate as many of the unintended consequences of action as possible. Unintended consequences of action in a social context are one of the most striking examples of 'doing what we do not intend to do'. Their existence highlights the distinction between action and agency — action is what we do, agency is what our action does. The fact that the social context of action introduces the factor of unintended consequences which become the unacknowledged conditions of future action breaks the link between action and agency which is always assumed. Action is not only shaped by the social world but is also as agency constitutive of social reality, and because it is that reality which provides the forum for the realisation of the Kingdom the process becomes theologically significant.

The second issue is the way in which action is conditioned by the institutional structures within which we

live. Initial exploration of this issue will provide the
opportunity to suggest a methodology by which theological
notions of 'structural evil' can be analysed. The notion of
'structure', although contentious in terms of social theory,
has become not only a theologically available concept, but a
theologically fashionable one (1). However, theology lacks
a systematic attempt to explore and define those structures
which are so clearly the repository of 'structural sin', and
is thus unable to speak with confidence of what salvation in
the structural context might mean. This can lead to a
simplistic view of 'salvation' as the adoption of alternative
political ideologies, or alternatively as the achievement of
some form of social change. Yet the concept of 'social
structure' is of fundamental theological importance. The
power of the Spirit to make us one, for which Jesus prays in
St John's Gospel, can only be operative in the context of
community existence, of group interaction in a recursive and
therefore historical context. It is only in a social context
that we can collectively be a church, only in a social
context that we can fulfil the Gospel demand to love our
enemies. It is surely not possible to theologise effectively
about these matters unless we gain a perspective on the
domain of the social which will enable us to endow it with
agreed content and meaning.

The idea of 'social structure' can be interpreted in
many different ways — widely and generally, as 'social
relations', or more narrowly as in the case of
'institutional' structures; it is this latter context that
the idea of structural rules or norms more particularly
applies. We can also talk more generally, for instance, of
technology and the structures, or patterns of existence, it
imposes on both society and institution. An alternative
perspective might focus on the political or economic
structures which form the parameters of existence in a given
society. All of these ideas need to be drawn into a unified
whole in order to establish a useful framework within which

to examine the actions of the person of faith. In this chapter I propose to situate this problem within one particular context – that of organisational structures. I argue that our participation as actors in organisational groups serves to condition our action in a variety of different ways, thus constraining our freedom to 'do what we intend to do'.

There are two questions which run like threads through the material dealt with in this chapter, questions which need to be answered if we are to draw conclusions as to the interpretation of action in a social context.
1. What is the relationship between person and structure? Is the social context of action in some senses external to the person, functioning as a determinant or constraint to his decisions? Or are person and structure inextricably bound together in some other kind of interrelationship?
2. What kind of autonomy can we accord to the person whose actions are seen in a social context? Does the acting person simply react in some functionalist sense to the exigencies of the system, or act merely as a carrier of its structural characteristics? Or is the person to be seen as an autonomous 'individual', whose social context serves merely as some kind of 'plastic creation'?
The next section will outline a framework of analysis which not only provides a precise delineation of the notion of 'structure', but does so without sacrificing the importance of the concept of agency, the capability to reproduce – or alter – that structure in the light of both intended and unintended consequences of action. The following sections will examine the way in which organisational structures, formed as they are for the specific tasks of decision and consequent action, constrain the actions of the person in such a way as to give a particular perspective to the notion of agency – one which decisively separates it from its basis in conscious intentionality.

ii. The social as context: agency and structure.

Social theory has taken a variety of positions on the relationship between person and structure on the one hand and on the issue of personal autonomy in a social context on the other (2). For the most part, these explanations have maintained one single perspective while sacrificing others. Functionalist or structuralist arguments disregard the person and see society as a constraint on action. Interpretative accounts based on notions of action and meaning pay no attention to problems of structure as constraining or enabling action. For theological purposes we need a more comprehensive framework which can contain our reflection on the nature of 'action for the Kingdom'. We need a vision of the way in which action continually serves to recreate the social world as structure and practice; we also need an understanding of how that action emerges as a consequence of the features of that world. This viewpoint has to be applicable not only in a general social context, but also particularly in the specific context of economic organisations, the paradigm institution in our society. This will enable us to develop a perspective on decision-taking which will highlight the constraints on individual action of that particular social context. To do this, however, we must first attempt to develop an adequate theretical framework — adequate, that is, in an analytical sense.

Giddens, drawing on the work of his predecessors (3), attempts to develop an approach which gives weight to the significance both of structure and of agency. The virtue of his presentation from a theological point of view is that it provides an integrated account not only of the relationship between the· individual and the social, but also of the dimensions of 'structure' in a way which can serve as a heuristic in theological contexts. Furthermore, Giddens does this without minimising the theologically important concept of agency as power to change — although not necessarily to control — the world (4).

Giddens rejects the idea that action is in any sense 'determined' by social forces. Social forces influence, rather than constrain action. There are different aspects to this process. The consequences of past action constitute the social forum for current action as they are reflexively monitored by agents. Questions of language and of meaning on the one hand, and the spatial/temporal constitution of society on the other, also form part of the forum. Societies are thus more than the sum of the individuals, they also have 'structural' properties which provide the context of action and shape social forces. But — and this is the crucial point — these structural properties of society are not to be seen as some kind of 'patterning' of social relations external to the actors, they are simply what is generated and reproduced by action, in ways not entirely controllable by those actors. There is no such thing as a distinctive category of structural explanation, only an interpretation of the modes in which varying forms of constraint influence human action (5) and form its context.

How should we characterise these 'structural properties'? Have they any kind of 'existence'? Social structure, argues Giddens, should be characterised as 'rules and resources', and is hence not to be specified as system-as-practice, but rather as the 'becoming of the possible'. Society (and here we can think in general or in more specifically organisational tems) is produced and reproduced as praxis in every historical moment in the context of its rules and resources within a linguistic mode —"the constitution of language as meaningful is inseparable from the constitution of forms of social life as continuing practices."(6). Every social item, as Marx says in Grundrisse (7) is only a vanishing moment in society; it is continually constituted and reconstituted.

Structures are produced and reproduced. The continuity of social reproduction is ensured by the fact that actors reflexively monitor social practice in the light of the unintended consequences of past action; these in turn become the unacknowledged conditions of future action. We make, but we cannot control our own history. Social activity is thus constituted not only spatially and temporally, but also paradigmatically in the sense that the structure, seen as rules and resources, is both context and outcome of that activity. 'Structure' is thus something internal to individuals as memory and practical consciousness of social practices, rather than something in any sense external. It is reified in discursive consciousness, and becomes historical reality in the context of action. 'Agent' and 'structure' thus do not form a dualism, but a duality.

The task of social theory — and theology — must therefore be to reformulate conceptions of human being and doing constitutive of social reproduction and social transformation, rather than as action-out-of-context. Such a perspective diverges from the emphasis of analytic philosophy on the connection between action, intention and purpose, because action and intention cannot be inevitably linked. Actions can have indirect consequences — a dismissal from employment, for instance, can lead to a suicide. The actor's intention may be achieved otherwise than by the agency of the actor, and behaviour may produde a different outcome to the one intended (8) — for instance, if enough people decide not to turn up for a meeting it will be cancelled. Purpose, too, must be divorced from agency, because purpose need not be translated into action, nor is it necessarily logically consistent with the agent's knowledge. Nor are motive and reason to be seen as the same thing, because reasons have to be given in institutional as well as individual terms. We can only study the phenomenon of the reproduction/ transformation of the institutionalised aspects

of social systems by the unintended consequences of action if
we can use developed notions of agency and intention in order
to identify what 'unintended consequences' are. The weakness
of functionalism is that it has no concept of agency, and
therefore no way of dealing with structural modification of
society.(9).

Looking at these ideas in more detail requires us to
make an initial distinction between structure, system and
what Giddens calls 'structuration'. 'Structure' is the rules
and resources, organised as properties of social systems,
enshrined, for instance, in the constitutions of nation
states or the articles of association of companies. In a more
specific sense 'structure' refers to the institutionalised
features or structural properties of social systems. These
will take the form of rules or codes governing relationships
which will be stabilised across time and space. These rules
will govern the way in which the society organises the
production, for instance, or education, or the political
dimension of societal life. Structural properties, or
insitutionalised features of social systems, will be
organised hierarchically into structural principles which
govern the reproduction of societal totalities. It has also
to be recognised, however, that structural principles can
operate in contradiction within a given societal totality
such as a nation—state. Alternative views may exist as to
how a given aspect of social life should be organised, and,
given the freedom to put these ideas into practice, groups
may elect to be governed by a variety of different codes.
If this is the case there will be conflict at different
levels between actors or groups.

The idea of 'system' refers to those reproduced
relations between actors or collectives which are organised
as regular social practices; these relations will be
conducted, as procedures or ways of behaving, according to
the rules or structural properties of that system. Relations

can be self-regulatory, as would be the case of they were purely functional, but they can also allow for information filtering and consequent change - i.e. reflexive self-regulation. Systems are often rendered functional by the use of non-human means. We talk about payments systems, for instance, when we refer to the way in which debts are settled. In this case we can discern the element of human agency, but also the existence of non-human (computerised) agency. In the case of the examination system the element of human agency is perhaps more pronounced, whereas stock control systems require very little human intervention. 'System', then, is concerned with relations, structure with the rules and resources which govern those relations. The second-order idea of 'structuration' refers to the conditions governing the continuity or transmutation of structures, and therefore to the reproduction of social systems. What is involved here is a study of the modes of social reproduction as done by actors using the relevant rules and resources in the context both of the unintended consequences and the unacknowledged conditions of action. These modes of social reproduction will govern the balance between continuity and change in any given social context. 'Structuration' is therefore a concept which expresses the dynamic dimension of structure and system.

Returning to the idea of structure as rules, Giddens argues that rules are to be seen not just as normative, but also as codes of signification. Rules in the general social sense are about ways of interacting in encounter in the looser sense of social practice rather than in the more formal sense of, say, a game of chess. They are formulas, techniques, proceedures for beginning, sustaining and terminating encounters. Harre (10) gives the example of the way in which we introduce people to one another. Rules are inherent in the constitution of social meaning; they also provide sanctions for social conduct. They are mainly known in practical consciousness rather than in discursive consciousness, which is the level at which they become articulated and hence interpreted — in other words, they are they are Schutz's 'cookbook recipes'(11). (Discursive and practical consciousness refer to psychological mechanisms of recall whereby the agent maintains an unarticulated understanding of the basis of action). This view of rules as norms is the most flexible possible. In certain social situations rules become something more specific — as in the case of laws or regulations governing conduct. In the context of formally constituted groups such as committees, for instance, the rules governing procedure are embodied in written formulae such as standing orders, although they can also be embodied in unwritten conventions of behaviour. But in everyday and non-organisational situations rules simply define the ways in which we deal with one another.

Resources provide the parameters for the operation of rules; together, therefore, they constitute social structure. Resources are also the means whereby structures of domination can be generatred which will facilitate the use of power in social situations. Resources are of two kinds — authoritative resources (human) and allocative resources (material). Allocative resources are the material features of environment, the means of material production, and produced goods themselves — in other words, the physical context of social existence. Authoritative resources refer to the way in which social life is organised, not merely in the narrower sense of organising human beings in association, but in the more diffuse sense of organising social time/space. In general day— to— day interaction social reproduction happens through the routinised conduct of agenta in the context of those resources. In organisations, on the other hand, there will be an element of monitoring and reflexive regulation of this proces which will be an essential element in institutional practice.

Social actors thus recreate social practices in a time—space context, using their knowledgeability to interpret and monitor past practice. This is a process which depends on rationalisation (intentionality as process) in the context of practical consciousness, rather than rationalisation at a level of consciousness where purpose, intention, reason and motive are articulated discursively. Giddens envisages a kind of hierarchy of motivation which extends all the way 'down' through discursive and practical consciousness to the unconscious (12). The depth of this internal hierarchy will reflect the life experience of the actor. Motivation generates a person's overall plans and projects rather than triggering specific action as such. So that action itself is seen as a continuous flow of conduct, and unacknowledged conditions of action stand outside the connecting links between motivation — rationalisation — reflexivity. So also do the unintended consequences which in their turn become the conditions of action. In other words, not every action is 'intended' in the narrowly rational sense of the word.(13) Most social interaction happens in a 'routine' manner, and social practices are simply recreated unless there is a real reason — arising, for instance, out of the monitoring of past action — for changing ways of interacting.

But the social actor is not only reflexive, he is also agent, the driving force in social process. Agency does not only involve intention, it involves capability, as well as power in the sense of transformative capacity excercised through resources. What the actor 'does' as outcome of motivation, rationalisation and reflexivity is different to what he 'does' in the consequential sense because the outcome of action includes unintended consequences which then form the unacknowledged conditions of action. Agency is thus best seen as involving events of which the individual is the perpetrator, rather than as resulting in 'acts' — events being the concrete social data, acts with all their consequences.

Agency happens in the context of 'co-presence'. Actors are 'positioned' in circumstances of co-presence, in daily time-space. The structural properties of social systems can therefore usefully be characterised as position-practice relations. This social 'positioning' is usually thought of as role. Goffman and others emphasise the 'given' character of role (14), but Giddens sees position as the more central idea, because he prefers to think of 'role' as implying the existence of attached rights and obligations (15), which happen specifically in an organisational context.

We now come to the central question of whether, or in what way, we should regard the actor as constrained by his social context - by society as such - in the carrying out of his decisions. There are clearly ways in which the idea of constraint is realistic. There are material constraints which derive from the character of the material world and from the physical qualities of the body. There are constraints in the sense of negative sanctions deriving from punitive responses on the part of some agents towards others. There are also 'structural' constraints which derive from the contextuality of action - ie from the given character of structural properties vis-a-vis situated actors - for instance in the case of a labour contract. Marx's 'relations of capitalism' is an example of such a structural constraint (16). The nature of constraint is clearly historically variable both in relation to circumstances and in relation to the forms of knowledgability that agents possess.

But it is simplistic to see human action as merely 'constrained' by the social context. Giddens argues that the correct` perspective is to see 'society' as not only constraining, but also enabling, action to take place. The inherent relation between structure and agency is that structure is recursively implicated in all social action. Structure provides the conditions for action, so that enablement is at least as important a perspective as constraint. It is through structure as rules and resources that agency happens, that power is exercised as a routine element in social reproduction. Actors are 'empowered' by structures, and agency-as-power is possible only because of the enabling property of structure. Power thus becomes something to be seen as as structures of social domination rather than as something excercised by persons.

The question then arises as to whether Giddens' concept of 'structuration' gives sufficient weight to constraint (17). Durkheim – and other structural sociologists – have seen constraint purely in terms of socialisation by institutions that predated and outlasted individual lives (18). But his perspective ignores the fact that such socialisation has also enabled the life of individuals as agents to take place, even though the time- space dimension will mean that actors have less of a reproductive transformative impact in the longer term. Durkheim sees social reproduction in terms of 'emergent properties' outside the consciousness of individuals, and social facts as external in a naturalistic sense. This is a view of constraint as causation which limits action, and it is replaced in the Giddens perspective of structuration by structure as implicated in freedom of action.

In fact, Durkheim's views are only one example of a genre of social theory which sees social process and change as some function of evolution, or historical determinism, or structural determinism. All the proponents of these ideas either tend to make general principles out of specific historical circumstances, or they argue as evolutionists, or in terms of biological models of social development. Human history cannot be evolutionary because it is reflexively constituted and therefore cannot be causal. Because it is continually constituted it is continually changing, and although it may embody elements of progress there can be no justification for believing that progress is linear.

Furthermore, none of these perspectives allow for the

existence of 'perverse' or 'emergent' effects — for the consequences of action which are unintended and unforeseen by the actor (19). We can think of these effects in two ways. On the one hand, there is the fact, always recognised by theology, that what we do as individual actors may have outcomes very different to those we intend. Some years ago an inquiry into a plane disaster heard that the pilot, always a short-tempered man, had been provoked into an argument by a colleague. He subsequently walked furiously across the tarmac to his plane, took off at too steep an angle and crashed, killing 118 passengers. Everyday life is full of such examples — the careless match which starts a fatal blaze, the casual conversation which changes a life.

But there is also another class of effect which can be termed the 'efects of composition' — the unintended consequences of social action by thousands of individuals acting together, doing the same thing because they all respond in the same routinised way to social situations. Individual agency becomes magnified as collective agency and 'overshoots', bringing consequences intended by nobody. For instance, if everyone tries to go to the seaside on a fine day traffic jams will prevent everyone getting there — a consequence of collective action. If everyone rushes to the bank to withdraw their deposits because they fear the bank might fail. The inevitable result of this collective belief will be a failure of the bank — the collective belief has acted as a self-fulfilling prophecy. Merton's classic example of this (20) is the way in which whites in the US after the First World War, by not allowing blacks from the South to join unions, created a class of scab labour; they then used the strike-breaking behaviour of the blacks as an argument against their unionisation on the grounds that they were clearly incapable of being loyal to a union.

The repercussions of collective agency can be far-reaching. The preference of United States consumers for hamburgers has led to the establishment of ranches in South America dedicated to the production of lean beef. The growth of this type of ranching has led to deforestation and hence to the destruction of the natural habitat of birds whose migratory habits have changed so that they no longer visit the United States. This has led in turn to a proliferation of pests in farming areas and a consequent loss of income by American farmers. The resultant social and political effects are no doubt experienced by those who choose to eat hamburgers, but are almost certainly not perceived by them as having anything to do with that choice.

The effects of unintended consequences on the dynamics of social change will depend on the forms such consequences take. Emergent effects can magnify or reinforce the existing direction of social action, as in the case of black racism cited above. They can have the result of reversing or neutralising the consequences of action, as in the case where groups (such as consumer groups) set up to fight power blocs have the effect of neutralising such power. They can inject a stabilising effect into a situation, as in the case where the development of industrial relations procedures results in the institutionalisation and therefore reduction of conflict. Alternatively, they can introduce multiple emergent effects, as in the case where individual choices to move out of inner city areas, or to opt for prestigious educational establishments, introduce deteriorating and segregating consequences into the systems in question. They can also produce new forms of social phenomena, as in the argument made by Parsons (21) that the development of the nuclear family was a direct social consequence of the division of labour.

The unintended consequences of social action can thus be good or bad. They can create costs or yield benefits on both an individual and a collective level. There are situations where collective benefit brings individual loss. For instance, it would appear that people become less satisfied and more frustrated with their relative standard of living the higher the overall standard of economic welfare in the community. Within the educational system, the improvement of opportunity for all and the creation of a meritocracy has had the effect of increasing competition and thereby disadvantaging those who for reasons of background or circumstance are less able to compete. Looked at from a different point of view, the widening of educational chances has contributed to the welfare of the less favoured, but has resulted in the marginalisation of all young people in that all feel themselves threatened by the risk of failure. In a different context, demands by workers in industrial countries for wage rises cause inflation and consequent recession in those countries as their competitiveness declines. The resulting reduction in demand for primary products lowers their prices and hence the incomes and standard of living of Third World producers. In an attempt to cope with this governments of those countries devote increasing amounts of land to cash crops so that the production of food for home consumption declines. During the height of the Ethiopian famine Ethiopian melons were on sale in the London fruit markets as Christmas fare for those who were contributing money for the relief of the famine.

Theology has always recognised the issue of responsibility for the unintended consequences of individual action. Aristotle and Aquinas both analysed the question in terms of willing and intention on the one hand and agency on the other. Judgement was a key component; responsibility was never taken further than the limits of agency, but actors were deemed to be responsible for the unintended consequences of which they were the agent but which might have been foreseen — the match in the forest, for instance. However, theology has always been individualist and has never tackled the issue of collective responsibility in a social context. We need a theological perspective on responsible action at a group level. Lonergan's work on economics, although not specifically theological, is one example (22) of this type of thinking. This unpublished work is based on the central idea that the phenomenon of economic fluctuations – booms and slumps – derives from an inadequate understanding by economists, economic agents and governments of 'discernible criteria' inherent in the productive process which can give guidance for responsible action. He has aimed at "working out an economic analysis that might yield an intrinsic basis for moral precepts in production, exchange and finance" (23). He believed that responsible behaviour was necessary both by the community of academic economists and by economic agents as a group; the former had the task of developing a more adequate method in economics which would convey the required understanding, the latter as producers and consumers needed to adapt their behaviour to the exigencies of cyclical behaviour in the economy. To do this would require a renunciation of self-interested behaviour. Lonergan was very aware of "the danger of self-interest coming to mean in economics the equivalent of Realpolitik in affairs of state". (24) Policy-makers, too, need to undertake the measures required to make the system function smoothly, altering policy so as to generate the rate of saving required at different phases of the cycle, rather than undertaking economic policies for short-term political gain.

I have spent some time in discussing Giddens' work and the issues which it raises because I believe that it can be normative for theology. In theological terms it gives us a profound view of society as continually reproduced. God created the world, but it is we who continually recreate the social order (25), and thus share in the work of creation. It is therefore we who are charged with the task of redeeming its sinful structures; we are thus not only co-creators but also co-redeemers. In the same way that action is self-transformative in a personal sense as praxis, so also is action socially transformative in a creative sense. Implicit in the idea of social reproduction in the context of rules and resources is freedom of choice. We make our own history, we choose whether or not to perpetuate existing historical forms. We are responsible for both our world and for our fellow humans within it. However, in retrospective terms we cannot control the course of our own history, because we cannot determine the unintended consequences of what we do, nor can we take account of the unacknowledged conditions of our actions. We are responsible, but we do not control; social systems get transformed in ways not intended. Here in the social context we see again the Pauline dilemma of Romans 7.14-25, where the outcome of action is other than intended, Whereas in a personal sense the reason for this is to be found in weakness or inconsistency, in a social sense it is to be found in the unintended consequences of action. This divorce of agency from action means that in a consequentialist sense there are real limits to our freedom as human persons. What we want to do — in the sense of achieve — we cannot do; what we do not want as the outcome of our actions is what in fact happens.

What is also theologically important — because social action is constitutive of the Kingdom — is how all this hinges on the question of power. The attribute of agency — as power to perpetrate events and recreate or alter structures — is different for each one of us. We all create and recreate our own histories, but the possibilities of doing this are limited for many people by the actions of others who are consciously involved in producing and reproducing structures which have a profound effect on the lives of everyone. In a world which becomes increasingly interdependent people's destiny becomes ever more dependent on processes, whether they be political, economic or financial, which they not only do not control, but — and this is the ultimate in powerlessness — which they do not even understand. A change in the exchange rate can halve the farmer's income. A rise in interest rates can bankrupt the businessman. A merger can wipe out thousands of jobs. These structural features of our world do not stand outside agency, they are not acts of God or forces of nature. They are events perpetrated and perpetuated by agents who act in commodity markets, financial markets, foreign exchange markets, who take decisions in multinational companies and international organisations. The inbuilt structural properties of market volatility and of company and organisational chains of command provide the dynamics which carry the consequences of action into worldwide spheres of influence. The small man is powerless. Even governments as elected representatives of ordinary citizens cannot stand against the power of decisions taken in structures linked worldwide. The ebb and flow of individual destinies are less and less attributable to personal actions and capabilities, more and more determined by events totally outside the experience and comprehension of the person.

iii.   The organisational context of action.

Action is thus both enabled and constrained by the social context. The particular consequences of this for the acting person are twofold. On the one hand the social context provides the factual basis for action and hence determines its moral character, as well as conditioning its morality in the wider sense of 'outcome morality'. On the other hand the socially determined character of action as praxis helps to mould our outlook and thus acts as a self-transformative influence. It then conditions future action, not only in the contextual sense but also in the sense that what we do makes us what we are.

The context in which all this happens is largely organisational. We now consider the way in which that particular social context conditions action. The characteristic of organisations is that they are social groupings formed and managed with a particular objective in view, whether it be economic or political. Much of what goes on in the day-to-day activity of organisations is structured towards the achievement of organisational objectives, and we are the instruments through which organisational functioning happens. Our own actions in that context will be at least partly constrained by this requirement. The most obvious example here is that of the company. Company objectives can be formulated in a variety of ways — the company may aim to increase its market share, for instance, or to improve its sales or its overall image. Managers within the company may believe that the company growth is the only way to ensure long-term security. But the objective which forms the basis of all company behaviour is the necessity to make the maximum possible profit, not only to satisfy shareholders, but to provide a hedge against the possibility of takeover should shareholder loyalty weaken. All decision-taking within the organisation will thus be taken in the light of this requirement.

Organisational constraint on action in a day- to- day context has three different dimensions. There is firstly the fact that our interaction happens as role performance within the group, which limits the freedom to function in a personal sense as beliefs and values might dictate. There is secondly the extent to which conformity is exacted by the group, and the way in which the necessity to conform results in distortion of perception, judgement and action. And finally there is the dynamic inherent in group decision-taking processes, which result in collective decisions characteristically different to those which would be taken by the separate individuals involved. All of this has feedback effects on future action both because it conditions what we become as persons, and because it creates the parameters which structure future decision-taking.

Groups are the 'natural' human collective unit. The

unit of social decision taking is always the group, and this
is particularly true in the organisational context. Biblical
references to the normative nature of the human group are not
hard to find. St.Paul, for instance, sees us as women and
men in partnership within the one body of Christ
(1Cor.10,17). Jesus himself assures us that he is present
whenever two or three are gathered together in his name
(Matt.18.20). The modern ecclesial context, too, emphasises
the dimension of human partnership and collaboration.
Laborem Exercens sees human work as a co-creative effort, not
only with each other but also in partnership with God.
However, we can usefully distinguish between the idea of
'group' in the sense of community and 'group' in the
closer-knit, more teleological sense. Groups within
organisations are of the latter kind, and it is in those
groups that we find the operation of the particular 'dynamic'
which acts as a conditioning influence on action.

Organisations can be conceived of in terms of a
structure which establishes hierarchy, authority and chain of
command. But they can also be seen as collections of people
working together in groups formed for purposes of task
performance, decision taking, and information handling (26).
Strategic decision-taking in particular needs the group
context, because complexity and uncertainty are better dealt
with by groups than by individuals (27). Groups are not
only needed in functional terms; in management terms too
there is a positive incentive to develop a group perspective
to organisational functioning, because people perform better
in groups. Research (28) shows that groups can constitute a
more potent source of motivation in the organisation than any
alternative structuring, even though there can be conflict
between organisational objectives and personal need
fulfillment. The reason for this is that membership of
groups is important to people, because groups provide a
'psychological home' for people within organisations (29), as
they do in society as a whole.

Groups exist at every level within an organisation – managers spend something like 80% of their working life in groups. They tend to have a shared communication network, shared sense of collective identity, shared goals, and a group structure (30). They can be formal; formal groups within organisations arise out of the division of labour – they are formally structured, whether temporary or permanent, task-oriented, and consciously organised. Committees, management teams, project/work groups, staff groups for specialist services – all of these are formally constituted groups. The optimum size of such groups will depend on the type of task, the urgency with which results are required, and the clarity with which the task is specified. But organisational groups can also be informal, constituting themselves on the basis of shared space and shared interests.

In both types of group there is 'people awareness'. Every group is in some sense a statement by members as to how the members of that group ought to behave. The stages of evolution through which every group goes (31) will include a stage at which the norms of group behaviour are laid down, either formally as rules of proceedure or implicitly as ways of behaving and relating are established. The strength of that normative structure will depend on the size of the group (32), the ease of entry and exit, the kind of activity in which it is engaged, and the organisational ethos within which it functions. Group processes will emerge as a sequence of interaction patterns between group members which will be conditioned by the structure of the group. For instance, the type of leadership, whether autocratic, democratic, or laissez-faire, will evoke appropriately different patterns of interaction, and this will in turn influence group structure and behavioural responses.

iv. Roles

The relationship between group structure and individual
behaviour expresses itself in individual role performance —
i.e. in the position-practice relations in which we function
in patterned interaction with others. The notion of role is
an active one, we 'play' a role, and we play it in the
context of the resources which serve as parameters to that
role. The corollary of that is that what we actually do is
specified by the norms governing the performance of that
role. Norms can be merely codes of expected behaviour, or
they can be more closely specified rules which stipulate
duties attached to the role which will imply a corresponding
nexus of rights.

The organisational position we occupy, our 'job
specification' is not at all the same thing as the role we
play. Role definition is something more diffuse than that —
something which encompasses not only how the organisation
requires us to function within our grouping, but also how we
opt to function. The roles we adopt are chosen as well as
imposed, and therefore may be more or less clearly specified.
In concrete terms, each one of us has a position within an
organisation, whether it be professor, manager, supervisor,
administrator. In each of these cases the roles we play will
be defined to the extent that the rules (norms, mores) which
govern their enactment are more or less clearly specified.
Roles within decision-taking groups, for instance, are
entirely specified in terms of powers and duties — the roles
of committee officers such as secretary, treasurer and so on
being a case in point. Work relationships in general,
however, will be less clearly structured, and we will have
greater freedom to interpret our roles there. The weaker the
sense in which we use the notion of role, the less does it
imply in terms of action — i.e. the less is action determined
by the nexus of rules which specify behaviour in that

particular role.

Our actions in relationship with others, the ways in which we 'play' our roles (33), are structured by the behavioural expectations which we learn in the process of socialisation as being appropriate to that particular form of relationship. 'Socialisation' in this context means adaptation to particular ways of behaving in that particular organisational context. Given our needs as persons, and given that our concept of person is derived from our social context, there will be a constant process of monitoring, interpreting and negotiating as we attempt to reconcile the needs of 'I' with the public expectations of 'me' — the relationship between our own self-concept and the expectations we have of ourselves on the one hand, and the expectations we see others have of us on the other. In other words, we experience ourselves both as subject and as object. We learn to see ourselves through the attitudes of others, and in the process we internalise our roles so that the expectations of others become the basis for our own self-direction. Roles are thus a means of socialisation and adaptation, both within the organisation and in a wider social sense, and it might be argued in consequence that a 'person' is simply built out of internalised roles from which it becomes increasingly difficult to exit (34).

How do we 'play' our organisational roles? To the extent that there are no clear directives it is up to us to choose our own 'style' of role performance. That style will emerge as an answer to personal questions about identity, power and aims (35). Roles within organisational groups can be functional — the friend and helper, the strong fighter, the logical thinker, or dramatic — the comedian, the organiser, the commentator, the deviant. People will adopt specific group maintenance roles — such as peacekeeper — or task roles — such as evaluator. The context is the group, and what matters is the way in which performance is perceived there. But it will not always be the case that the roles we play in groups are interpreted identically by each group member. Each of us has a perceived role and an enacted role – our role as we play it is not necessarily our role as seen by other group members. Our status within the group will depend on the extent to which the role we play meets the expectations of the group. Our formal status (which is dependent on task ability) is not necessarily the same as our social status – that accorded by the group, and the granting or withholding of such status will serve as an important lever on participants.

The roles we play as 'organisation persons' are multiple, and exist along a spectrum from the closely specified and more functional to the less functional and more 'dramatic'. Occupational role performance has a number of significant effects; perhaps the most central of these is the effect of role performance on our own personality. Studies have shown (36) that we tend to adopt the traits associated with the roles we perform; traits such as aggressivity and self assertion, or compassion and sympathy tend to become part of our character. In other words, we become what we do. The other side of this coin is the way in which role performance affects our perception of others. Instead of perceiving others 'in the round' we tend to make simplistic assumptions about them based on the roles they perform – in other words we tend to judge them in terms of the stereotypes or categories we associate with those roles. The feedback effect of this is that people then tend to conform to the stereotyped expectations others have of them – the so-called 'halo effect'(37). This is part of the mechanism whereby we adopt the characteristics associated with the roles we play. An example of this is the confrontational situation often experienced in the industrial relations field, where attitudes and responses become totally governed by stereotypes.

A further problem arises from the fact that we may ourselves be unclear about the dimensions of our role, and may experience great difficulty in establishing a satisfactory role performance in situations where our role is not clearly specified. Role ambiguity has the advantage that we have a degree of freedom in the shaping of our own role, but we lose the security of comprehension and perception. We become uncertain about our own position, we lose confidence and the sense of self-worth, and the result can be a diminution of ourselves as persons. This is a situation which often arises in cases where organisational restructuring creates administrative 'staff' functions where there is no clear operational brief, and where there is little effective group support. Role ambiguity often arises because of the deficiencies of role specification. But norms, when they are specified, can also be contradictory (38). Junior managers are supposed to show initiative, but to defer to the judgement of others. Workers must work hard enough to please the supervisors, but not be seen by their colleagues to work too hard in case management revises work loads upwards. It is also the case that roles are in fact heterogenous complexes of sub-roles. University lecturers are supposed to be both conscientious teachers and dedicated researchers, both intellectuals and experts on practical matters.

Often, too, we are overloaded as persons with a variety of different roles, not only at work but also in the rest of our lives. These roles may be incompatible - they may each impose priorities which conflict, or they may simply each demand a whole-time commitment. The obvious case is that of the working wife and mother, but as least as important is the situation of the man who feels that his job is taking him away from the needs of his family. In particular, such roles often demand different personal characteristics in their performance - aggression at work, gentleness in the home. The consequence of all this can be a degree of personal strain

which can manifest itself in tension, low morale and
behavioural problems.

The key question in all of this from a theological point
of view must be whether we become merely social actors,
playing a multiplicity of roles , or whether there remains a
self which exists independently of the roles we play, and
which retains a degree of freedom to choose a course of
action (39). The model of man which has always grounded
theological thinking is that of autonomous man (40) — the
conscious, rational, self—monitoring agent. Discussions of
the will and of autonomy have implied that there is a freedom
to act independently of constraints imposed by role
performance. It is clear that in one sense this is a more
reassuring view of man than Hollis's alternatives of
'plastic' man who is merely a cultural dope, whose actions
are entirely dictated by his social context, or 'theatrical'
man, whose actions are indeed determined by the requirements
of role play, for whom the world is merely a stage on which
he plays a part (41). But it does tend to minimise the
importance of institutionally structured social interaction
(42).

However, the crucial question which alternative
typologies leave unanswered is the extent to which there
remains a 'me' independently of the roles I play in my social
context. If each person presents many different faces to the
world depending on the context of interaction, is there
somehow a private face, and if so, what part does it play in
determining my actions? We can approach this question by
remembering that our concept of self is socially derived. It
is culture which defines the relationship of self to self and
self to others (43). But the assimilation of this conceptual
framework demands not only that we be conscious of it, but
also that we be self—conscious. It is only a degree of
self—consciousness that will allow us, for instance, to cope
with the fact that the boundaries between the public and the

private self are constantly shifting. If I am congratulated on a successful lecture, is it me who receives the praise, or is it the successful lecturer? How do I see myself, as lecturer or as me? Does my concept of self consist only of internalised roles, or does it somehow transcend those roles?

Clearly there is some concept of 'me' which is independent of my social roles, and self-consciousness will identify it. But it is not easy to specify what that private 'me' is, because it is only in a social context that we express ourselves. The key to why this is the case is not only that I play many roles and must therefore of necessity be self-consciously reflective about how I play them, but I also have a history which facilitates that self-reflection and enables me to some extent to transcend the roles I play because it teaches me to reflect more critically in the light of the past. The individual, in other words,

> "possesses a self and a history that is
> wider and deeper than any one role he plays,
> (so) that 'normal' role performance involves
> a projection of only part of the self—he
> responds to the role position—without—
> violating the life history — that
> constitutes his self." (44).

The independent self which exists is therefore not the outsider of existentialist literature, but the reflective and evaluative self existing within, but not indistinguishable from, the social self, a self whose metaphysical value can never be reduced to his social significance.

Clearly, then, in an organisational context each person retains the option of critical reflection on his own role performance. Unless he is operating under the most rigid of guidelines he can choose his own style of role play. The rules governing roles are more or less clearly specified depending on the role in question, and where the notion of appropriate behaviour is less clearly defined there is greater scope for the exercise of personal judgement and autonomy in the relationship (45). Indeed, he can even choose which style of role play he considers most appropriate to the problem in hand. Admittedly the overall constraints are the perceptions and expectations of the group, but even there reactions can often vary. All of this assumes, however, that the person retains the ability to be critical and reflective. In the measure that he is vulnerable to group pressure and dependent on group approval that ability may be diminished.

What, then, is the connection between being a moral agent in a social context and role performance (46)? Is being a moral agent simply assuming that ought follows from is, that it entails carrying out the rights and duties associated with a large number of roles — conforming, for instance, to professional codes of ethics? To maintain this would be to ignore problems of possible conflict between the norms governing different roles, as well as tensions between different expectations within the relationships belonging to the same role. And what about the situation where the demands of role performance conflict with moral judgement (47)?

Perhaps it is nearer to the truth to say that being a moral person is itself a role carrying with it associated rights and duties, the major one being the obligation of critical evaluation of action in a role context (48). Clearly this is because the agent undertook the role in the first instance, and he brings to it qualities of personal judgement and reflection. That judgement may dictate non-compliance with what is required in terms of role performance if it is felt to be immoral. More usually, perhaps, it may simply demand humane and compassionate treatment of others. The professional/client relationship, for instance, can be acted out in a variety of ways which are more or less caring (think, for instance, of the differing attitudes shown by social security officials). Organisational role performance demands from us as moral

266

agents the exercise of critical reflection on the effects of role performance, and the adoption of the maximum possible freedom of choice and action.

v . Conformity.

To what extent is the exercise of such autonomy possible in practice? Roles are the masks we wear; they constrain as well as enable our action. But role performance is a function of group structure, and I shall argue in this section that the dynamics of group participation both constrain autonomy and distort the processes of perception and judgement on which such autonomy necessarily depends.

The groups within which we function within organisations are not only formal groups. There also exist a myriad of informal groups — spontaneous interaction in ad hoc meetings, lunch clubs, etc. These are groups we choose to belong to because we use the groups we belong to, whether formal or informal, to fulfil needs which we cannot fulfil alone (49). Needs are not purely economic or material, and since we spend our lives in an organisational environment, it is in that context that other needs have also to be fulfilled. We tend to manipulate our surroundings so as to create need-fulfilling situations. Whereas formal groups are the ones we often see as fulfilling the more basic needs, the informal ones often fulfil the need to be appreciated, recognised, accepted, valued, useful. In fact, the line between the two is often indistinct — formal groups often develop ways of fulfilling these latter 'psychological' needs. The way in which all this happens may in practice be diffuse. People are often not really consciously aware of what they want or need, they are merely drawn to participate because they feel more at home as insiders than outsiders.

The drive for need fulfilment is a powerful one which

lies at the basis of much of our motivation. We tend to use
our influence in groups to gain support for our ideas and
projects, because we want to have the feeling of sharing in a
common activity (50). Above all, we need to establish a
satisfactory self-concept, and we can only do this in the
group. Psychological success is achieved when we succeed in
enhancing our own self-concept, psychological failure is when
we fail to achieve this, or when our self-concept gets
damaged. We constantly develop mechanisms to maintain and
preserve our self-concept. We tend to limit any possible
damage to it by trying to attribute the cause of any failure
to something/one other than ourselves (51). We can even
develop a personal desire for group success so that corporate
achievement can boost our own ego (52).

We bring our own personality, perceptions and
motivations to the groups in which we participate; our
resultant behaviour will depend on the interactions between
these and group processes. We need to feel that we belong to
the group, and that will demand conformity, but our
conformity will be contingent on whether or not we feel that
our own needs are being met. The calculation is often finely
balanced. There will be costs and rewards attached to group
participation — costs in the sense that we are forced to
modify our behaviour, rewards which come from belonging.
Groups develop norms (attached mainly to topics central to
the group) and the means to enforce our compliance with them.
Our need to belong must override any objections or doubts we
may have about those norms. (How, for instance, do we behave
towards group outsiders, even towards those to whom we feel
sympathetic, if the group norm dictates a hostile attitude?)
Norms set limits to the permissible in group conduct.
Enforcement of those norms can be vague, as in the case of
mere expectations of behaviour, or precise, as in the case of
institutional sanctions. Norms, in other words, can be
mandatory or non-mandatory. Many of the decision-taking
groups within organisations have a well-defined set of

mandatory rules. However, norms are never static, even when they become formally constituted rules. They can always be changed, either gradually or more deliberately by group decision.

Participation in a group is therefore going to involve, to a greater or lesser extent, the suborning of our own individual identity and autonomy to that of the group and its norms. Pressures to do this are not necessarily explicit (53), and there are levels of acceptanceof group norms. It is possible to comply overtly, but without conviction, for the sake of convenience. At the other extreme we can accept group norms to such an extent that they become internalised. But it will never be possible for the individual to reject group norms outright, given continued participation, because there will be subtle and diffuse processes at work which will gradually condition conformity. Conformity is imposed not merely by group pressure, but also by our own internal processes. The pressures from within ourselves to conform are particularly strong when the issue is ambiguous, when there is prolonged physical proximity, or when individuals lack support for their views. Not every one is equally likely to conform — the less intelligent, the less autonomous, less confident, more anxious, more conventional are more vulnerable to interior and exterior pressures to conform.

But it is not only we who lay ourselves open to being made to conform. Our conformity is also a function of the degree of power exercised on us in the social context. Social power is exercised to change cognition, behaviour, or emotion of the other (54). Power is not just an individual characteristic, it can also be seen as an interpersonal construct. There are different dimensions to power. Control of rewards is a source of power (55). So is interpersonal attraction, not just as charism but also because it makes for group cohesiveness. Control of punishment is also a source of power. But the type of power with the broadest base is 'referent' power, which is based on the desire to identify with the powerful. Power is the basis of the fact that our actions become subject to group approval. Sanctions on deviants include embarrassment, reprimand and exclusion. The power of a group to exact conformity depends on the sanctions at its disposal, the degree to which members value their group membership and their desire to avoid sanctions. The position of a deviant will depend on the power he can exercise to persuade others and the extent to which the group needs him and is therefore prepared to overlook his attitude.

The crucial point about power such as this is that it can only be exercised when permitted by acquiescent group members. The acquisition of power is an investment which entails costs, one of which is the responsibility which the exercise of power entails, both implicit and explicit. However, countervailing power is possible. This concept is often used in an intergroup context, as in the instance of the power of consumer groups to influence manufacturers' decisions, but it can also work within groups themselves. Milgram's research (56), which was used primarily to demonstrate compliance to authority in the face of an order to administer painful electric shocks to subjects, showed that a group can aid the individual to defy authority. In the situation where three people were given such an order obedience was considerably reduced by rebellion against the experimenter. If the individual is reassured that defiance is not abnormal, that his opinions about the legitimacy of the authority have back-up, and that the consequences of defiance are minimal, he will resist pressure to conform, and enough deviants will break the hold of the group. But this is the exception to the rule.

Power, then, is the source of pressure to conform, and it finds a willing partner in our own vulnerability. The kind of power and the degree of power will influence the outcome of the process. But it is not merely that we conform outwardly for the sake of appearances. Empirical research appears to indicate that the degree of conformity achieved by group pressure is more than merely superficial (57). Whether the pressure originates from outside or inside the person, it affects, conditions and changes our rational and affective processes — it is in a real sense 'mind bending', because the way we see, the way we judge, and the way we act will all undergo a process of change. As we work within groups our frame of reference, our perception, becomes more like that of the group. This will determine the meaning and interpretation we give to issues; we will gradually learn to see things in the same light as our colleagues. Our judgement will be affected in consequence. Muzafer Sherif (58) put people in a dark room and asked them to say which way a light was moving. The fact that the room was dark prevented them from having an objective frame of reference on which they could base their experience. Those subjects were subsequently tested in groups to ascertain whether they would modify their original judgements. The other research strategy was to test subjects firstly in groups, and after that test them individually to see whether they would modify the judgements they had already made in the group.

After the individually tested subjects were allowed to consult with each other their judgements tended to converge and become more similar. The anxiety of group members to conform to others led to the emergence of a group norm in terms of judgement, and in the experimental situation that norm remained even when the subjects were retested independently. When the subjects had originally been tested in a group context the judgement as to the appropriate norm was a group judgement. Subsequent individual testing did not result in any divergence from this. Sherif concluded that —

"The psychological basis of social norms..
is the formation of common frames of
reference as a product of the contact of

individuals. Once such frames of reference
are established and incorporated in the
individual, they enter as important factors
to determine or modify his reactions to the
situations that he will face .. In this
situation, within certain limits, there is
no 'right' or 'wrong' judgement ... Every
individual need not be aware of the fact
that he is being influenced in the group
situation.."(59).

Group pressure to conform will thus involve modification
of beliefs, values and attitudes. But its effect will be more
severe than this. Group pressure can also trigger the making
of assertions contrary to perceived and recognised fact — in
other words, induce a total loss of judgement and autonomy.
The most significant research project on this question, that
by Asch, tested the way in which people's judgements were
altered by the group context (60). In this investigation
subjects, (who were in fact strangers to one another) were
asked to pronounce on length of patently unequal lines. The
majority of the group were 'plants' who were instructed to
say that the lines were equal. The measure of conformity was
the number of times the volunteers (who were in the minority)
gave the wrong answer after they had heard the answer given
by the stooges. Every volunteer heard all the answers before
he was required to answer, and at the end there was a
discussion where each volunteer was asked to justify any
deviant answers. Various variations of the experiment were
tried, such as changing the size of the majority.

One fifth of the subjects remained independent, and
forty-two per cent were not appreciably affected by the
experiment, but the remainder experienced an insoluble
dilemma between their own perception and the evidence of
consensus. Subjects tried various strategies to resolve the
dilemma, including questioning the investigators to make sure

there was no mistake in the test procedure. They tended to see the difficulty as somehow arising from their own attitudes and performance, and to attempt an explanation in those terms. When attempts to improve their performance failed they began to doubt the validity of their own judgements, although the speed with which this happened tended to depend on individual characteristics. Even though the issue was clearly unambiguous, Asch's research found that the process of yielding to pressure happened in different ways (61).

1. There was genuine distortion of perception. Some people yielded to the majority in the full awareness that their estimates had been affected by that view and were therefore no longer objectively reliable. They did at least act according to their perceptions. Others were not aware that their perceptions were being distorted, and experienced cognitive confusion in consequence (62).

2. There was distortion of judgement. People's confidence in their own judgement was shaken as they came to believe that their perceptions were inaccurate. This is the classic legendary example of the 'emperor's new clothes'. In fact, part of this phenomenon is that it is the very people who have lost confidence in their own judgement who are most vociferous in maintaining and enforcing the party line. A classic example is that of women in the past who voluntarily confessed to witchcraft in an atmosphere of hysteria — did they genuinely believe they were witches?

3. There was distortion of action. Several people conformed, not because conformity was dictated by their perceptions or their judgement, but because they did not want to appear different, or possibly even inferior, to those who concurred with the majority. There were others who remained independent, sometimes with the independence born of confidence, sometimes with less confidence but a greater

regard for what they saw to be the truth.

There are important lessons to be learnt from this. One
question concerns the personal consequences of yielding. To
ask what kinds of person will yield to group pressure is a
different question from asking what does it do to them if
they yield. Trust, lack of fear and integrity of mind seem
to be the basic qualities distinguishing those who are
independent from those who yield. But what happens to the
self-concept of those who compromise the truth as they see
it? The related question concerns the consequences in terms
of ostracisation for those who refuse to conform. In a
situation where one member finds himself in moral
disagreement with the decisions of the group (63), the
options are few. One can ignore one's own attitude (like
Adolf Eichmann who signed the orders committing Jews to the
gas chambers) and comply in the carrying out of group
policies as a matter of duty. Alternatively, one can resign.
But resigning will in one sense achieve nothing – the group
will continue to do whatever they had planned to do anyway,
and resignation will deprive that member of the opportunity
to influence future decisions, given that all decisions of
social significance are made within a group context.
Admittedly such a step will be a positive sign – a sign that
the dissenting group member has not already been socialised
into moral numbness. It will also be a sign of protest which
may influence others to do the same and hence weaken the
credibility of that group, because – except in repressive
regimes – the power of groups does crucially depend on
majority compliance. There is no obvious line of action – the
decision can be morally agonising.

Another lesson concerns the dynamics of consensus.
Group decisions are arrived at by a variety of processes – by
authority, by majority and by consensus. But how is
consensus arrived at, and how dearly is it bought? Consensus
is important for social process, but efficient social process

cannot be bought at the cost of autonomy — "the act of
yielding is anti-social because it spreads error"(64). In
practice consensus cannot be achieved until the process of
discussion has managed to convince the waverers that their
fears and objections are groundless. And the issue can be
more complex than this. In the experimental situations cited
above the judgements involved were unambiguous ones,
requiring yes/no answers. But what if the facts/issues are
complex and it is difficult to come to a clear-cut decision?
What if it is easier to conform because it is impossible to
say why one objects to the majority viewpoint? A degree of
self-censoring so as not to appear foolish is an inevitable
element in all group processes (65) — one may agree simply
because it is the easy way out.

vi. Groupthink.

The exigencies of conformity and the dynamics of
consensus suppress freedom of judgement and action. But it
could be argued that this happens in the interests of some
greater good — that, for instance, group decision-taking is
more efficient than individual decision-taking, or more
likely to achieve a socially optimum situation, and that the
costs of consensus are worth incurring for that reason.
There is clear organisational evidence that, given proper
procedures, group decision-taking is efficient (66). But the
counterargument is that the suppression of individual
judgement necessary to achieve conformity has consequences
which are detrimental both to the quality of group
decision-taking and to its outcome.

The end result of the process of group conformity is
'groupthink' — a characteristic of situations where
cohesiveness in groups such as committees has resulted in the
complete suppression of dissent (67). The essence of the
phenomenon is that the participants in the group are quite

unaware that they have reached this situation. "Groupthink involves non-deliberate suppression of critical thoughts as a result of internalisation of the group's norms, which is quite different from deliberate suppression on the basis of external threats of social punishment" (68). When critical faculties, including moral judgement, have been suppressed people tend to suppress their own remaining deviant thoughts, regarding them as inappropriate in the situation where concurrence-seeking is the most dominant objective.

Janis looks at this phenomenon in the context of US political fiascos such as the Bay of Pigs incident, which appears in hindsight to be attributable not to individual stupidity but to some such process of 'group dynamic'. But no simple model of group pressure seemed appropriate to explain the decisions taken. The basis of decision-taking appeared rather to be one of shared illusion, maintained partly by the morale-boosting effect of loyalty even when individual consciences may have been troubled. The cosy feeling engendered by shared loyalty made people unwilling to risk losing this by rational consideration of alternative actions or attitudes. The depth of illusion was in no case more clearly manifested than by the way in which this we-feeling generated inside the group was paralleled by harshness to outgroups (69). Documentation shows, for instance, a total disregard of the humanity of enemy populations in Vietnam. Decisions and directives on how to kill, where to kill and when to kill are couched in language and in a manner which can only indicate a total suppression of ethical feelings on the part of participants.

'Groupthink' is an identifiable phenomenon in other organisational contexts, whether secular or ecclesial. Its symptoms include an illusion of invulnerability, which operates in tandem with a tendency to make light of the serious, particularly when the 'serious' involves a threat to the security of illusion or existence. There is a unanimity which is a consequence of the mental suppression of divergent views by participants. This unanimity is maintained even in hindsight, partly on the grounds that people respect the judgement and opinions of the others, partly because it is unpleasant to have to retrospectively think about or check on the rightness of the decision which has been made. The consequence of this is that the moral and ethical implications of decisions are swept under the carpet and not mentioned, not so much because the participants do not consider these aspects important, but because they genuinely believe that because all individual judgements concur the consensus must be a moral one. What this view does not take into account, however, is the fact that individual judgements have been subverted by the dynamics of consensus, and that the overall outcome is biased accordingly.

Consensus is maintained either by implicit or often by explicit self-censorship. No one discusses the relevant issues outside the group, and so decisions and the reasoning which led to them are never subject to the questions and criticism of those who might have a more detached view. The group as a whole thus tends to be far less risk-averse than any one individual. Problems inherent in decisions are rationalised so that excessive optimism prevails as to the feasibility and outcome of the chosen strategy. Janis cites Pearl Harbour as the outcome of a process where the American administration persuaded itself that the Japanese would never precipitate a war because the Americans were sure to win. There is recent evidence that UK intelligence knew what the Japanese had in mind, but that the American government was unwilling to listen.

Perhaps the most interesting facet of the phemomenon of 'groupthink' is the way in which the group handles dissent. Doubters are initially pressurised by 'domestication' — the group overtly accepts the dissenting position, but makes a joke of it. If dissent persists the dissenter is stereotyped

- as a troublemaker, a political radical, a religious freak, or whatever, depending on the context - as in 'what can you expect of a woman!'. Interestingly enough, much of the stereotyping has connotations of danger or threat. Dissenters may prefer to remain silent, and thereby avoid pressure, but silence will be interpreted as consent to consensus, so silence is not a viable option. Pressure on dissenters, if it is successful, has the eventual effect of breeding a maverick loyalty to group decisions. The victims of successful pressure will set themselves up as 'mindguards' who will be more diligent than anyone else in reinforcing the processes on which groupthink depends - as much as to say 'if this is what I lost my autonomy for I'm going to make sure that at least it works'.

Groupthink, by its very nature, reduces the efficiency of group decision-taking. Groups, as we have seen, do make better decisions in an organisational context than individuals because they can transcend the constraint of 'bounded rationality'. But this is only the case if they have proper objective proceedures. If groupthink exists there will be a failure to problem-solve effectively for a number of reasons, not least because there is no critical appraisal of the majority decision from the point of view of its disadvantages - the maintenance of self-esteem and emotional equanimity requires that critical procedures be avoided. The whole process of decision taking is subject to the consequences of faulty proceedures. Few of the possible alternatives are considered; there is a selective choice of information presented to the group, there is no assessment of the costs and benefits of alternatives, and there is no recourse to outside expertise.

Groupthink is not a necessary feature of organisational decision-taking: it can be avoided or negated in various ways. It is not difficult to create group situations where an element of questioning and discussion of doubt forms part

of the decision-taking process as a matter of course. The
component of criticism can be introduced in different ways,
not least by leaders who can deliberately instigate
situations where they lay themselves open to criticism.
Also, however, outsiders can be drafted in to the process as
advisers or observers. And it is above all essential that
those affected by decisions should be consulted and feedback
invited before the decision is finalised. This is essential
because of the tendency for groups to be less risk-averse
than individuals would be in similar situations. The
illusion of objective and participative decision-taking masks
the fact that the sharing of responsibility diffuses it to
the point where it is no longer clearly locatable, so that no
one person bears the burden of that reponsibility. In a real
sense people are no longer acting responsibly because their
judgemental processes have been so profoundly affected — only
those outside the group can then make objective judgements.

vii Group bias.

This study has sought to identify the ways in which the
determinisms of our world warp our ability to act
intelligently, reasonably and responsibly. In the particular
instance of action in a social context Bernard Lonergan has
recognised that the procedures of rational and affective
decision-taking can be warped by 'bias' (70). His analysis
highlights on a conceptual level the basic problems discussed
in this chapter.

Lonergan's notion of 'bias' — as that which impedes
rational and affectively motivated action — is seen to exist
on several levels, both within the individual and the group.
At the deepest level 'bias' springs from our unconscious
drives, which perhaps serve to generate the esteem needs
discussed earlier. But that is not the only bias affecting
the individual. There is also bias which exists at the
conscious level and which is seen as egoism — the deliberate

manipulation of the situation for personal gain. The basic
dynamic operative in the group situation is the need of each
participant for status and self-esteem; egoism translates and
realises these needs insofar as participants do and say that
which serves to fulfil those needs rather than what is
dictated by intelligent and moral judgement. The individual
always has a choice — he can opt for or against the option of
egoism. The choice is not necessarily always consciously
apparent, or — more often — it is not acceptable when
consciously perceived.

Egoism, then, is what causes individual action in
intersubjectivity to be guided by self interest. Its root is
to be found in the tension we all experience between being at
the level of intersubjectivity and being at the level of
detached intelligence. Egoism, as the spontaneous reaction
to intersubjective situations, interferes with the
development of intelligence —"it fails to pivot from the
initial and preliminary motivation, provided by desires and
fears, to the self-abnegation involved in allowing complete
play to intelligent inquiry". (71) The individual is clearly
aware of what is going on, because he is using his
intelligent and affective processes to discern and achieve
his own good at the same time as refusing to use them to
achieve the wider social good. The implication of this in
terms of the issue of conformity discussed earlier is that we
may conform not only because we are persuaded or seduced into
it but because we actively opt to conform because of
self-interest, in spite of the fact that what we are doing
contravenes our better judgement. In other words, we may opt
in cold blood to live with the tension between what we
consider reasonable and right and what we consider personally
expedient.

But 'bias' is seen not only at the individual level. At
the level of the group, too, the unit which is designed to
achieve social ends, there is often an imperfectly

intelligent response to the exigencies of each situation. This is because group responses are warped by the self-interest of the group, rather than motivated by the wider interests of society as a whole (and we have seen how the dynamic of consensus insures that those responses are uniform). Groups can thus be seen as having blind spots, 'bias', against the insights which would cast a critical eye on their own objectives and the ways in which they achieve them. The consequence which Lonergan forsees is an adverse development of the social order, which comes about because of the fact that the more powerful groups in society have the means to achieve their objectives at the expense of other groups. This distorts and twists the development of society in the sense that the resultant social order is the outcome of a power struggle rather than the realisation of any intelligently conceived practical ideal.

This is an insight which casts new light on our vision of the economic order. Economic organisations and groups are not just social groups in general - they are groups formed specifically for the purpose of achieving, not the common good, but their own overtly articulated objectives. For such groups altruism is not an option - they are bound, sometimes even by statute or charter, to work for the furtherance of their own aims at whatever cost, given that they remain within the law. It is then the powerful whose aims become normative within the social order - multinational companies, majority political parties, large trade unions, well-endowed universities, military cadres. The use of power within and by these groupings dictates the decisions which shape social forces and results in the structural properties of our world. Power and self-interest at group level, rather than intelligence and responsibiity, provide the motivation for and determine the character of group decision-taking and action in a social context. All of this is made possible by the compliance of individuals acting in one way or another in their own interests, or in the interests of their own self-preservation.

We can also extend this analysis to reflect on the role of government. There is a sense in which governments are simply self-interested groups writ large. Governments of nation states further their own interests, sometimes by means of armed conflict, against other states. In this they conform to the vision of a world twisted by self-interest. But in another sense governments, if they govern as elected representatives of the people, are there to redress the balance of power against the powerful and in favour of the powerless. They are there to restrain the activities of companies, control trade unions, tax the rich, denounce the ambitions of powerful interest groups. Governments can be judged in the measure that they conform to this view of their role; they can be criticised in the measure that they act to further their own ideological and financial interests.

===

NOTES – CHAPTER FIVE.

1. See Appendix IV.
2. Gaudium et Spes, para 25, see also eg. Gutierrez (1974), where the idea is used but not reflected on.
3. Giddens (1984) Introduction.
4. Functionalist/structuralist theories do not achieve this. Parson's actors are 'cultural dopes', says Giddens (1976 p.52), Althussers actors are 'structural dopes'. Parsons thinks purely in terms of social evolution on a biological analogy, and of behavour as adaptive to that exigency – i.e. he has no concept of agency. Language, technology, and religion serve only as evolutionary universals essential to cultural adaption. Giddens cites Thompson's (1978) critique of Althusser as offering a deficient account of agency and a deterministic conception of structure; human beings are only 'supports for production', and carriers of social practices.
5. Giddens (1984) p.213.
6. Giddens (1979) p.4
7. Quoted in Giddens (1984) p.53.
8. Boudon (1981) Ch.2.
9. "There is no such entity as a distinctive type of structural explanation in the social sciences; all explanations will involve at least implicit reference both to the purposive, reasoning behaviour of agents and to its intersection with constraining and enabling features of the social and material contexts of that behaviour". Giddens (1984) p.179.
10. Harre (1979) Ch.1.
11. Schutz (1970).
12. Giddens (1984) p.9. This suggestion of a hierarchy of consciousness avoids the Freudian extremes of reductionism

13. Time and space remove the likelihood of intentionality. Merton (1963) links unintended consequences (latent function) with functionalism.

14. Goffman's typology in e.g. (1963).

15. Giddens (1984) p.85.

16. Ibid. p.186.

17. Ibid. p. 169ff.

18. Durkheim (1895/1938).

19. Boudon (1982) p.1. sees the main task of the theoretical human sciences as identifying the non-intentional social repercussions of intentional human actions

20. Merton (1936).

21. Parsons (1949).

22. Lonergan (1981). For a lucid account of Lonergan's thinking on economics see Gibbons (1981).

23. Unpublished letter to Jane Collier 12.6.82.

24. Unpublished letter to Jane Collier 29.5.82.

25. Laborem Exercens para.4.

26. Likert (1961) Ch.8. pp.97-118 is the main proponent of the view which sees organisations as groups.

27. Gilligan et al (1983) p.35.

28. Quoted in Buchanan and Huczynski (1985) Ch.7.

29. Handy (1985) p.160.

30. See Asch (1952), Ch.9, also Homans (1951).

31. Groups go through identifiable stages - 'forming, storming, norming, performing'.

32. Robinson (1984) Ch.4.

33. See Emmet (1966) p.140.

34. See Wrong (1976) who talks about the 'oversocialised' conception of man.

35. Handy (1985) Ch.4.

36. Evidence quoted in Handy (1985) p.73.

37. Handy (1985) p.77.

38. Boudon (1981) p.41.

39. See Emmet (1966) p.152ff. for a discussion of this. J-P.Sartre (1957) sees role-playing as 'bad faith' - mauvaise foi.

40. See Hollis (1977).
41. Ibid. Ch.1.
42. See Ryan (1983) for discussion of the private and public self.
43. See Bensman & Lilienfeld —their essay in (1979), also Harre (1979).
44. Bensman and Lilienfeld (1979) p.8/9.
45. Boudon (1981) p.57.
46. See Downie (1971) p.128ff.
47. See account of Milgram's experiment in (1974), and discussion of his research in Eiser (1986).
48. Downie (1971) p.133
49. The most basic of the need classifications is that of Maslow (1970) who talks of basic needs such as those for food and shelter, and higher needs such as those for belongingness and ultimate self-actualisation.
50. For other views on needs see eg. McClelland (1981). See also Handy (1985) Ch.2, who talks about the need for power, the need for affiliation and the need for achievement.
51. 'Attribution theory' discusses this — see Argyris (1960).
52. See Zander (1981).
53. For a discussion of groups which aim to control/change the self-identity of members — eg AA, Jehovah's witnesses, see Jones (1984).
54. Cavanaugh (1984) in Kakabadse and Parker (ed).
55. See Collins and Guetzkow (1964) Ch.6.
56. Milgram (1974).
57. See eg. Crutchfield (1955). Here the experiment was designed to establish whether reactions of others influenced judgements on individual issues. Conformity is greater than when people answer individually.
58. Sherif (1936). Extract reprinted in Maccoby, Newcomb and Hartley pp.219-232. Other research cited in Eiser (1986) Ch.2.
59. Maccoby, Newcomb and Hartley (1966) pp.227-8

60. See Asch (1951), (1952).

61. Asch (1951) pp181-2.

62. See Humphrey (1986) for another discussion of distortion of perception.

63. Downie (1971) p.138ff.

64. Asch (1952) p.495.

65. See Zander (1981), essay on 'Harmony or Consensus'.

66. Handy (1985) Ch.6.

67. See Janis (1971).

68. Ibid. p.379.

69. The more cohesive the group the more rigid its approach to outsiders. For evidence see Sherif (1966).

70. Lonergan (1957) pp.218ff.

71. Ibid. p.220.

72. Much recent work on organisations focuses on this specific point. It seeks to investigate the way in which organisational decision-taking happens, given not only the self-interest of agents but also the existence of imperfect information. Problems such as the 'principal-agent problem' and 'moral hazard' are the result. See e.g. Clarke (1987).

CHAPTER SIX - CONVERSION.

i. Introduction.

The foregoing chapters offered an interpretation of Romans 7:18-25 in terms of present-day 'slavery to the law'. We are trapped in the mind-set imposed by our own presuppositions, ruled by the values of our culture, swayed by the norms of our group, and bewildered by organisational requirements to act on the basis of decisions which we did not make. We are thus blind to alternative visions, deaf to values which are not generally held, and paralysed by the pressures imposed by the social environment. So our actions are flawed; we do that which we do not want to do, and the consequences for both self and world are cumulative. This cumulative process is conceptualised by Lonergan's view of what he calls 'the cumulative process of decline'. In his introduction to Insight he says: -

> "The flight from insight blocks the insights that concrete situations demand. There follow unintelligent policies and inept courses of action. The situation deteriorates ..to provide the uncritical biased mind with factual evidence in which the bias is claimed to be verified ..we reinforce our love of truth with a practicality that is equivalent to an obscurantism. We correct old evils with a passion that mars the new good. We are not pure. We compromise".(1)

Is there any hope? As Christians we have to answer in the affirmative, because redemption is a reality not only for history but also for persons in their own individual lives; Jesus made the blind see, the deaf hear, and the paralysed walk. But redemption is not a magical or supranatural reality, it has to be something which translates into lived experience. Whatever the nature of the process, it has got to be a process of personal self-transcendence and transformation, and one which must be available and accessible to all, not merely to those who have faith in a purely religious sense. Faith will interpret the human reality in a particular way, but the reality must exist in an objective sense independently of faith, because we believe in a redemption which is for all, believers and non-believers alike.(2)

The reality in question is the phenomenon of conversion. Conversion is the reality of redemption experienced in our lives, not merely as a purely religious event or process, (although for the believer it will also have that dimension), but also as central to every aspect of thought and action. This chapter argues that conversion is one of the most fundamental of all human experiences, implying nothing less than a total transformation of the person, involving not only a change of heart, but a totally new view of the world which, for Christians, realises itself in commitment and action for the Kingdom.

Conversion is the coming of the Kingdom into our lives. The message of the Kingdom as preached by Jesus is that it is something that comes to us in the hiddenness and mystery of our own personhood. It breaks into our everyday existence as gift and surprise, as a message we discover cognitively and hear joyfully. Hearing the message of the Kingdom reverses our judgements, and changes our values. The reality of that message demands a response from us in terms of living and doing. Nothing appears to have changed, and yet everything has changed. We are the same, and yet we are new people.

The structures of the message of the Kingdom are paralleled by the structures of the process of conversion. Conversion is both cognitive and moral, and its consequences

are lived out in action. Intellectual conversion allows us
to relativise our cultural conditioning, to hear God's voice
and see God's work in a flawed world. Moral conversion is a
process of value reversal which culminates in moral autonomy.
Conversion in a social context entails becoming Christ in the
world; it frees us to be Christ for others.

ii. The basis of conversion

Conversion is a human experience religiously
interpreted. In characterising its subjective basis we can
draw on interpretations both sacred and secular. We can look
for common patterns of conversion, or common experiences, as
expressed in, for instance, the work of William James (3),
where feelings of love, joy, peace are described. We can
think of such moments, with Maslow, as 'peak experiences'(4).
Or we can look to the theologians who speak of the essence of
the conversion experience as an awakening (5), as response to
God's call (6) as repentance and 'metanoia' (Acts 26.18,
14.15), as death and rebirth into a new identity, as the
result of the exercise of a fundamental option or choice
which resolves the conflict within a divided self (7). We
can see it as essentially volitional, consequent upon a
chosen change of direction, or as an act of trusting, loving
surrender. We can view the experience as one of encounter and
unification — with the self of past and future (8), with the
real self which is the only one known to God (9), with the
new self (10) who is self-for-others, and ultimately
therefore with the God who is known and accepted in the core
of that encounter (11).

The idea which unifies all these perspectives is that of
a moving beyond the self. This is true in a purely spiritual
sense, where conversion can be seen as the discovery of the
'true' self, as opposed to the empirical object-self (12);
this does not involve the negation of 'self' so much as as
its realisation in 'authentic being'(13). However, it is

also true in a non-spiritual sense. The model which best explicates this is self-transcendence, the drive towards authentic personhood on all the levels on which we operate. Self-transcendence should not be confused with self-realisation or self-actualisation, because in terms of its outcome it reaches beyond the good of self to the good of others. Conversion as self-transcendence implies personal change, reinterpretation of what has gone before, and a reorientation of meaning and purpose for the future.

Conventional religious understandings of the phenomenon of conversion are often inadequate in that they fail to do justice to this much wider view of conversion for which, as I hope to show, there is ample evidence in Scripture. It is possible to argue that narrowly 'religious' views of the phenomenon of conversion are deficient in that they pay no attention to the developmental and behavioural dimensions of what is in essence an experiental reality, focusing rather on confessional and objectivist 'spiritual' aspects. At its weakest the idea of conversion is used merely to describe a change in 'adherence' to a particular confessional stance (14). Catholic views of conversion in particular show a legalism, a lack of biblical perspective, and a neglect of the existential implications for the lives of those who have experienced God's grace in a new and shattering way (15). Insofar as this is the case, such views do not accord with the scriptural evidence on the dimensions of conversion.

It is also not easy to find an empirical basis for this idea of conversion as self-transcendence. Disciplinary research on the objective phenomenon of conversion gives us some idea of the complexity of the topic without providing much in the way of useful insight or empirical foundations. Anthropologists, for instance, have concerned themselves with the way in which culture facilitates or impedes the movement from one religious group to another (16). Sociologists are interested in the part played by the group - ie the church -

in promoting, encouraging, validating and maintaining the adherence of those converted; they also explore the interactions between the aspirations of the convert and the survival needs of the group. Concepts of community and conversion are thus seen as inseparable. Psychologists, on the other hand, are more interested in the mental and psychological states which predispose towards conversion; they focus on the extent to which conversion is simply the result of suggestibility brought about by depression, tension or some other psychological state. Relevant to this, too, are the techniques used by cult groups, such as the Moonies, to gain and keep adherents. Psychoanalytic perspectives, on the other hand, look more deeply into the influences of childhood and the convert's subconscious impulses in affecting the liklihood of conversion.

All these perspectives give greater or lesser weight to the mental state and aspirations of the convert, the role of past and present socialisation, as well as to wider cultural factors. But they all focus on the process of conversion rather than on its content; they provide explanations of the 'who', 'when' and 'how' of conversion rather than attempting to give any account of its nature and substance. The approach to conversion thus ends up by being functional and objectivist, and at odds with the basic thrust of this dissertation, which attempts to derive an understanding of the acting person in the dynamic context of the Christian life. From this point of view what we need to recover is the characteristics of the conversion experience on the one hand, and the effect it has on the person's life on the other.

The problem for social scientists with this type of investigation is that evidence is very difficult to obtain. Gaventa (17) points to the limitations of empirical research in this area. There is not only the difficulty of establishing comparability between accounts of conversion experiences, there is also the problem of shifting interpretations of past experience, when retrospection and introspection become confused. There is therefore a methodological reason, as well as a theological one, for not relying on empirical evidence on the nature of conversion, but rather looking to scripture to provide us with clues as to its parameters.

In order to be able to identify what we are looking for, it is helpful in the first instance to estabish a typology of conversion. Gaventa establishes three senses of the word 'conversion' which may be identified in scripture. There is firstly conversion in the sense of 'metanoia', a 'turning round', where conversion entails a complete break between past and present. There is a sense of new identity, of wholeness rather than division. James (18) and Nock (19) both see conversion in this light. A less drastic interpretation is provided by the notion of 'alternation'(20), where conversion grows out of past experience. Nock makes the distinction between conversion proper and 'adhesion', which is simply the acceptance of a new belief system as a useful adjunct to the old, but the old is not necessarily rejected — as in the case where Christianity is superimposed on existing pagan ways of doing and worshipping. Perhaps a born Catholic comes to see greater meaning in his faith, or a non-churchgoer begins to worship again. Classic examples of this sense of conversion include the 'born again' experiences of evangelical Christians, who turn to Jesus as their Lord and renounce their past life.

A third category is that of conversion as transformation. In this case conversion entails a radically different way of seeing things. The experience does not form a continuity with past experience, as in the case of alternation. Nor does it involve breaking with the past; it simply involves seeing the present in a new way. There is a cognitive 'paradigm shift', a change in understanding, which

casts new light on all experience, and thereby creates the
necessity to reinterpret the past. The classic case to cite
here is the experience of Luther. Luther's 'tower
experience' was the culmination of a long process (21)
leading to a profound flash of insight. He had lived for many
years with a dislike of the words 'righteousness of God'
(Romans 1.17) because to him they suggested a righteous god
who punished the unrighteous sinner. He had also lived with
an understanding of conversion which led him to affirm (in
the Dictata) that the first conversion was the incarnation,
God's becoming man. There came a point where he had his own
incarnational experience, by which he came to see that the
phrase 'God's righteousness' is in fact a gift of God rather
than a quality of God, the gift by which the righteous live,
just as 'God's work' is what God does in us, 'God's wisdom'
and 'God's strength' are the gifts of His spirit.

Luther's own conversion thus occurred by the incarnation
of God as the Word breaking into his own heart and mind, and
by the Spirit revealing the meaning of the words of
scripture. There was therefore a marriage between two
perspectives — on the one hand his own earlier belief that
the source and substance of conversion was the incarnation of
God's Word in Christ, and on the other hand the nature of his
own conversion experience as the incarnation of God's word in
his heart. His own journey involved a gradual letting go of
the idea that conversion is something that can be worked for,
or even that we need to be disposed for it, and an acceptance
of the fact that we are converted to God by God's action,
because God was first converted to us.

The significant thing about Luther's experience was that
it was cognitive; it transformed his whole way of looking at
things. We find this same quality of 'transformation'
reflected in the conversion experience of Paul (22). It is
possible to argue that Paul's conversion certainly did not
entail a rejection of his past (he continued, for instance,

to acknowledge his Jewish roots), so that it was not 'conversion' in the first sense of our typology. Nor was it merely a natural development out of that past, whereby he was called to some new task or assignment. It was rather an experience, a gift, which caused him to see his world in a totally new way. The revelation by which God "was pleased to reveal his son to me"..(Gal.1:16), which caused him to exclaim "have I not seen Jesus our Lord"..(1Cor.9:1), was one which changed his perception of Jesus as a troublemaker into a vision of Jesus as messiah. The truth which had been hidden to him — although not to the Christians whom he had persecuted — was now discovered by him, forcing him to reinterpret everything he had previously taken for granted. Love had opened his eyes in joy.

Furthermore, everything which Paul had previously thought to be significant or worthwhile in his life and history now became irrelevant:"...as to the law a Pharisee, as to zeal a persecutor of the Church, as to righteousness under the Law blameless..."(Phil.3,6). Now all that is counted as loss, as "so much garbage"(Phil.3,8) because of the privilege of knowing the Lord. All his values are reversed. The consequence of this cognitive 'paradigm shift' was thus a fundamental change in values and commitments. His radical change in self-understanding is paralleled by a change in vocation — the only thing that matters now is to respond to the revelation (apokalypsis) which has been given to him by a God "who had set me apart from birth and called me through his grace, chose to reveal His son to me and through me in order that I might proclaim him to the Gentiles" (Gal.1,15-16). Paul's response entails a new way of living.

This picture of conversion is also portrayed in the Old Testament. Sklba's analysis of conversion in the O.T (23) indicates the presence of the same characteristics of conversion as we find in the letters of Paul.

"The classical prophets....hold in common a
profoundly personal encounter with God, a
moment of radical engagement with God
resulting in the shifting of their entire
horizon. In the light of that experience
all values were rearranged and the world
could no longer be viewed from the same
perspective. God himself appeared as one
who broke all prior images of himself, even
those most treasured by the nations of
Israel. The casual formulae of faith became
either ashes or burning coals in the mouths
of such prophets; they could never be the
same again, nor could their faith fit easily
into the catechisms of their contemporary
religious leaders. With that new intuition
into the nature and dealings of God came a
compelling vocation to speak forth..." (24)
It would thus appear that Paul's perspective on conversion is
totally in the prophetic tradition.

Although Paul never speaks of his conversion as such, it
is possible by examining the passages where he alludes to it
to discern the basic elements in the process.
1. The experience is sudden and shattering; he is "seized by
Christ"(Phil.3:12).
2. It results in a cognitive shift which causes him to
interpret both the present and the past in a totally
different way (Gal.1:11-17). More specifically, his view of
the happenings which surrounded the beginnings of the Church
is radically changed (1Cor.9:1-2, 15:8-10).
3. This cognitive shift in turn causes a fundamental change
in the value base by which Paul has lived, and by which he
has evaluated his own identity and status (Phil.3:7).
4. As his perceptions and values change, so also do his
commitments, as he now dedicates himself to preaching Christ

crucified (Gal.1:15-16).

Paul's view of his own conversion is also coherent with his view of what is entailed by conversion in others. As in the case of Luther, the subjective experience mirrors the objective view of the phenomenon. As Gaventa argues (25), conversion for Paul is not something the person does, it is an event brought about by God's action, a grace offered by God. When Paul uses the conventional conversion words 'epistrephein' and 'metanoun' he is not in fact speaking of conversion in the above sense, but rather in the sense of 'alternation' applied either to Jewish Christians who have fallen away and now repent (2Cor.7.9-10), Rom.2.4), or to Gentiles who turn back to their false gods, (Gal.4.8-9). Conversion as transformation, as the beginning of faith is spoken of as God's call (1Cor.1.2,9,26, Gal.1.6), God's purchase (1Cor.6.20, 7.23), God's liberation (Rom.6.17-18), God's grace (Rom 6.21-6). God's initative transforms persons; their response must be to allow that transformation to take place so that they become God's new creation (Gal.6.15, 2Cor.5.17) and witnesses to that grace. Paul sees that transformation as taking place in the first instance in the realm of perception .."be transformed (metamorphousthe) by the renewal of your mind.. "(Rom.12.2) It will then have implications both for commitment (Gal.6.1-6), and for community (Rom.15.1-3,5-6)

There is thus no conflict between Paul's own experience as reinterpreted and explained by him, and his own theology of what conversion is - although this interpretation is not necessarily consistent with other people's interpretations of what Paul's experience meant (26). It is an experience brought about by God's action; one which Paul considers intrinsic to the beginnings of faith, normative for all Christians, and definitive of Christian existence, rather than purely particular to himself. Paul's view of conversion also reflects the characteristics and requirements of the message of the Kingdom as preached by Jesus. If we accept that message as normative, we have to analyse the phenomenon of conversion in concrete terms relevant to everyday living. The argument of this dissertation has been that our response to God's call is flawed by our 'slavery'. If conversion involves cognitive paradigm-shift with a change in meanings consequent on reinterpretation of what has gone before, we will be liberated from bondage to our world-view. If it involves a change in values and hence commitments, the whole basis of action will be changed.

We owe to the work of Bernard Lonergan the fact that the concept of conversion is available to us in a form which enables us to discuss in a structured fashion the transformation of life and action to which Paul refers in his letters. For Lonergan, conversion entails a radical change of orientation, not merely a natural orientation of human intellect towards the transcendent, as was the view taken by Aquinas (27). He characterises conversion as a "vertical exercise of freedom" (28) which can move the person from one horizon to another and involves the reinterpretation of previous understandings. Lonergan distinguishes between intellectual conversion, moral conversion and religious conversion (29). Others working in that analytical framework have added the affective or emotional dimension as a salient part of the conversion process (30). Lonergan sees these conversions as grounded in, and running in parallel with, the experience of 'falling in love' with God, which is the heart of the Christian experience (31).

But, says Lonergan, conversion is not readily amenable to theological analysis because it is something that is personal to the life of each individual — in other words, it is difficult to discuss empirically (32). Conversion is not a change or a development, it is a transformation in the person which has consequences in terms of other changes and developments in his life. There are changes in

apprehensions; what was previously unnoticed becomes present.
New apprehensions take the form not of making new statements,
but of finding new meanings. There are changes in values,
which form the basis of change in the person and in his
relationships to others and to God. It is not so much a
matter of choosing new values as of a 'transvaluation of
values'. The person apprehends differently, values
differently, relates differently because in many ways he IS
different. It is the 'new world' of which Paul speaks, which
replaces the old order which is gone (2Cor, 5.17).

Conversion is thus a personal experience of
self-transcendence, a moving-beyond-the-self, but it also has
communal and historical dimensions as individuals and groups
create their world in new ways. Self-transcendence is
something dynamic, multidimensional, and historical. It is
dynamic because it is grounded in the drive of the human
spirit's search for meaning, truth, value and love. It is
multidimensional because it involves subsequent change and
development in key aspects of the person - the cognitive, the
affective or psychic, the moral and the spiritual or
religious. It is historical because it is related in specific
ways to the development potential which happens at different
moments in a person's life. The criterion of personal
authenticity thus becomes cognitive, moral and affective
self-transcendence, and for Christians "the Gospel demand
calling us to intelligent, responsible, loving service of the
neighbour requires no less than the fulfillment of this
fundamental drive for self-transcendence"(33). "Conversion
then is the fully responsible self-delineation of a man who
has become capable of maturity and authenticity, a man who
has realised that he will be what he becomes and that his
task is precisely to become authentically himself "(34).

If we accept that conversion is something which happens
in different dimensions of the person, we must also recognise
that reflection on that fact, in terms of the meaning given

to it, will take place in different realms of 'differentiated consciousness'. On a commonsense level, in the the everyday world of living, conversion is perceived as the way in which knowing, and hence actions, show the fruits of conversion — intellectually, morally and socially. On a theoretical level we can reflect on the way in which theory and praxis interact so that these conversions become transformative. On a spiritual and religious level, in the world of faith and grace, religious conversion, as the ultimate response to God's love, is perceived as salvific of self and world. Redemption is given, we stand redeemed in time and history as living proofs of God's mercy and not as witnesses to our own efforts. Conversion as a human phenomenon takes on all these meanings. On an everyday level we can notice the changes it brings in our lives, on a deeper and more dynamic level we can see it as transformative not only of our world but also of ourselves, and on a theological level we can reflect on the meaning of this in the light of the Kingdom which is both now and yet to come. As we reflect on intellectual and moral conversion, and on conversion in a social context, we bear these levels of meaning in mind.

iii. Intellectual conversion

Intellectual conversion is the cognitive dimension of conversion (35). Lonergan's notion of intellectual conversion involves what at first seems to be a very simple affirmation 'I am a knower'. This is an affirmation which can be made when one consciously grasps, and affirms, the structure of knowing — i.e the cognitional processes of experiencing, understanding and judging which together make up the methodology of that knowing (36). At the point where one becomes conscious of one's own cognitive capacities and operations, one enters into a 'differentiation of consciousness' as between the worlds of immediacy and the world mediated by meaning (37). In other words, one becomes aware that knowing is about how you know as well as about what you know. Instead of taking the view that knowledge is something 'out there' to be acquired or created by the performance of an 'external' set of operations, and that knowing is therefore like looking, the person comes to the realisation that knowing is an activity, a series of linked mental processes to which one can consciously attend. This realistion in turn introduces a capacity for, and the possibility of, critical reflective approaches, and a confidence that such approaches are valid. The difference in focus between the two approaches is between method and procedure on the one hand, and engagement, insight and reflection on the other; the process of coming to know will be defined in terms of the latter rather than the former (38).

The first consequence of intellectual conversion is therefore the "elimination of an exceedingly stubborn myth concerning reality, objectivity and human knowledge" (39). These are the myths about knowledge associated with rational empiricism. Knowing is not simply about looking. It is a process which begins with questions. Human wonder is as much about what the appropriate questions are as about the answers to those questions. Questions are answered by a twofold process of attending to and evaluating the evidence; in Lonergan's terms, both understanding and judgements of fact are brought to bear. Reality for the knowing subject is thus constituted by the affirmation that something is the case, rather than by any purely empirical manifestation. Reality can be further established by intersubjective agreement, but the important thing is that the real has been constituted by the process of coming to know rather than by the apprehension of what is 'already out there now'.

The rejection of naive realism has consequent implications for the notion of objectivity. The knowing subject who affirms the reality of his own cognitional processes will come to realise that objectivity is not guaranteed by the search for value-freedom, nor by scientific procedures which aim to see only what there is to be seen. It is rather the fruit of authentic subjectivity, relying on the adequacy of judgement in the cogntive operations of the knowing subject. Myths concerning objectivity and those concerning reality are closely allied in the sense that they are both rooted in a failure to distinguish between the world of the empirically immediate and the world mediated by meaning, which has to be accessed by cognitional processes. Lonergan distinguishes between the counterpositions of empiricism, where objective knowledge is sense experience, naive realism ,where knowledge is attained by looking, and idealism, where 'world' itself is ideal. The criterion of the real has to be found in the 'virtually unconditioned' of one's own judgement rather than in any of these positions (40).

The beginning of intellectual conversion is thus the possibility of self transcendence which stems from the fact that the knowing subject can affirm his own intelligence and his own rationality, and can in the process achieve intellectual self-realisation. But this is only the first of two stages in the process of intellectual self-transcendence. As well as self-affirmation there is also self appropriation. In the case of the first (41) one is making a judgement of fact about the fact that one is a knower; the logic is that 'if I were not a knower I would not be raising and answering the question' (42). In the case of the second, self-appropriation of one's own rational self-consciousness arises as one becomes familiar with the structures of cognitional operations (43). Essentially self-appropriation involves firstly experiencing cognitive operations, secondly understanding their interrelatedness, and thirdly affirming them as valid and worthwhile — in other words, applying cognitive procedures to cognition. Self-appropriation is thus about epistemological 'heightening of consciousness' by means of its objectification, and thus involves the acceptance of the exigencies of one's rational self consciousness in terms of critical reflection (44). Whereas self affirmation says 'I can do it, I do it', self appropriation asks 'how do I do it, can I do it better?'

This process is continual in the sense that it is constantly being evaluated. New questions always arise, old conclusions are continually challenged. Intellectual conversion both demands and in turn engenders an openness in which assumptions are constantly questioned, presuppositions criticised, ways of modelling the world challenged and evaluated in the light of the subject's own commitment to intelligent and critical reflectiveness. In fact all genuine scientific endeavour, all problem-solving activity, calls for the fruits of such conversion - 'is this the best way to do it?', 'is there another answer?', 'should I be thinking about this in another way?'. All questions of this type call for an understanding of and a confidence in one's own cognitional processes. Intellectual conversion lifts the whole cognitive process onto a 'second-order' level, where the conditions of possibility for knowledge are constantly brought under scrutiny. Because the realisation of what knowing is uncovers questions about the possibility of knowing itself, the validity of all modes of scientific thought is exposed to critical evaluation.

The implications of all this are that one may become aware of one's own imperfections in this regard. I may come to the realisation that my judgements of fact - quite apart from my judgements of value - tend to be too rash or too hastily made (45). Am I in the habit of making ill-considered judgements, of not paying sufficient attention to the evidence? And then again, am I prepared to accept that the process of knowing is not always a certain one, not so much in the sense that what holds today may not hold tomorrow, but in the sense that it is often not possible to make an unambiguous judgement about situations, about people, about potential outcomes? The clarity and validity of an insight in a theoretical context may not be easy to replicate in the context of human relationships. Am I prepared to affirm the continuing efficiency of my own cognitive performance in the face of ambiguity?

Finally, am I aware of the extent to which my cognitive processes are deeply conditioned by my historical, social and cultural context? The language I use places limits on my ability to conceptualise, the structures and frameworks of reality with which I operate tend to bias my judgement as to what is the case, and the underlying presuppositions I hold about 'world' determine the nature of my experience. The dynamics of culture are transmitted through and activated in cognitive and affective processes. Intellectual conversion, because it involves an awareness of these things, introduces a freedom into cognitive processes. Just as conversion in a religious context is thought of as turning away from the sinfulness of which one is increasingly aware, so intellectual conversion involves the freedom which comes from an awareness of the imperfections inherent, not in the nature or in the dynamism of one's own cognitional processes, but in their conditioning (46).

Intellectual conversion thus enables us to move to new horizons of thought. It is the subjective pole of 'horizon-shift' which enables us to make the fundamental move to what Lonergan calls 'basic horizon' – a position from which we can move to new horizons of thought. We are no longer trapped in a particular world-view; we can move beyond existing interpretations and develop a critical perspective on all interpretations and patterns of thought. But there is also an objective pole to this process which we must now consider. Modes of disciplinary thought and endeavour, ways of knowing in a scientific context, are themselves also in need of redemption. We look now at some

of the ways in which our academic culture has responded to
the call to conversion.

iv. Intellectual conversion in theory

I argued in Ch.3. that we looked at the world through a
nexus of 'grids' and 'filters' formed by our presuppositions
on the one hand and the theories by which we interpret
experience on the other. Basic presuppositions are
culturally conditioned; this means in effect that they are
the outcome of, and are based on, what we already know.
Knowledge in our Western world is 'scientific'; the fact that
science has enabled us to 'progress' as we have done has
ensured both that science has become the normative mode of
knowing and that its presuppositions have become enshrined in
thought. The hegemony of science as knowledge is based on
the view that reality is objective and empirically
accessible, that data about reality can be used to establish
and confirm laws which explain and predict the world, and
that the issue of meaning is non-significant because meaning
can either be clearly defined or it does not exist. This
hegemony has spread from the natural sciences to all forms of
knowledge, in particular to those which seek to explain
social reality. Here it gives rise to the belief that to
derive empirical explanatory theories of social behaviour
requires the derivation of basic laws and theories which
establish cause and effect in the social world. There is a
feeling that if we have not yet progressed so far as to be
able to do this, it is only because the social sciences are
not yet 'mature'.

There is a fundamental problem here. Social reality is
itself ultimately contingent on human action, and action, as
I have argued, is the outcome not only of volition but also
of conditioning. In other words theory in a social context
is ultimately bound up with the praxis it seeks to

illuminate. The way in which we think about ourselves is inextricably linked with the nexus of social forms which give content to that thought. 'Theory', if formulated, can thus not only be used to explain and predict, but also to control and manipulate (by those who make it and those who pay for it), because it is not only derivative of praxis but also conditions it.

The critique of science-as-knowledge arises not merely because it is clearly inappropriate when applied to social reality, but because its characteristics have consequences for society. It makes categorical distinctions not only between theory and practice, but between fact and value, description and evaluation. The positive is seen as rational, the normative as non-rational. So that whereas on the one hand theory is rational and objective, its application in policy terms is contingent on the choice of goals which are not amenable to scientific inquiry or analysis. Science has no interest in how it is applied, and will advise dispassionately on any application. Policy objectives are decided by political and social process; the role of the scientist is only to facilitate their achievement. Science itself is thus ideological; it is supposedly neutral with respect to ends, but the thrust of scientific endeavour is skewed towards the provision of means to achieve those ends (47).

Intellectual conversion enables us as subjects to see the world in new ways. If we see this as the subjective pole of conversion we can regard the objective pole as being characterised not only by Kuhnian paradigm shifts within specific disciplines, but by a fundamental questioning of the basic premises on which all scientific endeavour is conducted in both the natural and the social sciences. This process is nothing less than one of 'transcendental' self reflection on the conditions of possibility for knowledge as a whole. The critique of the epistemological tradition which one might

term 'science as knowledge' will then take several forms. I
discussed in Ch.3. the way in which observation is theory-
dependent, the formulation of experience is dependent on
concepts and language, and the modelling of reality is
socially conditioned. The critique is not only
epistemological, but also linguistic and metaphysical; its
particular focus is the inappropriateness of scientific
method and procedures for understanding the social world. It
negates the possibility of independence between theory and
language, theory and practice, fact and value, description
and evaluation. It rejects empiricist views of objective
reality, arguing rather for an interpretative process whereby
we search for truth rather than assuming that it can be
established. It relies on the category of meaning to
differentiate contexts of knowing, and thus requires the
scientist to move consciously between one realm of
consciousness and another — ie to differentiate his own
consciousness. That possibility opens up the way to knowledge
which is not scientifically accessible. The subjective and
the objective pole of intellectual conversion thus operate in
tandem.

To these differing perpectives we must add one other
form of critique. The perspective of 'critical theory' goes
beyond the rejection of empirical theory, beyond the advocacy
of the neccessity for interpretation if we are to understand
the social and political world (48). Its aim and interest is
a practical concern for the fate and quality of social life.
It challenges the received view that knowledge can of itself
bring good simply because we know more. It argues that
knowledge, because it is socially conditioned and thus
ideological, can be used for manipulation as well as for
enlightenment. The relationship between theory and practice
is therefore not just that social practice conditions theory,
but that theory conditions social practice because knowledge
and interest are interrelated. Theory guides praxis — ie
right action — and praxis is the verification, the truth, of

theory.

Theory is therefore not purely descriptive or explanatory of reality, nor is it value-neutral. Its role is rather to portray reality in a way which highlights the roots of social problems – unless theory serves to improve the human condition it is useless. It seeks, too, to expose the way in which the ideology embodied in language and thought forms distort the meaning of 'what is going on' in the world. Ideology critique will involve describing and accurately characterising the ideology, and interpreting it in a way which will reveal how it mirrors and distorts the underlying social and political reality. But it will also involve isolating and criticising the fundamental beliefs and interpretations which form the basis of the ideology, and discovering the material and psychological factors that sustain and reinforce it. The legitimising power of ideology will be weakened by the process of questioning and engaging in dialogue with its defenders. The end purpose is not to replace false consciousness with true consciousness, but to make it possible for theory in the widest sense to be self-reflective.

Ideology critique is the heart of intellectual conversion in its objective dimension. Ideological beliefs reflect and distort reality, although all who subscribe to them – and that includes all of us – consider that they are self-evident, valid, rational or reasonable and realistic. It is held to be natural, or even scientific, to hold the views current in the culture. The power of ideologies derives from the way in which they are used to justify and legitimise actions; ideology critique thus attacks the roots of intellectual blindness and social power because it makes people ask questions.

v. Moral conversion.

The essential characteristic of moral conversion is a shift in the criteria by which moral choices are made. Choices are made on the basis of values held; such values reflect what we consider to be 'the good' either in terms of ends or in terms of means, and are given to us primarily by the social environment we live in, because we are socialised into sharing in the meanings and values which constitute that world.

We can distinguish several facets of moral conversion. There is first of all the idea, reflected in all the structural theories of personal development (49), that the process entails a shift in the teleology of the moral decision from personal satisfaction to the value of the good of others. Lonergan (50) characterises moral conversion in this way. Such a change does not happen without an element of personal choice. Lonergan distinguishes between two possible types of moral choice which may be exercised. A horizontal exercise of freedom (51) - not the relevant one here - is a choice made within an already established horizon of perceptions and values. Although different moral choices may be made within this horizon, the basic valuations remain the same. A vertical exercise in freedom, on the other hand, involves a movement to a new horizon of thought and a new way of valuing. This may involve simply a deepening of the moral horizon, but it may also involve a critique of existing values and a radical shift to new values. Such a shift will force us to ask new questions about what we previously took for granted; it will also entail the creation of a radically new set of meanings in our lives. This is the 'foundational moral experience' and it happens partly at least because we opt for it in that we opt to choose our own values. Values were previously chosen by compulsion or given by conditioning; they are now adopted by choice (52).

Moral conversion also entails the realisation that moral choices made are self-transformative (53). Conversion, says Lonergan, occurs at that existential moment when the individual exercises 'vertical freedom' in choosing not only his own values, but also what he is to make of himself. Lonergan does not see the achievement of moral authenticity as merely as a shift from self-interest to altruism, but rather as a process whereby the person comes to realise, as a genuine horizon-shift, that choices affect him as much as they affect the object of choice, and that if he is to respond to the call to personal authenticity he must decide what kind of person he wants to become (54).

This is the dynamic element in moral conversion whereby we are called not only to continual self-transcendence, but to a awareness of the authenticity or otherwise of our own moral experience. Becoming a 'moral person' involves not only an option for the good, not only a shift in values, but the development of a heightened moral sense. Others too emphasise this latter aspect. Macquarrie (55) sees the development of conscience as the mark of moral maturity, which involves not only specific and general moral deliberation, but also the growth of self awareness. Niebuhr (56) sees such a growth in self-awareness as the striving for authenticity. Moral conversion is thus in one sense an everyday affair. Whereas the consequences of intellectual conversion happen in the realm of philosophy, science and scholarship, those of moral conversion happen in the realm of concrete living. The person becomes one who makes open-eyed and authentic moral choices as opposed to simply doing and choosing what others are doing and choosing (57).

But this begs a host of questions. For instance, under what circumstances is moral conversion likely to happen? For an answer to this we can turn to the theories and evidence provided by the developmental theorists, since it is clear that moral conversion is in some sense a development in the moral sensibility of the person. In particular, the work of Piaget, Erikson and Kohlberg is illuminating. However, it has to be recognised that none of these authorities provides us with answers. What the work of development theorists and psychologists does give us is a guide to the conditions of possibility for conversion. Each of the theories provides a criterion of personal maturity which is the specific normative thrust of personal development as evidenced in each of those theories. It is clear, for instance, that the conditions for intellectual conversion cannot exist until the person has reached some level of cognitive development (Piaget), that moral conversion demands a level of moral maturity where one is prepared to let go of moral certainties and risk the possibility of ambiguity (Kohlberg), and that affective conversion has to do with the ultimate resolution of crises in growth (Erikson).

It is in the work of Kohlberg that we find the most fruitful analysis of what moral conversion might entail. We also find here an aspect of the issue which enables us to take Lonergan's analysis a stage further (58). Lonergan's view of moral conversion runs in terms of self-affirmation, but he does not extend his analysis to explore what 'moral self-appropriation' might mean (59), although this would appear to be the logical extension of his analysis in a structural sense. Kohlberg, however, distinguishes three 'levels' of moral development, each with two stages (60). There is a 'preconventional' stage of moral development, where morality is heteronomous and egocentric, a 'conventional' stage where values are dictated by the group and self-respect is engendered by the regard of others. Beyond that, however, comes a 'post-conventional' moral stage where the person perceives that values are socially and culturally relative, and that there are values and rights prior to socially dictated norms. Ultimately, then, the converted person will follow self-chosen principles which are universal, and his moral judgements will be principled and autonomous. For Kohlberg, the fullness of moral conversion requires the attainment of this ' post-conventional' moral stance which is reached only in a maturity which sets little store by what 'the others think'.

It is clear that the stages of moral development represented by the post-conventional level are different in kind from the others located by Kohlberg. Gibb's critique (61) highlights the nature of this difference. Kohlberg's 5th and 6th post-conventional stages are to be regarded differently from the first four preconventional and conventional stages of moral development because they are not universal and unconscious and therefore 'natural' in the Piaget sense. In other words, they are not necessarily attained as a matter of development. The final two stages, however, are to be seen as existential rather than natural, requiring experiences of personal moral choice and responsibility. In other words, their attainment requires the making of a conscious option.

It is therefore possible to be more precise than Lonergan about the elements which might be required for moral conversion. Lonergan's view of moral conversion lies somewhere between Kohlberg's preconventional and the conventional levels. Basic moral conversion to conventional morality is then essentially uncritical, locating authority in absolutely given social values (62). But conversion involves not only the recognition of one's own moral consciousness but also the active decision to accept fully the exigencies of that moral consciousness in terms of progression. And that involves the choice not only of values rather than satisfaction as the basis for decision but of oneself — as opposed to principles — as the free and responsible orginator of the value expressed in one's decisions and choices (63). Critical moral conversion to a post-conventional stance goes beyond restricting one's own

311

horizon in terms of value, then, by grounding that horizon of
value in the reality of oneself as a critical, originating
value (64).

This perspective clarifies the relationship between
moral and intellectual conversion. As intellectual
conversion is a special instance of cognitive
self-transcendence in that it involves intellectual
self-appropriation, so too moral conversion is a special
instance of moral self-transcendence (65). Moral conversion
in the objective uncritical sense — where it is simply a
matter of making the option for the good of others - does not
presuppose intellectual conversion; it could be based simply
on religious motivation. But critical moral conversion
requires either explicit or at least implicit intellectual
conversion, because it requires a critical approach to
values, and thus has to be seen in the context of personal
development as a whole.

vi.   Moral conversion in practice.

We now consider the basis of 'authentic value'. Moral
conversion entails the adoption of a value nexus which is
consciously and reflectively chosen. In other words, moral
maturity does not involve simply the adoption of a new or
different scale of values given by a different social or
cultural milieu. It involves a critical and reflective
decision as to what must be the basis of moral choice for
that particular person. For the believer, as for Paul, that
basis is to be found in the life and person of Jesus.
Metanoia is not just repentance, it is also commitment, not
just a keeping of the letter of the law, but a radical
adoption of Gospel values by the disciple. The values
implicit in the parables and in the stories of the Kingdom
are a total reversal of the usually accepted priorities. The
stranger is accepted, the enemy loved, the poor are

preferred, the prodigal welcomed, the outcast drawn in.
Above all, rewards bear no relationship to what is deserved.
The values implict in these choices are totally opposed to
those given to us by social and cultural requirements — as
indeed they were for the Jews. At the most profound level
all the Gospel stories say the same thing — that the
ultimate intrinsic value is the god of the human person (66)
and that instrumental values are those which serve to achieve
the fullness of human living. It follows that these values
must relate to whatever provides for the needs of persons.
The needier they are, the greater their claim on us. Our own
ultimate need of salvation is satisfied by Jesus himself;
discipleship requires us to imitate his commitment to us by
our commitment to serve others. Openness to the message of
the kingdom thus involves a 'deconditioning' process, whereby
we shed the values we previously held, and adopt those of the
Gospel.

I discussed in Ch.4. the way in which the cultural nexus
of values which underpins our thinking about economic life
and material well-being is based fundamentally on the value
of self-interest. In a culture where the virtue of rational
thought is decisive, economics advances a definition of
rationality which runs in terms of the maximisation of
self-interest — thereby legitimating it, and the necessity of
consistency of choice in order to achieve that end (67).
Rational — ie self-interested — behaviour on the part of the
economic agent is both assumed and required. This clearly
presents problems. It would seem extraordinary to advocate
the pursuit of self-interest as uniquely rational, because
such an argument involves the implicit rejection of the role
of ethical considerations in economic decision-taking (68).
Furthermore, to maintain the rationality of self-interest
must consequently involve a negation of the importance or
validity of the moral conscience. Selfishness as a
requirement of rationality (which is itself a cultural
requirement of sanity) provides an insuperable constraint to

the moral development of the economic agent. This is not to say that people will always act selfishly; Sen quotes (69) the example of Japan where economic success is based on behaviour which is loyal and self-sacrificing rather than selfish. Non-selfish or altruistic behaviour may be well be more normal than the 'special-case' assumption of behaviour guided by self-interest (70). The point is that the advocacy of selfishness as an instrumental value serving the intrinsic value of rationality is totally at variance with the demands of the Gospel. Moral conversion must entail a rejection of this most fundamental of all economic values, and an adoption of what is normally considered to be the non-rational or irrational – a commitment to the welfare of others rather than self (71). This will in turn require a fundamental rejection of all notions of welfare-as-utility.

A transvaluation of values will involve a realisation that welfare has to do not with the fulfilment of wants but with the fulfilment of needs. Once we accept this we begin to see how one-sided is any definition of welfare which is purely economic. Our society, a 'welfare state', recognises the necessity for the provision of needs for those who lack the essentials of life. But the way in which this is done simply extends the principles of 'welfarism' to society at large, because we presume that we can know and understand what others need, and that it can be clearly defined in terms of commodities. Ignatieff (72) questions whether it is possible to speak for the needs of others, and indeed (73) whether it is possible to define what a particular group of human beings needs in order to flourish as persons. The clearest example of this (we are too close to our own welfare state to be able to use it as an example) is provided by the example of less developed countries and the misguided attempts of advanced societies to provide for their 'needs'.

To provide for the needs of those who cannot provide for their own is the hallmark of any moral community. But how do

we define those needs, and is it consonant with moral
maturity to provide for those needs as defined by the
providers — ie as socially constructed? (74). Furthermore,
needs can be provided as a matter of right, as a matter of
deserving, or as a matter of charity. Current political
ideology swings away from the first of these options and
towards the other two. But merit is not a Gospel criterion,
and charity creates the ambiguity of power on the one hand
and dependency on on the other. Also, we tend to
circumscribe categories of need (75), and in doing this we
negate the existence of other needs — the need for respect,
the need to be listened to, the need for dignity. Authentic
moral maturity means that we value the person in a way which
helps us to define needs not in terms of what people lack,
but in terms of what they must have in order to realise
themselves as human persons, and that we fulfil those needs
unconditionally.

Moral conversion will entail a reinterpretion of our
notion of justice. Justice is defined by us and by our
system in terms of distribution on the basis of merit derived
from our own efforts, or in terms of fairness in the sense of
equality of treatment. In theological terms we operate a
version of Pelagianism in economic values. But the Gospel
version of justice involves distribution according to need
(76). Needs vary in kind; some may be more urgent than
others. This kind of distribution will involve, in a world
where resources are finite, redistribution from the rich to
the poor and powerless. It will also involve the necessity
to correct the injustice which gave rise to the problem in
the first instance. Justice is thus clearly not attained by
equality of treatment, because need varies. It involves a
positive option in favour of those whose need is greatest,
irrespective of the merit of their case.

Freedom, too, takes on a new meaning. Culturally
speaking, freedom is always thought of in the context of

choice, economic or otherwise. Milton Friedman (77) sees
freedom of choice as an essential component of a 'free
market'. What he really means by freedom of choice is an
absence of coercion by government. Not only is this view
contingent on the assumption that freedom exercised by one
does not hinder the freedom of others, but it also implies
that all can compete equally. The arguments against this are
outlined in Ch.4. Freedom in this sense is a cultural myth;
its exercise creates as many barriers to freedom as it
negates.

   The problem about this view of freedom is that it is
limited to a view of freedom as 'freedom from' coercion in
the market. The only choice involved is the ability to
choose to compete against others in order to gain what they
lose. A wider – and more biblically based – sense of the
value of freedom must encompass not only aspects of 'freedom
from', but also the idea that freedom is 'freedom to' in a
genuine and creative sense. The scriptural value of freedom
has always to be historically and culturally interpreted;
scripturally freedom has the sense of liberation, not from
that which restrains one from aggression, but from that which
threatens, from danger or oppression – i.e.it liberates from
the aggressor. Cultural content is given to that by thinking
of the position of minorities, the inability of the poor to
provide food for their children, the existential burden of
despair, guilt and meaninglessness in people's lives, the
confusion of ignorance in a complex world, the loneliness of
isolation in a crowd. Freedom must be thought of as freedom
from the fear and alienation inherent in such situations.
But freedom must also mean 'freedom to' do what was hitherto
impossible – to relate to others in relationships (1John
3.23) and in community (11Cor.3.17), to actively reject
cultural divisions and taboos (Col.2.16–23, 1Cor.12.13, 7.22,
Gal.3.28, 4.7, 5.6), to live in the confidence of being made
whole and to be able to share that experience with others
(78). Such freedom is the fruit of liberation, of

redemption; it is a freedom of being as well as of doing, and it runs parallel with new ways of interpreting the meaning of welfare and of justice (79).

vii Conversion in a social context.

The introductory section of this chapter argued that the phenomenon of conversion, as well as having cognitive and moral dimensions, must also be seen in a communal and historical perspective, as those who have experienced 'conversion' act out their commitment to recreate their world. The converted person does not exist in isolation: not only is his self-identity contingent on his interaction with others in social groupings, but his actions are determined by the role he plays in the context of institutional and organisational norms within the structures of society. Somehow, then, there must be a social face to personal conversion; there must be some kind of dialectic between conversion of persons and conversion of structures, because redemption and the coming of the Kingdom are visions applicable to the history of communities as well as to those of persons. In order to analyse this we need firstly to remind ourselves of what action in a social context entails, and secondly we need to examine how such action is affected, changed or modified by conversion as a personal reality. The first issue is illumined by Giddens' analytical framework discussed in the last chapter, the second can be discussed in the context of the theological contribution of Arthur Rich.

It will be helpful at this point to give a brief account of the work of Arthur Rich, so that his ideas can be set in juxtaposition with those of Giddens. Rich sees 'the permanent task of a Christian faith' as being the achievement of human righteousness on all levels of existence, and this includes the achievement of an ethical social order. The core of his theology thus addresses itself to the problem of decisiontaking by the believer in an imperfect world, given that his decisions must be guided by "a decisive commitment to structural change that leads to a politically, socially and economically more just ordering of things in the interests of the disadvantaged of the world" (80), because human justice is an absolute value derivative of a Kingdom which is already come in Christ. Social ethics then becomes no less than "theology reflected in the mirror of what we do; it is a concern for the shape that is to be given to christian living in the modern world" (81).

Rich's concerns focus on three questions:
1. How do we arrive at an ethically responsible set of social structures?
2. How can we propose a theologically grounded solution to the first question when scripture gives us no clear lead?
3. What norms do the demands of love impose? (82)

The theological perspective from which he approaches these problems can be simply stated. Man is man in relationship — to God, to himself, and to others. With God he is co-creator of both self and world. But he lives with his historical declaration of autonomy by which he has set up his own will over and against that of God. He thus lives a monological as opposed to a dialogical existence (83), and this has consequences for action, for what he does to himself and to others. On the other hand, as a believer in the Christ-event, he lives with an eschatological perspective by which he knows that the Kingdom has already come in Christ. This entails a commitment to work for that Kingdom with an 'absolute hope' in spite of the existence of personal and social evil. This hope allows him to settle for the relative in the world in the knowledge that God will work through what is the relatively more acceptable, even though still imperfect human situation, because He cannot work through unattainable utopias. So he can live in the hope of a future which is on the one hand the result of the present and on the

other hand is that which approaches and beckons the present;
that hope sacralises the imperfect present and gives courage
to work for justice and for change within imperfect
structures. It is an important tenet of Rich's theology that
it is possible to live hopefully in a world where the signs
of the kingdom are not always apparent. But that is only
possible if we accept the premise, which is central to that
theology, that 'structural evil' has to be fought so that the
kingdom may be realised.

    In order to see how this might be possible we need to
give practical content to the concept of structure.
"Structures", says E.P.Thompson,

>   "are not a discovery of the last two
>   decades, with a lonely forerunner in Karl
>   Marx. As soon as we talk about
>   'organisation', (or 'organism'), about
>   'system', about 'the laws of supply and
>   demand', or about 'institutions' and about
>   'functionaries', we are talking about
>   structure; and we are likely also to be
>   talking about the way human behaviour is
>   ruled, shaped, ordered, limited, and
>   determined"(84).

Giddens, as we have seen, renders the concept precise by
seeing structure as rules and resources generated and
reproduced by action. Structure is thus dynamically
implicated in the freedom of action. But it is important to
be clear on the implications of this for the notion of
freedom itself. In a social context the links assumed to
exist between decision and action on the one hand, and action
and agency on the other, no longer exist. Social action
often occurs as role play, as fulfilling norms, as carrying
out the decisions of others. Decision and action are thus
separated. Even when decision and action are more closely
linked, there are unintended conseqences of action, so that

action and agency are divorced from one another. The
monitoring of consequences, both intended and unintended,
will have its repercussions on structure. Action is
monitored and rationalised in the light of consequences, and
this process provides the motivation and the unacknowledged
conditions of future action. In this way structure is
reproduced by us, and if structural evil exists it is we who
create it. It follows from this that any idea of freedom
which assumes that decision, action and agency are
inextricable is inadequate. So also is the idea that
personal conversion results in 'freedom from' social
constraints on action. The social world does not merely
constrain, it also enables our action (85).

The complexity of the idea of 'freedom' does not absolve
us from responsibility for the consequences of our actions.
We may not be 'free', but we are not powerless, we do
monitor, reflect on, and rationalise our actions. As we
create and recreate the structures of our world we are 'free
to' create our world, and in so doing we are co-creators with
God and thus responsible for what we create. Arthur Rich
argues that it is precisely in this creation of structures
that we participate in the ongoing task of creation (86).
Creation is not complete; the tension between the Kingdom
already come in Christ and not attainable until the eschaton
forces us to concern ourselves with the social forms and
institutions which are temporary but at the same time
carriers of the kingdom. This has always been the
understanding of Christian communities; Schillebeeckx reminds
us (87) that the response of early Christians to the life of
the Spirit within them was to attempt to discover new social
forms more in keeping with the spirit of the Gospel. The
value of Giddens' work from a theological point of view that
it enables us to see just how this human task of co-creation
is carried out. His theoretical and conceptual framework
identifies for us the mechanisms by which we create and
recreate, reproduce or change the structures of our world.

He thus provides us with a methodology which can ground and support the theological perspective provided by Rich's thought.

The exact relationship between conversion as a personal reality and conversion as the elimination of structural evil now becomes clearer. Just as personal conversion can only happen in the context of the social, so must social conversion be contingent on personal conversion. As we recreate social structures using existing rules and resources we can do so blindly, selfishly or unreflectively. There will be a dialectic of personal and structural evil: in the measure that we are 'unconverted' we will perpetuate evil structures — even though we may be personally charitable — simply because we will fail to see and to accept responsibility for consequences. Alternatively, in the monitoring of our actions we can be critical, reflective, and aware that the ' rules' and values which guided them must be continually subjected to the demands of the Kingdom.

This view of conversion as inextricably personal— and— social is consonant with the fact that Jesus's preaching about repentance had both a personal and a social dimension. The necessity for 'metanoia' arises because of sinfulness, but sinfulness is not just personal. Baum (88) argues that we have placed excessive emphasis on notions of personal sin and on the necessity for personal salvation, but we have neglected the task of discovering the meaning of social sinfulness, i.e. of structural evil (89). The two are intertwined, and so therefore are personal and social metanoia. It would be wrong to believe that structures would be put right if people were good — but it would be just as wrong to believe that changing structures would be sufficient to achieve a just world irrespective of the reality of personal evil.

We must now enquire as to the precise content of the

idea of social sinfulness, structural evil. Arthur Rich has commented that we owe to Karl Marx the fact that the idea has become theologically available to us (90). Marx saw social or structural evil as arising from the nature of the relations of production, and as defined in terms of the consequent injustice and oppression. This is an 'objective' or consequentialist view of structural evil. In this sense social sin is the failure to achieve a just, participatory and sustainable society, which is peaceful, harmonious and fully human. Injustice and oppression, power and individualism, selfishness and the misuse of resources are all examples of structural evil in a consequentialist sense.

But we must also consider the subjective aspect, and here we have a number of models. Social sin can be thought of as the collective bias explicated so well by Lonergan (91), the essence of which is blindness to insight. Blindness is also one of the biblical images which come to mind. In Isaiah 15:6, 9-10, and in Mt:13, 14-25 we find characterisations of blindness, deafness and hardness of heart. Rich says 'when man ceases dialogical existence and makes himself into the tribunal before which he has to answer'(92) he is no longer open to God's word. Man's estrangement from God gives rise to 'fundamental guilt' as his monological self assertiveness causes the rule of man over man and rejects the rule of God over man. Personal guilt thus arises when we perpetuate the consequent structures.

This notion of social sinfulness, which resides in the collective rather than in individual intentionality, is one way of giving meaning to the idea of original or inherited sin (Ps51 v.5). We are born into human situations where social evil is inbuilt — in the norms governing social action where outcomes are evil, in the perpetuation of unresolved conflicts in family, class or state (Cain and Abel), in the irresponsible use of resources. We are socialised in order

that we too may play our part in the maintenance of those
structures. We become actors and agents responsible for evil
consequences, both immediate and unintended. It is important
to remember here that in saying this we do not simply mean
that the structures we actually have are essentially evil.
No human structure would approximate to the Kingdom because
all structures are flawed. This is the essence of the whole
problem as Rich sees it, and this is why he places so much
emphasis on hope. In one sense there is nothing we can do to
bring about the Kingdom, but in another sense we do what we
do in the hope that God will work even in and through the
structures of our flawed world.

How can we characterise 'structural evil' in this
subjective or locational sense? Baum (93) suggests three
aspects of social sinfulness which we can see reflected in
the three issues discussed in Ch.5 — organisational
role-play, individual conformity in groups, and the dynamics
of group decision-taking.

1. There are firstly those social and institutional rules
and procedures which have as their consequence the
dehumanisation of those affected by them. Those whose
freedom and dignity are threatened can be employees within
organisations where work practices are alienating or pay is
insufficient to provide a decent standard of living. One of
the most urgent examples here is the activity of
multinational conpanies in newly industrialising countries,
where labour-intensive production processes are located in
low-wage countries with oppressive political regimes. But
this is simply an extreme example of the way in which all
capitalistic structures are fundamentally flawed. Rich (94)
points to the way in which work becomes a tradable commodity
while the worker has no say in the organisation of his own
working life. The same point is made by Pope John Paul II in
Laborem Exercens — "man is treated as an instrument of
production, whereas he...ought to be treated as the effective
subject of work and its true maker and creator" (95). Those

affected may also be outside the organisation, on the receiving end of such procedures. We can think here of those on social welfare or unemployment benefit, where there is often a deliberate attempt to demean recipients. We can think, too, of those in third world countries whose dependance on aid limits their own initiative and self-reliance. The other side of this coin is the sinfulness of structures which advantage people and thus promote selfishness - which is also a threat to dignity. Tax systems which provide loopholes, incentive and bonus systems, competitive educational systems - all these provide the occasion for the pursuit of personal gain at the expense of others.

2. In the second place, structural evil is embodied in the ideologies, symbols and modes of thought, which legitimise such norms and procedures, as well as in the language used to describe them, because language makes those structures possible. The exploitation of labour is legitimised by the ideology of the free market and of the profit motive, other consequences of institutional proceedures are legitimised by the value placed on achievement, by the importance given to competition, and by the ideology of growth. In this way false consciousness is created. Language structures thought and hence social practice. Language which reifies persons encourages practice which treats persons as things. Racial disharmony springs from a use of words ('wogs', 'Pakis'), which emphasises the 'otherness' of ethnic groups. Faith, too, can be presented as ideology, as an alternative world-view to atheism, rather than as a loving encounter with the living God in Christ (96).

3. Finally we can discern the presence of structural evil in the way in which the dynamic of collective decision taking blunts the exercise of individual responsibility and permits the practice of self-interest. Decision taking by groups - in particular those without formal decision-taking procedures

- gives the illusion that collective decisions are the outcome of free choices on the part of participants, but in fact these decisions are often the rational consequence of institutional distortions of information, prevailing norms of behaviour, and the influence of powerful individuals on the less powerful. Decisions taken in this way worsen the consequences of what are already adverse institutional procedures, and it has to be admitted that in a society where political decisions are usually taken in response to the activities of pressure groups, most public decision taking is of this nature.

It is possible to argue that structural evil is on the increase. Haughton (97) points to the fear which is engendered by the threats to safety of existence by factors such as pollution and nuclear proliferation, to the fact that thinking is controlled by the media, to the way in which decisions are taken by the faceless few — "from on high they plan oppression, they have set their mouths in the heavens, and their tongues dictate to the earth. So the people turn to follow them, and drink in all their words" (Ps 72). Reactions to all this vary. It is possible to join the dominant structures, either in fact or by identification. It is possible to ignore the whole issue of structural evil by either living mentally within a personal circle of existence — family, friends — which is comprehensible and controllable, or even by escaping totally into fundamentalism or superstition.

Is there a way out? In theological terms there has to be, because of the reality of redemption, and it has to be found within the perspective of 'metanoia'. Just as personal conversion involves a repentance which has cognitive and moral dimensions, so must the conversion of social structures involve a personal 'turning from', a distancing from 'false consciousness' and the growth of an awareness of evil wherever it exists. This process has been termed 'conscientisation'. Conscientisation (98) will involve not simply an awareness as 'prise de conscience', but the development of a critical and hence epistemological stance which will give rise to questions about the bases of all the structures of our world. This critical function will also be a prophetic one. The critical element will require us to work for the exposure of ideologies and false consciousness, the prophetic function will involve the attribution of responsibility for injustice and suffering to their perpetrators. Nor will the church itself as a human institution be exempt from critique (99). Injustice to persons within church structures, modes of decision-taking by hierarchical bodies, and the use of religion for ideological purposes can all be criticised. Baum argues (100) that where it is the task of critical theology to reflect on social praxis, as has been done in Latin America, the role of the church in that situation must be included in that critique. This role becomes mandatory for theology in situations of human injustice; the church thus functions as both human institution and prophet in such situations.

Conversion in a social context thus presupposes intellectual and moral conversion, because it requires the exercise of a critical stance and a questioning of received cultural and social values. And just as personal conversion involves personal recreation, so will conversion in a social context involve a commitment to the recreation of society in closer accord with Gospel values and the promise of the kingdom. Grace as the renewal of life thus applies in a collective as well as in an individual context.

viii   <u>Social conversion in practice.</u>.

How is all this to come about? We normally speak of conversion as if it were something which happened within the person, in the heart and mind. In the case of conversion in a social context, concrete action must be the vehicle by which the phenomenon is externalised. But what do we do? How do we in our everyday lives as converted persons overcome unjust structures, remembering that we ourselves are part of the process whereby such structures are generated and reproduced? It is tempting to believe that there is something we can do in the sense of achieve, that if we were only brave enough, or strong enough, or powerful enough we could succeed in banishing injustice. But this is an unproductive view, simply because none of this can ever be the case. To think like this therefore only gives us a licence to despair, or to forget about the issue and do nothing.

This is where Rich's approach is so fruitful. The key to the above dilemma, according to Rich, is to be found in being rather than in doing. Given the relativity of human existence – ie the fact that no one humanly attainable situation can be specified as 'the Kingdom, what is required is 'right action' within social structures. 'Right action' will be defined not in terms of achievement, but in terms of the fact that it springs from an authentic humanity. Authenticity, it will be remembered, is the ideal towards which self-transcendence strives. Rich suggests a number of criteria for being authentically human in this fullest and most Christian sense of the word – in other words, criteria for action by the converted person (101). The basis of these criteria (102) is theologically solid, because it is to be found in the grounding of one's existence in relationship with Another, who addresses but also demands, answers but also makes us answerable. That Other is no less than

> "Jesus Christ, in whom the Father-God
> becomes transparent, who in the intimacy of
> dialogical existence calls us to
> collaboration and thus to a life in the
> freedom of an active, creative and critical
> responsibility... We are not lords of
> creation, but functionaries with the mandate
> to bring God's healing will into worldly
> existence" (103).

Rich's criteria for being authentically human within the structures of everyday existence are formulated in the following terms -:

1. Being human will entail maintaining a critical distance from the world (Romans 12.2), thus not betraying that which is to come for that which is present and thereby denying the reality of hope. The realisation that the existing social order is only temporary gives us the courage to challenge existing structures and to work for better ways of doing things. But we must not absolutise any existing social order because that puts 'system' before righteousness. All human situations must be constantly held up to the mirror of God's justice, and maintaining a critical distance demands that we see all such situations 'through the eyes of Christ'.

2. Being human will mean realising that even changing structures will not free us from evil or bring about the Kingdom. Our critical stance, which is therefore also prophetic, will on the one hand refuse to idolise any historical reality, and on the other will not allow us to be unrealistic or escapist about existing social situations, since these are the only ones we - and God - have to work with.

3. Being human is working with existing laws, customs, and standards, but at the same time giving priority to our Christian commitment to others within those structures. This follows from the fact that no one structure can approximate

to the Kingdom — all human structures are flawed, and injustice will be part and parcel of all structures. But it is possible to make the workings of existing structures more just on a personal level. Rich uses here the example of Phil.4:8, where Paul exhorts Philemon to treat his slave as the law of love would dictate. The suggestion is that existing structures be relativised and reformulated so as to highlight the relational element: Jesus came not to bring a new law but the questioning of all laws in the light of the law of love. This perspective of relativising will allow us to see that freedom from the law and service to others within that law, although apparent opposites, are part and parcel of the same thing, because it is love which allows us to transcend the bonds imposed by the law.

4. Being human is being radical rather than extremist (104). Being radical is aiming for the totality rather than settling for the partial. Extremism, which is only interested in abstracts, must be fought with the radicality of the relational, otherwise we lose ourselves in pragmatism or ideology.

5. Being human involves living with others in solidarity and brotherhood. It involves allowing others to share what we are, have and do, so that we realise our co-humanity in action with and for others. This is the criterion which asks us to remember that we are human 'with' others (105), even though on the face of it we have little or nothing to do with them. We exist in co-humanity with the marginalised of the world, with the elderly, with criminals, with the forgotten. We exist in solidarity with all those with whom we work. We are co-human with our political enemies, with killers and rapists, with those who injure us, simply because we share with all men God's life and God's promise.

6. Being human on a structural or institutional level translates solidarity into the encouragement of participation in power, rights and decision-taking. Participation is dialogical — we must strive to live with others as we live

with God. Participation is thus proper to what man is. The
model before us is that of the early Christian communities,
where each person was valued and listened to, and where all
shared in decision-taking.

7. Being human is being practical in that we take into
account the 'facts of the matter' in each situation,
assessing them on the one hand from technical and
sociological points of view, but on the other hand from the
point of view of the law of love. It is remembering that it
is impossible to lay down principles to be applied
irrespective of the situation. Only an analysis of the
circumstances will reveal what is required.

What can we take from all this? The first point to be
made is that Rich's whole perspective is deeply
incarnational. It is what we are in the world that counts,
not what we do. His criteria specify some of the things that
being fully human might imply in terms of action. Being
'human' in this sense will be sufficient to transform our
world, because it will mean that Christ is present and active
through us. This in turn will endows persons and structures
with value and meaning, and our participation in structures
and relationships with people will become the means whereby
the Kingdom is realised.

The second point is that the criteria must be taken in
their entirety, rather than singly, as a set of parameters of
the shape of the Christian presence in the world. Some of
these criteria are attitudinal - words like 'realise',
'accept' are used to introduce them. Some are behavioural;
they dictate the quality of our relationships. One, that of
participation, refers to the structural rather than the
personal level. There is no specified form of that
behaviour, however, simply that we should act towards others
in love. This perspective settles once and for all the
question of whether there is such a thing as 'Christian
ethics': Rich would argue that there is only the ethics of a

Christian (106).

We must also be aware of the positive note which is struck by these 'criteria'. We are to be critical, but not to waste time criticising or being negative about existing structures. Every day is a piece of history, every action and every word makes that history. We are to live as Christs within the structures which exist. This clearly implies that there will be times when we protest, times when we subvert, but we will always take seriously the fact that our creational role requires us to be positive and constructive.

Although these criteria form a totality, it is perhaps worthwhile to reflect on the implications of each one for concrete living in an institutional environment. The criterion of 'critical distance',although Rich specifies it in terms of an awareness of the 'temporariness' of existing structures, will also have the effect of causing us to be aware of the kind of roles we play and their consequences. It will make us personally less vulnerable in group contexts, and more careful not to be swept away by the dynamics of 'groupthink'. Our attitude may well be deemed 'radical' by colleagues, but perhaps that is no bad thing. 'Radical' always has connotations of 'dangerous', but that is because it is conflated with 'extremism'. For Rich (107) radicality and extremism are opposites, the distinction being that extremism divorces itself from existing reality, whereas radicality grows from and beyond it.

The second criterion is the one which sets us free from the idea that we need to achieve anything. To use the criterion of success in our efforts, or of achievement, is not an option available to us — we 'preach Christ crucified', Christ who was a failure in human terms. Since there is no nprovement in the social situation which can be defined as he Kingdom' there is no specific outcome which can be med success or failure. We do what we can, and leave the

results to God. This is the necessary mind-set in the light
of the existence of 'unintended consequences', because even
if we do aim for and achieve a given outcome, we never know
whether its ramifications are good or bad in the end.

The other side of this coin is that we are precluded
from idealising any particular world system or social form,
any political party or creed as that which will achieve the
kingdom. Rich (108) points to the fact that both capitalism
and Marxism are simply alternative forms of power structure
which render others powerless. The danger in identifying a
particular political, social or economic strategy as one
which will bring about the Kingdom is that we sacralise the
human demand for social change. What begins as an effort to
work for the Kingdom often ends up by giving priority to
emancipation as an end in itself, and to control over men by
men. Nor can the organisational church at different
historical periods be exempt from these strictures. "God",
says Schillebeeckx, "cannot be used for human ends"(109).
Faith or religion has nothing to say about the specification
of a human order which is in line with God's plan. Faith
does not create a human order, faith creates the person and
persons make the world in fidelity to the Spirit. Faith
demands that we love, and in loving we may be able to create
flashes of God's Kingdom in the world. The commitment of the
believer "makes possible rational criticism of man and
society and the furthering of their good without recourse to
a dreamed-up state of salvation, and without the fiction of a
healed or reconciled world in the limits of our history"
(110).

Having said that, however, and having said that
withdrawal is not an option open to us, it is only possible
to work for change within an institutional context. The
prophet who 'cries in the wilderness' has still a function,
but that role does not belong to everyone. We can relieve
the social effects of injustice by means of personal charity,

but we can only affect the source of that injustice if we become part of the structures which create it, whether they be political parties, industrial or governmental organisations, or the church itself. Our strategy may well then involve a mixture of protest, compliance, and subversion as we struggle for change.

The third of Rich's criteria, that of relationality, demands of us that we focus on that structural level where the Kingdom is really built. Structure may be 'rules and resources' but it is created in intersubjectivity by persons. Norms and procedures may dictate unequal relations between persons, but they cannot dictate or impose inhumanity. Even institutional situations at their most bestial allow for the excercise of some humanity. This is not to say that the structural framework is to be accepted unquestioningly. The forum within which change can be worked for may present itself, but it will not be today and it may not be tomorrow, and in the meantime God continues to work in history.

The criterion of co-humanity or brotherhood reminds us that our roles as persons are not only played out within the structures in which we participate. We have a real role, perhaps yet to be identified, in relation to all humanity, and particularly towards those whom the Gospel calls us to serve. The 'option for the poor' has to be a lived reality in everyday existence: the specific translation of this in organisational contexts is to be found in our attitude to those who are weaker than we are, those who are marginalised by group processes, those who are manipulated. But that option has also a wider context within the community, and within the world as a whole, and the commitment to the poor can translate itself in strange ways. We are only asked to regard the challenge as an ongoing one, and to remain open to ways of response.

Participation is something which can be formalised on a

structural level. It is also something which can be implemented on an interpersonal or small-group level - 'don't tell them, ask them'. Allowing people to articulate what they feel about their own concerns and their own functioning in a work situation removes the element of dehumanisation inherent in hierarchical organisational structures. Again, it is not so much what is done, but how it is done. Participation as a mode of decision-taking, even on a very small scale, respects the dignity of the person and it is thus less likely to result in decisions which threaten the dignity of others.

With the last of his criteria Rich puts the emphasis on the concrete situation as the normative focus for decision-taking given the attitudes and the behaviour patterns already discussed. It is only in the tension created by the confrontation between criteria and the concrete situation that it is possible to say which ought to be done, or to generate 'maxims' which can guide action (111). The status of such maxims is clear - their application is relative not only in the sense that they apply to the particular situation, but they are also relative to the absolute criterion of a humanity acting in faith, hope and love. This criterion is theologically grounded, whereas the grounding of situation-specific maxims is to be found purely in the technical and social understanding necessary to generate them.

I have argued that Arthur Rich gives us a theologically grounded specification of 'criteria for a new humanity' within social structures. We now need to ask whether we can regard this as a complete specification. Rich's approach has strengths and weaknesses. A major strength is the tightness of the assemblage of theological 'building blocks'. There are those who would see as a major weakness the lack of universal principles or maxims to guide behaviour in all circumstances; however, such a criticism would be based on a belief in the existence of an 'objective ethic'. On this ground Rich cannot be faulted (112): he stands squarely in the tradition of one who has heard the Gospel which supersedes the Law. We can also regard Rich as having developed a genuinely 'political' theology, if we take as normative for such a theology the fact that it is grounded "...not on concepts and ideas, but on the dynamics of historical and social human subjects striving to live out the call to conversion, metanoia, or exodus as intellectual, moral, social and religious imperatives" (113). Above all, Rich's approach provides concrete and practical recommendations for those who are committed to the cause of working for justice in the world. The Justice and Peace movement in the Roman Catholic Church, for instance, reflects on the question of changing unjust structures, but there is little practical discussion as to the methodology which should ground this reflection or give rise to action – other than the very general idea of using 'social analysis'. Rich makes of the commitment to justice a feasible and practical option in the context of everyday existence.

However, there is a major lacuna in what is otherwise, theologically and pastorally, a creative viewpoint. Nowhere in the development of Rich's ideas does one find any hint of of a dynamic perspective. We live in faith, hope and love, but we also live, as Giddens has pointed out, in a time–space context, and since our view of time is linear, we must have some view of process. We have already said that there is no reason to hope that the world is made any better by our efforts, or that the Kingdom is brought any nearer. Is there then nothing we can say about the dynamic context of what Rich is saying? What happens over time? I believe there is one perspective which can be developed here, which will introduce notions of process into Rich's theology. It is a perspective which can be said to be located not in 'world' but in 'person'.

ix. Person and praxis.

Rich's theology is about action for the Kingdom. In academic terms it belongs to the genre of theologising which maintains the 'primacy of praxis'. Lamb, who distinguishes five variants (114) of the theory–praxis relationship within theology, sees this type of theology as including several differing perspectives depending on whether praxis is understood as cultural–historical activity, liberal sociopolitical reform, or Marxist revolutionary praxis (115). What all these have in common is an emphasis on praxis as social activity. Theologies of praxis then become reflections on possibilities of redemption through social change.

There is also another sense of the word praxis – ie praxis as doing in the sense of conduct. This is the Greek as opposed to the Marxist sense of the word. Praxis in the fullest sense is thus life lived individually and socially, it is both orthopraxis and social action. However, theologies on the 'liberation' end of the praxis spectrum (116) tend to concentrate on the second sense of the word, on the more of less deterministic outcome of social transformation. God's people must be liberated from unjust structures as the chosen people were liberated by the Exodus. But it is possible to give due weight to the 'primacy of praxis' in theology without adopting simplistic ideas about 'changing the world'. We may not choose to accept the premise that active intervention to achieve a given mode of social change is necessarily redemptive in the theological sense of the term, even though we are obliged to accept the reality of a redemption to be realised in history.

Rich's theology of praxis is not about changing the world, it is about working for the Kingdom. It thus combines both senses of the word 'praxis'. It is based on the New rather than the Old Testament, on the concept of a Kingdom which comes much more mysteriously than any dramatic liberation—event, a Kingdom which is actualised by a God working in history through those with faith in Jesus Christ who love their fellow men in hope. Structures will then be transformed by 'orthopraxis', by decision—taking in faith, hope and love, although this is not necessarily the same thing as saying that the intention is to bring about social change. The intention is to love; we can say little about outcomes in terms of what that love achieves.

What we can say is that just as there is a socially transformative aspect to social praxis, so also must there be a personally transformative aspect to orthopraxis, and it this which may provide the ultimate explanation of the way in which God's saving power becomes actualised in human existence. "All theologies of praxis" says Tracy (117) "... implicitly or explicitly insist that personal transformation is the key to theological truth as 'speaking the truth". In other words, it is not possible to theologise about 'changing the world' unless that theology includes the perspective of self-transformation.

This perspective of self—transformation is the development which is lacking in Rich's analysis. Because he does not develop the idea of personal transformation, we have no way of visualising how the attitudes and behaviour patterns which Rich sees as being constitutive of the Kingdom can result in any form of change. But praxis is totally transformative, of self and of world, and of world because of self. We become what we do. As Tracy says '(118), "Any individual becomes who he/she is as an authentic or inauthentic subject by his actions in an intersubjective and a social—historical world with other subjects and in relationship to concrete social and historical structures and movements." Orthopraxis follows; our actions spring from what we are. Being, doing and becoming form a triad; in the process there arises a dialectic between self-transformation and 'changing the world'.

But how does this come about — how can we precisely characterise the process. This is where we return to Lonergan. The model of action presupposed in this study has been based on Lonergan's philosophy of consciousness. Action is based on experience, understanding, judgement and decision — mental processes which run parallel to the canons of scientific method. But in his later years Lonergan extended his views on method, prompted by what he saw as the demise of the scientific 'age of innocence' where human authenticity could be taken for granted (119), and the arrival of an age where 'human authenticity was in question'. This development is the outcome of the inevitable social process whereby "the shortcomings of the individual become the accepted practice of the group, (this)..can become the tradition accepted in good faith by succeeding generations"(120). In other words, social sin, structural evil spreads through the community from individual to group to tradition, and thus becomes embodied and endemic in cultures and in societies.

But this process has to be reversible. In other words, there has now to be more to human authenticity then being intelligent, reasonable and responsible. 'Method as praxis' requires a reverse orientation, a 'hermeneutic of suspicion'. Whereas empirical 'scientific' method moves upwards through experience, understanding, judgement and decision, so 'method as praxis' moves down through those same procedures. This happens as action and its consequences demand of us as authentic persons that we make an evaluation, a judgement of the value and disvalue in each action — in Giddens' terms, that we monitor actions reflexively. We are thus engaged in both a hermeneutic of suspicion and a hermeneutic of recovery (121) as we discern what is good and condemn what is bad in what we do. This process of evaluating and judging must necessarily lead to fresh understandings, fresh insights.

It will thus change our perceptions and in this way affect
our future cognitional processes and actions (122). And just
as this happens on a personal subjective level, so too on an
objective and disciplinary level will 'scientism' in the
human sciences be replaced by a more evaluative and
humanising scientific stance.

Orthopraxis, right action, is thus reflective and
dialectical. Above all, the interaction between being and
doing is dynamic and liberating. On a personal level it
means that we become more aware, more critical, more
confident as we become surer of our ground and our values.
The socially transformative aspect comes about because of the
consequence of this in terms of our effectiveness. We create
and recreate our world, but we also heal others in the
measure that we are healed. Lonergan (123) sees the creative
aspect translated in history as, so to speak, the upward
movement of human development, where insight, understanding
and judgement give rise to appropriate action. But there is
also development from above downward that springs from love,
and that is the healing process.

> "Where hatred only sees evil, love reveals
> values. At once it commands commitment and
> joyfully carries it out, no matter what the
> sacrifice involved. Where hatred reinforces
> bias, love dissolves it, whether it be the
> bias of unconscious motivation the bias of
> individual or group egoism, or the bias of
> omnicompetent, short-sighted common sense.
> Where hatred plods around in ever narrower
> vicious circles, love breaks the bonds of
> psychological and social determinisms with
> the conviction of faith and the power of
> love"(124).

In short, then, it is orthopraxis as self-transformation
which allows God to create and to heal in history. But it is
not only healing which is required, but also creativity,

because, as Lonergan points out, what is needed is not only the healing of structural sin, but the creation of structures which are free of bias, free of exploitation, free of injustice. We can only do this in the measure that we allow our disciplinary thought and practical action to be governed by the criteria of the Gospel.

==

NOTES - CHAPTER SIX

1. Lonergan (1957) p.xv Introduction.
2. This belief is supported by empirical evidence. The research done by the Religious Experience Unit in Oxford confirms that such experience is common even for those without faith. See Hardy (1979), esp.pp.25-9 for a classification of the characteristics of this experience.
3. James (1902).
4. Maslow (1970).
5. See Barth (1958) Vol.IV/2.
6. Rahner (1975).
7. Augustine; Confessions Book 7:VI,VII XI.
8. See Jung (1971).
9. Merton (1973). The idea of a 'true self' known only to God is basic to Merton's spirituality. The 'false self' is the imperfect self of everyday existence. As we grow towards God we uncover more of the true self, while the 'false self' fades. Final human integration is the full flowering of that self. See Conn (1986) for a study of Merton and conversion.
10. Niebuhr (1963)
11 Rahner op.cit.
12. Merton op.cit.
13. Conn (1986) p.22, who notes that neither self-sacrifice nor self-fulfillment are acceptable images of conversion. Self transcendence, as our response to the drive of the human spirit for meaning, truth, value and love, involves a moving beyond the self in all the dimensions of our existence.
14. Nock (1933).
15. For a critical analysis of conversions in Catholic theology see Curran (1976).
16. Rambo (1982) provides a bibliography of current research on conversion from different disciplinary perspectives.

17. Gaventa (1986) p.7.
18. James op.cit.
19. Nock. op.cit.
20. See Travisano (1970). In psychological terms this form of conversion is associated with maturity in the sense of integration, where the person integrates all his past experience, including his religious affiliations, into a new and meaningful whole.
21. For one analysis of this see Harran (1983) pp.182ff.
22. What follows relies heavily on Gaventa's approach.
23. Sklba (1981). For an alternative presentation see eg. 'Grace and conversion in the Old Testament' by Dom Marc-Francois Lacan in Conn(1978).
24. Ibid p.69.
25. Gaventa op.cit. p.40ff.
26. Ibid p.147ff. For instance, we may cite the descriptions in Acts 9, 22, and 26, where Luke's accounts of Paul's conversion, as well as of other conversions, reveal more about the Lukan understanding of what conversion is than they do about Paul's conversion as such. For Luke, conversion is to be seen not so much as cognitive, but rather as a break with and a rejection of the past, because conversion is understood by him primarily as a beginning, for the individual and for the Church.
27. See Lonergan (1968) p.160.
28. Lonergan (1971) p.237.
29. Ibid p.238.
30. See Doran (1981), Gelpi (1977). The major contribution made by Lonergan's account of conversion is the indentification of conversions as intellectual and moral as well as religious. Doran, Gelpi and others have argued that conversion must also take place in the psychic, affective or emotional aspects of the personality. But this is not the only gap in Lonergan's analysis. It can also be argued that he fails to take account of continual aspects of conversion, as well as

of social and ecclesial aspects - see eg. Dorr (1975). However, this criticism can be countered by a reference to Lonergan's later work on 'method as praxis', which is the subject of the final part of this chapter.

31. Lonergan (1971) p.242.

32. Lonergan (1974), pp.65-7.

33. Conn (1986) p.24.

34. Butler (1975) p.325.

35. For accounts of this see Conn (1976), (1978), (1986).

36. See Ryan (1981).

37. Lonergan (1971) p.238.

38. Intellectual conversion must then be a 'condition of possibility' for doing philosophy. Lonergan argues that it must also form the basis of 'doing theology'. See (1971) pp.270/1.

39. Ibid 238.

40. Ibid pp.238-9. For other references see Conn (1986) fn.48p.315.

41. Lonergan (1957) Ch.11.

42. Op.cit. p.329.

43. Op.cit. p.xviii.

44. Lonergan (1971) p.13.

45. Conn (1986) p.122 cites the example of Elizabeth Bennett in Jane Austen's 'Pride and Prejudice' as someone who made a judgement which was both prejudiced and based on insufficient evidence.

46. Lonergan (1971) p.52.

47. Bernstein (1979) p.51. This author discusses the extent to which conversion, or paradigm-shift, has occurred in social theory. For a critical discussion of the lack of such a shift in economics see Hodgson (1988) esp.Ch.1

48. For a comprehensive list of references to authors of the Frankfurt school see eg. Lamb (1980a) p.55,fn.3.

49. Major representative sources of these ideas include Erikson (1965), Piaget (1968), and Kohlberg (1981), (1984).

50. Lonergan (1971) p.240.

51. Lonergan takes this concept from de Finance (1962) p.287ff - see Lonergan (1971) p.237.

52. Happell and Walter (1986) p.38.

53. Lonergan (1967), p.242.

54. Conn (1986)p.18.

55. Macquarrie (1970).

56. Niebuhr (1963).

57. Lonergan (1967) p.242.

58. Conn (1976) p.395.

59. Lonergan (1971) p.13ff. gives a structured account of self-appropriation, but does not discuss it in the context of moral self-appropriation in this particular sense.

60. Kohlberg (1976) p.35.

61. Gibbs (1977).

62. Lonergan's analysis (1971) p.49ff on good of order appears particularly uncritical of existing social forms.

63. Conn (1976) p.377.

64. Conn (1986) p.27, see also Conn in Lamb (1981b) p.371. for another discussion of the same issue.

65. Conn (1976) p.394.

66. Redemptor Hominis. Pope John Paul sees man as being at the centre of all things, endowed with infinite value by the God who created and redeemed him and in whose image he is made.

67. See eg. Koutsoyannis (1979) Ch.23 for one standard textbook presentation of this point.

68. Sen makes this argument in (1987).

69. Ibid p.18.

70. See Collard (1978) for a discussion of what constitutes altruism.

71. Ibid, see also Benn and Mortimore (1976) for a discussion of non-rationality.

72. Ignatieff (1984).

73. Ibid p.12.

74. Seabrook (1986),'Needs and commodities'. In Ekins (ed)

(1986).

75. Rawls (1972) p.92. See Rich (1984) pp.207ff who, although he draws parallels between his own methodology and that of Rawls, points out that Rawls fails to take into account the consequences of unrestricted economic freedom.

76. Lonergan (1971) p.47ff.on typology of needs in the context of the human good. For a discussion of various norms of justice see Gordon (1980) also Greenberg & Cohen (ed) (1982), Ch.12.

77. Friedman (1980).

78. Schillebeeckx (1980) p.479ff outlines the biblical concept of freedom.

79. As autonomous moral agents what we choose is not so much values, but interpretations of socially given values which are more akin to those of the Gospel.

80. Rich (1969) p. 88. The English-language source on the work of Arthur Rich is Tonks (1984).

81. Op.cit.p.88.

82. Strohm (ed.) (1980), Introduction.

83. This idea is developed in Rich (1968).

84. Thompson (1978) p.339.

85. Thompson (1984) ch. argues that Giddens' views on structuration do not give enough weight to structure as constraint on action. Constraints may in fact bind, leading to 'single exit' solutions, because the range of options available to individuals and groups is differentially distributed and structurally circumscribed.

86. Rich (1975) Ch.3.

87. Schillebeeckx (1980) p.562.

88. Baum (1975) Ch.9.

89. Gaudium et Spes paras. 25-31, 34, 35.

90. Cited by Tonks in an unpublished paper given in Selly Oak in 1983.

91. See Ch.5, section viii of this dissertation. Also Lonergan (1957) Ch.7, (1971) pp.243/4.

92. Tonks (1984) p.310.

93. Baum (1975) p.201.

94. Rich (1973) Ch.1.

95. Laborem Exercens p.25.

96. Rich (1962) Ch1.

97. Haughton (1980).

98. See eg. Freire (1974).

99. Haughton op.cit.

100. Baum op.cit.

101. The specification of these criteria vary as between sources - for an overview see Strohm (1980) pp.22-28, Tonks (1984) pp.169-181. The most recent reworking is to be found in Rich (1984) pp.173-201. This source includes the criterion of 'mitgeschopflichkeit' - creatureliness.

102. Rich (1984) pp.174ff.

103. Op.cit.pp.178/9.

104 See Tonks (1984) p.192 fn.77, who points out that radicality was an included as an earlier criterion, but was later dropped from the list.

105. Ibid p.176.

106. Ibid p.21.

107. Ibid p.192 fn.82.

108 Rich (1973) Ch.1

109. Schillebeeckx (1980) p.774.

110. Ibid p.777.

111. Rich (1984) Ch.8.

112. For other criticisms of Rich's approach see Tonks op.cit. pp.281ff.

113. Lamb (1982) p.120.

114. Ibid Ch.3.

115. Ibid p.68. For another discussion of this see Tracy (1981a) Ch.9

116. For an overview of various strands of liberation theology see Kirk (1979). A more critical view of this is provided by Novak (1986).

117. Tracy (1981a) p.42.

346

118. Tracy (1981b) p.35.
119. Lonergan (1985) p.156
120. Ibid p.151/2.
121. Lamb (1982) p.129 acknowledges this as Ricoeur's terminology.
122. Giddens also speaks of a process of monitoring and rationalisation of action, but he says nothing as to the perspective out of which this is done. In other words, Giddens' actor is free to create and recreate structures to suit his own purpose, whether that be evil or good. Lonergan's actor, on the other hand, evaluates from a basis of human authenticity, as would Rich's actor.
123. Lonergan (1985) p.106.
124. Ibid p.106.

==

CONCLUSION

Theology is hope seeking understanding

This study has used insights from several different disciplines in its discussion of the problems of living out an 'option for the Kingdom'. The value of such insights, as 'acts of understanding' (Lonergan) is that they can provide theology with tools of analysis and critique to be used in the task of reflecting on 'praxis' in the light of the word of God. These insights have been of different kinds. They have been critical in the sense that they have provided counterarguments to prevailing intellectual positions such as reductionism. They have also been destructive in the measure that they have rejected the hegemony of particular knowledge claims (positivism), challenged the validity of metaphysical assumptions ('market forces'), and exposed the ideological status of cultural beliefs, both ontological and axiological. Insights have been ethical where they have highlighted the poverty of cultural interpretations of basic human values of welfare, justice and freedom. They have been constructive insofar as they have formulated 'models of man' more in tune with scriptural ideas. And finally, they have been structural where they have provided frameworks within which to analyse the 'domain of the social'.

There are two final issues which need to be raised. One of these concerns the methodology used in this study and its limitations, the other concerns the overall implications of the analysis. On the question of methodology, the basic task, as we have seen, has been to create a modern interpretation of Romans 7.18-25. All interpretations have their limitations. This interpretation is heavily biased in favour of one specific and narrow cultural context. The context is neither sufficiently wide to encompass the

English-speaking world community, nor is it wide enough to embrace the Western European context. The rationale for this limitation is to be found in the necessity to be specific. The wider the illustrative context chosen, the greater the level of generality. It is not so important that the reader should be able to empathise with everything which has been said. It is far more important that the approach should provide a method which can be used by others to reflect on the cultural context of their own particular faith experience. Other reflections may well engender analyses which are different because, for instance, they spring from very different cultural perspectives.

However, there are certain 'ground rules' which can be suggested. There are also some reservations which should be made.

1. The importance of locating faith in experience is central. Faith can be a variety of things, but if it is not part of experience and recognised as such it will have no result in terms of lived praxis. Only that which is experienced and affirmed and validated and judged to be the case can have consequences in terms of action.

2. The Kingdom is the symbol for that which defines the way in which we have to translate our faith into our lives. The exhaustive linguistic analysis of the characteristics of the Kingdom in Chapter 1 is designed to emphasise the fact that the notion of 'Kingdom' has more than merely symbolic or mythological value for us. In the measure that it is possible to give concrete content to the idea by identifying its attributes, it is possible to find its practical relevance for our everyday lives.

3. The selection of various accounts of action in Chapter 2 is necessarily arbitrary, and is by no means an exhaustive catalogue of explanations of action. This does not detract from the central point of the argument, which is that we need to develop a more rounded view of action if we are to locate

the ways in which it is culturally conditioned. There is a sense in which no reductionistic account of action can allow for the possibility of conditioning because by definition such accounts are 'objective' and 'value—free'. An adequate model of man must therefore characterise action in a way which makes it possible to locate the dimensions of such conditioning. For the purposes of this exercise it might well be possible to vary the approach of the study at this point, but the choice of model would still have to be subject to this criterion.

4. In choosing to focus on the influence of economic reasoning and economic motivation on the conditioning of action, I am aware that I make an arbitrary choice which excludes other possible lines of approach. However, I feel that it is true to the spirit of the study to opt for the particular area of human experience with which I am most familiar.

5. I also have to admit that to characterise the discipline of economics as I do is to paint a radically critical picture. The image of economics presented here is not, however, a distorted one. The perspective which is highlighted in these pages is that which is perceived culturally and legitimated and popularised ideologically. In fact, the ideological use of the basic tenets of traditional economic theory over the last ten years has done much to raise awareness of the fundamental problems which it embodies. There is a growing body of critique which has been encouraged by the fact that a discipline which has considered itself 'scientific' can become so overtly ideological. Chapter 3 makes the point that all science is ideological, but this is not the general perception or expectation; science is generally considered to be the antithesis of ideology. The growth of this critique is effectively limited, however, by the tightening of research funding, the evaluation of institutions as to their dominant position, and individual necessity for job security and renewal of

contracts.

6. With regard to values, there is an issue which is logically prior to the analysis in Chapter 4 of cultural interpretations of received values. It may be the case that what one culture perceives as basic values may not be those chosen by another culture. The most obvious point to be made here is that other cultures may interpret the 'good' not in terms of personal welfare, but rather in terms of the group, the tribe, or the state.

7. The 'organisational' context of action requires to be looked at in greater depth. This is one area which would benefit from a cross-cultural comparison, since it must obviously be the case that outcomes in terms of the conditioning of action will be affected by such factors as cultural peceptions of authority, power and status.

8. Working for the Kingdom demands the intellectual freedom and the moral autonomy outlined in Chapter 6, and this must be a conclusion whose validity transcends the narrow cultural context. In adopting the theology of Arthur Rich I am aware that I have again committed the interpretation to the context of Western industrial capitalism. Rich's attempt to uncover and construct a 'theology of being' in a world of imperfect structures works from a theological point of view. However, any attempt to create such a theology, however general the behavioural and attitudinal recommendations, can do no more than reach towards truth. In fact, the whole of this enterprise has to be relativised in the light of a Gospel which has a habit of casting changing lights on the human situation in order to illumine the darkness and the ambiguity. None of it can be the last word: it is offered, therefore, as no more than a sign of a hope which seeks understanding in a confused and confusing human situation.

There are two implications which arise from this study. One involves the manner of 'doing' theology (theory), the other concerns the living out of a faith commitment (praxis).

Theology needs to establish a real dialogue with other disciplines so that it can use such insights to reflect cogently on the human situation. Faith must speak not only to culture, but also through the use of cultural forms of every kind. It must speak not only through the obvious forms of ritual, myth and symbol, but also through other media which can communicate its content – language and the printed word, art, film, television. But faith also has to use disciplinary thought forms, and the understanding which they achieve, to interpret the historical situation as God sees it. Lonergan argued that theology must take serious account of the power and force of disciplinary contributions if it is to have anything to say to audiences outside the purely academic. In fact, one of the central ideas of his later writings was that it was possible to speak in terms of a 'metamethod' which structured the parameters of all disciplinary endeavour, including that of theology. Within this framework the theologian could move freely from one discipline to another,

Both of these views – that 'doing theology' requires an openness to other disciplines – and that all disciplinary activity is subject to a commonality of method – negate the force of a certain type of 'cultural imperialism' to be found within disciplines – best exemplified by the fact that practitioners have to be chartered, qualified, certified, graduated, incorporated before they can practice. Such 'imperialism' has two specific consequences for theology. On the one hand theologians – or bishops – may be tempted to pronounce on matters of political, social or economic significance without any real technical understanding of the issues involved. On the other hand, theologians may consider that politics, economics or sociology are such obscure disciplines that their paradigms are barred to them: they may thus remain silent because they lack the expertise to say anything meaningful.

The dialogue between theology and other disciplines is not only necessary for interpretative purposes. There is an essential role for a prophetic voice to be exercised in our society by those who hear the word of God and reflect on it. The prophetic voice is not merely a critical voice, it is also the voice which gives hope and encouragement to those who pray the God's Kingdom may be established "in our lifetime and in our days . . even speedily and at a near time". People need to see and hear 'signs of the Kingdom' in their own culture and their own language. The prophetic voice can convey the hope of this Kingdom because such hope is both the basis from which theology springs and the outcome of the search for understanding which it represents. This is why the prophetic utterance must not lose its force or its power to convince simply because it has to confine itself to generalities for lack of disciplinary competence.

The second implication to be drawn from this study concerns the person of faith, the 'subject' of this dissertation. We have all at one time or another been persuaded to believe, to value and to practice what is deemed culturally acceptable. Our cultural symbols, myths, rituals, forms of social interaction and discourse all embody presuppositions and values which appear so self-evident as to be unassailable. As economists — and also practitioners of other disciplines — we are on the one hand caught in a climate of opinion where doubt has been expressed about the wisdom and relevance of what we do — witness the many references to critical material in this dissertation. On the other hand we exist in a situation, as we saw earlier, where our livelihood, our research and in the end our thought is ideologically pressured and politically manipulated. It is all too easy to flow with the tide. We may do so for purely instrumental reasons, we may not even realise the extent to which we succumb to effective conditioning. In the measure that we do so we weaken, or even negate, the force of our 'option for the Kingdom.'

What I have aimed to do in this study is to delineate the conditions of possibility for freedom from these cultural 'determinisms' in terms of the idea of conversion. The converted person is intellectually critical enough to be aware of the way in which cultural conditioning works, and awareness is the beginning of freedom. He has rejected the values offered or imposed by the environment, and instead knowingly chooses values which may be at odds with those held by others. But such a person does not stand apart or 'outside' the group; he is 'alongside' his colleagues, his family, his community. He is critical without being judgemental, radical without being utopian. Above all, he is present to and for others; he listens to needs, he engages with the problems of others, he is the peacemaker, the optimist, the one who gives others a sense of their own worth and their own dignity. Such a person carries the message of the Kingdom into human situations because he is at the same time hearer of that message and part of the structures of the world in which that Kingdom must be realised. He lives in the hope of the coming of the Kingdom, and is thus the one who will discover signs of that Kingdom in communities, in industrial and political situations. As a critical, detached and autonomous moral person he will create those signs wherever he is because he is prepared to allow God to act through him. He lives in the freedom of hope, in the serenity of coherence, and in the unity of metanoia and praxis.

===

Appendix One

Praxis

In view of the ambiguities which accompany the use of
the word 'praxis' both in theology and in the social sciences
(1), I think it is important to define the sense in which the
word is used in this dissertation. It is best to begin by
locating the origins of the various forms of the concept of
"praxis". Aristotle's tripartite division of human activity
into theoria, poiesis and praxis presents a unified picture
of human contemplation, making and doing. One flows into the
other. However, the historical emphasis on praxis has moved
from the understanding of man as knower and thus the primacy
of theoria to an emphasis on the individual person as agent
who "makes the world" (2), and subsequently to an emphasis on
praxis as something other than individual. There are two
separate strands in this development, the Hegelian and the
Marxist. The Hegelian notion of praxis is never individual.
Praxis is the praxis of the Spirit which realises itself in
history (3). The rational element in this realisation
constitutes consciousness; our consciousness of that rational
element forms theory. Theory is thus the rational
articulation of praxis. Theory may be individual, but
praxis, as the objectified relationship between consciousness
and world, is not.

Marx develops two notions of praxis(4). The distinction
is between "blind" praxis, which is enforced by external
structures such as the relations of production (5), and
creative praxis which changes those structures. This
contrasts with Kant's "moral action" which was non-creative
in a social sense, Marx sees creative praxis as creative not
only of society but of self. Praxis embodies theoria and
relates it to practical ends by means of poiesis,
'manipulative knowledge' (6).

It is thus a Marxian insight — but not only a Marxian one — that praxis is self-transforming; that "any individual becomes who he/she is as an authentic or inauthentic' subject by their actions in an intersubjective and as social/historical world with other subjects and in relation to concrete social and historical structures and movements" (7). But the above definition needs to be supplemented by two "riders". We must distinguish clearly between "praxis" in the sense of "what I do" from the objectified sense of "praxis" in the sense of "what is done" — as in "social praxis". We also have to be clear that the emphasis here is on faith praxis — transformative action which springs from a faith commitment (8). The second is that our faith does not tell us the right thing to do. We do what the faith commitment tells us to do without any idea of whether it is the right thing to do or not. So we cannot say in an a priori sense that we ought to engage in social praxis to transform unjust social structures. It may be the case that that is what our faith will require us to do in the concrete situation in which we find ourselves, but we cannot lay it down as a moral imperative arising from our faith (9). It is God who is responsible for the realisation of the Kingdom, given the nature and quality of our actions. Norms for faith-as- action have to come therefore neither from theory, nor from a purely intuitive response, nor are they to be found in revelation (10). They derive rather from the dialectical gospel-life relationship which is mediated by theological reflection in such a way as to generate those norms. But because faith-as-praxis is not only personally transformative but also socially transformative praxis will not only generate but also change and correct that reflection.

Praxis, then, is "that human activity which modifies and fashions not only man's exterior existence but also the interior dimension of life. The effects of praxis are part of man's very being; it is the salvific activity 'par excellence'. In a certain metaphysical framework, praxis is that activity by which the potentiality of the human being is actualised (11)". Orthopraxis is thus anything which serves as salvific in the sense of achieving human fullness. "Every action which leads to the perfection of man in the concrete existential situation in which he is engaged is authentic praxis" (12).

Notes

1. As Avis says (1982) p.533, "no self-respecting theologican nowadays can put two words together without one of them being praxis."
2. Bernstein (1972) p.7.
3. See e.g. Lane's account (1984) p.38.
4. As analysed in Alvin Gouldner (1980). Also see Lamb's essay in Lamb (ed) — Generalised empirical method and praxis. Quoted Davis p.15.
5. Lane (1984) p.40.
6. This framework forms the basis of Habermas' analysis of the way in which we have lost the unity between the Aristotelian triad. Poesis, manipulative knowledge, has been alienated from praxis, praxis in turn has been alienated from theoria. Habermas (1974), p.41ff.
7. Tracy — Theologies of praxis, in Lamb (ed) p.35/6.
8. Ibid.fn. p.36.
9. The concrete problems in spelling out the practicalities of social praxis are enormous. For instance, how can we know what the achieving of 'social justice' entails in advance of the particular instance. See Marstin (1979) p.11 for different definitions of social justice.
10. See Lamb (1982) Ch.3.
11. Panikkar (1971) pp.239/9.
12. Ibid.

Appendix Two

The Kingdom of God in Judaism.

What kind of understandings formed the background to Jesus' preaching? The Hebrew word for 'Kingdom' — malkuth — has connotations both of rule and of realm. If we conceive of realm as that process by which God begins to govern as king, because he is creator and hence lord of the universe, we can then think of his rule as the final state of affairs by which he reigns in power. The word thus throws up two ideas, that of process and that of power. The Jews are unique in the story of man's relationship with the transcendent because they see God's intervention as a historical process. As Ladd argues (1)

> "Israel's hope is ....rooted in history, or
> rather in the God who works in
> history....The other Semitic religions were
> nature religions and did not develop a sense
> of history, but the Hebrews developed an
> interest in history because of their concept
> of God whose activity was to be experienced
> in history".

Israel thus understands God's rule as a historical process working towards a final, decisive act of intervention.

The Jewish experience of God is also that of an active, powerful God, whose rule is characterised "not by a latent authority but by the exercise of power, not by an office but by a function...not a title but a deed"(2). God's kingship is dynamic, he comes to deliver, to judge and to save. He renews the face of the earth (Ps.47, 93), he sustains his people (Ps.96, 97, 98), He wins victory over evil (Ps.99), he brings righteousness and justice. The Jewish understanding of God's rule found in the Pentateuch is in fact composed of two separate strands of tradition. One of them, the older, is the understanding of a powerful God who makes a covenant with his people over time – a conception which originates in Canaan and is common in near-eastern myth and was subsequently borrowed by the Jews (3). The other is a belief in a God who saves; history thus becomes salvation-history. This view is based on a conception of time which is punctilinear – ie composed of a series of events. Festivals are the celebration of the fact that the time for sowing or for the harvest has arrived (Eccles.). They are also the celebration of times past when God has intervened on behalf of his people. They are, in other words, salvation events. The idea that there is a time for everything is the basis of the prophetic hope, of which the messianic hope is just one expression. God, who has shown his saving power in the past, will come finally and decisively to conquer his enemies and take possesion of his Kingdom.(Is.52:11seq, 40seq).

The post-exilic failure led to a shift in understanding. It was possible that the final and decisive salvation event was to be interpreted more eschatologically – ie as something in some sense further away. Two separate expectations then arose. One assumed that the eschatological event would take place within human history. Another newer expectation saw the event as taking place outside history. God's saving activity would happen in the context of the ending of the present era, and the creation of a new era. Amos and Isaiah believe that God's rule is both present and future in the sense that present history gets its significance from the fact that God is about to break into human history and visit his people in order to make the whole of creation new (Amos 9:11-15). The whole of present history is thus interpreted in the light of that future event. Catastrophes are interpreted as God's judgement, reprieves are seen as signs of God's care and a foretaste of the final saving act by which God will redeem his people. Eventually this eschatology took on nationalistic overtones. The specific form that God's saving act would take would be the sending of a messiah, who would be a son of David (Amos 9:11, Is.9:6, 11:1, Mich1:5seq, Jer.23:5, Ezch.34:23, 37:24, 37:25-7). Initially it was felt that the role of the messiah would be to administer the Kingdom which God would establish, but the later belief was that the messiah would actually be the one to establish God's rule. There was no suggestion (except in the belief of the Zealots) that God's rule would in any sense be a political one.

This eschatological expectation of the Kingdom remained current until the time of Jesus. We find evidence of this not only in the Gospels, but also in the Kaddish, the prayer said daily in the synagogue...."may he establish his Kingdom in your lifetime and in your days and in the lifetime of the house of Israel even speedily and at a near time."(4). However, there had emerged a new apocalyptic strand of literature by 200 BC which also structured the expectations current at that time. This thinking was characterised by a dualism (see Book of Daniel) which saw God's sovereign action to redeem his people finally and decisively as happening independently of man's cooperation outside the historical framework. God would create a new and purified earth, a new age would dawn after God had finally conquered the powers of evil. This kind of perspective led to a discarding of the significance of what was happening in the present, since the coming of the Kingdom would not take place in this era. It also led to a kind of passivity in an ethical sense (5) because it would be God who would choose both the time of final salvation and those who were to be saved (the 'righteous remnant'). The apocalyptic perspective encouraged people to look for 'signs and portents' as they tried to predict the time which God would choose.

Although both the evangelists and Paul witness to the fact that apocalyptic and eschatological hopes formed the background to what must have been the expectations of Jesus' hearers, the concept of 'Kingdom ' as such was not of central importance in late Judaism. Rabbinical teaching saw God's rule as a continuum over time which is perceived clearly only in events such as Sinai and the Exodus, and in the future coming of the messiah. At other times it remains concealed, but becomes realised when a man in obedience to the Torah accepts the yoke of the Kingdom and submits himself to the one God. Rabbinical teaching was therefore ambiguous as to whether redemption would come at a fixed time or only if man did penance. The emphasis on the establishment of the Kingdom in late Judaism had shifted to a focus on the coming of the messiah; God's rule or reign was an aspect of that event which primarily interested the Zealots who saw it as a political development.

The background to Jesus' proclamation of the Kingdom was thus a varied series of understandings of the word. Some of those understandings were adopted by him in his proclamation; some, such as the more apocalyptic expectations, were rejected. And to existing understandings of the nature of God's activity represented by that symbol he added others which were his own.

Notes.

1. Ladd (1974) p.52.
2. Schnackenberg (1963) p.13.
3. See Perrin (1976) p.16ff.
4. Perrin (1963) p.19.
5. Ladd op.cit.p.91.

=======================================

Appendix Three

Lonergan's notion of consciousness.

Lonergan's position on consciousness can be briefly
stated as follows. The focus of Lonergan's concern is the
subject, who is characterised by a dynamic and intentional
consciouness. Cognitional processes by their intentionality
make objects present to the subject and by consciousness
these same processes make the subject present to himself (1).
The drive of conscious intentionality is what grounds the
'unrestricted desire to know', which is continually expressed
in questioning. Knowing happens in a structured fashion
through experience, understanding and judgement; a key moment
in this process is the insight which happens as the
transition between experience and understanding (2). Another
key moment happens in the process of self-appropriation of
one's cognitional activities, whereby the subject affirms
that he is a knower - this happens as a moment in judgement.
It is in that process of self-appropriation that the
subject's consciousness becomes 'differentiated'; as his
knowledge of the world expands he moves through a series of
'moving viewpoints', experiences 'horizon-shift'. His
differentiated consciousness experiences different worlds,
differently mediated by meaning. There is thus an
unrestricted potential for human development, both on an
individual and on a group basis (3).

For Lonergan, consciouness is therefore the ultimate
ground of cognitional theory. Consciousness thus acquires a
central role in any analysis of action as cognitive.
Consciouness as awareness of self is immanent in the
cognitional operations of the subject (4). It is
consciousness which enables the subject to be present to
himself, to attend to himself in the process of knowing, as

well as to be aware of the presence of the object to him. He is aware of himself experiencing, understanding and judging, and thus of himself as the 'subject' of these operations. So consciousness is not merely cognitive, it is also constitutive. It brings into being the mental operations of which it is conscious. If, for instance, we are conscious of our own rationality, it is that consciousness which constitutes our rationality (5). It is in becoming conscious of our intelligence that we become intelligent in a functional sense; it is when we are aware of being critical that our critical faculty comes into being.

Lonergan sees this process as resulting in a consciousness which is capable of being 'differentiated' in the following manner.

Empirical consciousness is simply the awareness or experience of one's perceptual or experiental functioning as opposed to the awareness of the object of perception. It is an awareness of ourselves as seeing, hearing, perceiving, rather than an awareness of what is seen. The object of experience is thus the experiental process itself.

Intelligent consciousness is the understanding of one's own processes of inquiry, understanding and linguistic hypothesis formation. This is much more difficult to achieve. We have to attend to the process of our own understanding of the world until we understand how it is that we understand.

Rational or reflective consciousness is the affirmation of the self as making judgements about what is or is not so, it is the mode of consciousness in which we are able to declare that we are knowers in the sense that we find in the structures of our own consciousness those cognitional structures which are presupposed by that statement. In other words, we affirm the reality of one's experienced and understood experiencing, understanding, judgement and deciding.

The fourth level of consciousness is the responsible. This is the level where we reflect not only on the cognitive

but also on the moral component of what we do (6). It is the
level where we consciously decide to

> "operate in accordance with the norms
> immanent in the spontaneous relatedness of
> one's experienced, understood, (and)
> affirmed experiencing, understanding,
> judging and deciding. It is the level, in
> other words, where consciousness becomes
> conscience" (7).

Notes

1. Lonergan (1971) p.8.

2. Lonergan maintains that insight is preconceptual, but this
position is not tenable if we accept the increasing
importance given to the linguistic mediation and
interpretation of experience and understanding in
contemporary philosophy.

3. See Lonergan (1971) p.6ff.

4. Ibid.

5. Tyrell (1974) p.77.

6. Ibid p.15.

7. Ibid pp.268/9. See also Lonergan (1974) 'The Subject'p.80

==

Appendix Four

The individual and the social.

Fundamental problems exist within the perspective of
social theory on the question of the relation between the
individual and the social, largely because of the tension
between the two opposing poles of social—man—as—subject and
social—man—as—object. We understand ourselves as persons, as
subjects in intersubjectivity, and yet a 'scientific' dictate
of objectivity would require us to "render the world, and
human beings in the world, an object" (1). This tension
finds its expression in the polar opposition between
interpretative, or hermeneutic approaches to sociology, and
empirical approaches which maintain the possibility of
establishing 'social facts' capable of being tested and
verified (2).

The search for scientific respectability dictated that
the beginnings of social science in the nineteenth century
should erect the ideals of precision, unity, universality and
the validity of laws as the aims of social investigation.
These became embodied in the positivistic approach to
sociology, which sees all social entities — people,
structures and the ways in which they interact — in
quantifiable terms. Comte, for instance, simply assumed that
the development of science "edged closer and closer to human
life, moving through physics, chemistry and biology to the
creation of sociology, the science of human conduct in
society" (3) Social laws were seen as having the same form
as natural laws; action in a social context was also governed
by such laws — motive, for instance, can be seen as a
law—like proposition concerning agents behavioural
disposition.

The necessary agenda for this was to establish behavioural psychology as the foundation for the study of social reality. J.S.Mill, for instance, considered that the scientific study of society is primarily about discovering causal sequences by setting up regularities in patterns of action and making generalisations about them (4). Action, he argued, is based on motivation; predictable human motivation will thus lead to regularity of behaviour within social institutions. Causality was the key to understanding the relationships and events within society. Society is thus an ordered behavioural construct, and the study of society became scientifically respectable insofar as it provided a causally-related nexus of explanation (5).

Mill emphasised causality; Pareto, too, sought scientific respectability, but in his case the emphasis was on empiricism (6). The only concepts permissible in social scientific study were empirical ones. He argued that people's behaviour is not influenced by their ideas, but rather by a means-ends calculus. Logical action is that designed to achieve the result which the actor wants; the actor must want the result and know what will achieve it. Action can clearly be non-logical in a variety of ways, but it is then not intelligible and not amenable to scientific investigation (7).

The key problem with the 'scientific' approach in social theory is the existence of what Giddens (8) calls the 'double hermeneutic' of social science. Social reality, the subject of scientific study, is on the one hand produced by the actions of those involved in its creation, but it is also interpreted by them in terms of the meanings which arise as a consequence of their attempts to understand and explain their actions; these attempts are in turn based on their own knowledge and beliefs about those actions. This process can happen only within a context of shared meanings and assumptions (9). To put it more technically, the double hermeneutic can be seen as "relating both to entering and grasping the frames of meaning involved in the production of social life by lay actors, and reconstituting these within the new frames of meaning involved in technical conceptual schemes" (10). It is thus not possible to analyse behaviour in a social context without a prior attribution of meaning to that behaviour – a meaning which is based on both subjective and intersubjective intepretations, and which is carried in the concepts used to discuss it which themselves stem from social existence. Furthermore, the meaning of an action is not simply given by the agent's intentions, but depends on a system of social relations which allow us to discuss the ascription of responsibility (11). The meaning of actions thus also depends on their social interpretations. It can also be the case that the social interpretation of an action will often differ from the agent's interpretation – history, said Hegel, is made by people who do not realise what they are doing (12). Actions have unintended consequences; their social meaning must also include these.

The social scientist thus has to be aware that there is a philosophical problem about the nature of social reality to be handled before the problems of empirical research can be tackled (13). Social action needs to be explained in the first instance by specifying conceptual relations rather than by isolating causal dependencies as such. But the problem here is that the social scientist is himself part of the reality he is observing, he is a 'participant observer'. His own scientific investigations themselves constitute a form of social action which serve to change the reality he is observing. Many of the concepts used in the general understanding of social life – group, class, society – are themselves a product of the observational process; they enter into social meaning structures and hence into our experience of social reality in the same way as commonsense concepts and meanings. It can therefore be argued that social theory has more effect on 'world' than natural science, because reflection on social process enters into, and creates, the universe it describes (14) — social theory and social praxis are thus interactive.

It is clear, then, that neither positivism nor rationalism can be appropriate philosophical stances for the social scientist, because both the positivist and the rationalist are likely to bypass the central question of the significance of social phenomena (15). The former will simply miss the significance, the latter will distort it by imposing a conceptual system of thought onto the social situation. To confine the study of action in a social context to a consideration of rational action within causal patterns of social process is to bypass both the complexities of human motivation for action and the attribution of social meaning to that action (16).

A more adequate perspective requires us to see that social action as process is interactive, and it is that interaction which constitutes society — society has no existence which is separate from the sum total of actions and ways of behaving. Furthermore, action consitutes or creates society in ways not intended by actors. The fact that action is institutionalised within structures can well introduce a separate focus for concern, because it creates the aspect of power and hence influences the direction and pattern of social change. But whatever model we use has to see the relationship between action and structure as duality rather than dualism, to realise that action creates structure while structure influences action.

The question of the 'scientific' nature of social theory is thus clearly related to another tension — that of the primacy of the individual versus society in terms of the relevance of perspective. Social science itself has at one time or another adopted all possible positions along this spectrum. If we choose to focus on the person, is he actor, reactor, or agent? We can characterise the individual as self in intersubjectivity, 'social self' (17), or as a behavioural unit (18), or as constrained by society, or as totally conditioned by society (19). Society itself can be seen as system (20), or mechanism (21), or organism (22), or structure (23). The choice between these viewpoints will reflect not merely pragmatic, historical or cultural factors, it will reflect genuinely different ways of looking at the world, geniunely different perspectives on social reality.(24).

We can start with those who emphasise the individual actor, with the idea of a person as existing in intersubjectivity, as a 'social self'. This person will have as 'cultural baggage' a set of presuppositions and ways of viewing the world, culturally given patterns of rationality, and values imbibed from his environment. George Herbert Mead (25) saw social reality emerging at the point where gesture and interpretative response facilitate the mutual emergence of 'shared selves'. The self becomes socialised (26) as each person participates in the other's view of himself and thus internalises the other. Self-consciousness is the outcome of this. But Mead's social self exists only prior to action, and thus creates no concept of society — social reality is merely potential. Furthermore, Mead's social self is paradoxical in that he emerges in social experience through communicating, but the social process of communicating itself presupposes selves (27).

Mead gives us the self-conscious self emerging in a social context, but a self without intentionality or agency. In this respect Weber's actor is more convincing (28). His action is related to his inner mental states — not in the sense of psychological states, but in the sense of states which trigger purposive action. Purposive action is to be distinguished from behaviour on the one hand, and from social action — i.e. objectively observable action — on the other.

Action is 'meaningful' - but it is to be interpreted in terms of the meaning intended by the actor, his Verstehen, rather than in terms of some objectively valid meaning. Because action is purposive it is causal, not only in Mill's sense of choice causing action, but in the sense that the end or goal determines the form of action. Social phenomena are therefore subject both to causal explanation and to interpretative understanding (29).

The self-as-object is thus implicit in Weber as in Mead, but the difference is that the meaning of action intended by the acting self is expressed in terms of ends. Action is thus 'Zweckrational'; the rational actor uses expectations of behaviour of others - and events - to calculate what he should do to achieve his desired objectives. This is the standard way in which rationality is understood in the social sciences. But Weber admits that there are other possible interpretations of actions - action can be Wertrational - i.e. done because it is good and has value in itself, or it can be affectual (governed by emotions) or traditional (done from force of habit).

Weber's actor does more and achieves more than Mead's 'social self'; he is at least intentional. But the typology of action provided gives us nothing more than a series of 'ideal types'. Human action is much more likely to be a mixture of these types, with any given action containing elements of each. Nor can we assume that the whole notion of teleological action is non-problematic. Purposes and ends can be subconscious, they can be incoherent, inconsistent or non-empirical. It is also not clear how the means-ends calculation is to be interpreted, as neither rationality nor logic survive cultural transformation unaltered. Can we say, for instance, that ritual or magical practices are zweckrational? Nor does Weber distinguish, as Hesse (30) points out, between value relevance which can be eliminated by pragmatic considerations and values which are built into the very structure of causality on which the action rests.

However, there are ways in which Weber's ideas can be extended. One way is to ask ourselves how the actor attaches meaning to what he does in the context of the fact that action has a temporal structure. Meaning is not only given by what the actor intends in a teleological sense. It is also constituted in reflective consciousness as it brings to light what was intended retrospectively. Schutz's "Phenomenonology of the Social World" attempts to extend Weber's ideas by providing them with a philosophical grounding deriving from Husserl and Bergson (31). He makes a genuine attempt to investigate the generation of social order in a temporal context, rather than simply assuming it. He sees social order as being generated by intentional consciousness in an intersubjective context. That consciousness, which grounds meaning, has a time dimension. It operates within the intersubjective world, the locus of encounter of the conscious self with the other, the scene of the self's action directed towards others. That world thus provides "both the domain of action and the epistemic context for action" (32). More practically, what Schutz attempts is an analysis of the properties of commonsense thought and action — i.e. the quality of our belief in everyday life and the kinds of learned interpretative schemes or cookbook recipes we have for leading it.

Schutz's basic criticism of Weber is precisely that he does not recognise the 'time structure' of action, the fact that an act can be ongoing or completed. He thus fails to account for the differing kinds of motivation governing action. Action can be done 'because of' something, or 'in order to ' achieve something. This omission results in a failure to clarify the status of meaning because the structure of intentionality is not fully analysed. Meaning is a certain way of looking at experience. It is thus bound to the way in which action is conceived of and interpreted.

But action is what I am doing now, what I intend to do, or what I did, and my experience of action depends on what kind of action is in question. I give meaning now to what I did and what I will do as well as to what I am doing now, and that meaning forms the nexus of my present experience. The particular kind of meaningful experience I have is thus contingent on the temporality of action as well as on the reflective moment of consciousness which arises from the awareness of action.

Social action, says Schutz, is all project-directed. Its goal is the meaning of the act taken to realise it — the projected act. The intentional unity meant is thus independent of the intending. The whole meaningful structure of the social world is underpinned by the projection of acts. But the temporality of action introduces distinction of motivation, a two-way flow between project and action. Action is motivated by the project; action is done 'in order to' when the action is projected. The intended project thus provides the motivation. But action done 'because' is action which motivates the project in the sense that interpretation of past acts forms the project as it stands today.

The project thus defines the span and meaning of action. Social science thus has to explain the project, its content, its relation to sequences of events, prior conditions and underlying regularities. But that explanation can be retrospective, explaining in terms of 'because', or it can be prospectively reflective, as the project expresses in a reflected consciousness the meaning and motive of action as it looks forward. We understand the total complexity only by applying our 'cookbook recipes', our learned interpretative schemes, which are our subconscious stores of knowledge.

Schutz has reminded us that it is not sufficient to explain action in terms of purpose, we must also explain it in terms of meaning in a way which allows for the possibility

of reinterpretation and redescription. But he does not
succeed in reconstituting social reality as an 'object world'
of social relationships; he is, as Giddens says 'weddded to
the standpoint of the ego'. His scheme is thus incapable of
taking into account that most important aspect of any action
– the consequences it may have for others. There is also the
problem of which kind of meaning enters into the
interpretation of action – it can be subjective meaning, in
terms of reasons, or it can be objective meaning – i.e. the
meaning that society bestows on action and carried in
language, conceptual schemes, philosophies and moral codes.
This question is particularly relevant for social scientific
study, because it is objective meanings which are accessible
to social scientists. Phenomenological sociology is in
consequence profoundly non-empirical and it thus creates
suspicion among social scientists in the 'scientific'
tradition: it conveys at best understanding rather than
explanation.

Mead, Weber and Schutz form a continuum; they work from
the self to the social, but without providing a satisfactory
account of agency. Others start from the perspective of the
social. The original emphasis on the social came from
Durkheim, whose opposition to psychologism led him to
initiate a study of the effects of social influences on human
activity. Constraints on individual behaviour originate not
in inner mental drives, but in society itself, and these
constraints can be objectified and redefined in terms of
'social fact'. Social facts are actions, whether of a set
nature or not, capable of excercising external constraint
over the individual (33). They are 'things (34), external
manifestations of some internal reality. The establishment
of social facts requires the social scientist to leave behind
his pretheoretic concepts and ideas – because they form a
"veil drawn between the thing and ourselves" (35) – and
proceed scientifically from things to ideas.

A social fact will be something generalised throughout society. As external manifestation, it presents the reality of a collective consciousness in institutional or customary terms. The problem then arises as to where this collective consciousness is located, because, as the 'social', it cannot logically exist outside all individuals. Here lies the weakness of Durkheim's portrayal of the 'social': in his effort to avoid emphasising the psychological origin, he confuses the nature of social reality by objectifying it into social fact, and in the end produces a theory in which the individual is determined by a society which has no identifiable characteristics.

Durkheim was an empiricist, and thus a positivist in the Comtean sense. Latter-day positivism (in the Vienna-school sense) influenced the development of the approach he originated in such a way that the objective social reality studied by social scientists became not empirical social facts but 'society' in the abstract (36). In order to be able to apply the canons of logical positivism to that abstraction it became necessary to give it a logical shape. Organic and anthropomorphic models of society became fashionable, and this led to the situation where

> "the wise refusal to reject individual
> psychological factors as sole determinants
> of social behaviour led to the opposite kind
> of reductionism, the refusal to accept any
> individual psychological factors. A society
> without people (thus) becomes the proper
> stable object of sociology"(37).

The structural-functional (or simply functional) analysis of human action sees it as dictated by (38) the requirements of "equilibrium" — social science's version of mechanism. Functionalists see social reality as a structural whole and social action as simply the process of functional adaptation. Talcott Parson's early work (39) lays some emphasis on action – actors are goal–oriented, select means, are constrained by environment and by the way in which their emotional/moral make–up influences their judgement. Actors are totally socialised, however, both ego and id, as they internalise rigidly accepted norms and values, these latter being both elements of personality and components of society. The system itself is seen as teleological – which raises the interesting question as to what dictates the goal of the system itself (40). It is directed by a need to survive or grow, or is there some external force (such as perhaps the process of technological change) which dictates the pattern of change? The process of transformation of the system happens because of the adaptive behaviour of the organisms (people), who themselves are also transformed in the process. Functionalist explanation thus evaluates positively all those processes which enhance the values of a given system, and takes a negative view of conflict, withdrawal, tension, and deviance – even though it regards values as non–rational. These values, uncritically accepted, thus become the criterion for what is functional in social process.

How are we to model this system? The founders of modern anthropological functionalism, Radcliffe Brown and Malinowski, adopted a biological analogy (41). Talcott Parsons, however, evolved the kind of adaptive formulation (42) which showed how the interaction between functional adaptation (what people do) and functional survival worked. To achieve social goals social units – ie people – have to adapt both externally and internally. They have to become the kind of people who function in the required way. This is achieved by a process of integrating internalised norms and values and expressing that internalisation in appropriate action – appropriate, that is, in the light of the goals of the system.

As an explanation of human action functionalism is profoundly deficient. In its emphasis on dynamic eqilibrium it is closely allied to the mechanistic models of the behaviourists, thus lacking both spatial and temporal dimensions. Cultural values assume the role played by impulse in behavioural sociology: human agency is reduced to outcome of the internalisation of values as the actor accepts the values of his culture without question. Functionalism does not recognise the possibility that social norms are negotiated and pluralistic rather than dictated in some imperialistic fashion. In denying any substantive role to reason it fails to see social life as actively constituted by the doings of its members, Furthermore, although functional analysis purports to explain the coherence of social reality and the way in which future social reality is implicitly embodied in present states of affairs its analysis is retrospective —

> "Social process is actually constituted in prospective intentionality, but functional analysis objectifies this process in retrospect, and then makes functional evaluations as if this were a mere prospective analysis, thus creating an illusion of evolutionary determinism"(43).

Notes

1. Dageneis (1972) p.xi.
2. There is a clear interest in social science as science for control purposes, which reflects social interest in science generally. Thomas (1979) p.1. discusses how methodologies follow scientific methodologies with a lag. Also see Radnitsky (1970) Vol.2.p.125.
3. Giddens (1976) p.12.
4. Mill (1865) .
5. He did admit, however, Ibid (p.466) that "it is not possible that events which depend on complications of causes can be made the subject of a true induction by observation

and experiment".

6. Pareto (1935)

7.. This, as Winch points out (1958) p.122, makes scientific intelligibility the norm for all intelligibility, and excludes the majority of social phenomena from social study.

8. Giddens (1976), p.79.

9. Thomas (1979) p.74 notes that "there is no more confused area in the philosophy of social science than that of the problem of meaning...So poor have most formulations of the problem of meaning been that writers have often missed the complexity of the issue at hand". Lonergan in MIT provides a useful account – he discusses sources, carriers and acts of meaning. Anglo-Saxon philosophy is narrower, it sees meaning as carried in concepts; language, in other words, is fundamental to the structure of social reality. Natural events, as Winch points out (1958) p.132, happen independently of concepts, but the character of human actions and consequent events is determined by concepts. Concepts, in other words, settle for us the form of experience we have of the world.

10. Giddens (1976) p.79.

11. Simon (1982) Ch.2.

12. Quoted Simon (1982) p.39.

13. Winch (1958) p.9ff.

14. For instance, ideas about soverignity have become an essential part of the reality they helped to establish. Giddens (1976) p.xxxv.

15. Fay and Moon (1977) p.213

16. Social science has failed to control but also failed to adopt the criticist position which would have allowed it to make a genuine contribution to the shaping of society.

17. Mead (1967).

18. e.g.Skinner (1948).

19. e.g.Radcliffe Brown (1952).

20. e.g. Bertalanffy (1981).

21. Functionalists such as Merton (1963) and Parsons (1949).

22. e.g. Comte (1975).

377

23. e.g. Levi-Strauss (1968).

24. See Winter's (1966) 'styles' — manipulative/behaviourist, consensual/functionalist, oppositional/alienative.

25. In Mind, Self and Society (1967).

26. Dageneis (1972) p. 86.

27. Winter (1966) p. 25-7.

28. See eg Schutz in Emmet and Macintyre (1970) for an account of Verstehen .

29. As Hollis (1977) p.112 says —"teleology is simply a licence to read off causal connections in a certain way".

30. Hesse (1980) p.187ff.

31. Natanson (1974).

32. Ibid. p.36.

33. Quoted Dageneis (1972) p.78 from Durkheim (1938).

34. Filmer (1972) p.37.

35. Durkheim (1938) p.15.

36 Dageneis (1972)p.88.

37. Ibid. p.88.

38. Agassi (1977) p.266 sees functionalism as social science's version of relativism — "each to his own custom".

39. Eg. Parsons (1949).

40. Rex (1961) p.66.

41. Radcliffe-Brown (1952). See p.178ff. in particular.

42. In Parsons et al. (1953).

43. Winter (1966) p.188.

==

BIBLIOGRAPHY

ACHINSTEIN Peter (1968) — Concepts of science; a
    philosophical analysis. Baltimore: Johns Hopkins Press.

ACHINSTEIN Peter and BARKER S.C.(ed) (1969) — The legacy
    of logical positivism. Baltimore: Johns Hopkins Press.

ACTON H.B.(1971) — The morals of markets: an ethical
    explanation. London: Longmans.

AGASSI Joseph (1977) — Towards a rational philosophical
    anthropology. The Hague: Martinus Nijhof.

ALTHUSSER Louis (1979) — Reading Capital. London: Verso
    Editions.

ANDRESKI Stanislav (1972) — Social sciences as sorcery.
    London: Andre Deutsch.

ANTAKI Charles (ed) (1981) — The psychology of ordinary
    explanations of social behaviour. London: Academic
    Press.

ANTHONY Peter (1977) — The ideology of work. London:
    Tavistock Publications.

AQUILA R.E.(1977) — Intentionality: a study of mental acts.
    Pennsylvania and London: The Pennsylvania State
    University Press.

ARGYRIS Chris (1960) — Understanding organisational
    behaviour. London: Tavistock.

ARISTOTLE — Basic Works. R. Mc Keon (ed). New York 1964.

ARMSTRONG D.M.(1968) — A materialist theory of the mind.
    London: Routledge and Kegan Paul.

ASCH.S.E.(1951) — Effects of group pressure upon the
    modification and distortion of judgements.
    In GUETZKOW (1951)(ed).

ASCH.S.E.(1952) — Social Psychology. New Jersey: Prentice
    Hall.

AUGUSTINE ST. — Confessions of St.Augustine. Tr.F.J.Sheed,
    London: Sheed & Ward.

AUNE Bruce (1977) — Reason and action. Doordrecht/Holland
    and Boston/USA: Reidel Publishing Co.

AVIS P.D.L.(1982) — In the shadow of the Frankfurt school;
    from critical theory to critical theology.
    Scottish Journal of Theology.35.6, pp.529-540.

AYRES C.E.(1980) — Ideological responsibility.
    In SAMUELS (ed) (1980).

BANDSTRA A.J. (1964) — The law and the elements of the
    world. Kampen: J.H.Kok.

BARKER B. (1977) — Absolutisation of the market. In
    DWORKIN (ed) (1977).

BARNES Barry (1974) — Scientific knowledge and sociological
    theory. London: Routledge and Kegan Paul.

BARTH Karl (1936/58) — Church Dogmatics.
    Tr.G.W.Bromily. T & T Clark, Edinburgh.

BARZUN J.M.(1964) — Science, the glorious entertainer.
    London: Secker and Warburg.

BAUER Peter (1984) — Reality and rhetoric; studies in the
    economics of development. London: Weidenfeld and
    Nicholson.

BAUM Gregory (1969) — Faith and doctrine; a contemporary
    view. New York: Newman Press.

BAUM Gregory (1975) — Religion and alienation. New York:
    Paulist Press.

BAUMRIN Bernard (ed) (1963) — Philosophy of science; the
    Delaware Seminar. New York: Interscience Publishers.

BEARDSLEE W.A.(1970) — Uses of the proverb in the synoptic
    gospels. Interpretation 24,1, pp.61-73

BECKER Gary — Altruism, egoism, and genetic fitness.
    Journal of Economic Literature,14,3,pp.817-826

BENN G.I.and MORTIMORE G.W.(1976) — Rationality and the
    social sciences. London: Routledge and Kegan Paul.

BENN G.I.and GAUSS.G.F.(ed)(1983) — Public and private in
    social life. Beckenham, Kent: Croom Helm.

BENSMAN Joseph and LILIENFELD Robert (1979) — Between
    public and private: the lost boundaries of the self.
    London, Free Press: Collier Macmillan.

BENSUSAN-BUTT D.M.(1978) — On economic man.
    Canberra: Australian National University Press.

BERGER Peter et al (1974) — The homeless mind.
    Harmondsworth: Penguin.

BERGER Peter and LUCKMAN Thomas (1971) — The social
    construction of reality. Harmondsworth: Penguin.

BERNSTEIN R.J. (1972) — Praxis and action. London:
    Duckworth.

BERNSTEIN R.J.(1979) — The restructuring of social and
    political theory. Philadelphia: University of
    Pennsylvania Press.

BERTALANFFY Ludwig von (1981) — A systems view of man.
    Boulder, Colorado: West View Press.

BLATT John (1983) — How economists misuse mathematics.
    In EICHNER (ed) (1983a).

BLOOR David (1976) — Knowledge and social imagery.
    London: Routledge Direct Editions.

BLUM Fred (1970) — Ethics of industrial man. London:
    Routledge and Kegan Paul.

BOLAND Lawrence (1979) — A critique of Friedman's critics.
    Journal of Economic Literature,17,2, pp.503–522.

BOND E.J.(1983) — Reason and value. Cambridge: Cambridge
    University Press.

BONHOEFFER Dietrich (1965) — Thy kingdom come. In
    GODSEY (ed) (1965).

BOUDON Raymond (1981) — The logic of social action.
    London, Routledge and Kegan Paul.

BOUDON Raymond (1982) — The unintended consequences of
    social action. London: Macmillan.

BOULDING Kenneth (ed) (1984) — The economics of human
    betterment. London: Macmillan.

BOULDING Kenneth (1967) — The basis of value judgements
    in economics. In HOOK (ed) (1967).

BRENTANO Franz (1874) — Psychology from an empirical
    standpoint. London: Routledge and Kegan Paul, 1973.

BRITTEN Samuel (1973) — Is there an economic consensus?
    London: Macmillan.

BROMBERGER Sylvain (1963) – A theory about the theory of theory and about the theory of theories. In BAUMRIN (ed) (1963).

BUBER Martin (1970) – I and Thou. Edinburgh: T.&.T Clark.

BUCHANAN A.T.(1985) – Ethics, efficiency and the market. Oxford: Clarendon Press.

BUCHANAN D.A. and HUCZYNSKI A.A. (1985) – Organisational behaviour. London: Prentice Hall.

BULTMAN Rudolf (1967) – The old and the new in the letters of St. Paul. Richmond, Virginia: John Knox Press.

BULTMAN Rudolf (1951/5) – Theology of the New Testament 2 vols. New York: Scribners.

BUNGE Mario (1979) – A systems concept of society – beyond individualism and holism. Theory and Decision, 10,1, pp.13-30.

BURKE T.P.(ed) (1968) – The Word in history. London: Collins.

BUTLER B.C.(1975) – Bernard Lonergan and conversion. Worship, 49,6,pp.329-356

CAMPBELL Joseph.(ed) (1971) – The portable Jung. New York: Viking Press.

CAMPBELL Keith (1971) – Body and mind. London: Macmillan.

CAPRA Fritz (1979) – The tao of physics. London: Fontana.

CAPRA Fritz (1982) – The turning point. London: Wildwood House

CARTWRIGHT D.P.(ed) (1959) – Studies in social power. Ann Arbour: University of Michigan Press.

CAVANAUGH M.S.(1984) – A typology of social power in KAKABADSE Andrew and PARKER Charles (ed).

CENTORE F.F.(1979) – Persons; a comparative account of six possible theories. Westport, Conneticut: Greenwood Press.

CHASE R.X.(1983) – The development of contemporary macroeconomics; vision, ideology and theory. In EICHNER (ed) (1983a).

CHISHOLM R.M.(1976) – Person and object. London: Allen and Unwin.

382

CLARKE Roger (1985) — Industrial Economics. Oxford:
    Basil Blackwell.

CODDINGTON Alan (1972) — Positive economics.
    Canadian Journal of Economics 5,1,pp.1-15.

COLLARD D.A.(1978) — Altruistic Economics. Oxford: Martin
    Robinson.

COLLINS B.E. and GUETZKOW H.S.(ed) (1964) — A social
    psychology of group processes for decision-making.
    New York: Wiley.

COMTE Auguste (1975) — Physique Sociale. Paris, Herman.

CONN W.E.(1986) — Christian conversion; a developmental
    interpretation of autonomy and surrender. New York:
    Paulist Press.

CONN W.E.(1981) — Moral development; is conversion
    necessary? In LAMB (ed) (1981b).

CONN W.E.(ed)(1978) — Conversion; perspectives on personal
    and social transformation. New York: Alba House.

CONN W.E.(1976) — Bernard Lonergan's analysis of
    conversion. Angelicum, 53, 3 pp.362-404.

COOPER D.E.(1980) — Moral relativism. In FRENCH et al.
    (1980)(ed).

CORCORAN Peter (ed) (1975) — Looking at Lonergan's method.
    Dublin: Talbot Press.

CRANFIELD C.E.B. (1964) — St. Paul and the law.
    Scottish Journal of Theology 17,1, 43-68.

CROSSAN J.D. (1975) — The dark interval; towards a theology
    of story. Illinois: Argus Puplications.

CROSSAN J.D. (1973) — In parables; the challenge of the
    historical Jesus. New York: Harper and Row.

CROWE F.E.(1977) — An exploration of Lonergan's new notion
    of value. Science et Esprit XX1X, 2,pp.123-143.

CRUTCHFIELD R.S.(1955) — Conformity and character.
    American Psychology, 10, pp.191-8.

CULLMAN Otto (1951) — Christ and time. London: SCM Press.

CURRAN Charles (1976) — Christian conversion in the
    writings of Bernard Lonergan. In McSHANE (ed) (1976).

DAGENEIS J.J.(1972) — Models of man; a phenomenological critique of some paradigms in the human sciences. The Hague: Martinus Nijhoff.

DANTO A.C.(1973) — The philosophy of action. Cambridge: Cambridge University Press.

DAVIDSON, Donald (1963) — Actions, reasons, and causes. Journal of Philosophy 60,23,pp.685-700.

DAVIDSON, Donald (1980) — Essays on actions and events. Oxford: Clarendon Press.

DAVIS Charles (1981) — Lonergan's appropriation of the concept of praxis. New Blackfriars, pp.114-126.

DAVIS W.D. AND DAUBE D.(ed)(1956) — The background of the New Testament and its eschatology. Essays in honour of C.H.Dodd. Cambridge: Cambridge University Press.

DEANE Phyllis (1978) — The evolution of economic ideas. Cambridge: Cambridge University Press.

DEI VERBUM; Dogmatic Constitution on revelation. In VATICAN COUNCIL (2nd): Documents.

DEWEY John (1916) — Essays in experimental logic. Chicago: University of Chicago Press.

DODD C.H. (1935) — The parables of the Kingdom. London: Nisbet.

DORAN Robert (1981) — Psychic conversion and theological foundation: towards a reorientation of the human sciences. California: Scholars Press.

DORR Donal (1972) — Religious experience and Christian faith. In SURLIS (ed) (1972).

DORR Donal (1975) — Conversion. In CORCORAN (ed) (1975).

DOWNIE R.S. (1971) — Roles and Values. London: Methuen .

DUESENBERRY J.S. (1962) — Income, savings, and the theory of consumer behaviour. Cambridge, Mass.: Harvard University Press.

DUHEM Peter (1906/62) — The aim and structure of physical theory. New York: Athanaeum.

DUMONT Louis (1977) — From Mandeville to Marx. Chicago: University of Chicago Press.

DUNN J.G.D.(1975) — Rom.7.14-25 in the theology of Paul. Theologische Zeitschrift 31,5,pp.257-273.

DURKHEIM Emile (1895/1938) — The rules of sociological method. 8th.ed. G.E. Catlin (ed) Cambridge: Cambridge University Press.

DWORKIN Gerald (ed) (1977) — Markets and morals. Washington: Hemisphere Publishing Co.

EDEL Abraham (1979) — Analysing concepts in social science. New Brunswick, New Jersey: Transaction Books.

EKINS Paul (ed) (1986) — The living economy. London: Routledge Kegan Paul.

EICHNER Alfred (ed) (1983a) — Why economics is not yet a science. London: Macmillan.

EICHNER Alfred (1983b) — Why economics is not yet a science. In EICHNER (1983a) (ed).

EISENSTADT S.N. (1981) — The schools of sociology. In SHORT (1981)(ed).

EISER J.R.(1986) — Social Psychology. Cambridge: Cambridge University Press.

ELKANA Yehuda (1979) — Science as a cultural system. In MATHIEU and ROSSI (1979) (ed).

ELLIS Adrian and KUMAR Krishnan (ed) (1983) — Dilemmas of liberal economics. Studies in Fred Hirsch's Social Limits to Growth. London, Tavistock.

ELSTER Jon (1983) — Explaining technical change. Cambridge: Cambridge University Press.

ELSTER Jon (1979) — Ulysses and the sirens: studies in rationality and irrationality. Cambridge: Cambridge University Press.

EMMET Dorothy (1984) — The effectiveness of causes. London: Macmillan.

EMMET Dorothy (1979) — The moral prism. London:Macmillan.

EMMET Dorothy (1966) — Rules, roles and relationships. London: Macmillan.

EMMET Dorothy and MACINTYRE Alasdair.(ed) (1970) — Sociologica theory and philosophical analysis. New York: Macmillan.

ERIKSON Eric (1965) — Childhood and society. Harmondsworth: Penguin.

385

EVANS Donald (1980) — Faith, authenticity and morality.
Edinburgh: Handsel Press.

FAY B.C.and MOON S.M. (1977) — What would an adequate
philosophy of the social sciences look like?
Philosophy of the Social Sciences 7,pp.209-227.

FEIGL H. and MAXWELL G.(ed) (1962) — Minnesota Studies
in the Philosophy of Science.Vol.3. Minneapolis.

FEYERABEND Paul (1962) — Explanation, reduction and
empiricism. In FEIGL and MAXWELL (1962) (ed).

FILMER Paul et al.(1972) — New directions in sociological
theory. London: Collier Macmillan.

FINDLAY J.N. (1970) — Axiological ethics. London:
Macmillan.

FINANCE J.de (1962) — Essai sur l'agir humain. Rome:
Gregorian University Press.

FINE Ben (1980) — Economic theory and ideology.
London: Edward Arnold.

FISHER A.L. and MURRAY G.B. (1969) — Philosophy and
science as modes of knowing: selected essays.
New York:Appleton-Century-Crofts Meredith Corporation.

FLEW Anthony (1978) — A rational animal and other
philosophical essays on the nature of man. Oxford:
Clarendon Press.

FOA Bruno (1982) — Marshall revisited in the age of DNA.
Journal of Post-Keynesian Economics 5, 1 ,pp.3-17.

FOLEY D.K. (1975) — Problems v. conflicts: economic
theory and ideology. American Economic Review
65, 2 ,pp.231-6.

FOUREZ G.(1979) — Liberation ethics. Philadelphia: Temple
University Press.

FREIRE Paolo (1974) — Conscientisation. Month 7,5,
pp.575-8.

FRENCH J.R.P. and RAVEN B.H. (1957) — The bases of social
power. In CARTWRIGHT (ed) (1957).

FRENCH P.A., VEHLING T.E., WETTSTEIN H.K.(ed)(1980) —
Studies in ethical theory. Midwest Studies in
Philosophy Vol.3. Minnesota: University of Minnesota
Press.

FRIEDMAN Maurice (1967)   —   To deny our nothingness:
    contemporary images of man. Chicago: University of
    Chicago Press.

FRIEDMAN Milton (1980)   —   Free to choose.   London: Secker
    and Warburg.

FRIEDMAN Milton (1953)   —   Essays in positive economics.
    Chicago: University of Chicago Press.

FULTON G. (1984)   —   Research programmes in economics.
    History of Political Economy 16, 2, pp.187-205.

GAUDIUM ET SPES: Pastoral Constitution on the Church
    in the world. In VATICAN COUNCIL (2nd) 1962-5.

GALBRAITH J.K.(1957) —   American Capitalism; the concept of
    countervailing power.   London: Blackwell.
    Revised ed. 1980.

GAVENTA B.R.(1986)   —   From darkness to light; conversion
    in the New Testament. Overtures to Biblical Theology 20.
    Philadelphia: Fortress Press.

GELPI Donald (1977)   —   Charism and sacrament; a theology of
    Christian conversion.   London: SPCK.

GEORGESCU-ROEGEN Nicholas (1979)   —   Methods in economic
    science. Journal of Economic Issues 13,2,
    pp.317-328.

GEUSS Raymond (1981)   —   The idea of a critical theory:
    Habermas and the Frankfurt school.   Cambridge: Cambridge
    University Press.

GIBBONS Michael (1981)   —   Insight and emergence; an
    introduction to Lonergan's circulation analysis.
    In LAMB (1981b).

GIBBS John (1977)   —   Kohlberg's stages of moral judgement —
    a constructive criticism.   Harvard Educational Review,
    47, 1,   pp.43-61.

GIDDENS Anthony (1984)   —   The constitution of society.
    Cambridge: Polity Press.

GIDDENS Anthony (1979)   —   Central problems in social theory.
    London:Macmillan.

GIDDENS Anthony (1976)   —   New rules in sociological method.
    London: Hutchinson.

GILKEY Langdon (1983) – The creationist issue: a theologian's viewpoint. Concilium, 166, pp.55-69.

GILLIGAN C, NEALE B, MURRAY D. (1983) – Business decision-making. London: Philip Allen.

GODSEY J.D.(ed) (1965) – Preface to Bonhoeffer; the man and two of his shorter writings. Philadelphia: Fortress.

GOFFMAN Ernst (1963) – Behaviour in public places. New York: Free Press.

GOLDMAN A.I.(1970) – Theory of human action. New Jersey: Prentice Hall, Englewood Cliffs.

GORDON H.S. (1980) – Welfare, justice and freedom. Columbia: Columbia University Press.

GORDON Scott (1977) – Social science and value judgement. Canadian Journal of Economics, 10,4. pp.529-546.

GOULDNER Alvin (1980) – The two Marxisms; contradictions and anomalies in the development of theory. London: Macmillan.

GREENBERG J. and COHEN R.L.(ed) (1982) – Equity and justice in social behaviour. New York: Academic Press.

GUETZKOW H.S.(ed) (1951) – Groups, leadership and men. New York: Carnegie Press.

GUTIERREZ Gustavo (1974) – A theology of liberation. London: SCM Press.

HABERMAS Jurgen (1976) – Legitimation crisis. London: Heinemann.

HABERMAS Jurgen (1974) – Theory and practice. London: Heinemann.

HABERMAS Jurgen (1971) – Knowledge and human interest. London: Heinemann.

HABERMAS Jurgen (1970) – Towards a rational society. London: Heinemann.

HAHN Frank (1982) – The invisible hand. Lloyds Bank Review, April.

HANDY Charles (1985) – Understanding Organisations. Harmondsworth: Penguin.

388

HANSON N.R. (1958) – Patterns of discovery. Cambridge:
Cambridge University Press.

HAPPELL Stephen and WALTER J.(1986) – Conversion and
discipleship, Philadelphia: Fortress Press.

HARDY Alister (1979) – The spiritual nature of man; a study
of contemporary religious experience. Oxford:
Clarendon Press.

HARE R.M. (1952) – The language of morals. Oxford:
Oxford University Press.

HARNACK A. von (1901) – What is Christianity? New York:
G.B.Putnam. English translation by J.B.Saunders.

HARRAN Marion (1983) – Luther on conversion; the early
years. New York: Cornell University Press, Ithaca.

HARRE Rom (1979) – Social being; a theory for social
psychology. Oxford: Blackwell.

HARRE Rom (1984) – Personal being. Cambridge, Mass: Harvard
University Press.

HARRIS Bob and HARVEY John (1981) – Attribution theory from
phenomenal causality to intuitive social scientist and
beyond. In ANTAKI (1981) (ed).

HARSANYI J.C.(1982) – Morality and the theory of rational
behaviour. In SEN & WILLIAMS (1982) (ed).

HARVEY A.E. (1982) – Jesus and the constraints of history.
London: Duckworth.

HAUGHTON Rosemary (1980) – Is there hope for a tree? –
a study of the emerging church. Unpublished paper.

HAUSMAN Daniel (1981) – Capital, profits and prices.
New York: Columbia Press.

HAYEK Fredrich (1976) – The mirage of social justice.
London: Routledge & Kegan Paul.

HAYEK Fredrich (1960) – The constitution of liberty.
London: Routledge & Kegan Paul.

HEBBLETHWAITE Peter (1977) – The Christian-Marxist
dialogue. New York: Paulist Press.

HEILBRONNER R.L.(1973) – Economics and a 'value-free'
science. Social Research, 40,1, pp.129-143.

HESSE Mary (1983) – Cosmology as myth.
Concilium 166, pp.49-54.

HESSE Mary (1980) — Revolutions and reconstructions in the philosophy of science. Sussex: Harvester Press.

HICKS John (1979) — Causality in economics. Oxford: Blackwell.

HICKS John (1974) — The crisis in Keynesian economics. Oxford: Blackwell.

HIRSCH Fred (1977) — Social limits to growth. London: Routledge & Kegan Paul.

HODGSON Geoffrey (1988) — Economics and institutions. Cambridge: Polity Press.

HOLLENWEGER Walter (1982) — Umgang mit Mythen. Munich: Chr. Kaiser Verlag.

HOLLIS Martin (1977) — Models of man. Cambridge: Cambridge University Press

HOLLIS Martin and NELL Edward (1975) — Rational economic man: a philosophical critique of neo-classical economics. Cambridge: Cambridge University Press.

HOMANS G.C. (1951) — The human group. London: Routledge and Kegan Paul.

HOOK S.M. (ed) (1967) — Human values and economic policy. New York: University Press.

HORNSBY Jennifer (1980) — Actions. London: Routledge and Kegan Paul.

HORTON Robin and FINNEGAN Ruth (ed) (1973) — Modes of thought: essays on thinking in Western and non-Western societies. London: Faber and Faber.

HUDSON W.D. (ed) (1969) — The is/ought question. London: Macmillan.

HUGHES G.J. (1978) — Authority in morals: an essay in Christian ethics. London: Heythrop Monographs.

HUME David (1885) — A treatise of human nature. London: Clarendon Press.

HUMPHREY Nicholas (1986) — The inner eye. London: Faber.

HUTCHINSON T.W. (1977) — Knowledge and ignorance in economics. Oxford: Blackwell.

IGNATIEFF Michael (1984) — The needs of strangers?.
    London: Chatto and Windus, Hogarth Press.

JAMES WILLIAM (1902) — The varieties of religious
    experience. New York

JANIS I.L. (1971) — Groupthink. Psychology Today. Nov.

JEREMIAS Joachim (1954) — The parables of Jesus.
    London: SCM.

JEVONS William (1871) — Theory of political economy.
    Harmondsworth: Penguin Edition 1970.

JOHN PAUL II, Pope (1981) — Laborem Exercens; encyclical
    letter on human work. London: CTS.

JOHN PAUL II, Pope (1997) — Redemptor Hominis. London: CTS.

JOHNS R.D. (1976) — Man in the world; the political
    theology of J.B.Metz. Missoula, Montana: Scholars
    Press.

JONES R.K. (1984) — Ideological groups. Aldershot:Gower.

JULICHER Adolf (1888–1910) — Die Gleichnisreden Jesu.
    2 vols. Tubingen: JCB Mohr (Paul Siebeck).

JUNG Carl–Gustav (1971) — The stages of life. in
    CAMPBELL (1971) (ed).

KAKABADSE Andrew and PARKER Christopher (ed) (1984)–
    Power, politics and organisations. Chichester: Wiley.

KAMARCK A.M. (1983) — Economics and the real world.
    London: Blackwell.

KASEMANN Ernst (1980) — Commentary on Romans. Michigan,
    Grand Rapids: William B.Eerdmans Publishing Co.

KASPAR Walter (1980) — An introduction to Christian faith.
    London: Burns & Oates.

KAYSEN C. (1967) — The business corporation as creator of
    values. In HOOK (ed). (1967).

KAYSEN Peter (1989) — It may be art, but what is it worth?
    Independent 6.3.89.

KENNY Anthony (1979) — Aristotle's theory of the will.
    Newhaven: Yale University Press.

KINLOCH G.C. (1981) — Ideology and contemporary
    sociological theory. New Jersey: Prentice–Hall.

KLAPPHOLZ Kurt (1964) — Value judgements and economics.
British Journal for the Philosophy of Science
15,58, pp.97-114.

KNOOR-CETINA K.D. (1981) — Social and scientific method,
or what do we make of the distinction between the
natural and the social sciences.
Philosophy of the Social Sciences
11, pp.335-359.

KOCKELMANS J. (1983) — On the impact of the human sciences
on our conception of man and society.
In TYMIENIECKA (1983) (ed).

KOENIG F.(1972) — Problems of believing today.
In SURLIS (1972) (ed).

KOHLBERG Lawrence (1986) — The philosophy of moral
development; moral stages and the idea of justice.
San Francisco: Harper and Row.

KOHLBERG Lawrence (1984) — The psychology of moral
development. London: Harper and Row.

KOHLBERG Lawrence (1981) — The philosophy of moral
development. London: Harper and Row.

KOHLBERG Lawrence (1976) — Moral stages and socialisation.
In LICKONA (1976) (ed).

KOHLBERG Lawrence (1971) — From is to ought; how to commit
the naturalistic fallacy and get away with it in the
study of moral development. In MISCHEL (1971) (ed).

KORFF W. (1968) — Empirical social study and ethics.
Concilium,5, 4, pp.5-18.

KORTIAN Garbis (1980) — Metacritique: the philosophical
argument of Jurgen Habermas. Cambridge: Cambridge
University Press.

KOUTSOYANNIS A. (1979) — Modern microeconomics.
Basingstoke: Macmillan.

KROEBER A. and KLUCKHOHN C. (1952) — Culture: a critical
review of concepts and definitions.Papers of the
Peabody Museum of American Archaeology and
Ethnology,47. Cambridge,Mass.

KUHN Thomas (1961) — The structure of scientific
revolutions. Chicago:University of Chicago Press.

LACAN M-F (1978) — Conversion and grace in the Old
Testament. In CONN (1978) (ed).

LADD G.E.(1976) - The presence of the future. London: SPCK.

LAKATOS Imre (1978) - Philosophical Papers Vols.1&2 . Cambridge: Cambridge University Press.

LAKATOS Imre and MUSGRAVE Alan (1970) - Criticism and the growth of knowledge. Cambridge: Cambridge University Press.

LAMB Matthew (1982) - Solidarity with victims. New York: Crossroad.

LAMB Mattthew (1981a) - Generalised empirical method and praxis. In LAMB (1981b) (ed).

LAMB Matthew (ed) (1981b) - Creativity and method; essays in honour of Bernard Lonergan SJ. Milwaukee: Marquette University Press.

LANE Dermot (1984) - Foundations for a social theology; praxis, process and salvation. Dublin: Gill and Macmillan.

LANE Dermot (1981) - The experience of God; an invitation to do theology. Dublin: Veritas Publications.

LARAIN Jorge (1979) - The concept of ideology. London:Hutchinson.

LATSIS S.J.(ed) (1976) - Method and appraisal in economics. Cambridge: Cambridge University Press.

LAWSON Hilary (1986) - The fallacy of scientific objectivity. The Listener, 20.2.86.

LEACH Edmund (1970) - Claude Levi-Strauss. London: Fontana.

LEHRER Keith (ed) (1966) - Freedom and determinism. New York: Random House, New York.

LEIJONHUFVUD Axel (1976) - Schools, revolutions and research programmes in economics. In Latsis (1976) (ed)

LEVI-STRAUSS Claude (1968) - Structural anthropology. London: Allen Lane.

LEVINSON H. (1972) - An effort towards understanding man at work. European Business, Spring.

LICKONA Thomas (ed) (1976) - Moral development and behaviour. New York: Holt Rinehart and Wilson.

LIKERT Rensis (1961) - New patterns of management.

New York: McGraw Hill.

LIPSEY Richard (1979) — An introduction to positive
economics. 5th ed. Loondon: Weidenfeld and Nicholson.

LOASBY B.J. (1976) — Choice, complexity and ignorance.
Cambridge: Cambridge University Press.

LONERGAN Bernard (1957) — Insight: a study in human
understanding. London: Longmans Green & Co.

LONERGAN Bernard (1967) — Collection: Papers by Bernard
Lonergan. New York: Herder & Herder.

LONERGAN Bernard (1968) — Verbum: word and idea in Aquinas.
London: Darton Longman and Todd.

LONERGAN Bernard (1971) — Method in theology. London:
Darton, Longman and Todd.

LONERGAN Bernard (1974) — A second collection. London:
Darton Longman and Todd.

LONERGAN Bernard (1981) — An essay in circulation analysis.

Unpublished manuscript.

LONERGAN Bernard (1985) — A third collection. New York:
Paulist Press.

LOWE Adolph (1984) — On economic knowledge. New York:
M.E.Sharpe, Inc.

LOWE Adolph (1967) — The normative roots of economic value.

In HOOK (1967)(ed).

LOWE Adolph (1951) — On the mechanistic approach in
economics. Social Research 18,4,pp.403–434.

LUGG Andrew (1983) — Explaining scientific belief.
Philosophy of the Social Science,13, pp.265–278.

LUMEN GENTIUM: Dogmatic Constitution on the Church.
In VATICAN COUNCIL (2nd). 1962–5.

LUTHER Martin (1522) — Preface to the Epistle to the
Romans. In Works of Martin Luther, Miekkenberg Press,
Philadelphia, 1932.

LUTZ M.A.and LUX K. (1979) — The challenge of humanistic
economics. California: The Benjamin/Cummings
Publishing Co.Inc.

McALISTER Linda (ed) (1976) — The philosophy of Brentano.
London: Duckworth.

McCLELLAND D.C. (1961) — The achieving society. Princeton:
D.Van Nostrand Company Inc.

MACCOBY Eleanor et al. (1966) — Readings in social
psychology. London: Methuen.

MACGREGOR G.H.C. (1954) — Principalities and Powers; the
cosmic background of Paul's thought.
New Testament Studies,1,1, pp.17-28.

MACH Ernst (1906) — Erkenntnis und Irrtum. Leipzig:
J.A.Barth.

MACHLUP Fritz (1978) — Methodology of economics and other
social sciences. New York: Academic Press.

MACHOVEC Milan (1976) — A Marxist looks at Jesus.
London: Darton, Longman and Todd.

MACINTYRE Alistair (1971) — Against the self-image of
the age. London: Duckworth.

MACINTYRE Alistair (1981) — After virtue. London:
Duckworth.

MACKIE J.L. (1977) — Ethics: inventing right and wrong.
Harmondsworth: Penguin.

MACQUARRIE John (1970) — Three issues in ethics. New York:
Harper and Row.

MCSHANE Philip (ed) (1976) — Foundations of theology:
papers from the international Lonergan conference 1970,
Notre Dame, Indiana: University of Notre Dame Press.

MANNHEIM Karl (1936) — Ideology and Utopia. London:
Routledge and Kegan Paul

MANNING D.J. (1980) — The form of ideology.
George Allen and Unwin, London.

MARSHALL H. (1977) — Preaching the Kingdom of God.
Expository Times, 889, pp.13-16

MARSTIN Ronald (1979) — Beyond our tribal gods: the
maturing of faith. Maryknoll:Orbis Books.

MASLOW A.H. (1970) — Religious values and peak experiences.
New York: Viking.

MASTERMAN Margaret (1970) — The nature of a paradigm.
In LAKATOS and MUSGRAVE (ed) (1970)

MATHIEU Vittorio and ROSSI Paolo (1979) — Scientific
culture in the contemporary world. Milan: Scientia.

MATTHEWS R.C.O. (1981) — Morality, competition, and
efficiency. Manchester School,19,4,pp.289-309.

MEAD G.H.(1967) — Mind, self, and society: from the
standpoint of a social behaviourist. Chicago:
Phoenix Books.

MEINONG Alexis (1968) — Gesamtausgabe. Graz: Akademischer
Druck- u. Verlagsanstalt.

MENNELL Stephen (1974) — Sociological theory, uses and
unities. London: Nelson.

MERTON Robert (1963) — Social theory and structure.
New York: Glencoe Free Press.

MERTON Robert (1936) — The unanticipated consequences of
purposive social action. American Sociological Review,
1,6, pp.894 - 904.

MERTON Thomas (1973) — Ccontemplation in a world of action.
New York: Doubleday Image Books.

METZ J-B.(1965) — Unbelief as a theological problem.
Concilium, 6.

METZ J-B. (1978) — Followers of Christ. New York: Paulist
Press.

MILGRAM Stanley (1974) — Obedience to authority. London:
Tavistock.

MILL John Stuart (1973) — A system of logic. Collected
Works of Mill. Toronto: University of Toronto Press.

MINFORD Patrick (1983) — Unemployment; cause and cure.
Oxford; Robertson.

MISCHEL Theodore (1971) — Cognitive development and
epistemology. New York: Academic Press.

MISHEN Ed (1969) — Costs of economic growth. Harmondsworth:
Penguin.

MORGENSTERN Oskar (1963) — On the accuracy of economic
observations. Princeton: Princeton University Press.

MORRRIS Desmond (1977) — Manwatching; a field guide to human behaviour. London: Verona Press.

MORRIS Desmond (1969) — The naked ape. London: Corgi.

MUNBY D.L. (1956) — Christianity and economic problems. London: Macmillan.

MURDOCH Iris (1970) — The sovereignty of good. London: Routledge & Kegan Paul.

MUSGRAVE Alan (1981) — Unreal assumptions in economic theory — the F-twist untwisted. Kyklos, 34. pp.377-387.

MYRDAL Gunnar (1953) — The political element in the development of economic theory. London: Routledge & Kegan Paul.

MYRDAL Gunnar (1958) — Value in social theory. London: Routledge & Kegan Paul.

NAGEL Ernst (1963) — Assumptions in economic theory. American Economic Review Supplement,53,2, pp.211-219.

NAGEL Thomas (1979) — Mortal questions. Cambridge: Cambridge University Press.

NATANSON M.A.(1974) — Phenomenology, role and reason; essays on the coherence and deformation of social reality. American Lectures Series Publications 914, 2Springfield, Ill.

NESSEL Muriel (1984) — Indicators of human betterment. In BOULDING (1984) (ed).

NEWMAN J.H. (1947) — An essay in aid of a grammar of assent. New York: Longmans Green & Co. 2nd.ed.1870.

NIEBUHR H.R. (1960) — Radical monotheism and western culture. London: Faber and Faber.

NIEBUHR H.R. (1963) — The responsible self; an essay in Christian moral philosophy. New York: Harper and Row.

NIELD Ronald (1982) — The case for the reconstruction of economics. Business Economist, Winter.

NOCK A.D. (1933) — Conversion. Oxford: Oxford University Press.

NOVAK Michael (1986) — Will it liberate; questions about liberation theology. New York: Paulist Press.

NYGRENS Anders (1951) — Christ and the forces of destruction. Scottish Journal of Theology. 4,4, pp.363—375.

O'DONNELL R.M. (1982) — Keynes, philosophy and economics; an approach to rationality and uncertainty. Ph.D. Cambridge.

OLTHUIS J.M. (1968) — Facts, values and ethics. Assen: Van Goren.

OTTO Rudolf (1923) — The idea of the holy. London: Oxford University Press.

OUTHWAITE William (1983) — Concept formation in social science. London: Routledge & Kegan Paul.

PANIKKAR Raimundo (1971) — Faith as a constitutive dimension of man. Journal of Ecumenical Studies, VIII,2, pp.223—254.

PANNENBERG Wolfhart (1975) — Theology and the kingdom of God. Philadelphia: Westminster Press.

PARETO Vilfredo (1935) — The mind and society. New York: Harcourt Brace.

PARSONS Talcott, BALES F.F., & SHILS E.A. (1953) — Working papers in the theory of action. New York: Free Press.

PARSONS Talcott (1956) — Elements pour une theorie d'action. Paris: Plon.

PARSONS Talcott (1949) — The structure of social action. London: Allen and Unwin.

PERRIN Norman (1963) — The kingdom of God in the teaching of Jesus. London: SCM.

PERRIN Norman (1967) — Rediscovering the teaching of Jesus. London: SCM.

PERRIN Norman (1976) — Jesus and the language of the kingdom. London: SCM.

PHILLIPS D.Z. and MOUNCE H.O. — Moral practices. London: Routledge & Kegan Paul.

PIAGET Jean (1968) — Six psychological studies. New York: Random House Vintage.

PIGOU A.C. (1952) — The economics of welfare. London: Macmillan, 4th.ed.

398

PITT J.C.(ed) (1979) — Philosophy in economics.
Doordrecht: D.Reidel.

PLATT J.R. (ed.) (1965) — New views on the nature of man.
The Monday lectures. Chicago: Univeristy of Chicago
Press.

POLANYI Karl (1945) — The great transformation.
London: Gollancz.

POLS Edward (1982) — The acts of our being. Amherst,
Mass.: University of Massachussets Press.

PRATT Vernon (1978) — The philosophy of the social
sciences. London: Methuen.

PRICHARD H.A.(1949) — Acting, willing and desiring,
in Moral Obligation. Oxford University Press,
Oxford.

QUINE W.van O. (1964) — From a logical point of view.
Cambridge, Mass: Harvard University Press.

RADCLIFFE-BROWN A.R.(1952) — Structure and function
in a primitive society. London: Cohen and West.

RADNITSKY Gerald (1970) — Contemporary schools of
metascience. Vols 1 & 2. Goteborg: Akademiforlag.

RAGAZ Leonhart (1971) — Die Gleichnisse Jesu; seine
sociale Botschaft. Hamburg.

RAHNER Karl (1979) — The foundation of belief today.
In Theological Investigations 16. London:
Darton, Longman and Todd.

RAHNER Karl (1978) — Foundations of Christian Faith;
an introduction to the idea of Christianity. London:
Darton, Longman and Todd.

RAHNER Karl (1975) — 'Conversion' in Encyclopedia of
theology; the concise Sacramentum Mundi. New York:
Seabury Press.

RAHNER Karl (1973) — Belief today: three theological
meditations. London: Sheed and Ward.

RAHNER Karl (1968) — Theology and anthropology.
In BURKE (1968) (ed).

RAHNER Karl (1967) — Some thoughts on a good intention.
In Theological Investigations 3. London:
Darton Longman and Todd.

RAHNER Karl (1966) — Nature and grace. In Theological Investigations 4. London: Darton,Longman and Todd.

RAHNER Karl (1965) — Concerning the relationship between nature and grace. In Theological Investigations 1. London: Darton, Longman and Todd. (Also p.396)

RAMBO L.R. (1982) — Current research on religious conversion. Religious Studies Review, 8, 2, pp. 146–159.

RAUSCHENBUSCH Walter (1960) — A theology for the social gospel. New York: Apex Books.

RAWLS John (1972) — A theory of justice. Oxford: Clarendon Press.

REICKE B.I.(1951) — The law and this world according to Paul. Journal of Biblical Literature 70 pp.259–276.

RESCHER Nicholas (1979) — Economics v. moral philosophy: the Pareto principle as a case study of their divergent orientation. Theory and Decision,10,3, pp.169–179.

RESCHER Nicholas (1972) — Welfare: the social issues in philosophical perspective. Pittsburg: University of Pittsburg Press.

RESCHER Nicholas (1969) — Introduction to value theory. New Jersey: Prentice Hall.

RESCHER Nicholas (1967) — Values and the explanation of behaviour. Philosophical Quarterly, 17, 67, pp.130–136.

RESCHER Nicholas (1966a) — Practical reasoning and values. Philosophical Quarterly, 16, 63,pp.121–136.

RESCHER Nicholas (1966b) — Distributive Justice; a constructive critique of the utilitarian theory of distribution. Indianapolis: Bobbs Merill Company.

REX John (1961) — Key problems of sociological theory. London: Routledge & Kegan Paul.

RICH Arthur (1984) — Wirtschaftsethik; Grundlagen in theologischer Perspektiv. Gutersloh: Gutersloh Verlag, Gerhard Mohn.

RICH Arthur (1975) — Socialethik im Industriezeitalter. Lectures given in the University of Zurich 1974–5.

RICH Arthur (1973) — Mitbestimung in der Industrie;
eine socialethische Orientierung. Zurich: Flamberg
Verlag.

RICH Arthur (1969) — Zwingli als socialpolitiker Denker.
Zwingliana, X111, 1 pp.67–89.

RICH Arthur (1968) — Personal und strukturell Boses
in der menschlichen Existenz.
Theologische Zeitschrift, 24 pp.320–337.
Translated by H.Tonks and reprinted as Appendix II of
Tonks (1984) p.303ff.

RICH Arthur (1962) — Glaube in politischer Entscheidung;
Beitrage zur Ethik des Politischen. Zurich: Zwingli
Verlag.

RICHARDS Stewart (1983) — Philosophy and sociology of
science.
London: Blackwell.

RICOEUR Paul (1961) — The symbolism of evil. Boston:
Beacon Paperback.

RIGAUD J. (1979) — Science and culture.
In MATHIEU and ROSSI (ed) (1979).

RIKHOF Herwi (1981) — The concept of church. London:
Sheed and Ward.

RITSCHL Albrecht (1900) — The Christian doctrine of
justification and reconciliation. Edinburgh:
T & T Clark.

ROBBINS Lionel (1932) — An essay on the nature and
significance of economic science. London: Macmillan.

ROBINSON Joan (1964) — Economic Philosophy.
Harmondsworth: Penguin .

ROBINSON Mike (1984) — Groups. Chichester: John Wiley
and Sons.

ROGERS Carl (1961) — On becoming a person. Boston:
Houghton Mifflin Co.

RORTY Richard (1980) — Philosophy and the mirror of nature.
Oxford: Blackwell.

ROSENBERG A. (1979) — A skeptical history of
microeconomics. In PITT (ed).

ROSS S.D. (1971) — The scientific process. The Hague:
Martinus Nijhoff.

RUBERY Jill (ed) (1988) — Women and recession. London:
Routledge and Kegan Paul.

RYAN Alan (1983) — Private selves and public parts.
IN BENN & GAUSS (1983) (ed).

RYAN Alan (1970) — The philosophy of the social sciences.
London: Macmillan.

RYAN W.J.F (1981) — The transcendental reflection according
to Edmund Husserl and intellectual conversion according
to Bernard Lonergan. In Lamb (1981b) (ed).

RYLE Gilbert (1949) — The concept of mind. New York:
Barnes and Noble .

SAMUELS Warren (ed) (1980) — The methodology of economic
thought. New Brunswick: Transaction Books.

SANDERS E.P.(1977) — Paul and Palestinian Judaism. London:
SCM.

SARTRE J-P.(1957) — Being and nothingness. London: Methuen.

SCHELER Max (1961) — Resentiment. New York: Free Press of
Glencoe.

CHILLEBEECKX Edward (1983) — Jesus: an experiment in
Christology. London: Collins, Fount Paperbacks.

SCHILLEBEECKX Edward (1980) — Christ: the Christian
experience in the modern world. London: SCM.

SCHILLEBEECKX Edward (1968) — Faith and self-understanding.
In BURKE (1968) (ed).

SCHLEIERMACHER F.D.E. (1928) — The Christian faith.
Edinburgh: T & T Clark.

SCHNACKENBERG Rudolf (1968) — God's rule and man's kingdom.
New York: Herder and Herder.

SCHNEIDER H.K.(1974) — Economic man: the anthropology of
economics. New York: Macmillan Press.

SCHUMACHER E.F. (1980) — Good work. London: Abacus.

SCHUMACHER E.F. (1974) — Small is beautiful. London:
Abacus.

SCHUMPETER J.A. (1954) — History of economic analysis.
London: George Allen and Unwin.

SCHUTZ Alfred (1970) — Rationality in the social world.
In EMMET and MACINTYRE (1970) (ed).

SCHWEITZER Albert (1911) — The quest of the historical
    Jesus. London: Adam and Charles Black.

SCITOVSKY Tibor (1977) — The joyless economy. Oxford:
    Oxford University Press.

SEABROOK Jeremy (1986) — Needs and commodities.
    In EKINS (1986) (ed).

SEABROOK Jeremy (1984) — Face to faith. Guardian,
    26.11.84.

SEGUNDO J.L. (1973) — Grace and the human condition.
    New York: Orbis Books, Maryknoll.

SELLARS Wilfred (1966) — Fatalism and determinism.
    In LEHRER (1966) (ed.).

SEN Amartya (1987) — On ethics and economics.
    Oxford: Blackwell.

SEN Amartya (1984) — Resources, values and development.
    Oxford: Blackwell.

SEN Amartya (1982) — Choice, welfare and measurement.
    Oxford: Blackwell.

SEN Amartya (1981) — Poverty and famines: an essay in
    entitlement and deprivation. Oxford: Clarendon.

SEN Amartya (1970) — Collective choice and social welfare.
    San Francisco: Holden Day Inc.

SEN Amartya (1967) — The nature and classes of prescriptive
    judgements. Philosophical Quarterly, 17,66,
    pp.46–62.

SEN Amartya and WILLIAMS Bernard (1982) — Utilitarianism
    and beyond. Cambridge: Cambridge University Press.

SHACKLE G.L.S. (1972) — Epistemics and economics.
    Cambridge: Cambridge University Press.

SHERIF Muzafer (1936) — The social psychology of group
    norms. New York: Harper.

SHERIF Muzafer (1966) — Group conflict and cooperation.
    London: Routledge & Kegan Paul.

SHILS Edward (1974) — Faith, utility and the legitimacy
    of science. Daedalus, 103, 3, pp.1–16.

403

SHORT J.F.(ed) (1981) — The state of sociology.
    London:Sage Publications.

SIMON Brian (ed) (1957)   —   Psychology in the Soviet Union.
    London: Routledge and Kegan Paul.

SIMON Herbert (1976)   —   From substabtive to proceedural
    rationality.   In LATSIS (1976) (ed).

SIMON Herbert (1957)   —   Models of man, social and rational.
    New York: Wiley and Sons.

SIMON M.A. (1982)   —   Understanding human action.   New York:
    State University of New York Press, Albany.

SKINNER B.F. (1972)   —   Beyond freedom and dignity.
    London: Jonathan Cape.

SKINNER B.F. (1948)   —   Walden Two. New York: Macmillan.

SKLBA R.J. (1981)   —   The call to new beginnings; a biblical
    theology of conversion.   Biblical Theology Bulletin,
    11, pp.67-73.

SKOLIMOWSKI Henryk (1974)   —   The scientific world-view
    and illusions of progress.   Social Research ,
    41, 1. pp.52-82.

SLATER, P.,WIEBE D., and HORVATH T. (1981)   —   Three
    responses to faith and belief; a review article.
    SR:Studies in Religion/Sciences Religieuses,
    10, 1, pp.113-126.

SMELSER Neil (1962)   —   Theory of collective behaviour.
    London: Routledge and Kegan Paul.

SMITH Adam (1776)   —   The wealth of nations; an enquiry into
    the nature and causes of liberty.   Indianapolis
    Library Classics 1981

SMITH Adam (1759)   —   Theory of moral sentiments.
    D.Raphael and A.Macfie (ed). Glasgow 1976.

SMITH W.C. (1979)   —   Faith and belief.   Princeton N.J:
    Princeton University Press.

SPERY R.W. (1965)   —   Mind, brain and humanist values.
    In PLATT (ed).

SPIELBERG Herbert (1976)   —   Intention and intentionality in
    the Scholastics, Brentano and Husserl.
    In McAlister (1976) (ed).

STONE G.P.& FARBERMAN H.P.(ed) (1970) — Social psychology
through symbolic interaction. Waltham, Mass.:
Ginn-Blaisdell.

STRAWSON P.F. (1959) — Individuals: as essy in descriptive
metaphysics. London: Methuen.

STREETEN Paul et al.(1981) — First things first; meeting
basic needs in development countries. New York: Oxford
University Press.

STROHM Theodor (ed) (1980) — Christliche Wirtschaftsethik
vor neuen Aufgaben. Festgabe fur Arthur Rich. Zurich:
TVZ Verlag.

SUPPE Fredrick (ed) (1977) — The structure of scientific
theories. Illinois: University of Illinois Press.

SURLIS Paul (ed) (1972) — Faith; its nature and meaning.
Dublin: Gill and Macmillan.

TARASCIO V.J.(1980) — Value judgements in economic science.
In SAMUELS (1980) (ed)

TAYLOR Charles (1971) — Interpretation and the
sciences of man. Review of Metaphysics,25,pp.3-51.

TAYLOR P.W.(1980) — On taking the moral point of view.
In FRENCH et al.(1980) (ed).

TAYLOR Richard (1966) — Action and purpose. New Jersey:
Prentice Hall, Englewood Cliffs.

TAYLOR-GOOBY Peter (1983) — The distributional complex
and the moral order of the welfare state.
In ELLIS AND KUMAR (1983) (ed).

THOMAS David (1979) — Naturalism and social science:
a post-empiricist philosophy of social science.
Cambridge: Cambridge University Press.

THOMPSON E.P. (1978) — The poverty of theory and other
essays. London: Merlin Press.

THOMPSON J.B. (1984) — Studies in the theory of ideology.
Cambridge: Polity Press.

TILLICH Paul (1959) — Theology of Culture. New York
Cambridge University Press.

TISDELL C.A. (1976) — Rational behaviour as a basis for
economic theories. In BENN and MORTIMORE (1976) (ed).

TISDELL C.A. (1975) — Concepts of rationality in economics.
Philosophy of the Social Sciences,5, pp.259-72.

TITMUSS R.M.(1973) — The gift relationship.
    Harmondsworth: Penguin.

TONKS Harold (1984) — Faith, hope and decision—taking;
    the Kingdom of God and social policy—making.
    Frankfurt: Verlag Peter Lang.

TORRANCE T.F. (1980) — Christian theology and scientific
    culture. Belfast: Christian Journals.

TORRANCE T.F.(ed) (1980) — Belief in science and in
    Christian life. Edinburgh: The Handsel Press.

TRACY David (1981a) — The analogical imagination.
    London: SCM.

TRACY David (1981b) — Theologies of Praxis.
    In LAMB (1981a) (ed).

TRACY David (1970) — The achievement of Bernard Lonergan.
    New York: Herder and Herder.

TRAVISANO R.V.(1970) — Alternation and conversion as
    qualitatively different transformations.
    In STONE & FARBERMAN (ed) (1970).

TRIGG Roger (1980) — Reality at risk: a defence of realism
    in philosophy and science. Sussex: Harvester Press.

TYMIENIECKA A—T (ed) (1983) — The phenomenology of man
    and the human condition. Boston/London: D.Reidel
    Publishing Co.

TYRRELL Bernard (1974) — Bernard Lonergan's philosophy
    of God. Dublin: Gill and Macmillan.

ULLMAN—MARGALIT Edna (1977) — The emergence of norms.
    London: Clarendon Press.

VATICAN COUNCIL (2nd) 1962-5 — The documents of Vatican II.
    Ed.W.M.Abbott. London: Angelus Books.

VESEY G.N.A.(ed) (1978) — Human values. Sussex:
    Harvester Press.

VON CRANACH Mario and HARRE Rom (1982) — The analysis of
    action. Cambridge: Cambridge University Press.

VON MISES Ludwig (1949) — Human action. London: William
    Hodge and Co.

VON RAD Gerhard (1965) — Old Testament theology Vol.2.
    Edinburgh: Oliver Boyd.

VON WRIGHT G.H. (1971) — Explanation and understanding. London: Routledge and Kegan Paul.

WALHOUT Donald (1978) — The good and the realm of values. Indiana: University of Notre Dame Press.

WEISS Johannes (1892) — Jesus' proclamation of the Kingdom of God. Philadelphia: Fortress Press (1976)

WEISSKOPF W.A. (1979) — The method is the ideology: from a Newtonian to a Heisenbergian paradigm in economics. Journal of Economic Issues, 13,4, pp.869—884.

WEISSKOPF W.A. (1977) — Normative and ideological elements in social and economic thought. Journal of Economic Issues, 11,1, pp.103—118.

WEISSKOPF W.A. (1973) — The image of man in economics. Social Research, 40, 3, pp.547—563.

WEISSKOPF W.A. (1971) — Alienation and economics. New York:E.P.Dutton & Co. Inc.

WERNER Stark (1958) — The sociology of knowledge. London: Routledge & Kegan Paul.

WILDER A.N. (1956) — Kerygma, eschatology and ethics. In DAVIS AND DAUBE (1956) (ed).

WILES Peter (1983) — Ideology, method and neoclassical economics: a general and coherent Weltanschauung. In EICHNER (1983a) (ed).

WILES Peter and ROUTH G. (ed) (1984) — Economics in disarray. London: Blackwell.

WINCH Peter (1958) — The idea of a social science and its relation to philosophy. London.

WINTER G. (1966) — Elements for a social ethic: scientific perspectives on social progress. New York: Macmillan.

WISEMAN Jack (ed) (1983) — Beyond positive economics. London: Macmillan.

WITTGENSTEIN Ludwig (1961) — Tractatus Logico-philosophicus. London. Routledge & Kegan Paul.

WITTGENSTEIN Ludwig (1975) — Philosophical remarks. Oxford: Blackwell.

WOGAMAN J.P. (1977) — Christians and the great economic debate. Philadelphia: Westminster Press.

WOODHAM—SMITH Cecil (1962) — The great famine. London:
    Hamish Hamilton.

WOTYLA Karol (1979) — The acting person. Dordrecht:
    D.Reidel Publishing Co.

WRONG Denis (1976) — Sceptical sociology. New York:
    Free Press.

YARNOLD Edward (1974) — The second gift. Slough:
    St. Paul Publications.

ZANDER Alvin (1981) — Groups at work. San Francisco:
    Jossey—Bass Publishers.

==

STUDIEN ZUR INTERKULTURELLEN GESCHICHTE DES CHRISTENTUMS
ETUDES D'HISTOIRE INTERCULTURELLE DU CHRISTIANISME
STUDIES IN THE INTERCULTURAL HISTORY OF CHRISTIANITY

Begründet von/fondé par/founded by
Hans Jochen Margull †, Hamburg

Herausgegeben von/edité par/edited by

Richard Friedli
Université de Fribourg

Walter J. Hollenweger
University of Birmingham

Theo Sundermeier
Universität Heidelberg

Jan A.B. Jongeneel
Rijksuniversiteit Utrecht

Band 20 Arturo Blatezky: Sprache des Glaubens in Lateinamerika. Eine Studie zu Selbstverständnis und Methode der "Theologie der Befreiung".

Band 21 Anthony Mookenthottam: Indian Theological Tendencies. Approaches and problems for further research as seen in the works of some leading Indian theologicans.

Band 22 George Thomas: Christian Indians and Indian Nationalism 1885-1950. An Interpretation in Historical and Theological Perspectives.

Band 23 Essiben Madiba: Evangélisation et Colonisation en Afrique: L'Héritage scolaire du Cameroun (1885-1965).

Band 24 Katsumi Takizawa: Reflexionen über die universale Grundlage von Buddhismus und Christentum.

Band 25 S.W. Sykes (editor): England and Germany. Studies in theological diplomacy.

Band 26 James Haire: The Character and Theological Struggle of the Church in Halmahera, Indonesia, 1941-1979.

Band 27 David Ford: Barth and God's Story. Biblical Narrative and the Theological Method of Karl Barth in the Church Dogmatics.

Band 28 Kortright Davis: Mission for Carribean Change. Carribean Development As Theological Enterprice.

Band 29 Origen V. Jathanna: The Decisiveness of the Christ-Event and the Universality of Christianity in a world of Religious Plurality. With Special Reference to Hendrik Kraemer and Alfred George Hogg as well as to William Ernest Hocking and Pandipeddi Chenchiah.

Band 30 Joyce V. Thurman: New Wineskins. A Study of the House Church Movement.

Band 31 John May: Meaning, Consensus and Dialogue in Buddhist-Christian-Communication. A study in the Construction of Meaning.

Band 32 Friedhelm Voges: Das Denken von Thomas Chalmers im kirchen- und sozialgeschichtlichen Kontext.

Band 33 George MacDonald Mulrain: Theology in Folk Culture. The Theological Significance of Haitian Folk Religion.

Band 34 Alan Ford: The Protestant Reformation in Ireland, 1590-1641. 2. unveränderte Auflage.

Band 35 Harold Tonks: Faith, Hope and Decision-Making. The Kingdom of God and Social Policy-Making. The Work of Arthur Rich of Zürich.

Band 36 Bingham Tembe: Integrationismus und Afrikanismus. Zur Rolle der kirchlichen Unabhängigkeitsbewegung in der Auseinandersetzung um die Landfrage und die Bildung der Afrikaner in Südafrika, 1880-1960.

Band 37 Kingsley Lewis: The Moravian Mission in Barbados 1816-1886. A Study of the Historical Context and Theological Signifcance of a Minority Church Among an Oppressed People.

Band 38 Ulrich M. Dehn: Indische Christen in der gesellschaftlichen Verantwortung. Eine theologische und religionssoziologische Untersuchung politischer Theologie im gegenwärtigen Indien.

Band 39 Walter J. Hollenweger (Ed.): Pentecostal Research in Europe: Problems, Promises and People. Proceedings from the Pentecostal Research Conference at the University of Birmingham (England) April 26th to 29th 1984.

Band 40 P. Solomon Raj: A Christian Folk-Religion in India. A Study of the Small Church Movement in Andhra Pradesh, with a Special Reference to the Bible Mission of Devadas.

Band 41 Karl-Wilhelm Westmeier: Reconciling Heaven and earth: The Transcendental Enthusiasm and Growth of an Urban Protestant Community, Bogota, Colombia.

Band 42 George A. Hood: Mission Accomplished? The English Presbyterian Mission in Lingtung, South China. A Study of the Interplay between Mission Methods and their Historical Context.

Band 43 Emmanuel Yartekwei Lartey: Pastoral Counselling in Inter-Cultural Perspective: A Study of some African (Ghanaian) and Anglo-American viwes on human existence and councelling.

Band 44 Jerry L. Sandidge: Roman Catholic/Pentecostal Dialogue (1977-1982): A Study in Developing Ecumenism.

Peter Kern

Ethik und Wirtschaft
Leben im epochalen Umbruch:
Vom berechnenden zum besinnenden Denken?

Frankfurt/M., Bern, New York, Paris, 1990. 174 S.
ISBN 3-631-42393-4   hardcover DM 43.--/sFr. 39.--

Die vielfältige Ethik-Diskussion in der Wirtschaft wird in diesem Buch vor die existentiellen Herausforderungen des Atomzeitalters gestellt: Möglicher atomarer Holocaust, tiefgreifende Ökologieprobleme und das Elend der armen Länder sind Themen, die zentral in den Dialog zwischen "Ethik und Wirtschaft" einbezogen werden müssen. Die gegenwärtige Wirtschaftsethik stellt sich diesen Problemen nur in unzureichender Weise. Damit bekommt die Ethik eine bloße Alibifunktion in der Wirtschaft.
Mit dem Konzept eines "ökosophischen Managements" soll versucht werden, auch in der Wirtschaft ethisch legitimierbare Antworten auf die Herausforderungen des epochalen Umbruchs zu geben.

Aus dem Inhalt: Doppelmoral in der Wirtschaft? - Ethische Herausforderungen an die Wirtschaft im epochalen Umbruch - Technokratische Optimisten - untergangsprognostische Pessimisten - New-Age-Denken - Ökosophisches Management

Verlag Peter Lang Frankfurt a.M. · Bern · New York · Paris
Auslieferung: Verlag Peter Lang AG, Jupiterstr. 15, CH-3000 Bern 15
Telefon (004131) 321122, Telex pela ch 912 651, Telefax (004131) 321131
– Preisänderungen vorbehalten –

Peter Ernst

**Beruf als Verantwortung – Ausbildung
zur Verantwortung**
Eine sozialethische Studie zu Wandlungen
des Berufsverständnisses und zur Stellung
der Berufsausbildung in der theologischen Ethik
der Gegenwart

Frankfurt/M., Bern, New York, 1987. X, 328 S.
Europäische Hochschulschriften: Reihe 23, Theologie. Bd. 309
ISBN 3-8204-0198-9   br./lam. DM 82.--/sFr. 68.--

Die Lage des Menschen in der modernen hochindustrialisierten Ge-
sellschaft mit ihrer starken Akzentuierung von Wirtschaft, Prosperität,
Produktion und technischem Fortschritt hat seine berufliche Existenz
und damit einhergehend auch die Berufsausbildung in eine tiefe Sinn-
krise geraten lassen. Das Bemühen, durch Aufgreifen der Aus-
bildungsproblematik ein sozialethisches Defizit abzubauen, setzt daher
eine Reexaminierung des Berufsgedankens unter Berücksichtigung
unterschiedlicher Berufsbegriffe und -vorstellungen, aber auch der
konkreten gesellschaftlichen, wirtschaftlichen und technischen
Bedingungen beruflicher Existenz des Menschen voraus. In der
Perspektive evangelischer Ethik geht es in diesem Problemzusammen-
hang und vor dem Hintergrund einer Neuinterpretation des insbeson-
dere von Martin Luther im Lichte des Rechtfertigungsgeschehens ent-
falteten reformatorischen Berufsgedankens vor allem darum, unter
Aufzeigen von Elementen einer sozialethischen Theorie des Berufes
den Versuch zu unternehmen, die gegenwärtig als so außerordentlich
virulent empfundene Frage nach dem Sinn des Berufes und der Berufsausbildung durch den Hinweis auf eine sinnstiftende Größe einer
Antwort näherzubringen.
Aus dem Inhalt: Säkulare Berufsbegriffe – Rechtfertigung und Sinn –
Der Berufsgedanke Luthers – Evangelische Sozialethik und Beruf –
Beruf als Verantwortung – Ausbildung zur Verantwortung.

Verlag Peter Lang Frankfurt a.M. · Bern · New York · Paris
Auslieferung: Verlag Peter Lang AG, Jupiterstr. 15, CH-3000 Bern 15
Telefon (004131) 321122, Telex pela ch 912 651, Telefax (004131) 321131
- Preisänderungen vorbehalten -